This cat that's stuck halfway out of the hole always runs to me when I come home from work. Odd for a cat. Her name's "Moto-kyu." Don't be lulled into a false sense of security by her cuteness or she'll bite you and ask for food. She's my entertainment while I'm drawing *Muhyo*.

—Yoshiyuki Nishi

Yoshiyuki Nishi was born in Tokyo. Two of his favorite manga series are *Dragon Ball* and the robot-cat comedy *Doraemon*. His latest series, *Muhyo & Roji's Bureau of Supernatural Investigation*, debuted in Japan's *Akamaru Jump* magazine in 2004 and went on to be serialized in *Weekly Shonen Jump*.

MUHYO & ROJI'S

BUREAU OF SUPERNATURAL INVESTIGATION

VOL. 2
The SHONEN JUMP Manga Edition

STORY AND ART BY
YOSHIYUKI NISHI

Translation & Adaptation/Alexander O. Smith
Touch-up Art & Lettering/Mark Griffin
Design/Izumi Hirayama
Editor/Amy Yu

Editor in Chief, Books/Alvin Lu
Editor in Chief, Magazines/Marc Weidenbaum
VP of Publishing Licensing/Rika Inouye
VP of Sales/Gonzalo Ferreyra
Sr. VP of Marketing/Liza Coppola
Publisher/Hyoe Narita

MUHYO TO ROZY NO MAHORITSU SODAN JIMUSHO © 2004 by
Yoshiyuki Nishi. All rights reserved. First published in Japan in
2004 by SHUEISHA Inc., Tokyo. English translation rights in the
United States of America and Canada arranged by SHUEISHA Inc.
The stories, characters and incidents mentioned in this
publication are entirely fictional.

No portion of this book may be reproduced or transmitted in
any form or by any means without written permission from the
copyright holders.

Printed in the U.S.A.

Published by VIZ Media, LLC
P.O. Box 77010
San Francisco, CA 94107

SHONEN JUMP Manga Edition
10 9 8 7 6 5 4 3 2 1
First printing, December 2007

www.viz.com www.shonenjump.com

THE WORLD'S
MOST POPULAR MANGA

PARENTAL ADVISORY
MUHYO & ROJI'S BUREAU OF SUPERNATURAL INVESTIGATION
is rated T for Teen and is recommended for ages 13 and up.
This volume contains fantasy violence.
ratings.viz.com

SHONEN JUMP MANGA EDITION

Muhyo & Roji's

Bureau of Supernatural Investigation

BSI

Vol.**2** **Premonition**

Story & Art by **Yoshiyuki Nishi**

Dramatis Personae

Toru Muhyo (Muhyo)

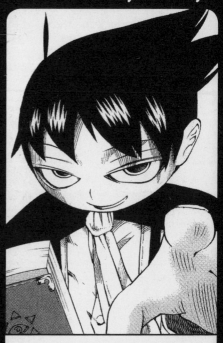

Genius elite practitioner of magic law, one of the youngest to achieve the highest rank of "Executor." Always calm and collected (though sometimes considered cold due to his tendency to make harsh comments), Muhyo possesses a strong sense of justice and has even been known to show kindness at times. Sleeps a lot to recover from the exhaustion caused by his practice. Likes: *Jabin* (a manga). Dislikes: Interruptions while sleeping.

Jiro Kusano (Roji)

Assistant at Muhyo's office and a "Second Clerk," the lowest of the five ranks of practitioners of magic law. Roji cries easily, is meek and gentle, and has been known to freak out in the presence of spirits. Frustrated that he always seems to be getting in Muhyo's way, Roji has devoted himself to studying magic law. Likes: Tea and cakes. Dislikes: Scary ghosts and scary Muhyo.

Kenji

Troublemaker who wrecked Muhyo and Roji's office sign because he thought they were a sham. But ever since Muhyo and Roji rescued him from a marauding ghost, Kenji seems to have taken a liking to them and often finds excuses to hang out at the office.

The Story

Toru Muhyo and Jiro Kusano practice magic law at Muhyo & Roji's Bureau of Supernatural Investigation. Magic law is a newly-established practice for judging and punishing the increasing crimes committed by spirits; those who use it are called "practitioners." Muhyo, widely regarded as a genius, attained the topmost of the five ranks of magic law, "Executor," at a young age. Meanwhile, his assistant Roji remains at the lowest rank, that of "Second Clerk." Things at the office are business as usual until Muhyo and Roji receive a late-night phone call from pianist and former child prodigy Aya Shiratori asking for help with a spirit who appears at night and plays her grand piano. Muhyo sentences the spirit, a manifestation of the envy Aya's audiences felt for her, but oddly, the spirit doesn't attack Aya herself. Muhyo's suspicions are confirmed when they find the flyer Aya used to contact them. On the flyer, the symbol for magic law is different than normal: the white and black parts of the symbol have been reversed. This inverted mark is the sign of a betrayer–a clear sign that this case was a setup. The target wasn't Aya, it was Muhyo, and Muhyo has an idea who was behind it: a man named "Enchu." But who is this Enchu, and why is he after Muhyo...?

CONTENTS

Article 6: **Unfading** 7

Article 7: **Nana's Photos** 27

Article 8: **Daddy** 47

Article 9: **Roji's Pen** 69

Article 10: **Presence** 93

Article 11: **Premonition** 115

Article 12: **Madness** 135

Article 13: **Pride** 157

Article 14: **Together** 179

2

ARTICLE 6
UNFADING

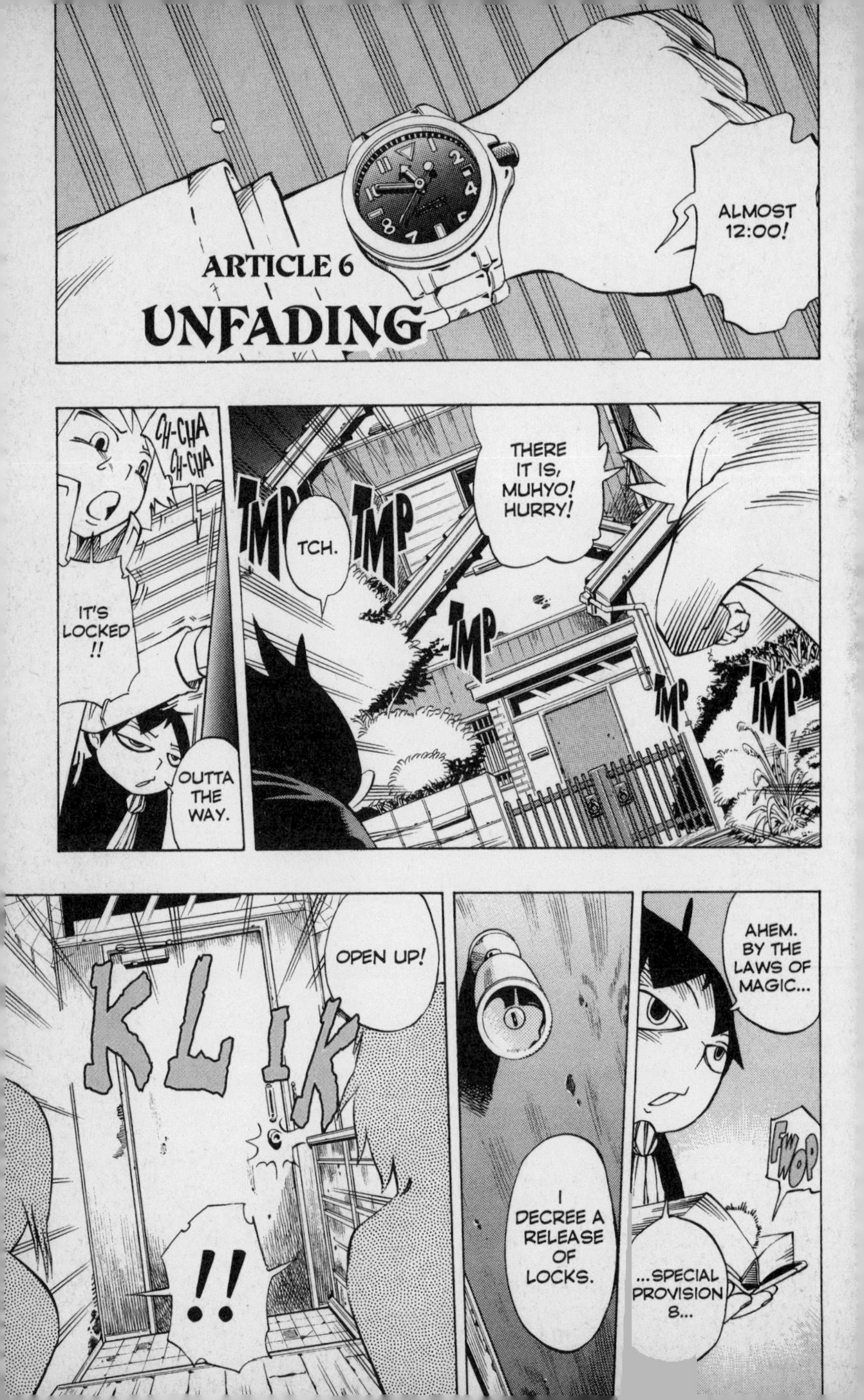
ALMOST 12:00!
THERE IT IS, MUHYO! HURRY!
TMP TMP TMP TMP TMP
TCH.
CH-CHA CH-CHA
IT'S LOCKED !!
OUTTA THE WAY.
AHEM. BY THE LAWS OF MAGIC...
FWOP
...SPECIAL PROVISION 8...
I DECREE A RELEASE OF LOCKS.
OPEN UP!
KLIK
!!

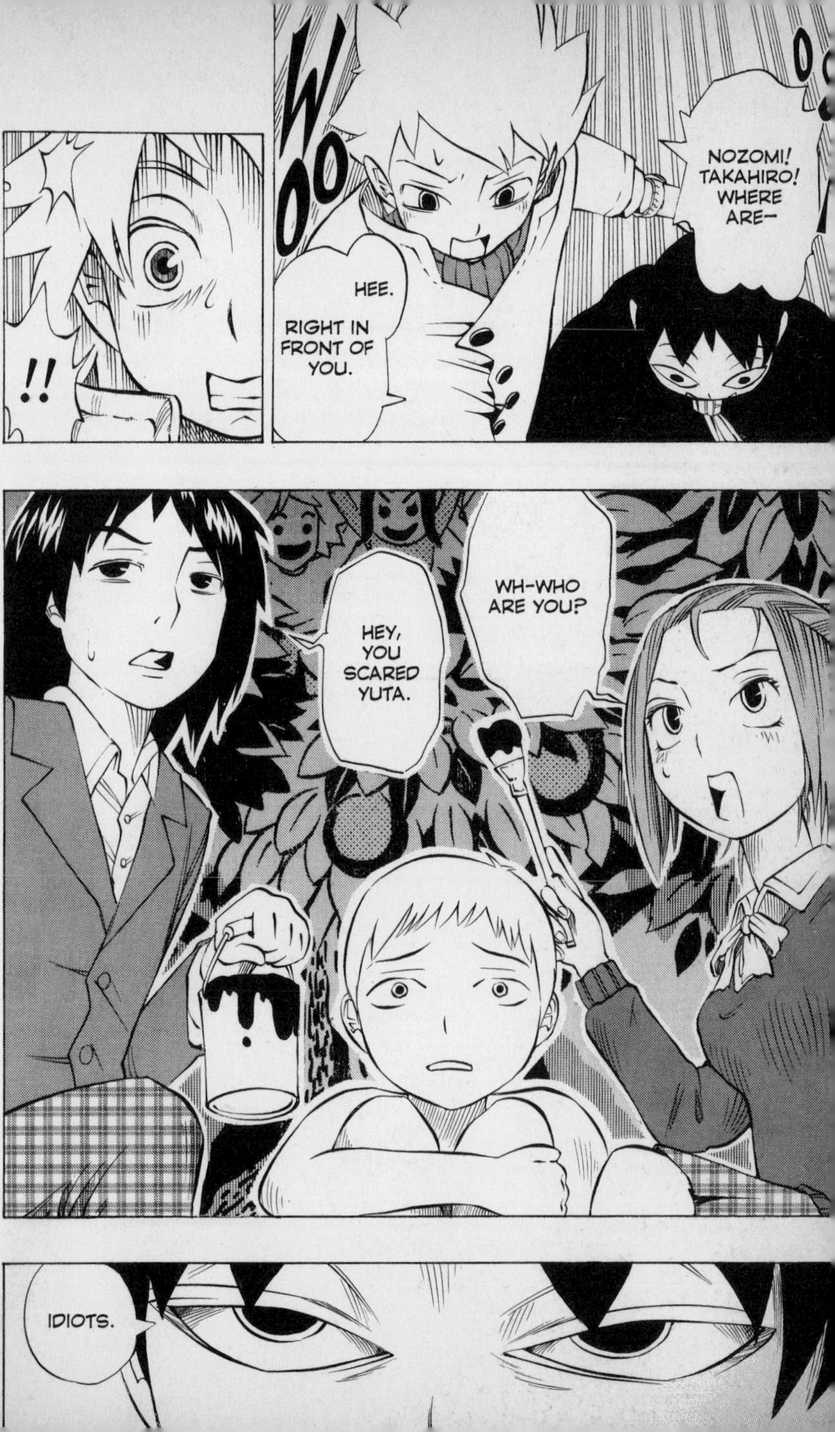
NOZOMI! TAKAHIRO! WHERE ARE—
WOO
HEE.
RIGHT IN FRONT OF YOU.
!!
WH-WHO ARE YOU?
HEY, YOU SCARED YUTA.
IDIOTS.

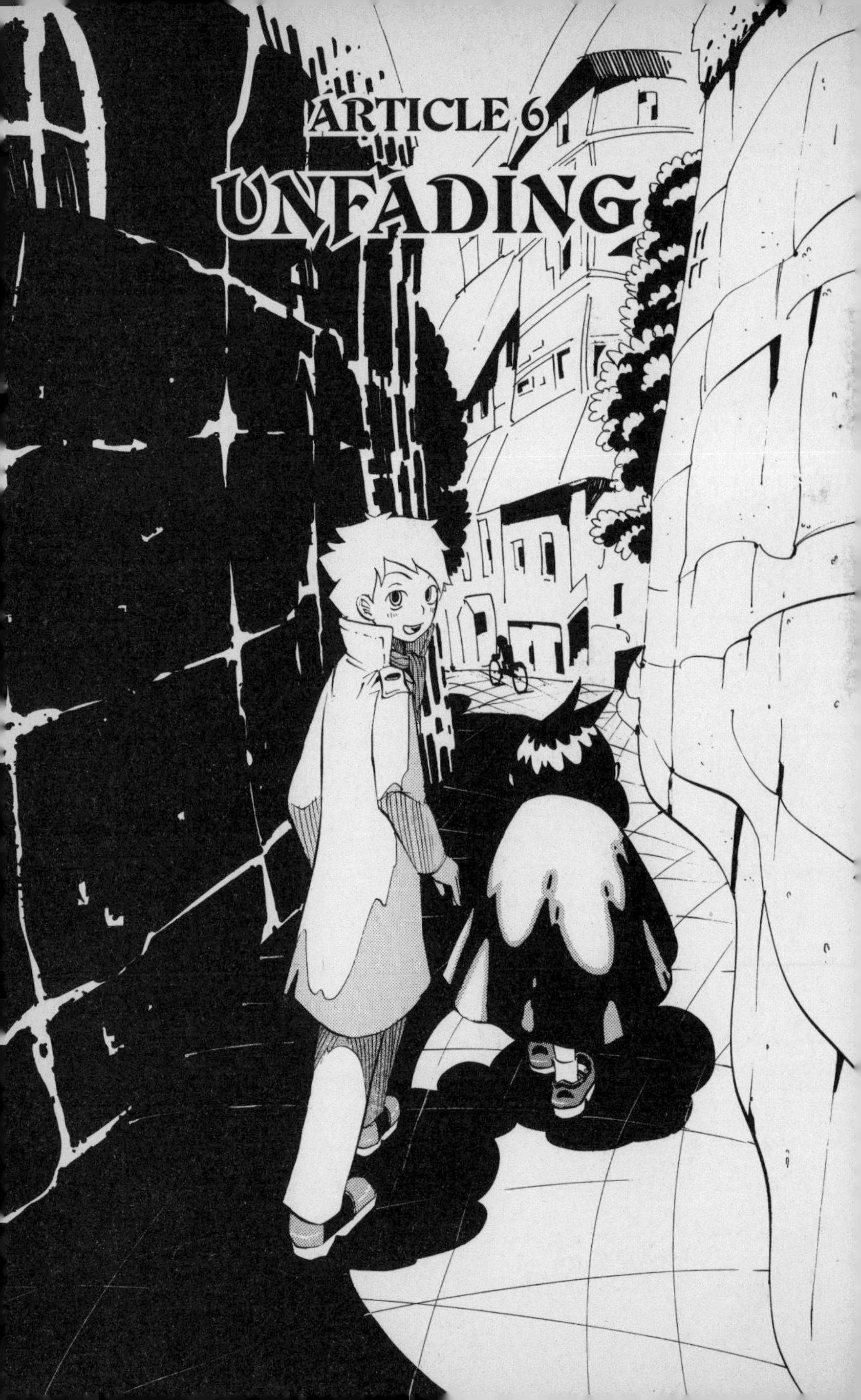
ARTICLE 6
UNFADING

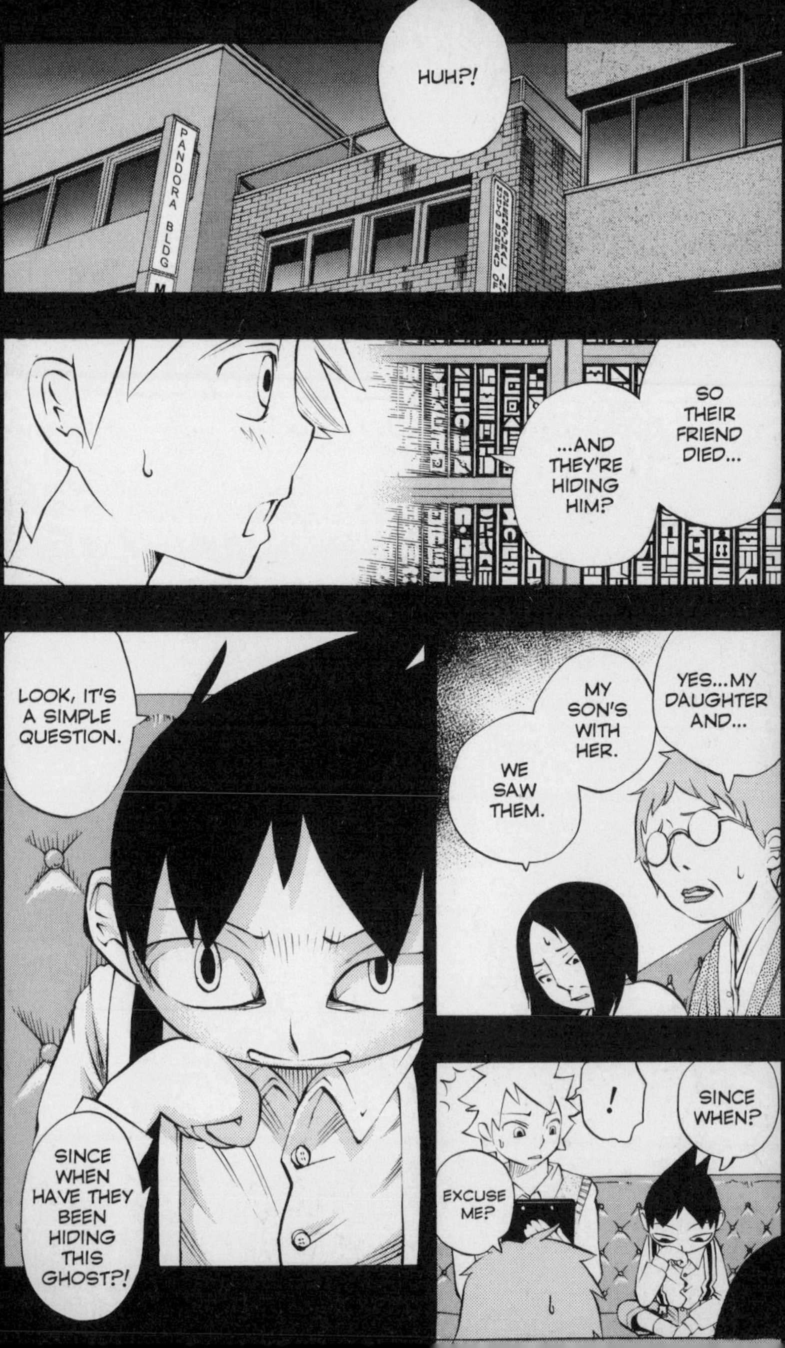
HUH?!
PANDORA BLDG
SO THEIR FRIEND DIED...
...AND THEY'RE HIDING HIM?
YES...MY DAUGHTER AND...
MY SON'S WITH HER.
WE SAW THEM.
SINCE WHEN?
!
EXCUSE ME?
LOOK, IT'S A SIMPLE QUESTION.
SINCE WHEN HAVE THEY BEEN HIDING THIS GHOST?!

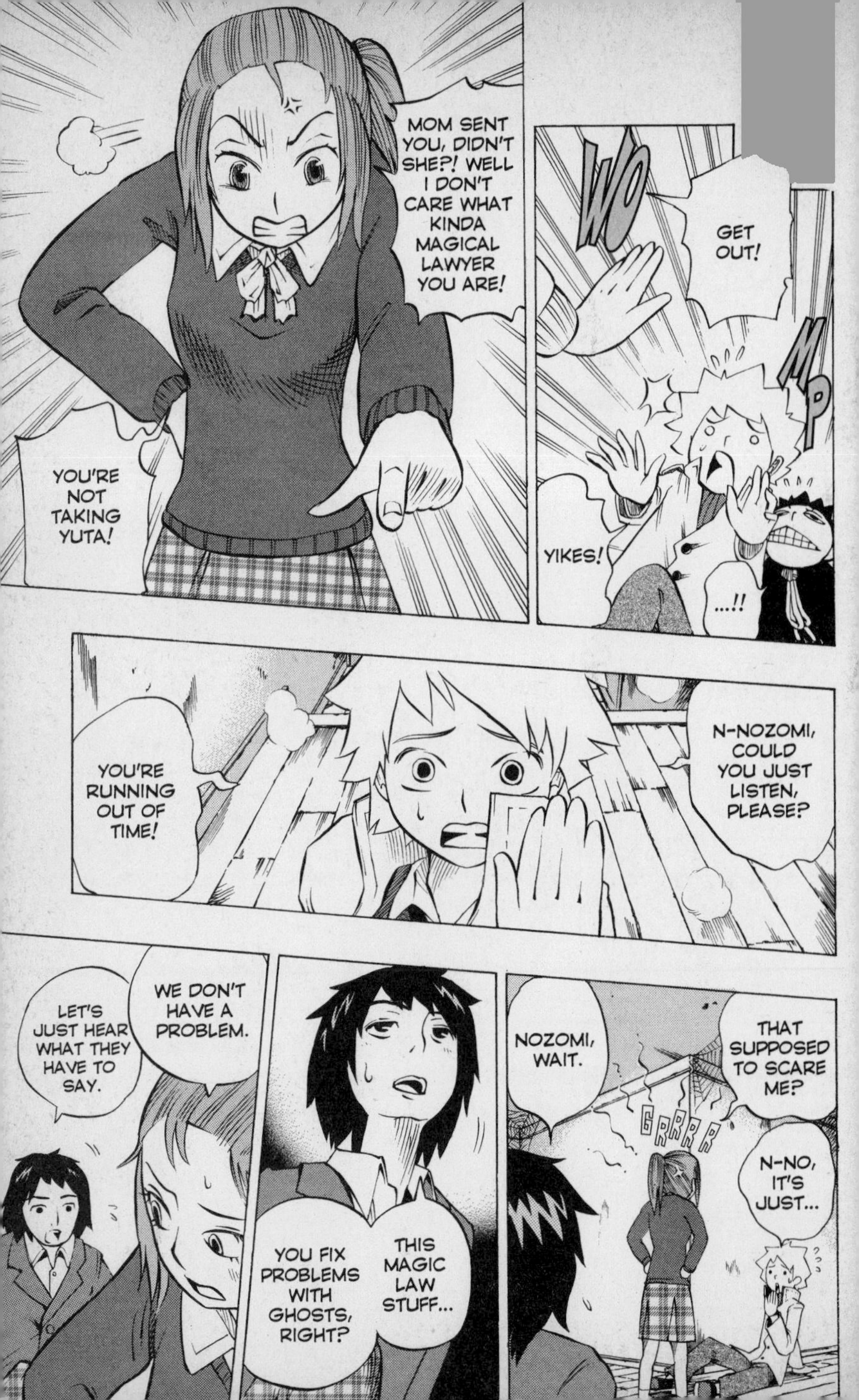
WOMP
GET OUT!
...!!
YIKES!
MOM SENT YOU, DIDN'T SHE?! WELL I DON'T CARE WHAT KINDA MAGICAL LAWYER YOU ARE!
YOU'RE NOT TAKING YUTA!
N-NOZOMI, COULD YOU JUST LISTEN, PLEASE?
YOU'RE RUNNING OUT OF TIME!
THAT SUPPOSED TO SCARE ME?
NOZOMI, WAIT.
GRRRR
N-NO, IT'S JUST...
THIS MAGIC LAW STUFF...
YOU FIX PROBLEMS WITH GHOSTS, RIGHT?
WE DON'T HAVE A PROBLEM.
LET'S JUST HEAR WHAT THEY HAVE TO SAY.

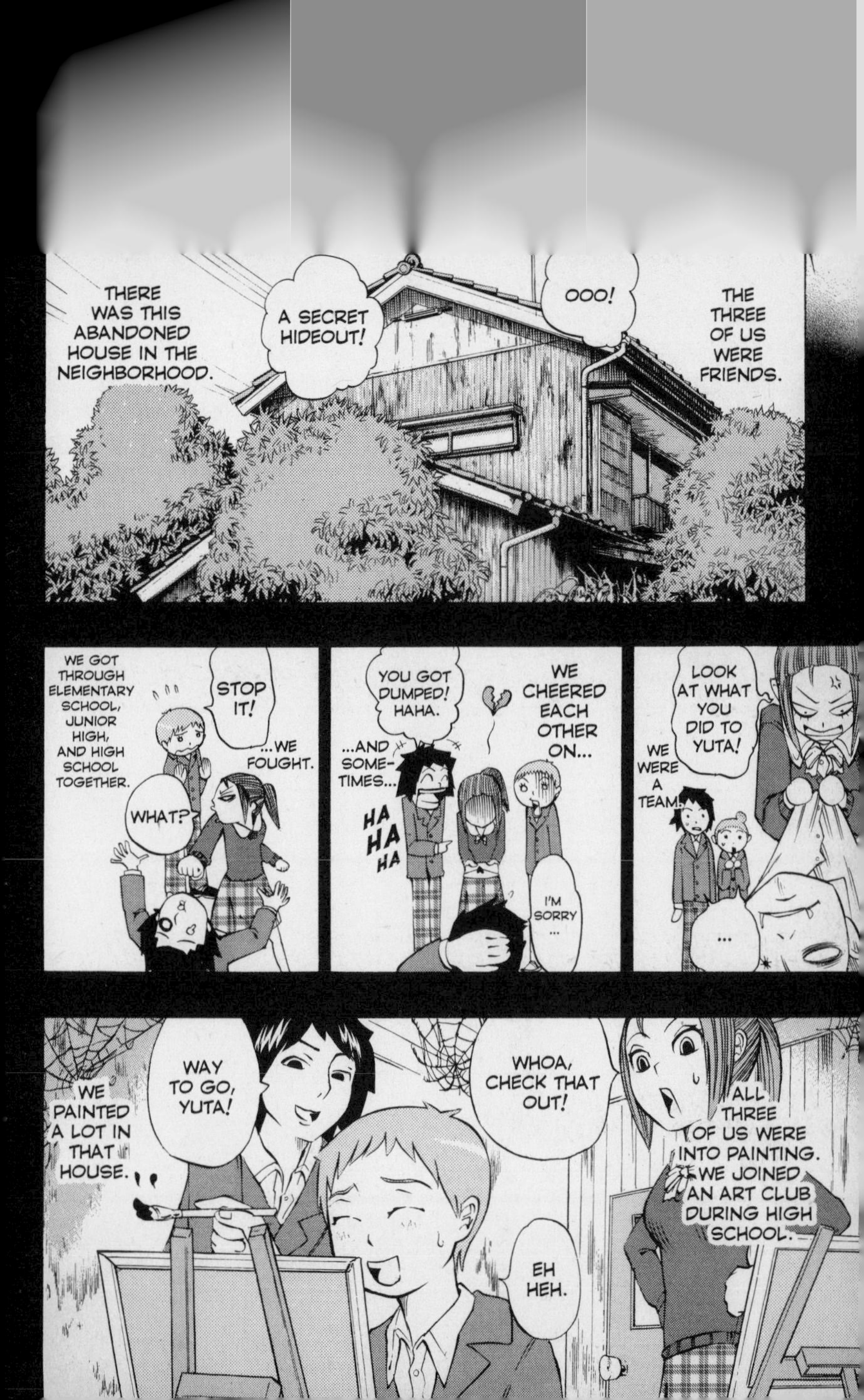
THE THREE OF US WERE FRIENDS.
OOO!
A SECRET HIDEOUT!
THERE WAS THIS ABANDONED HOUSE IN THE NEIGHBORHOOD.
LOOK AT WHAT YOU DID TO YUTA!
WE WERE A TEAM.
...
WE CHEERED EACH OTHER ON...
YOU GOT DUMPED! HAHA.
...AND SOMETIMES...
HA HA HA
I'M SORRY ...
STOP IT!
...WE FOUGHT.
WE GOT THROUGH ELEMENTARY SCHOOL, JUNIOR HIGH, AND HIGH SCHOOL TOGETHER.
WHAT?
ALL THREE OF US WERE INTO PAINTING. WE JOINED AN ART CLUB DURING HIGH SCHOOL.
WHOA, CHECK THAT OUT!
EH HEH.
WAY TO GO, YUTA!
WE PAINTED A LOT IN THAT HOUSE.

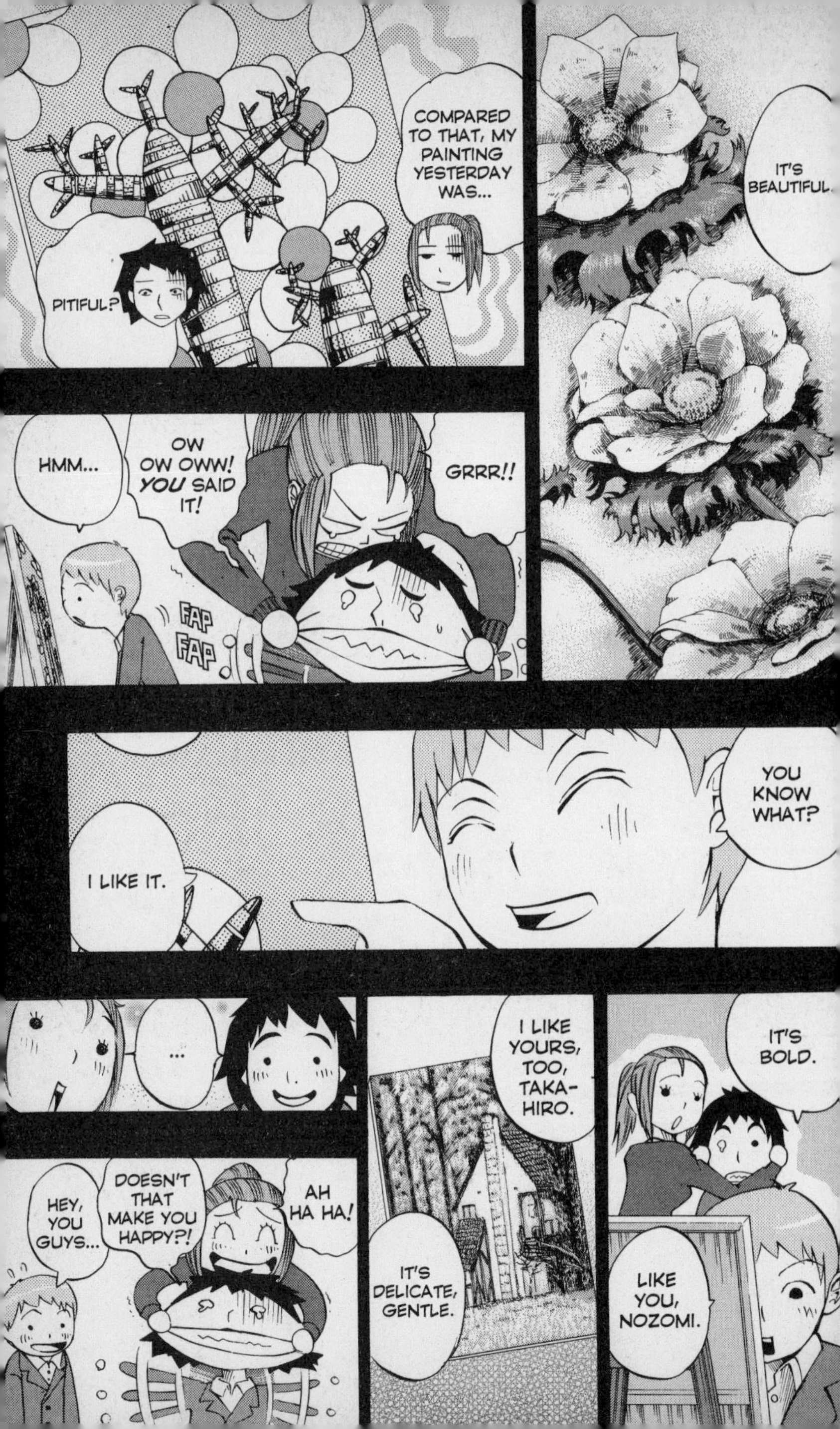
IT'S BEAUTIFUL.
COMPARED TO THAT, MY PAINTING YESTERDAY WAS...
PITIFUL?
GRRR!!
OW OW OWW! YOU SAID IT!
HMM...
FAP FAP
YOU KNOW WHAT?
I LIKE IT.
IT'S BOLD.
LIKE YOU, NOZOMI.
I LIKE YOURS, TOO, TAKA-HIRO.
IT'S DELICATE, GENTLE.
...
AH HA HA!
DOESN'T THAT MAKE YOU HAPPY?!
HEY, YOU GUYS...

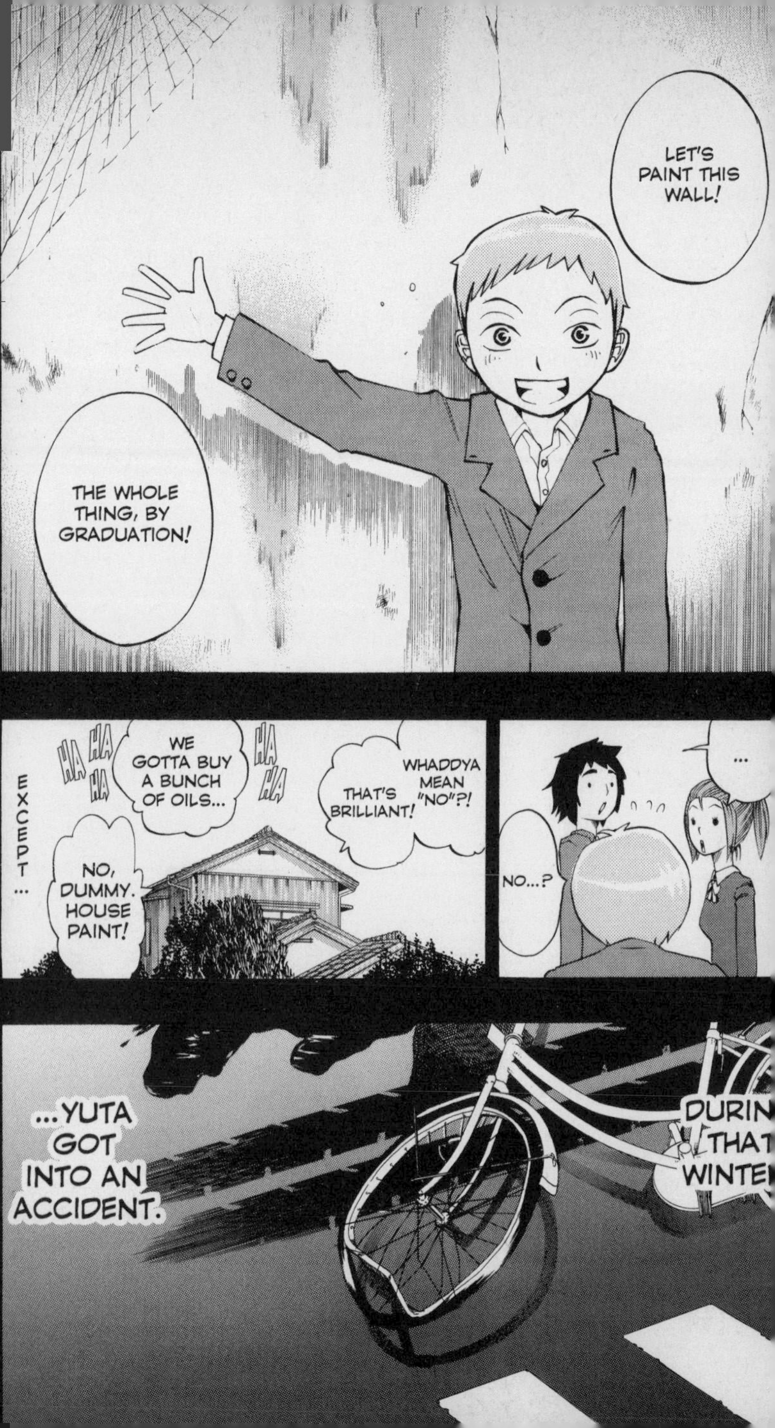
LET'S PAINT THIS WALL!
THE WHOLE THING, BY GRADUATION!
...
NO...?
WHADDYA MEAN "NO"?!
THAT'S BRILLIANT!
HA HA
WE GOTTA BUY A BUNCH OF OILS...
HA HA HA
NO, DUMMY. HOUSE PAINT!
EXCEPT...
DURIN THAT WINTE
...YUTA GOT INTO AN ACCIDENT.

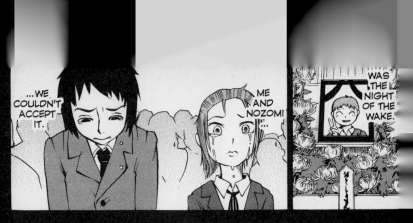

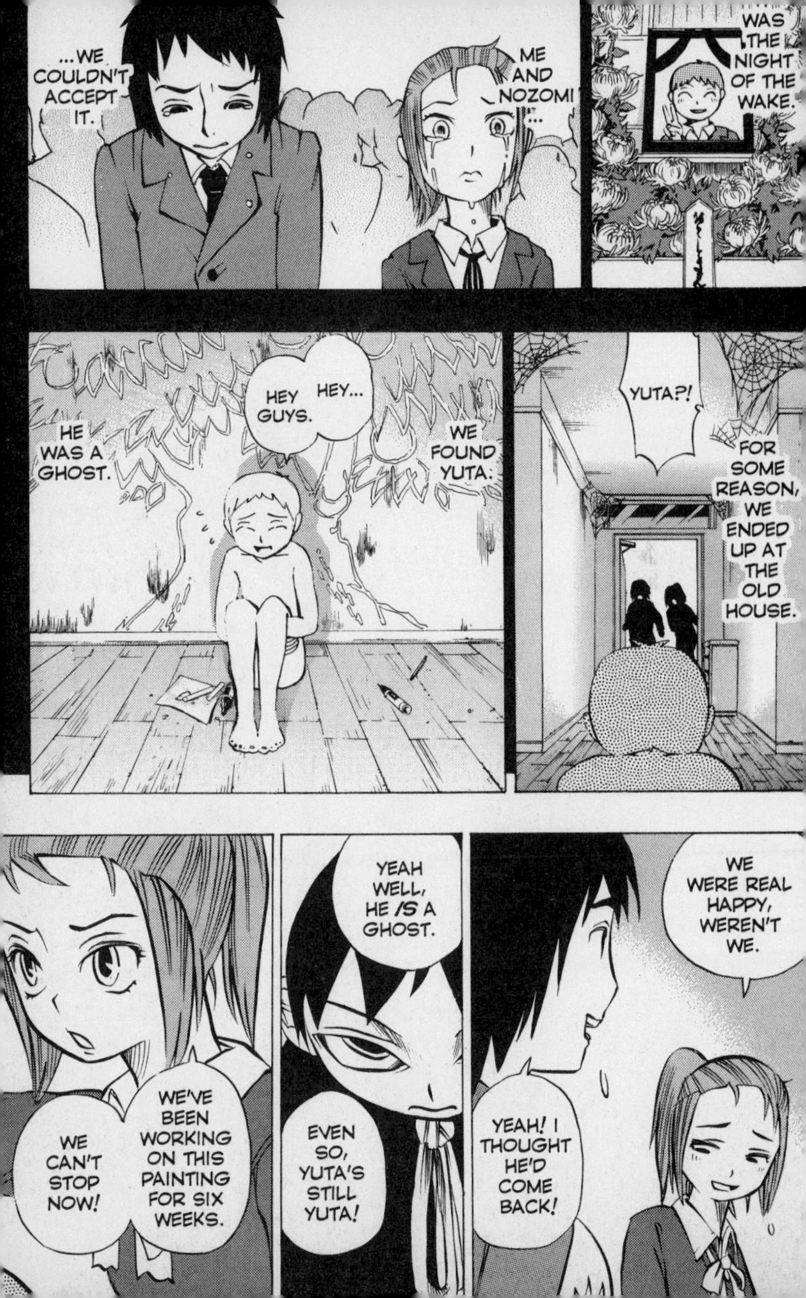
WAS THE NIGHT OF THE WAKE.
ME AND NOZOMI...
...WE COULDN'T ACCEPT IT.
FOR SOME REASON, WE ENDED UP AT THE OLD HOUSE.
YUTA?!
WE FOUND YUTA.
HEY...
HEY GUYS.
HE WAS A GHOST.
WE WERE REAL HAPPY, WEREN'T WE.
YEAH! I THOUGHT HE'D COME BACK!
YEAH WELL, HE *IS* A GHOST.
EVEN SO, YUTA'S STILL YUTA!
WE'VE BEEN WORKING ON THIS PAINTING FOR SIX WEEKS.
WE CAN'T STOP NOW!

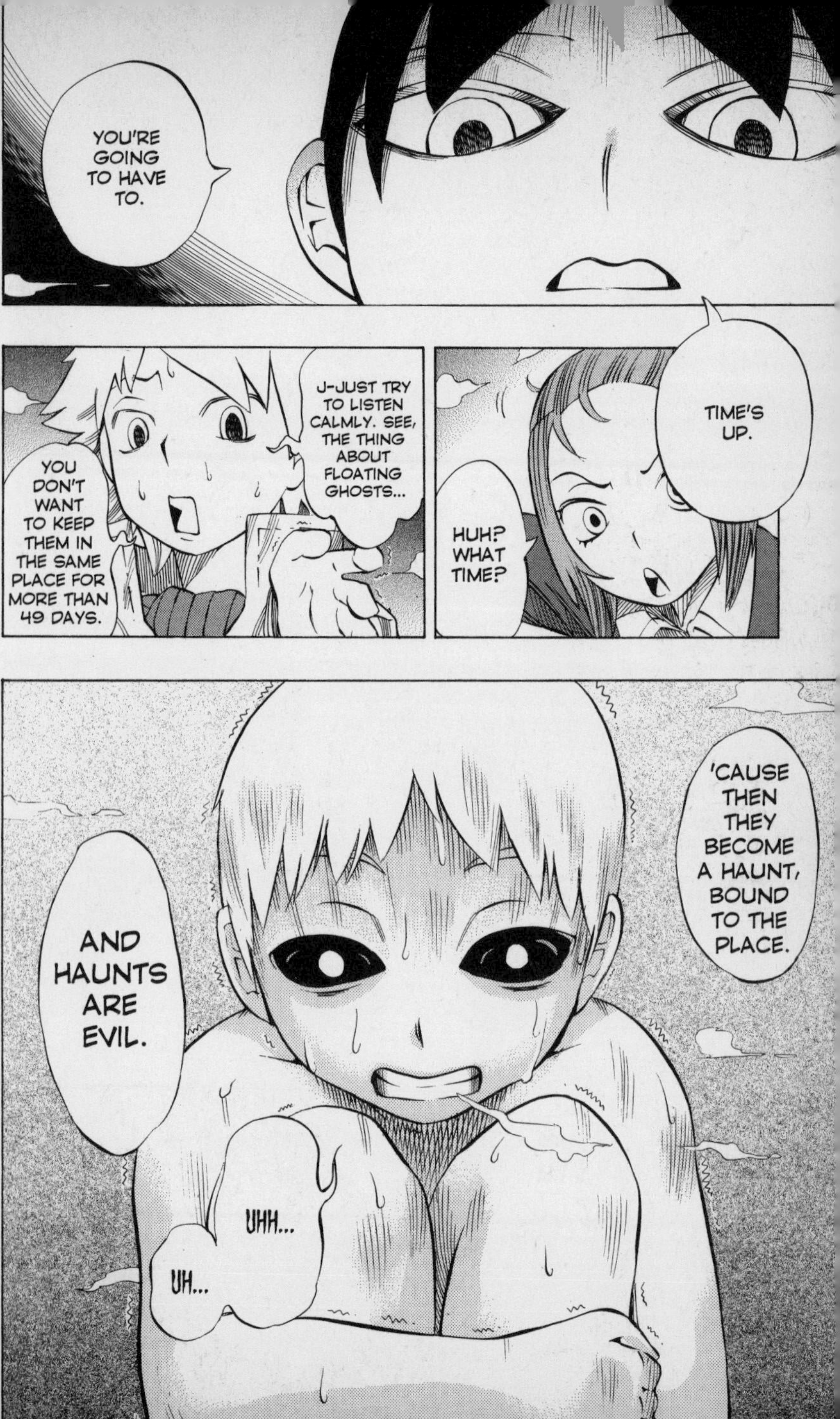
YOU'RE GOING TO HAVE TO.
TIME'S UP.
HUH? WHAT TIME?
J-JUST TRY TO LISTEN CALMLY. SEE, THE THING ABOUT FLOATING GHOSTS...
YOU DON'T WANT TO KEEP THEM IN THE SAME PLACE FOR MORE THAN 49 DAYS.
'CAUSE THEN THEY BECOME A HAUNT, BOUND TO THE PLACE.
AND HAUNTS ARE EVIL.
UHH...
UH...

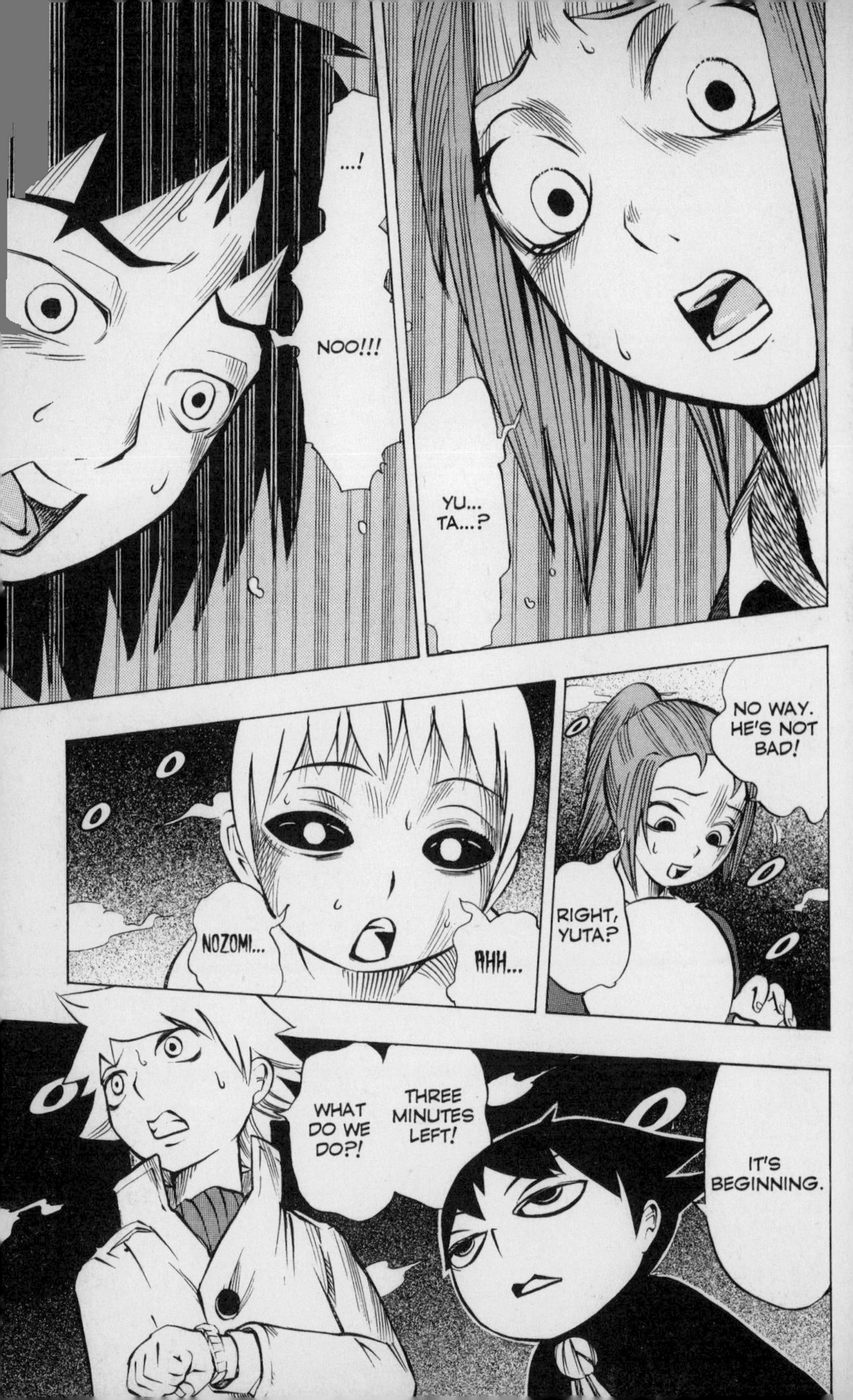
YU... TA...?
...!
NOO!!!
NO WAY. HE'S NOT BAD!
RIGHT, YUTA?
AHH...
NOZOMI...
IT'S BEGINNING.
THREE MINUTES LEFT!
WHAT DO WE DO?!

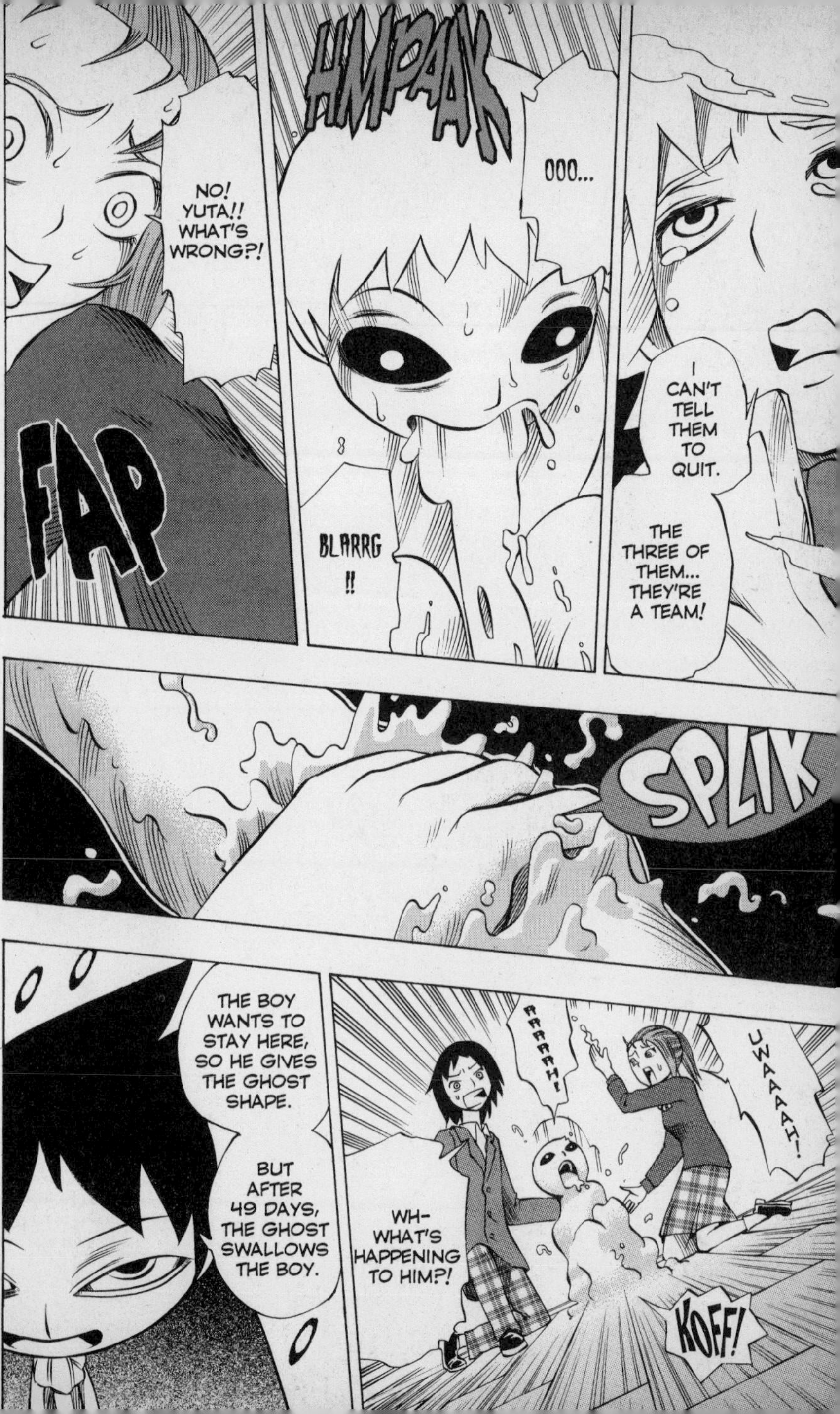
I CAN'T TELL THEM TO QUIT.
THE THREE OF THEM... THEY'RE A TEAM!
HMPAK
OOO...
BLARRG!!
NO! YUTA!! WHAT'S WRONG?!
FAP
SPLIK
UWAAAAH!
ARRRRH!
WH-WHAT'S HAPPENING TO HIM?!
KOFF!
THE BOY WANTS TO STAY HERE, SO HE GIVES THE GHOST SHAPE.
BUT AFTER 49 DAYS, THE GHOST SWALLOWS THE BOY.

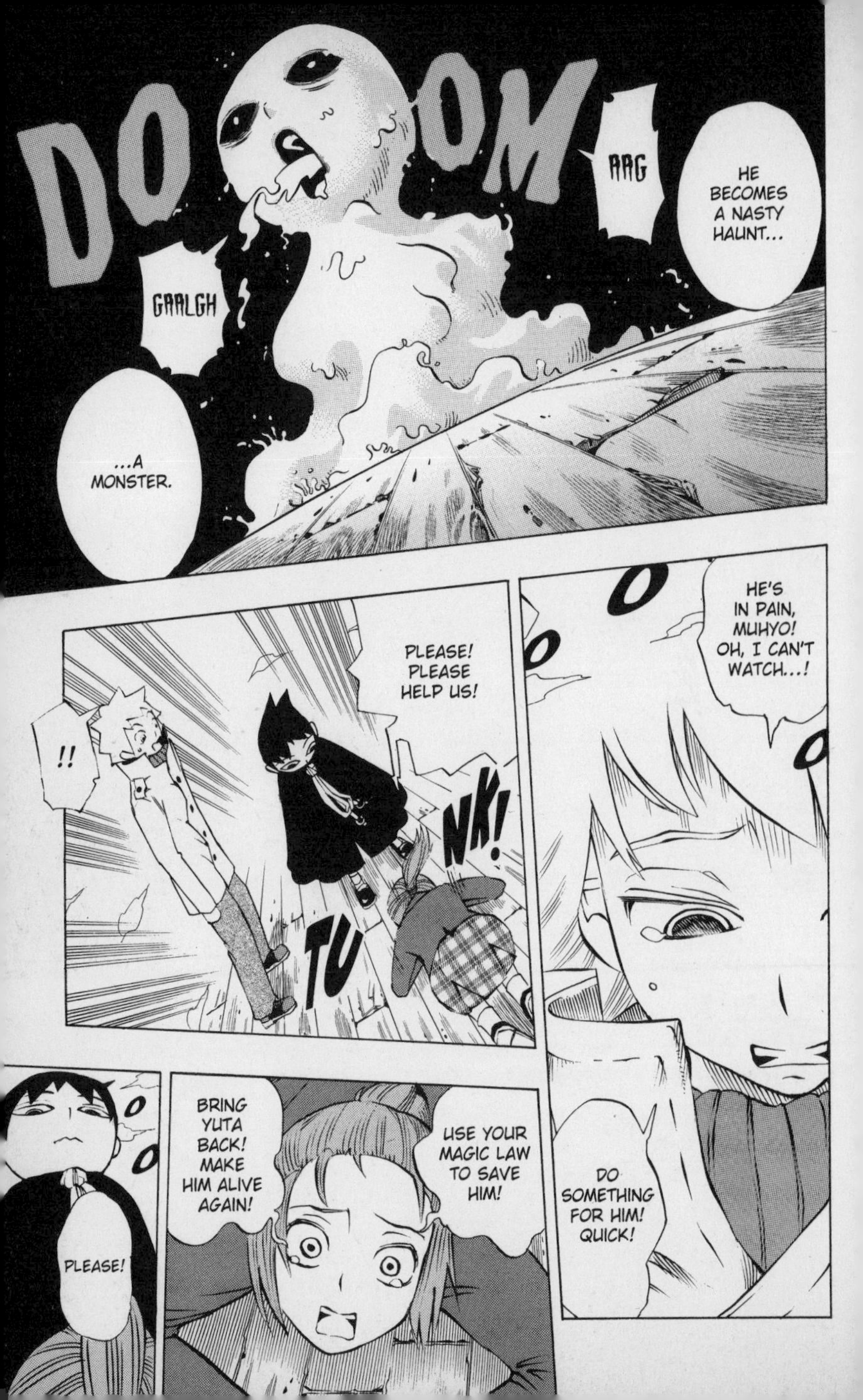
HE BECOMES A NASTY HAUNT...
ARG
DOOOM
GAALGH
...A MONSTER.
HE'S IN PAIN, MUHYO! OH, I CAN'T WATCH...!
DO SOMETHING FOR HIM! QUICK!
PLEASE! PLEASE HELP US!
TUNK!
!!
USE YOUR MAGIC LAW TO SAVE HIM!
BRING YUTA BACK! MAKE HIM ALIVE AGAIN!
PLEASE!

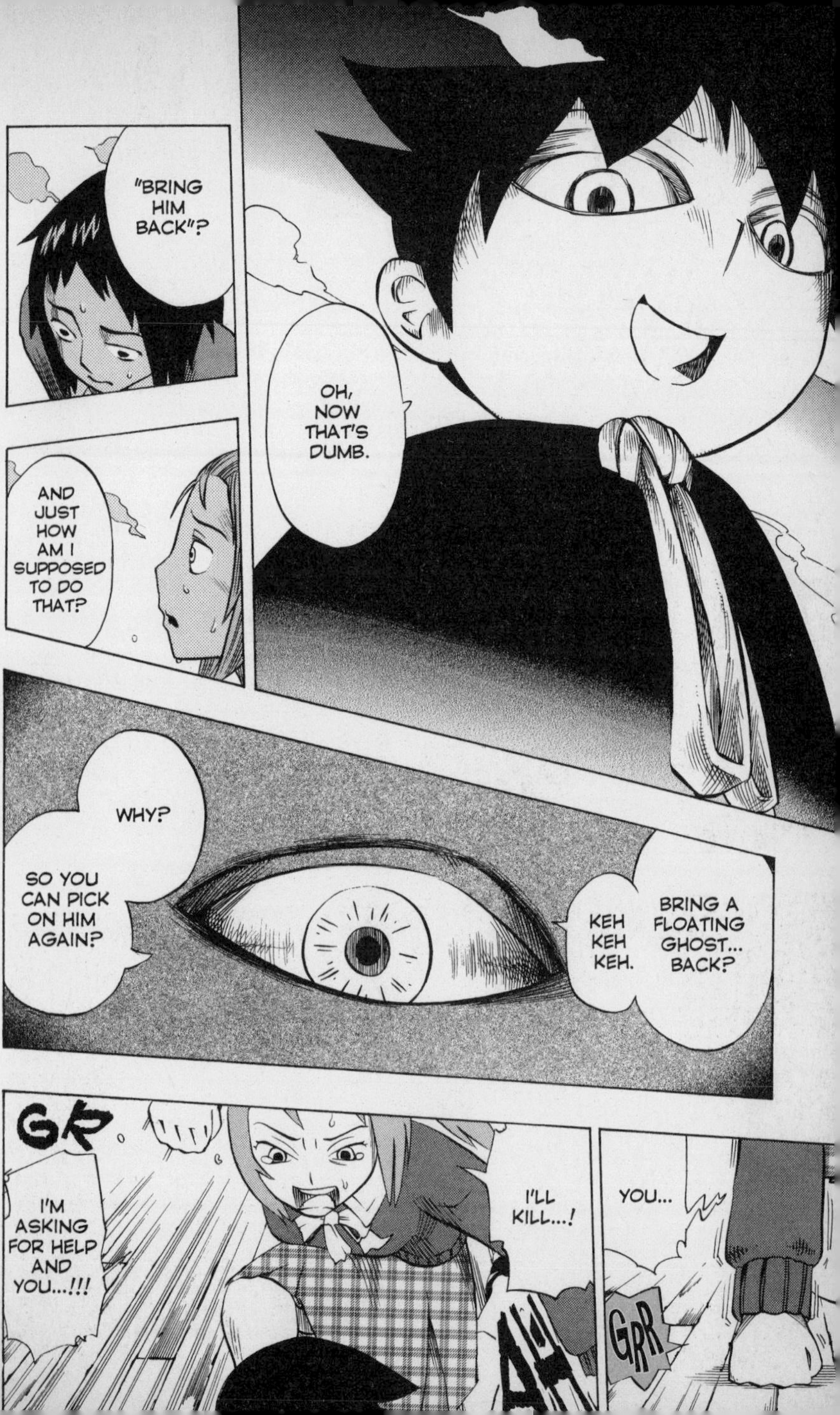
OH, NOW THAT'S DUMB.
"BRING HIM BACK"?
AND JUST HOW AM I SUPPOSED TO DO THAT?
BRING A FLOATING GHOST... BACK?
KEH KEH KEH.
WHY?
SO YOU CAN PICK ON HIM AGAIN?
YOU...
GRR
I'LL KILL...!
AH
GR
I'M ASKING FOR HELP AND YOU...!!!

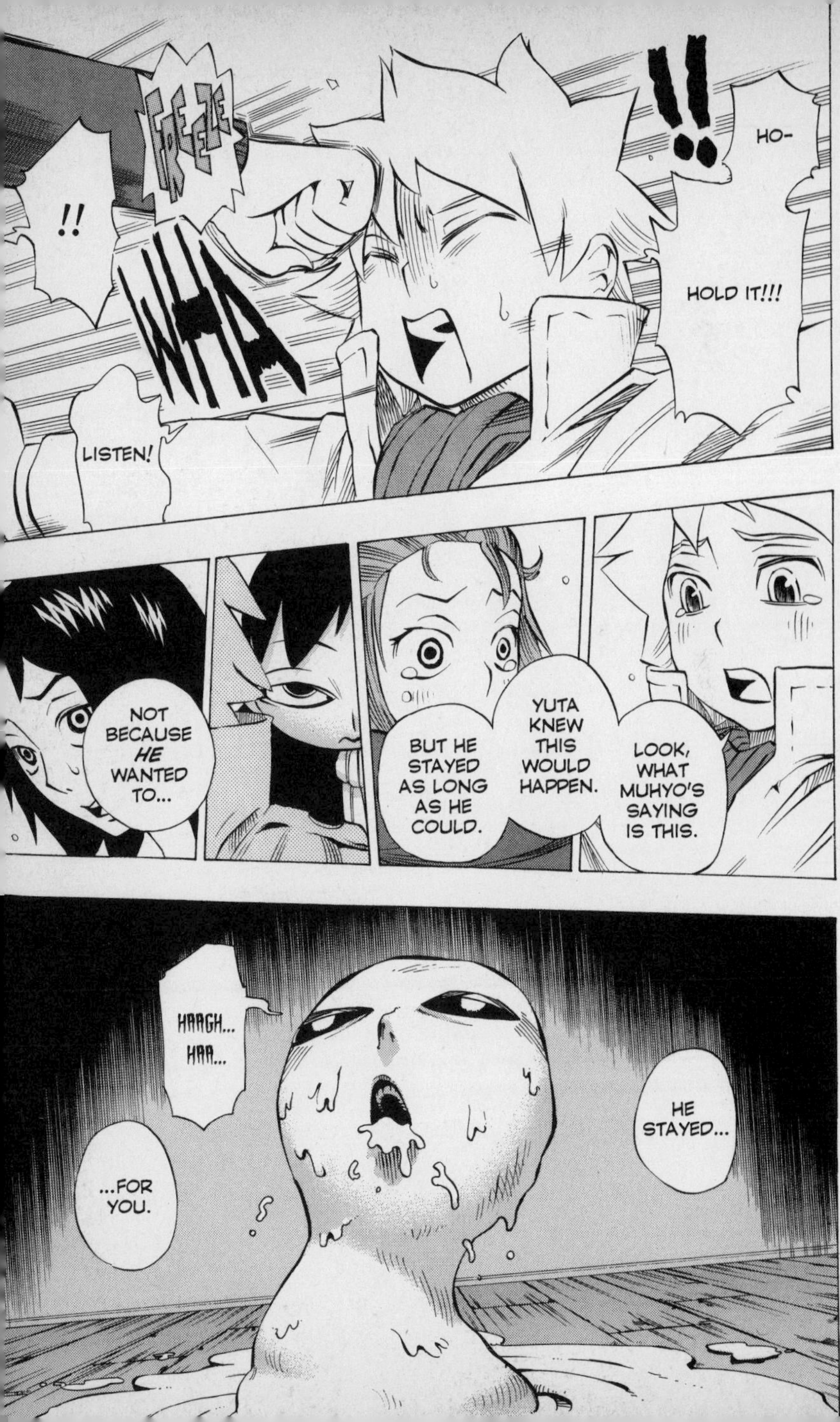
!!
HO-
HOLD IT!!!
FREEZE
!!
WHA
LISTEN!
LOOK, WHAT MUHYO'S SAYING IS THIS.
YUTA KNEW THIS WOULD HAPPEN.
BUT HE STAYED AS LONG AS HE COULD.
NOT BECAUSE *HE* WANTED TO...
HE STAYED...
HAAGH... HAA...
...FOR YOU.

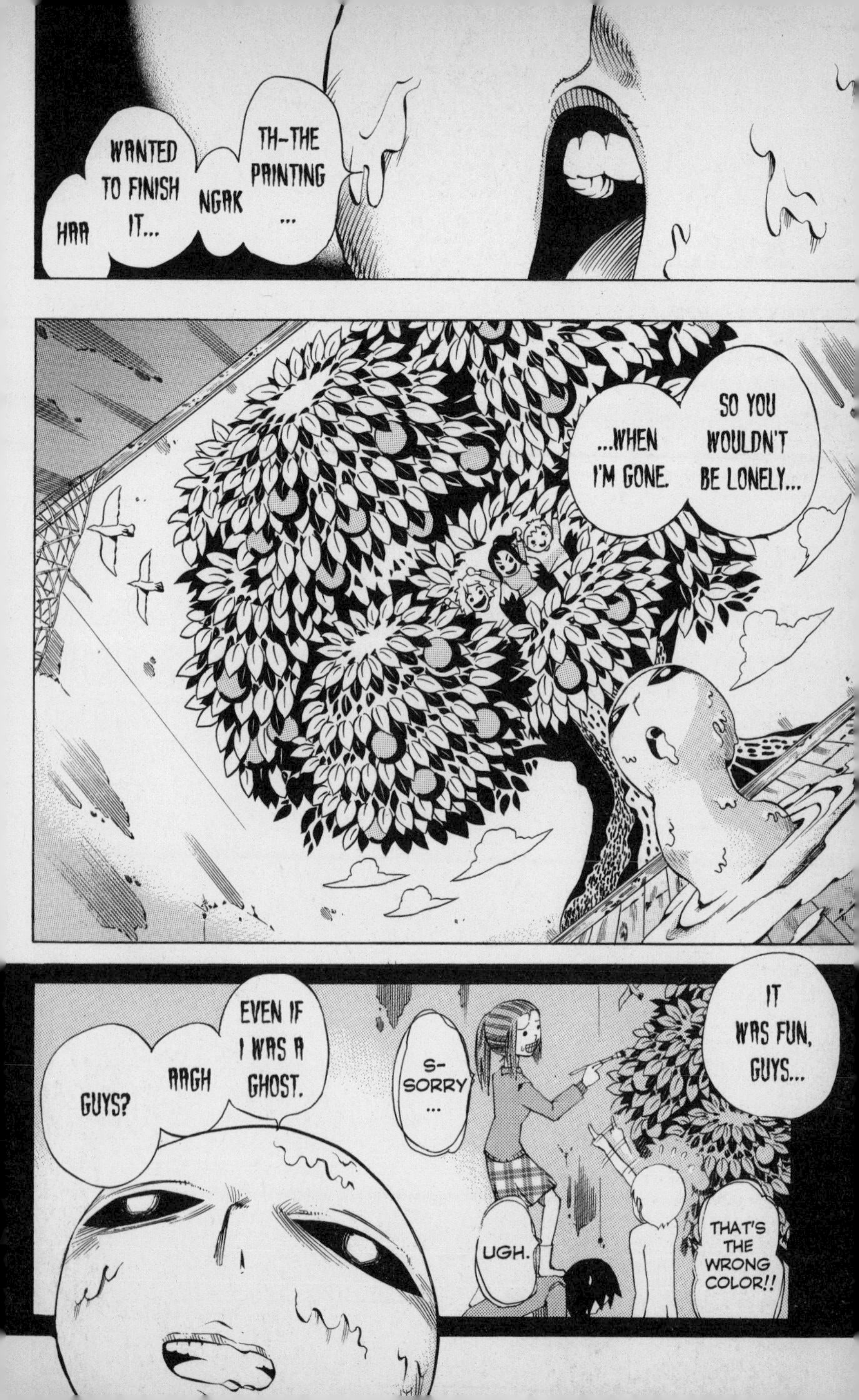
TH-THE PAINTING ...
NGAK
WANTED TO FINISH IT...
HAA
SO YOU WOULDN'T BE LONELY...
...WHEN I'M GONE.
IT WAS FUN, GUYS...
THAT'S THE WRONG COLOR!!
UGH.
S-SORRY ...
EVEN IF I WAS A GHOST.
AAGH
GUYS?

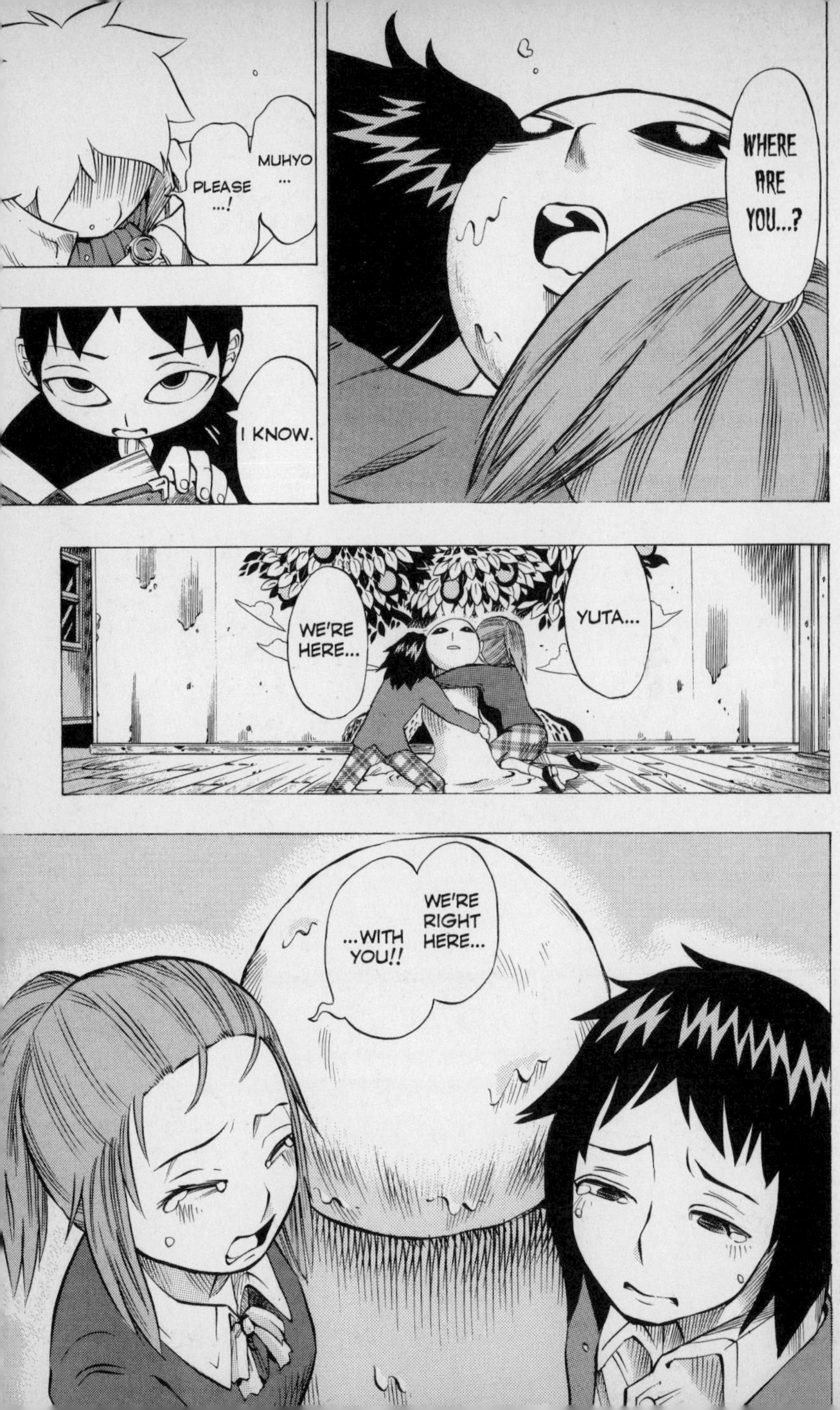
WHERE ARE YOU...?
MUHYO...
PLEASE...!
I KNOW.
YUTA...
WE'RE HERE...
WE'RE RIGHT HERE...
...WITH YOU!!

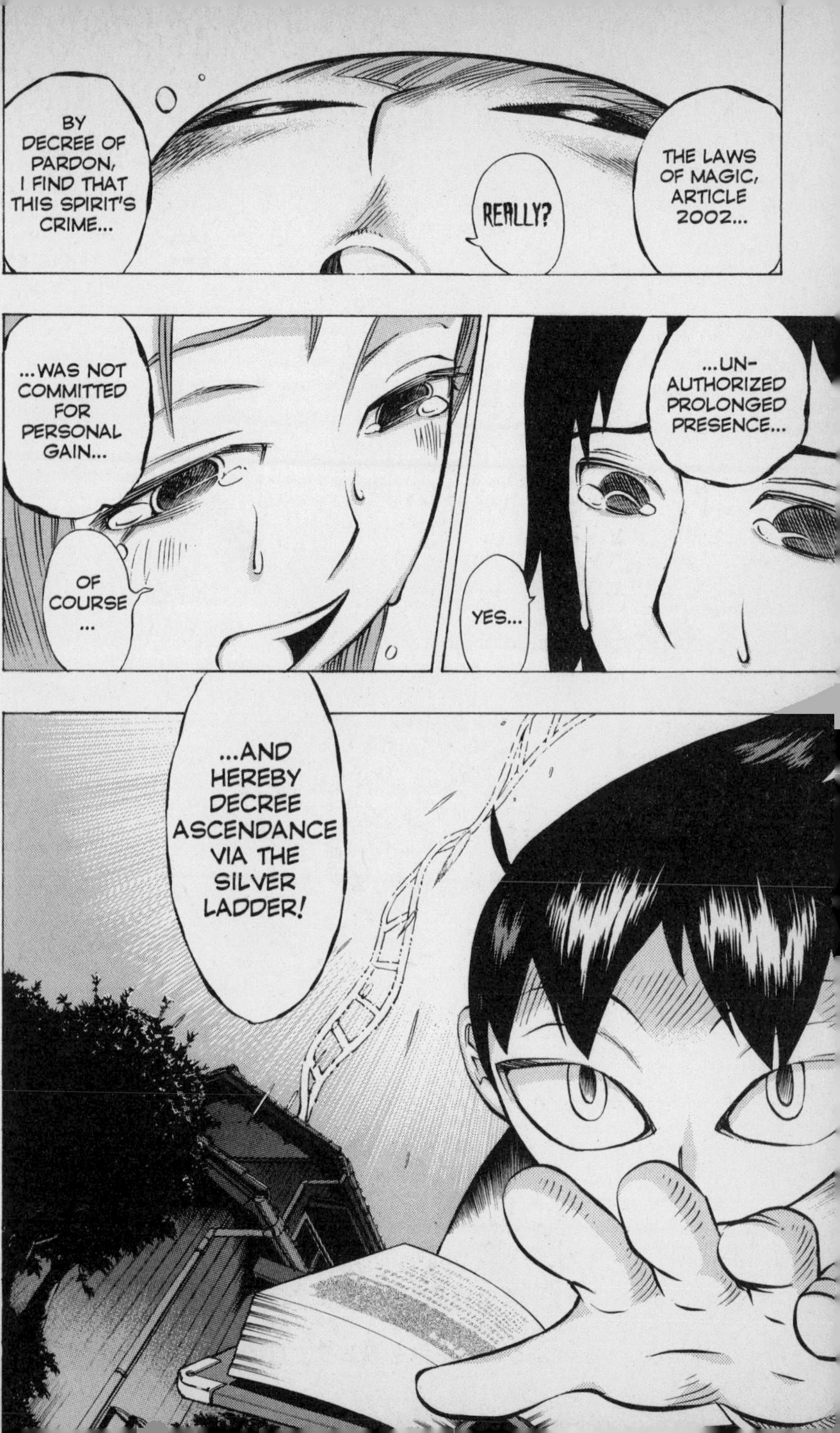
THE LAWS OF MAGIC, ARTICLE 2002...
REALLY?
BY DECREE OF PARDON, I FIND THAT THIS SPIRIT'S CRIME...
...UN-AUTHORIZED PROLONGED PRESENCE...
YES...
...WAS NOT COMMITTED FOR PERSONAL GAIN...
OF COURSE...
...AND HEREBY DECREE ASCENDANCE VIA THE SILVER LADDER!

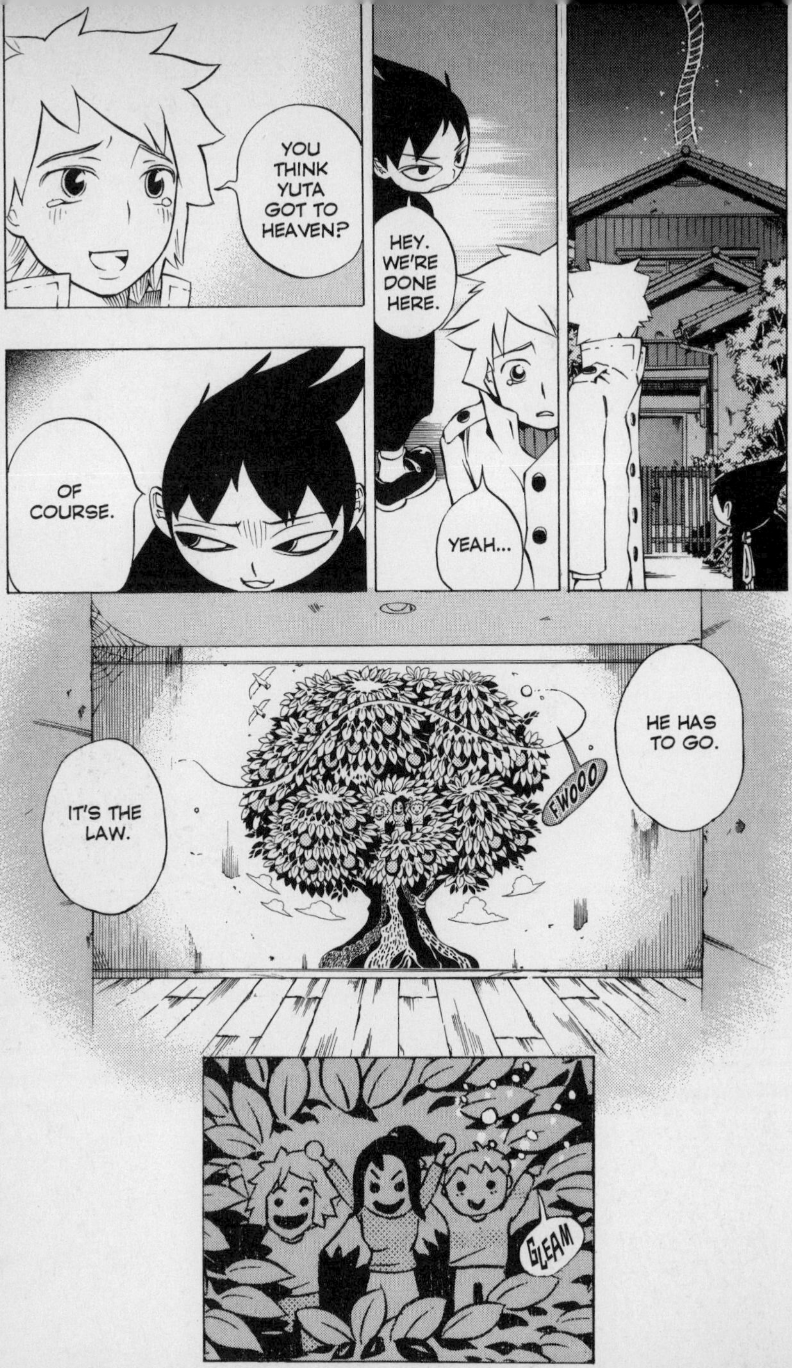
HEY. WE'RE DONE HERE.
YEAH...
YOU THINK YUTA GOT TO HEAVEN?
OF COURSE.
HE HAS TO GO.
FWOOO
IT'S THE LAW.
GLEAM

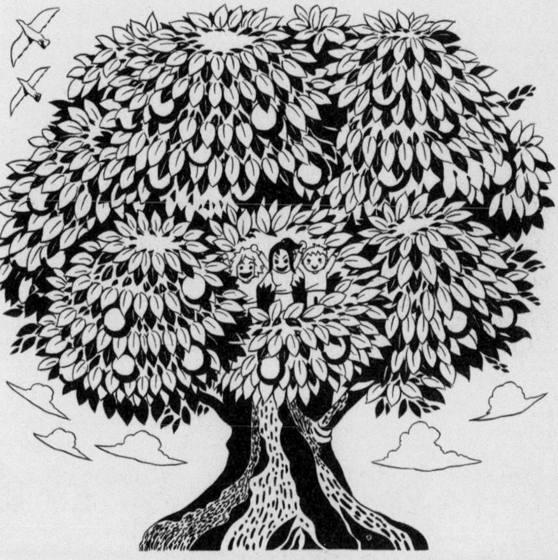
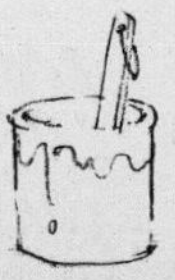

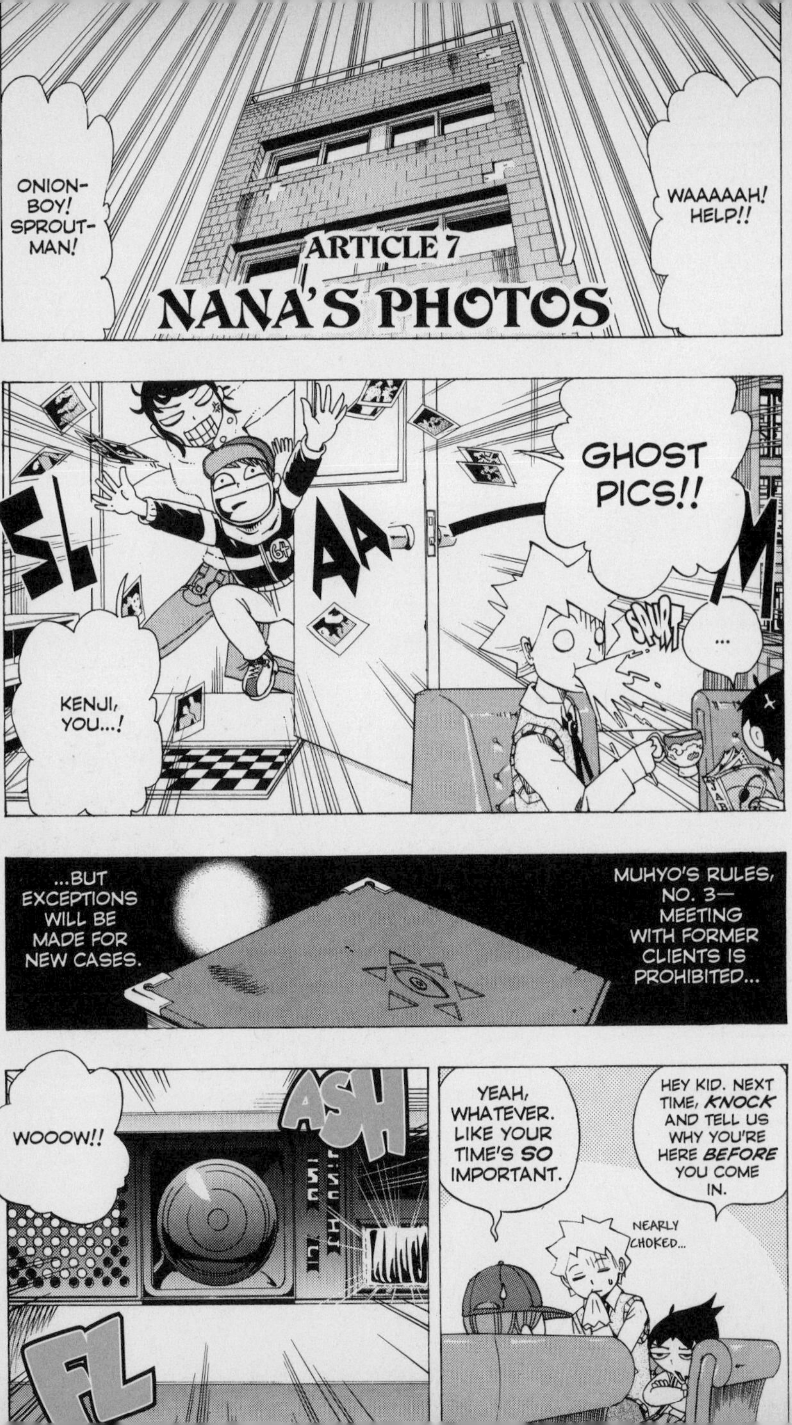

WAAAAAH! HELP!!
ARTICLE 7
NANA'S PHOTOS
ONION-BOY! SPROUT-MAN!
GHOST PICS!!
M
...
SPURT
AA
SL
KENJI, YOU...!
MUHYO'S RULES, NO. 3—MEETING WITH FORMER CLIENTS IS PROHIBITED...
...BUT EXCEPTIONS WILL BE MADE FOR NEW CASES.
HEY KID. NEXT TIME, KNOCK AND TELL US WHY YOU'RE HERE BEFORE YOU COME IN.
YEAH, WHATEVER. LIKE YOUR TIME'S SO IMPORTANT.
NEARLY CHOKED...
ASH
WOOOW!!
FL

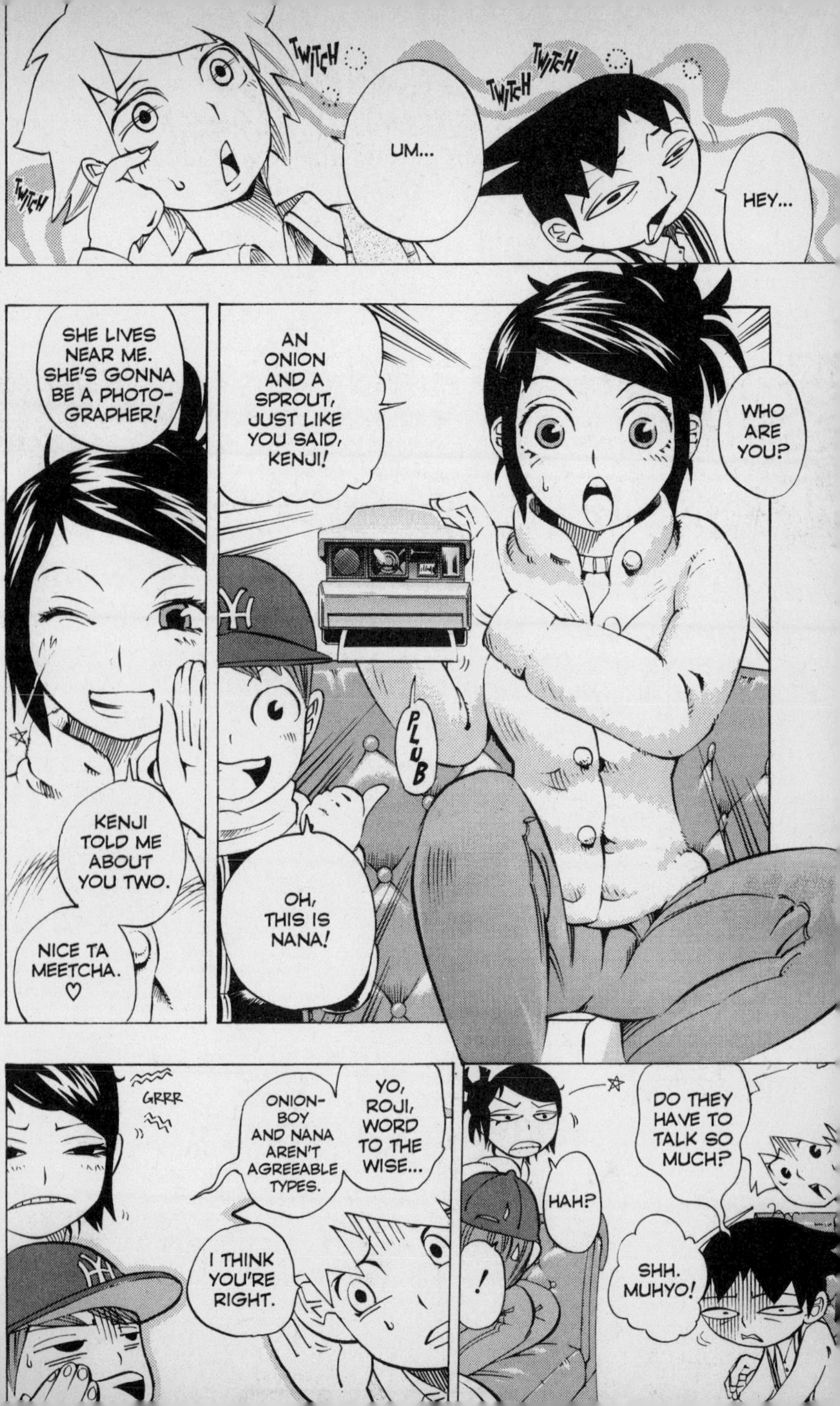
TWITCH
TWITCH
HEY...
TWITCH
UM...
TWITCH
WHO ARE YOU?
AN ONION AND A SPROUT, JUST LIKE YOU SAID, KENJI!
PLUB
OH, THIS IS NANA!
SHE LIVES NEAR ME. SHE'S GONNA BE A PHOTO-GRAPHER!
KENJI TOLD ME ABOUT YOU TWO.
NICE TA MEETCHA. ♡
DO THEY HAVE TO TALK SO MUCH?
HAH?
SHH. MUHYO!
!
YO, ROJI, WORD TO THE WISE...
ONION-BOY AND NANA AREN'T AGREEABLE TYPES.
GRRR
I THINK YOU'RE RIGHT.

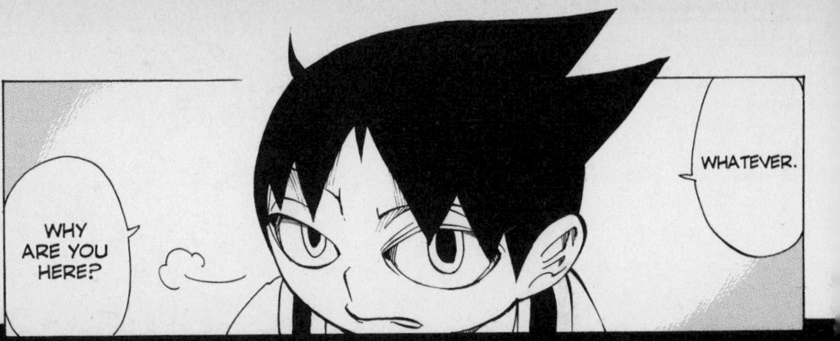
WHATEVER.
WHY ARE YOU HERE?

ARTICLE 7
NANA'S PHOTOS

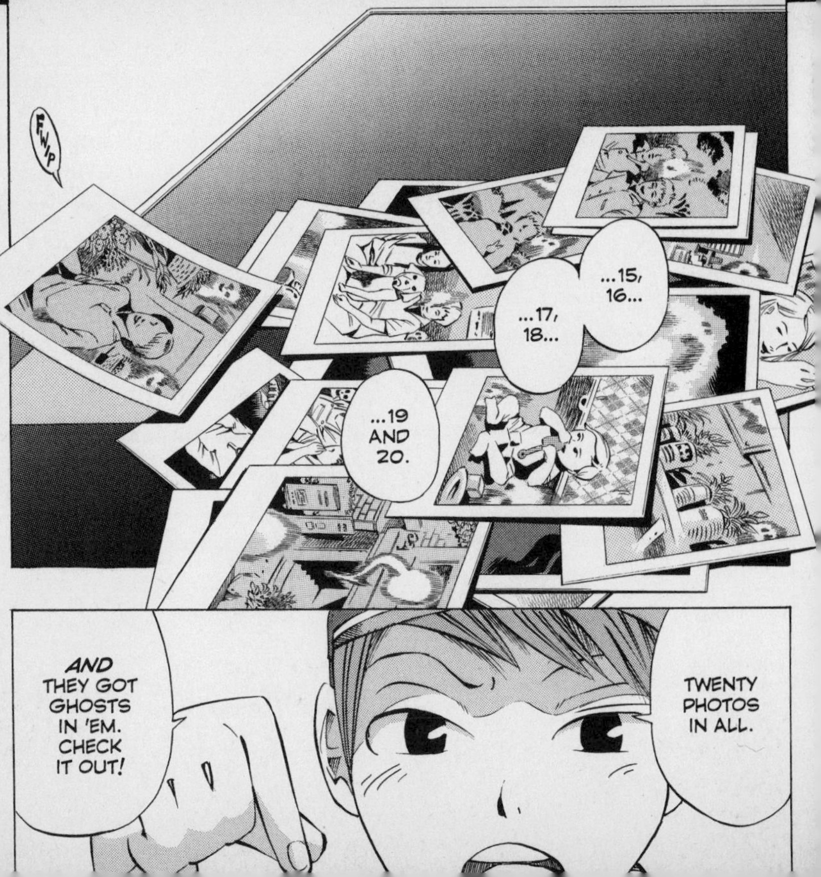
FWIP
...15, 16...
...17, 18...
...19 AND 20.
TWENTY PHOTOS IN ALL.
AND THEY GOT GHOSTS IN 'EM. CHECK IT OUT!

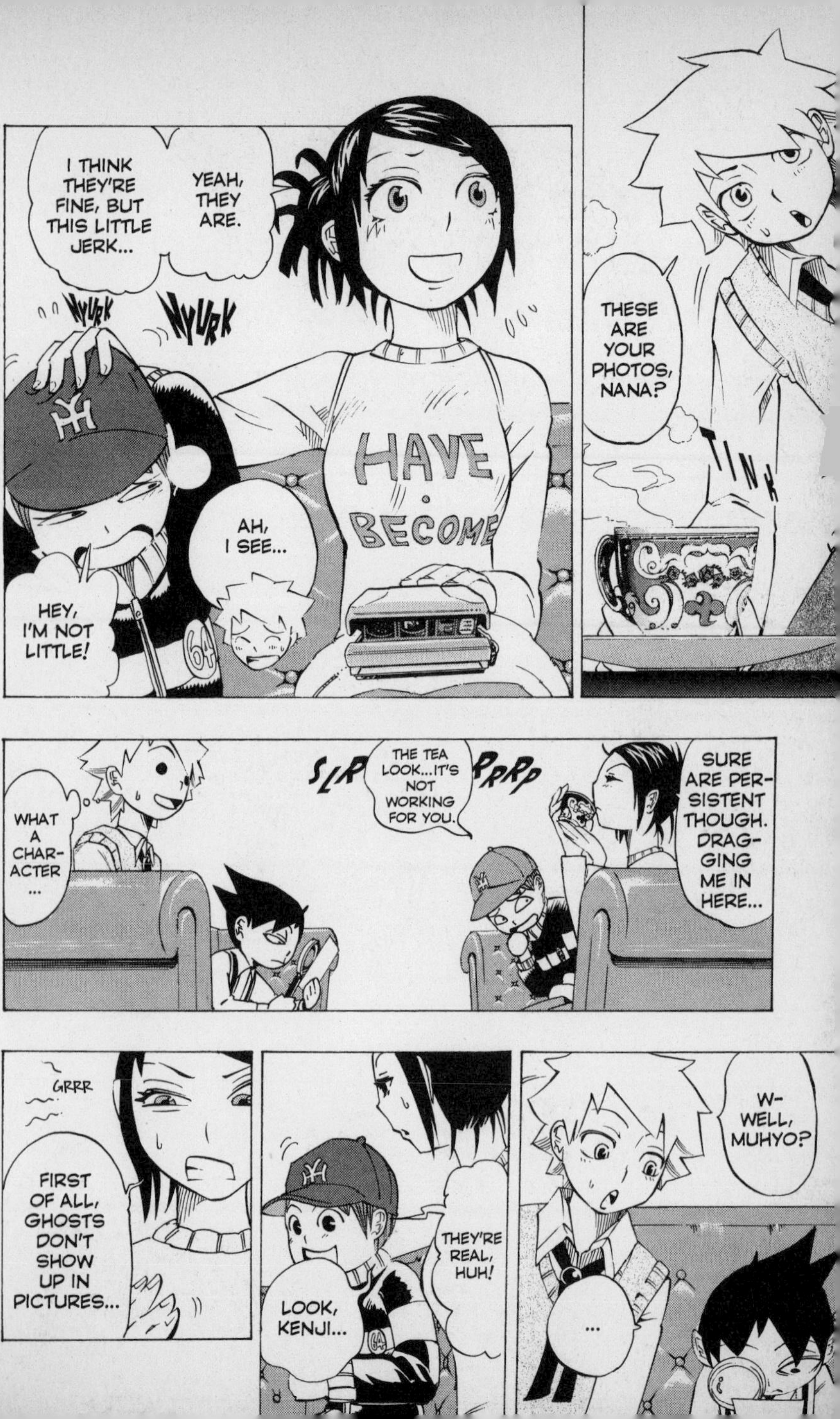
THESE ARE YOUR PHOTOS, NANA?
TINK
YEAH, THEY ARE.
I THINK THEY'RE FINE, BUT THIS LITTLE JERK...
NYURK
NYURK
HAVE • BECOME
AH, I SEE...
HEY, I'M NOT LITTLE!
SURE ARE PERSISTENT THOUGH. DRAGGING ME IN HERE...
SLRRRRP
THE TEA LOOK...IT'S NOT WORKING FOR YOU.
WHAT A CHARACTER...
W-WELL, MUHYO?
...
THEY'RE REAL, HUH!
LOOK, KENJI...
GRRR
FIRST OF ALL, GHOSTS DON'T SHOW UP IN PICTURES...

READ THIS WAY

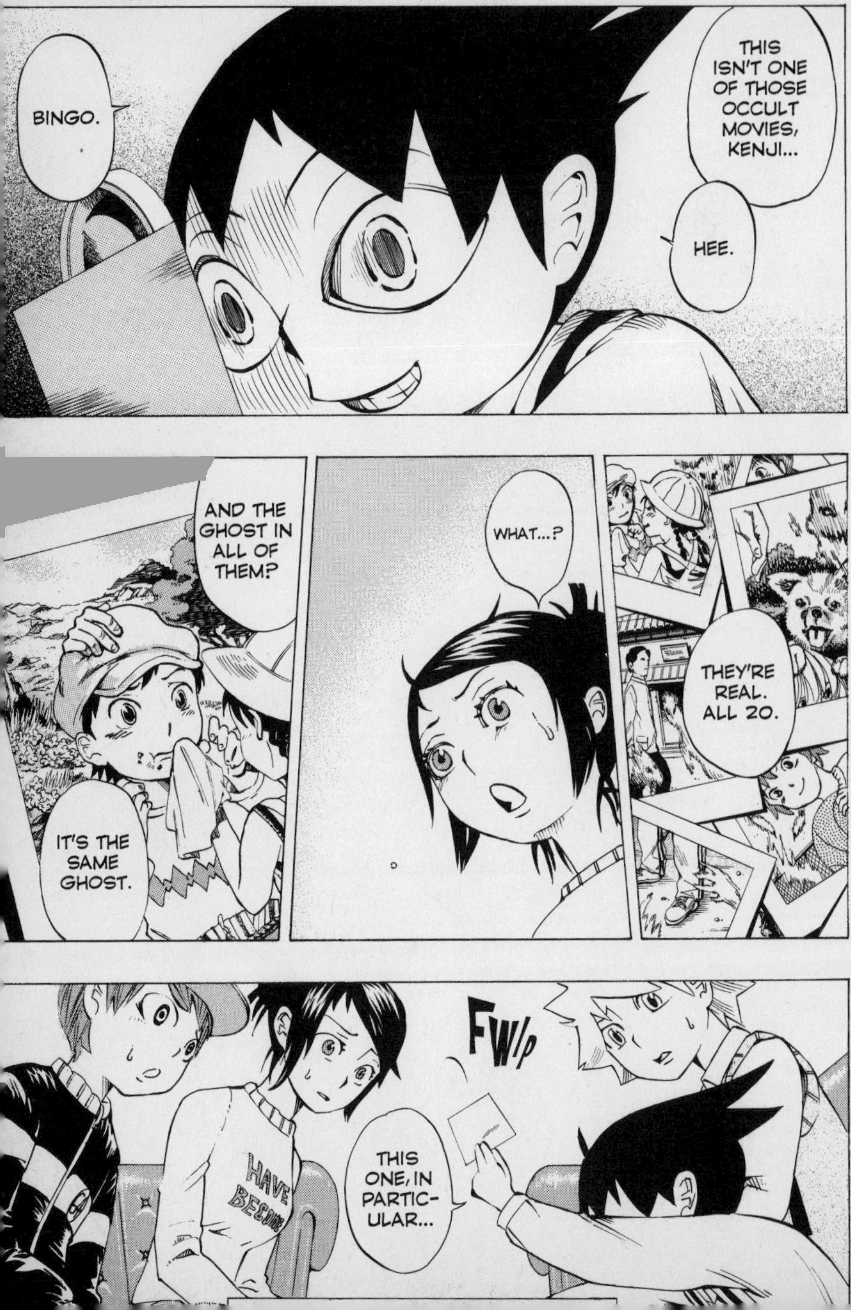
THIS ISN'T ONE OF THOSE OCCULT MOVIES, KENJI...
HEE.
BINGO.
THEY'RE REAL. ALL 20.
WHAT...?
AND THE GHOST IN ALL OF THEM?
IT'S THE SAME GHOST.
FWIP
THIS ONE, IN PARTICULAR...

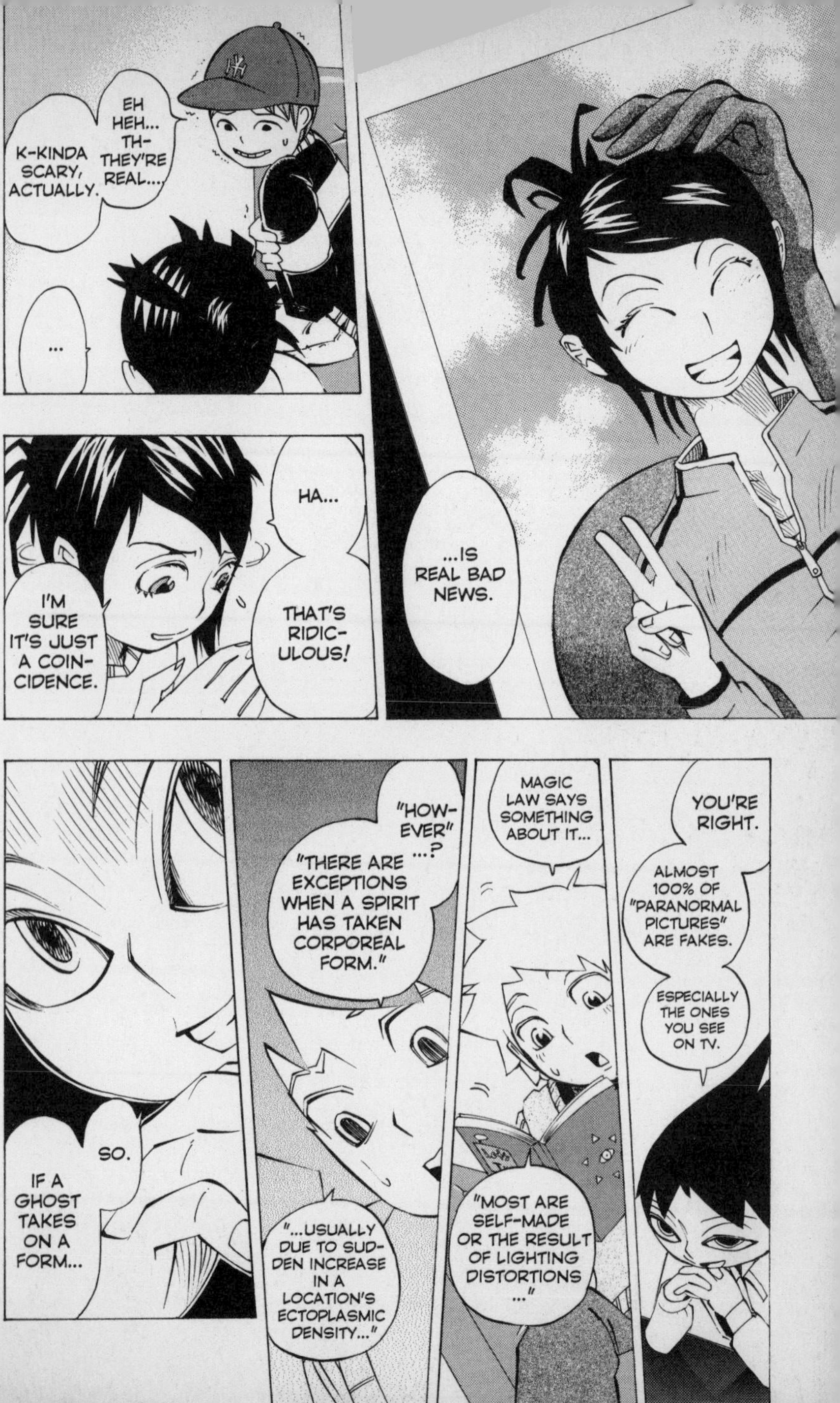
...IS REAL BAD NEWS.
EH HEH... TH-THEY'RE REAL...
K-KINDA SCARY, ACTUALLY.
...
HA... THAT'S RIDICULOUS!
I'M SURE IT'S JUST A COINCIDENCE.
YOU'RE RIGHT.
ALMOST 100% OF "PARANORMAL PICTURES" ARE FAKES.
ESPECIALLY THE ONES YOU SEE ON TV.
MAGIC LAW SAYS SOMETHING ABOUT IT...
"MOST ARE SELF-MADE OR THE RESULT OF LIGHTING DISTORTIONS..."
"HOWEVER"...?
"THERE ARE EXCEPTIONS WHEN A SPIRIT HAS TAKEN CORPOREAL FORM."
"...USUALLY DUE TO SUDDEN INCREASE IN A LOCATION'S ECTOPLASMIC DENSITY..."
SO.
IF A GHOST TAKES ON A FORM...

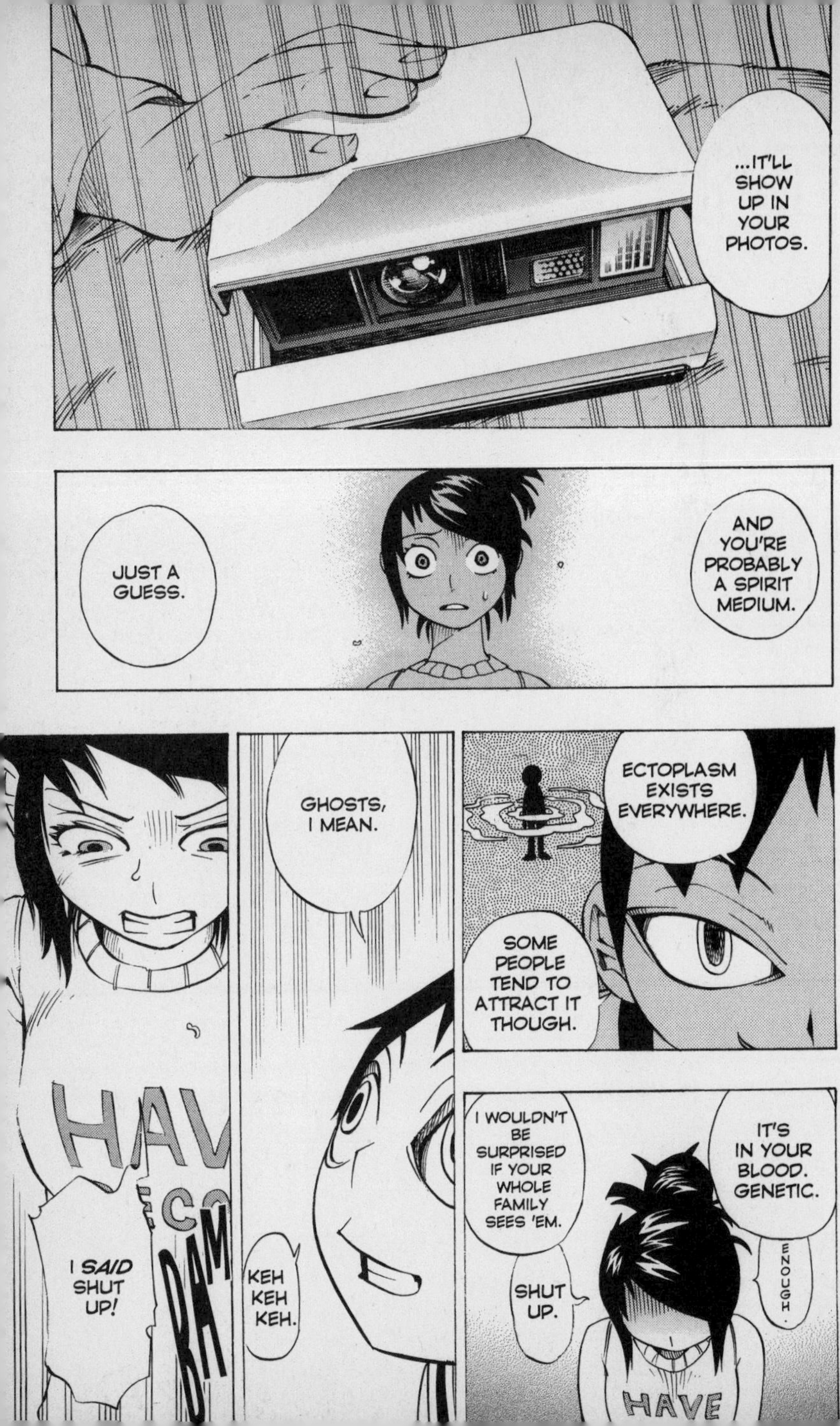
...IT'LL SHOW UP IN YOUR PHOTOS.
AND YOU'RE PROBABLY A SPIRIT MEDIUM.
JUST A GUESS.
ECTOPLASM EXISTS EVERYWHERE.
SOME PEOPLE TEND TO ATTRACT IT THOUGH.
IT'S IN YOUR BLOOD. GENETIC.
ENOUGH.
I WOULDN'T BE SURPRISED IF YOUR WHOLE FAMILY SEES 'EM.
SHUT UP.
GHOSTS, I MEAN.
KEH KEH KEH.
I *SAID* SHUT UP!
BAM

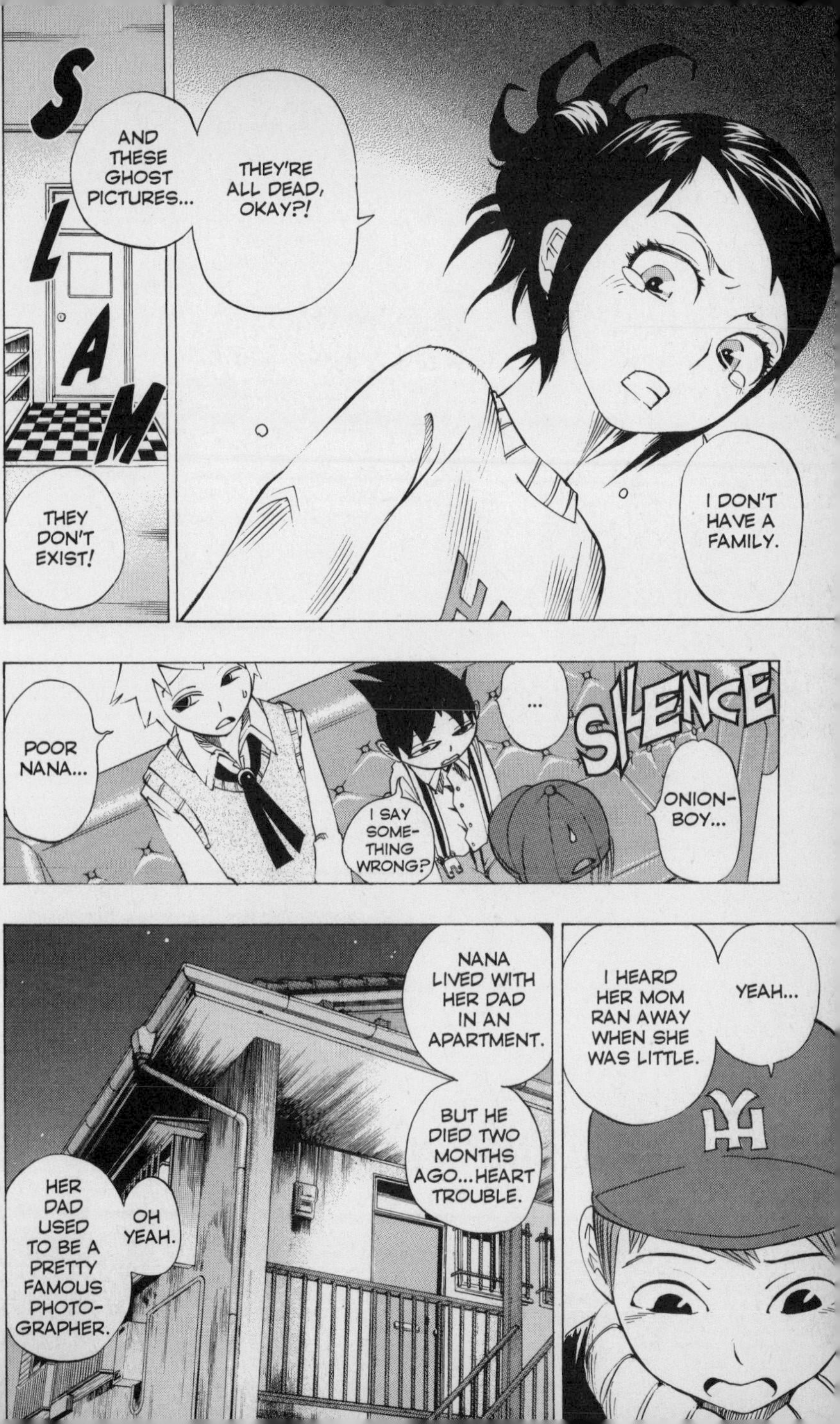
I DON'T HAVE A FAMILY.
THEY'RE ALL DEAD, OKAY?!
AND THESE GHOST PICTURES...
THEY DON'T EXIST!
SLAM
SILENCE
ONION-BOY...
...
I SAY SOMETHING WRONG?
POOR NANA...
YEAH...
I HEARD HER MOM RAN AWAY WHEN SHE WAS LITTLE.
NANA LIVED WITH HER DAD IN AN APARTMENT.
BUT HE DIED TWO MONTHS AGO...HEART TROUBLE.
OH YEAH.
HER DAD USED TO BE A PRETTY FAMOUS PHOTOGRAPHER.

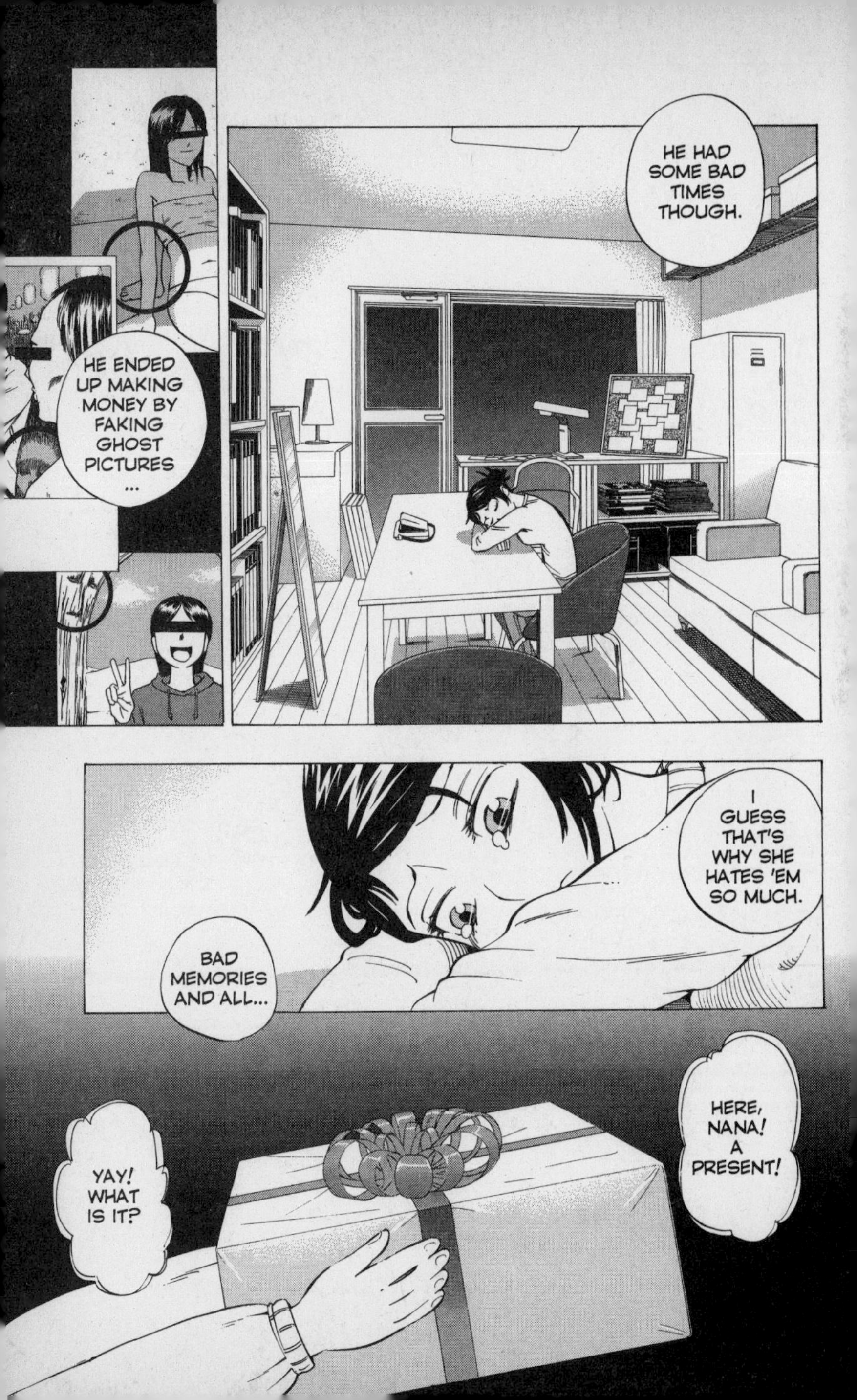
HE HAD SOME BAD TIMES THOUGH.
HE ENDED UP MAKING MONEY BY FAKING GHOST PICTURES ...
I GUESS THAT'S WHY SHE HATES 'EM SO MUCH.
BAD MEMORIES AND ALL...
HERE, NANA! A PRESENT!
YAY! WHAT IS IT?

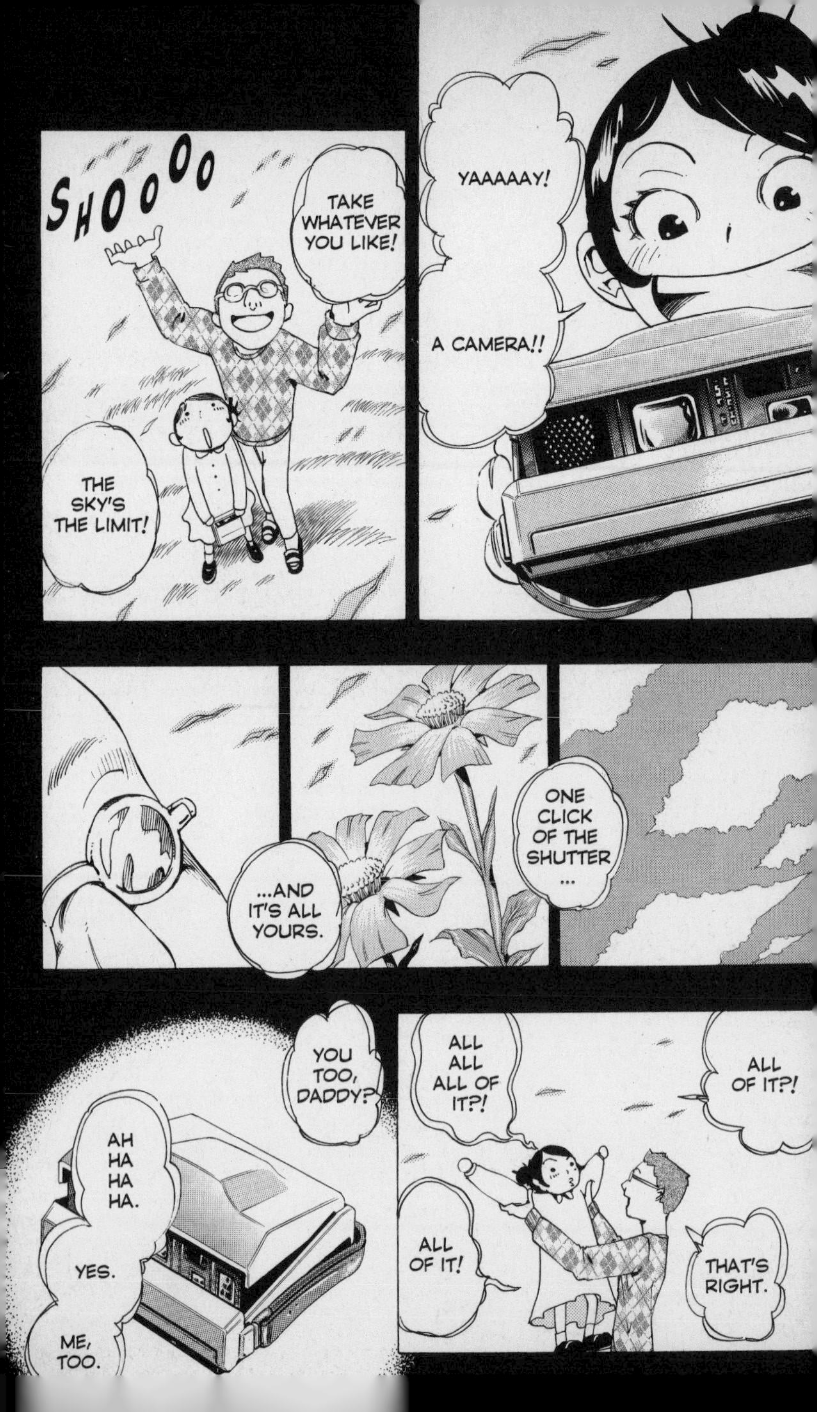
YAAAAAY!
A CAMERA!!
SHOOOOO
TAKE WHATEVER YOU LIKE!
THE SKY'S THE LIMIT!
ONE CLICK OF THE SHUTTER...
...AND IT'S ALL YOURS.
ALL OF IT?!
ALL ALL ALL OF IT?!
THAT'S RIGHT.
ALL OF IT!
YOU TOO, DADDY?
AH HA HA HA.
YES.
ME, TOO.

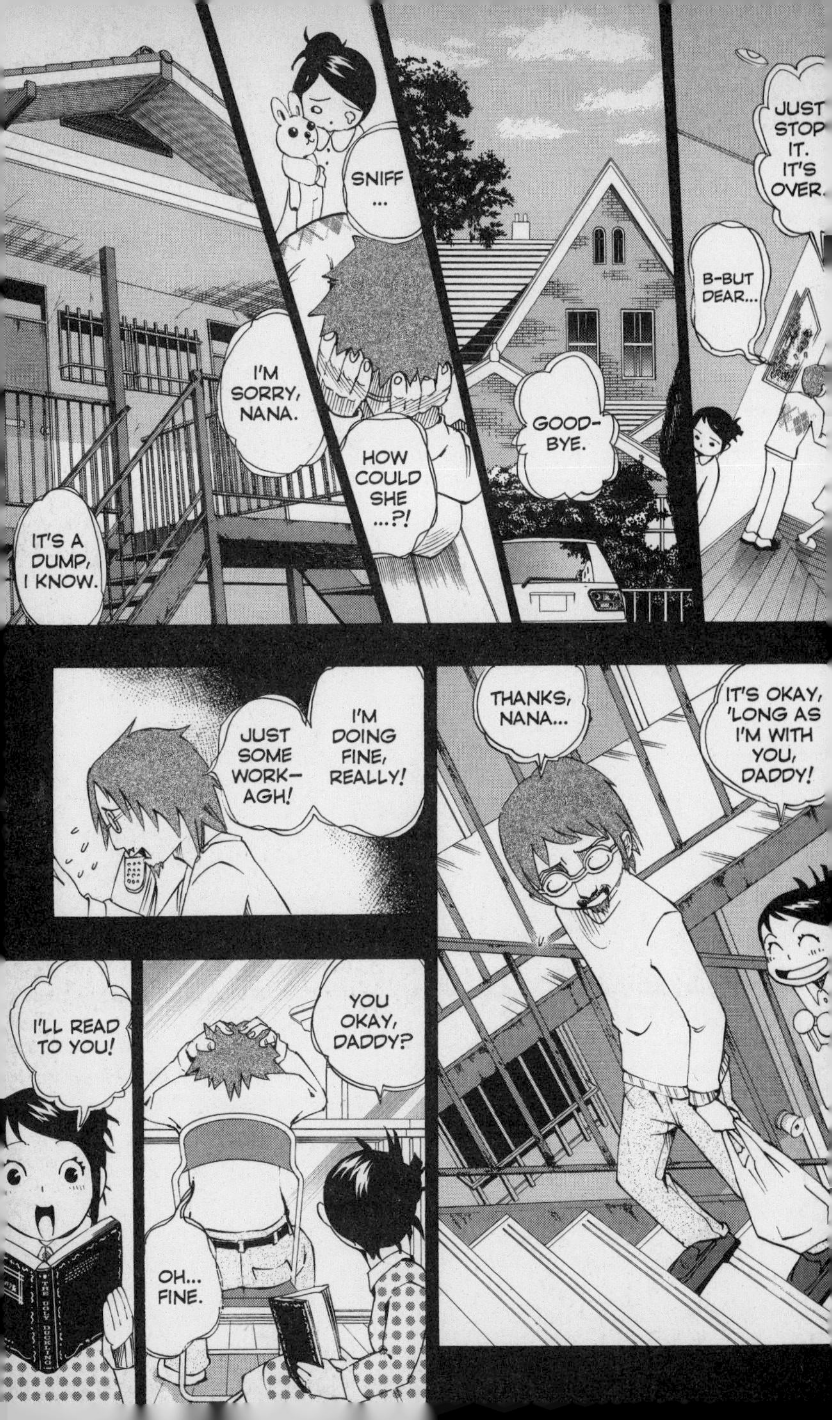
JUST STOP IT. IT'S OVER.
B-BUT DEAR...
GOOD-BYE.
SNIFF ...
HOW COULD SHE ...?!
I'M SORRY, NANA.
IT'S A DUMP, I KNOW.
IT'S OKAY, 'LONG AS I'M WITH YOU, DADDY!
THANKS, NANA...
I'M DOING FINE, REALLY!
JUST SOME WORK—AGH!
YOU OKAY, DADDY?
OH... FINE.
I'LL READ TO YOU!

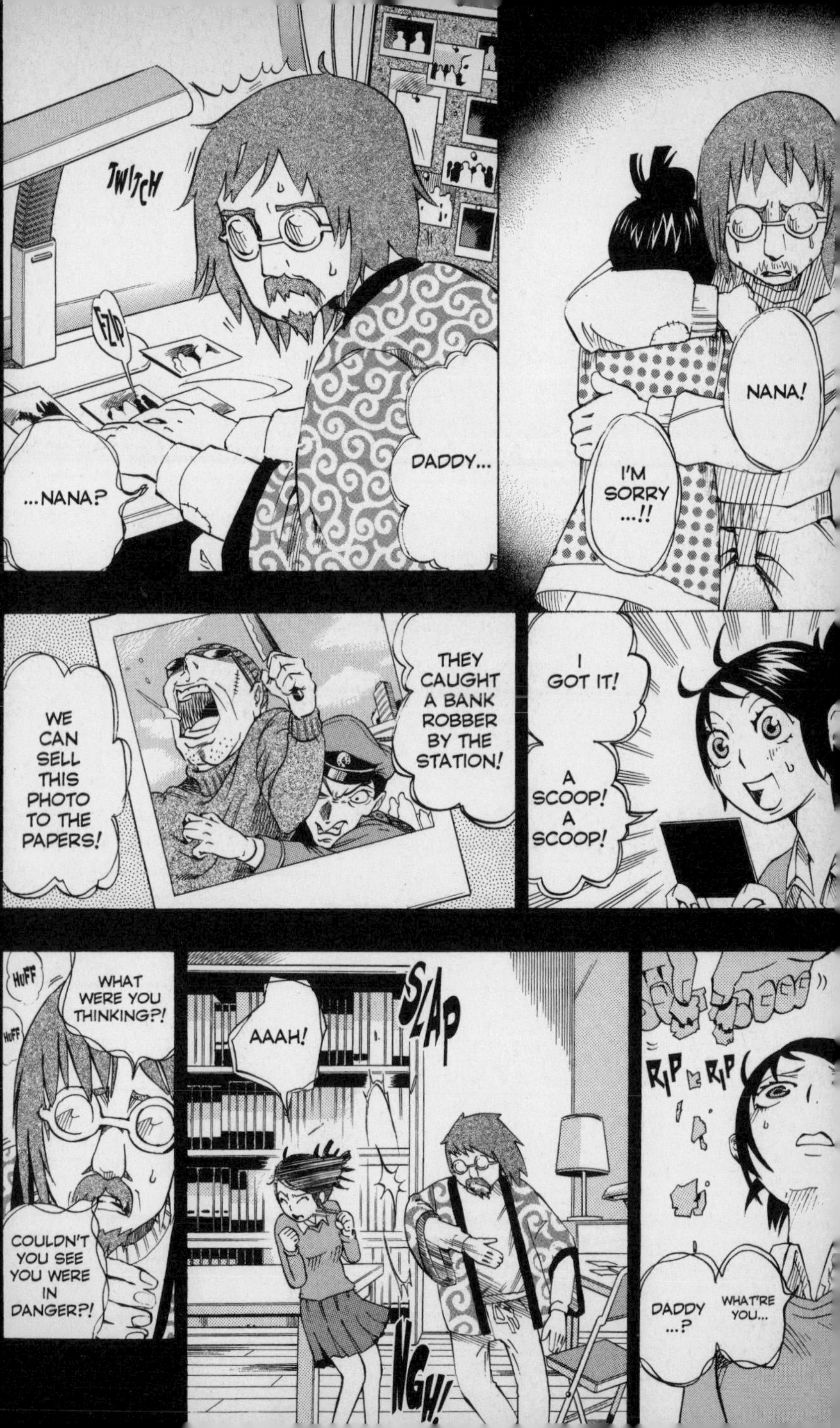
NANA!
I'M SORRY ...!!
TWITCH
FZIP
DADDY...
...NANA?
I GOT IT!
A SCOOP! A SCOOP!
THEY CAUGHT A BANK ROBBER BY THE STATION!
WE CAN SELL THIS PHOTO TO THE PAPERS!
RIP RIP
WHAT'RE YOU...
DADDY ...?
SLAP
AAAH!
NGH!
WHAT WERE YOU THINKING?!
HUFF
HUFF
COULDN'T YOU SEE YOU WERE IN DANGER?!

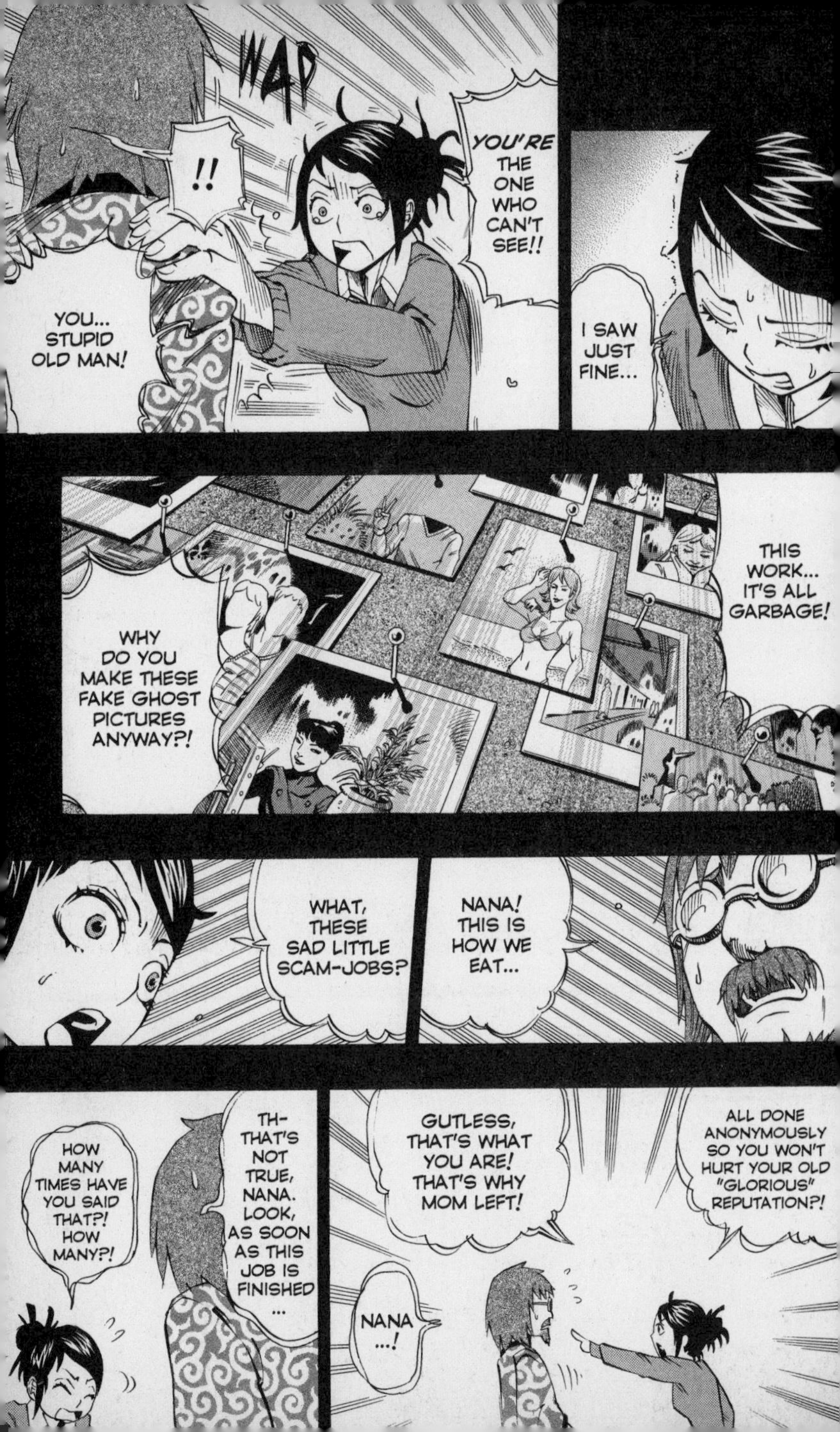

I SAW JUST FINE...
YOU'RE THE ONE WHO CAN'T SEE!!
WAP
!!
YOU... STUPID OLD MAN!
THIS WORK... IT'S ALL GARBAGE!
WHY DO YOU MAKE THESE FAKE GHOST PICTURES ANYWAY?!
NANA! THIS IS HOW WE EAT...
WHAT, THESE SAD LITTLE SCAM-JOBS?
ALL DONE ANONYMOUSLY SO YOU WON'T HURT YOUR OLD "GLORIOUS" REPUTATION?!
GUTLESS, THAT'S WHAT YOU ARE! THAT'S WHY MOM LEFT!
NANA ...!
TH-THAT'S NOT TRUE, NANA. LOOK, AS SOON AS THIS JOB IS FINISHED ...
HOW MANY TIMES HAVE YOU SAID THAT?! HOW MANY?!

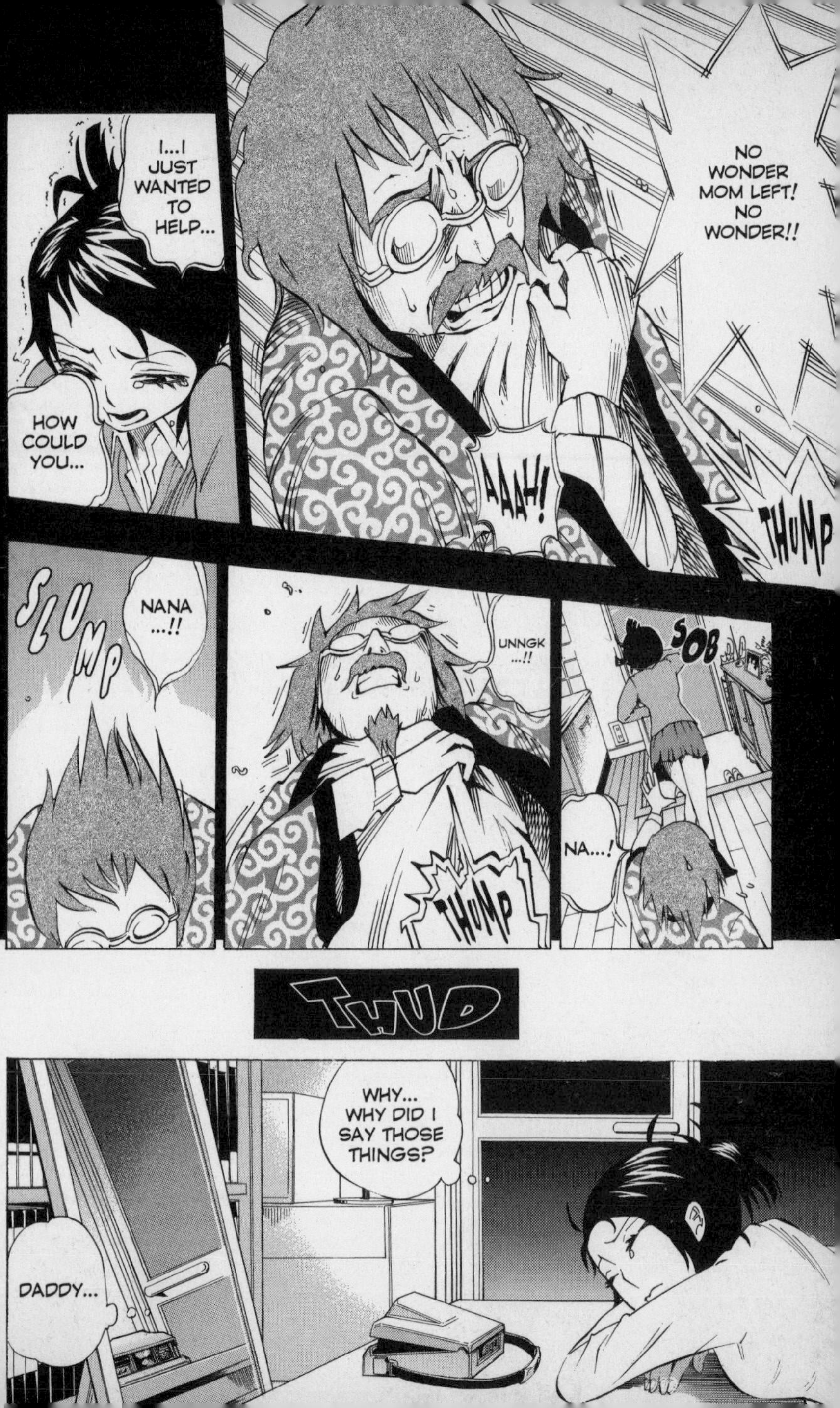
NO WONDER MOM LEFT! NO WONDER!!
AAAH!
THUMP
I...I JUST WANTED TO HELP...
HOW COULD YOU...
SOB
NA...!
UNNGK ...!!
THUMP
SLUMP
NANA ...!!
THUD
WHY... WHY DID I SAY THOSE THINGS?
DADDY...

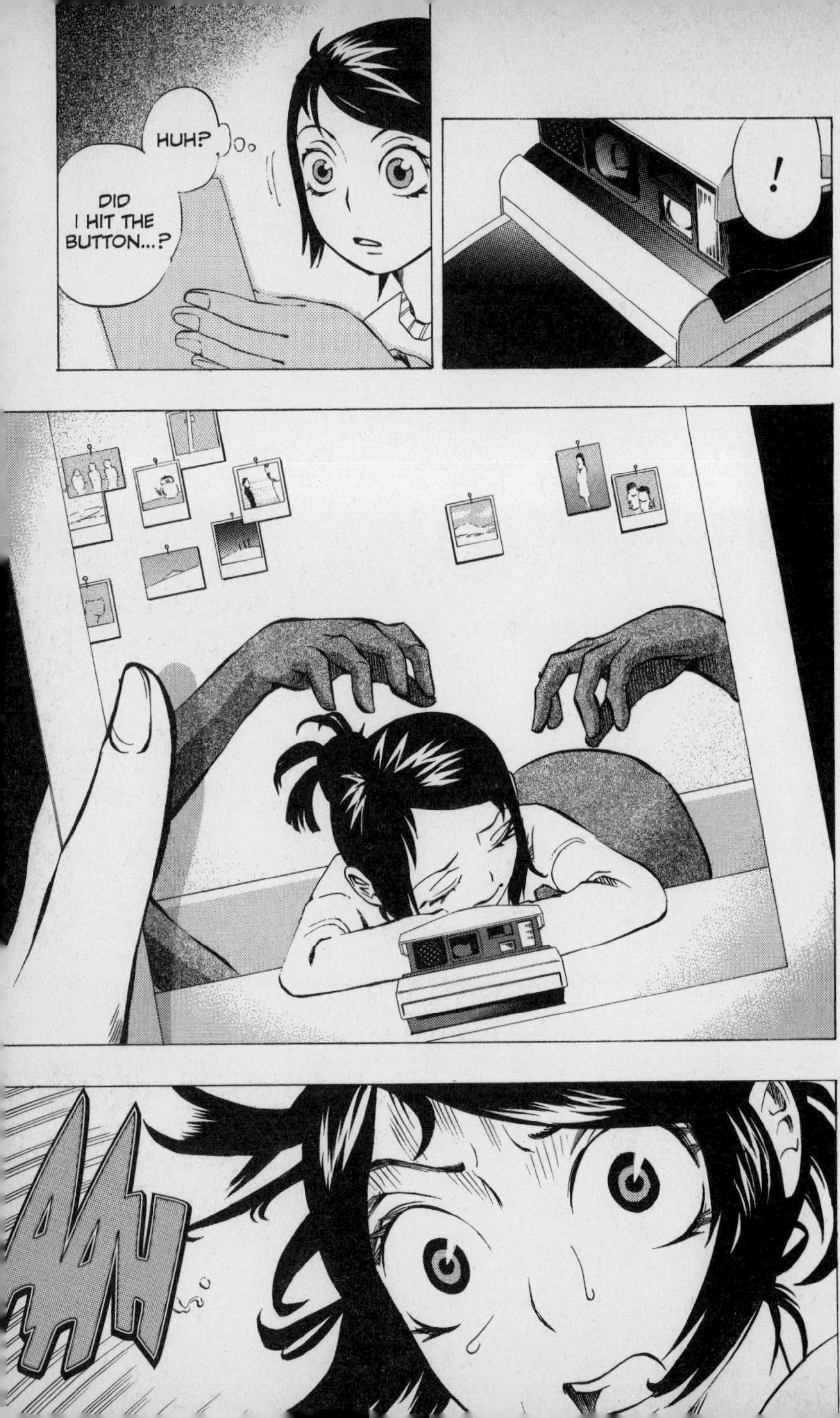
!
HUH?
DID I HIT THE BUTTON...?

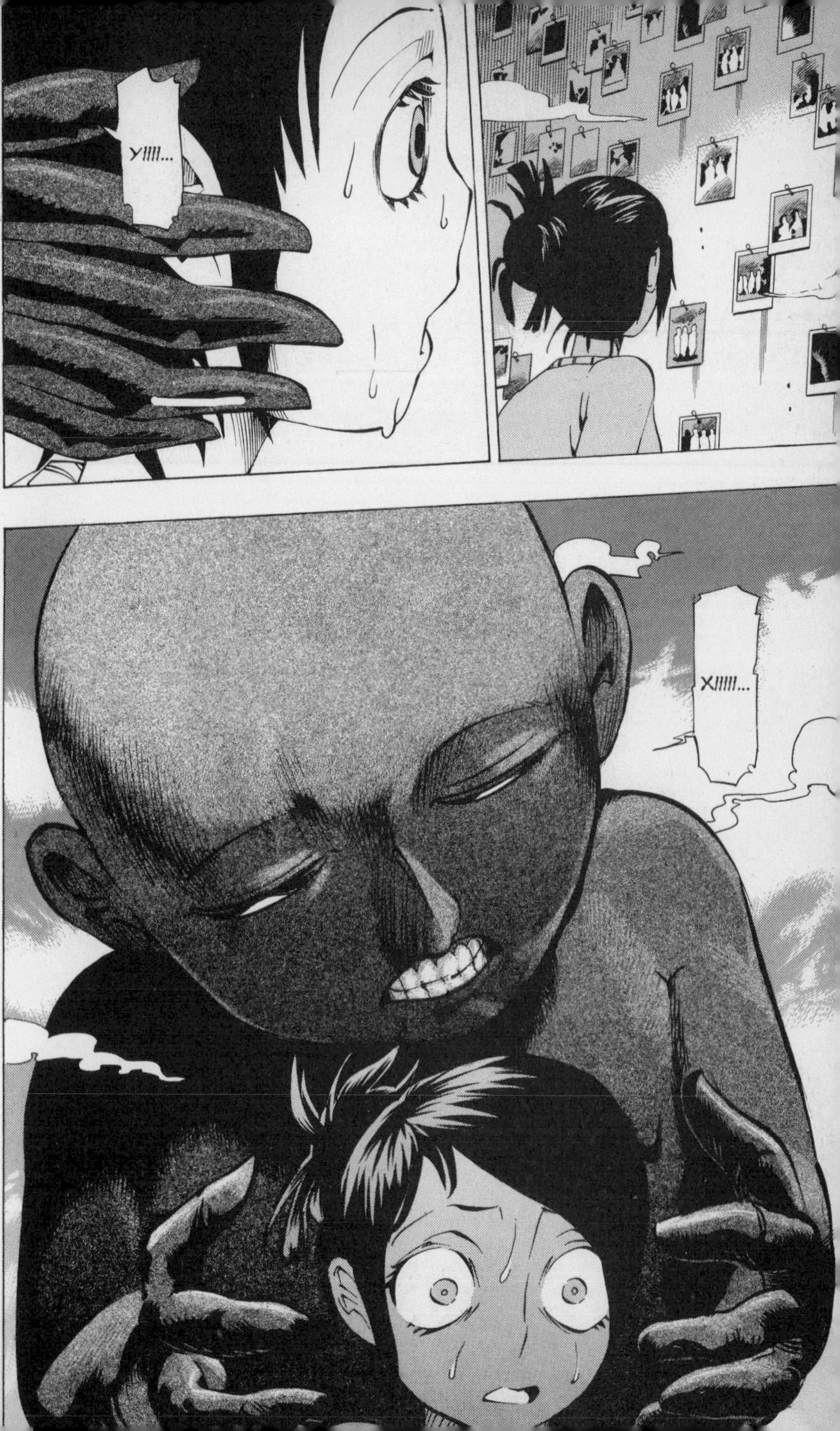
YIIII...
XIIIII...

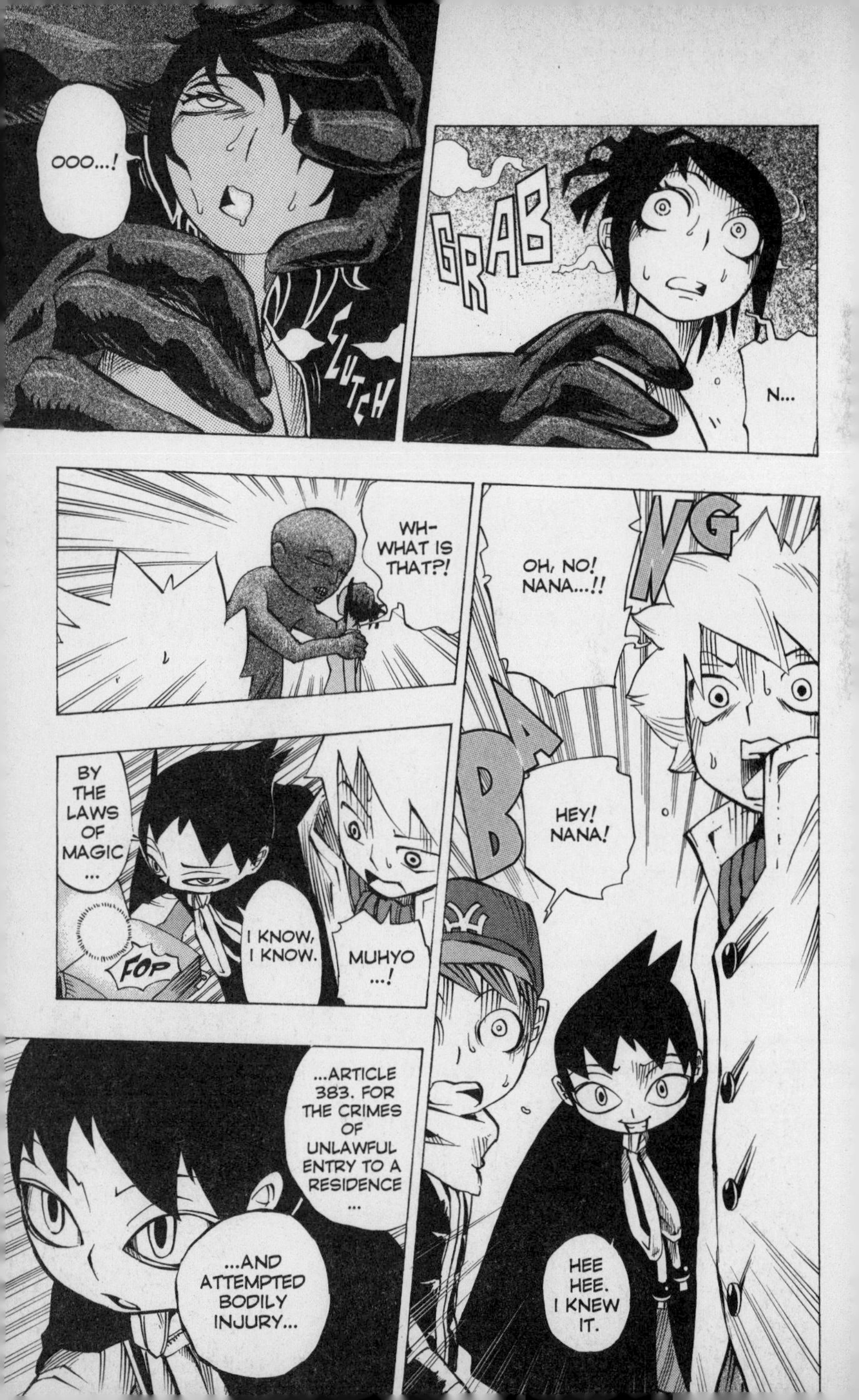
GRAB
N...
OOO...!
CLUTCH
NG
OH, NO! NANA...!!
BA
HEY! NANA!
HEE HEE. I KNEW IT.
WH- WHAT IS THAT?!
BY THE LAWS OF MAGIC ...
MUHYO ...!
I KNOW, I KNOW.
FOP
...ARTICLE 383. FOR THE CRIMES OF UNLAWFUL ENTRY TO A RESIDENCE ...
...AND ATTEMPTED BODILY INJURY...

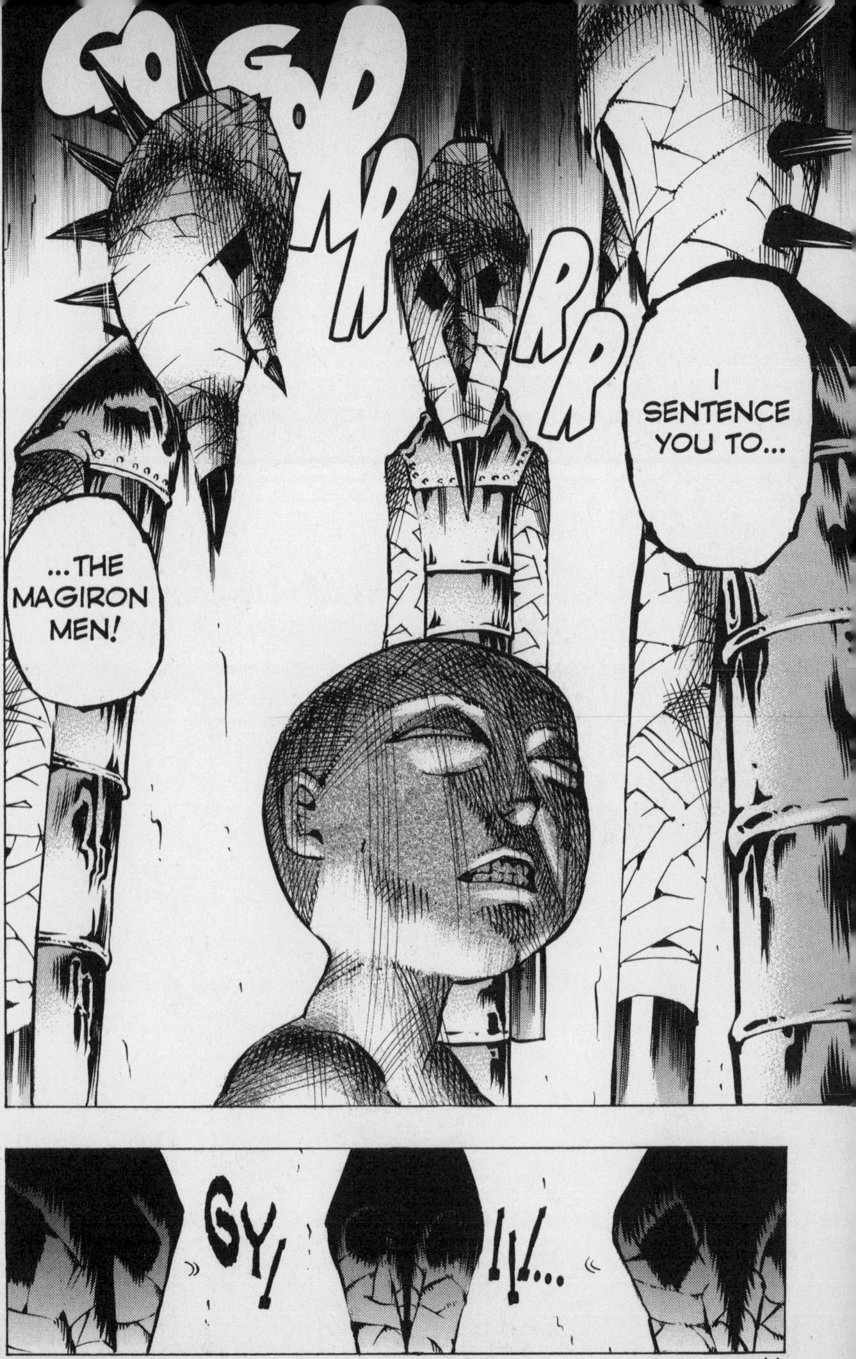
I SENTENCE YOU TO...
...THE MAGIRON MEN!
GY!
I!...

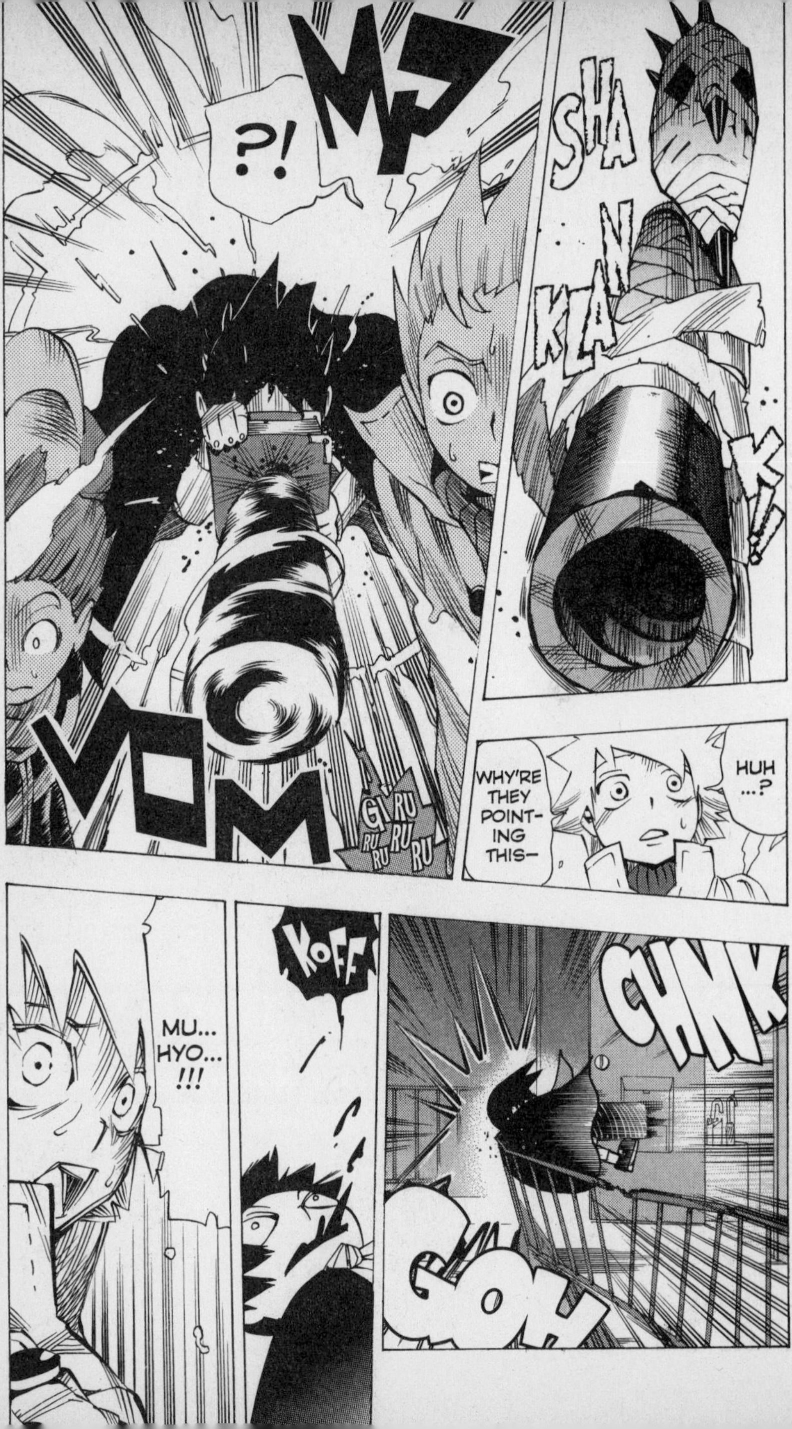
SHAN
KLANK!!
HUH ...?
WHY'RE THEY POINTING THIS—
?!
VOOM
GIRURURURURU
CHNK
GOH
KOFF
MU... HYO... !!!

NANA TAKENOUCHI
BIRTHDAY: JULY 7
HEIGHT: 164 CM
LIKES: ROJI'S TEA,
  GOOD SHOTS (SCOOPS),
  HOT SPRINGS (TRAVEL)
TALENTS: PRESSING THE
  SHUTTER BUTTON, TAKING
  QUICK SHOTS, HIDING CAMERAS
NOT GOOD WITH: FREE TIME

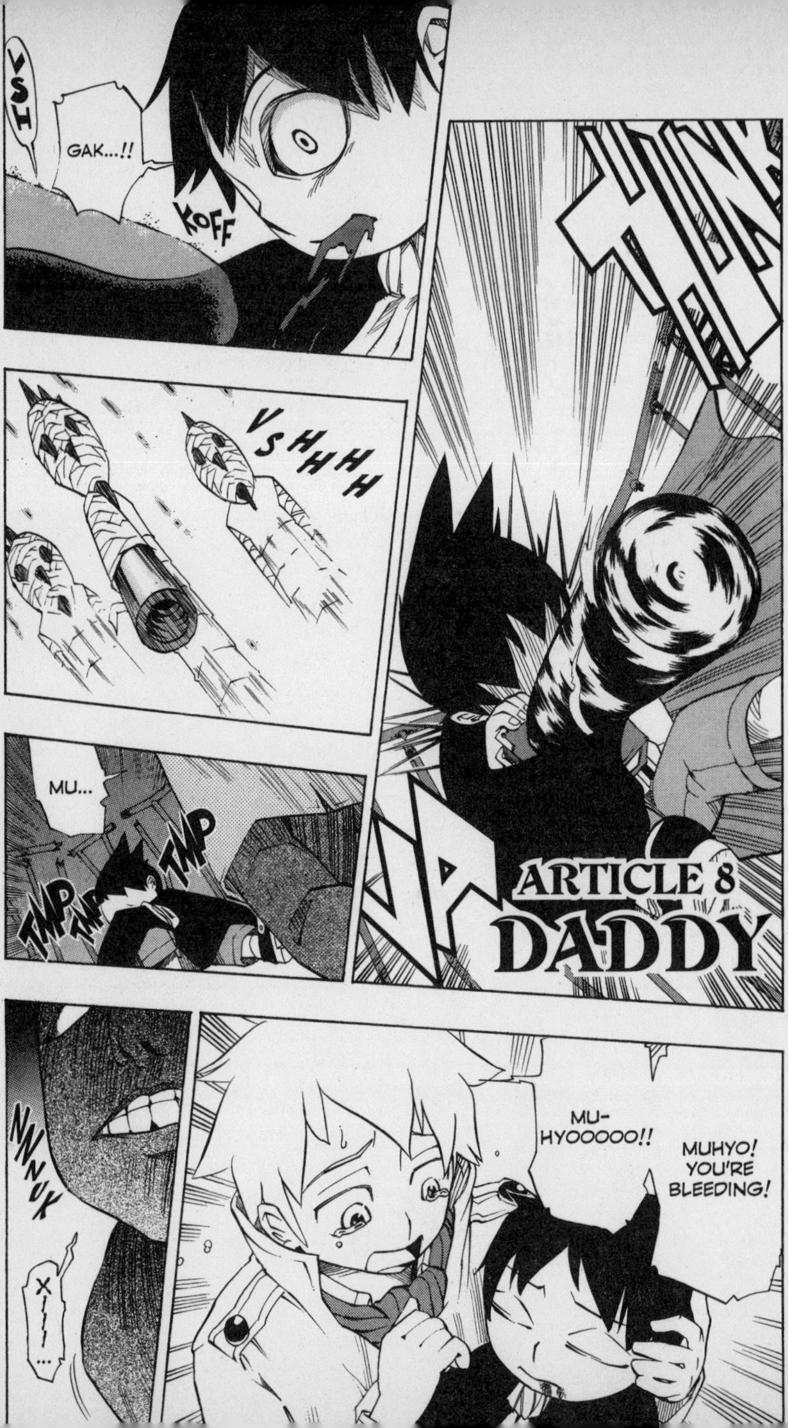
ARTICLE 8
DADDY
VSH
GAK...!!
KOFF
VSHHHHH
MU...
TMP TMP TMP
MU-
HYOOOOO!!
MUHYO! YOU'RE BLEEDING!
NNNUK

ARTICLE 8
DADDY

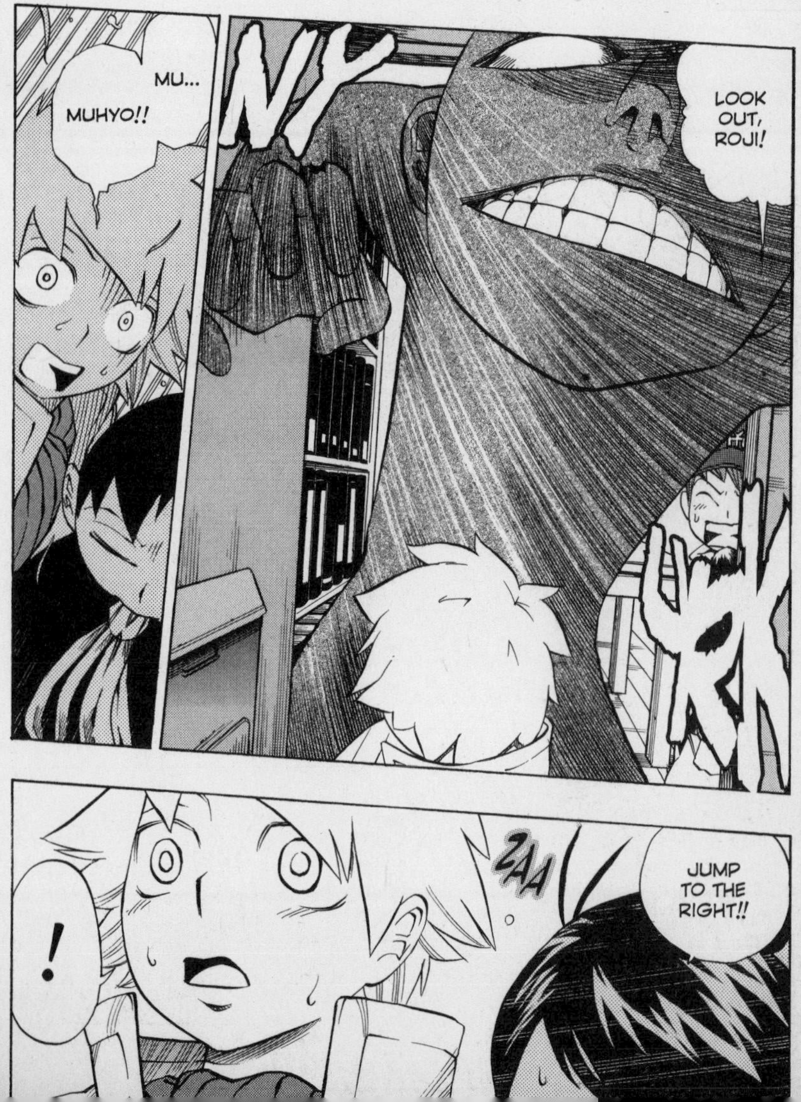
LOOK OUT, ROJI!
NY
MU... MUHYO!!
JUMP TO THE RIGHT!!
ZAA
!

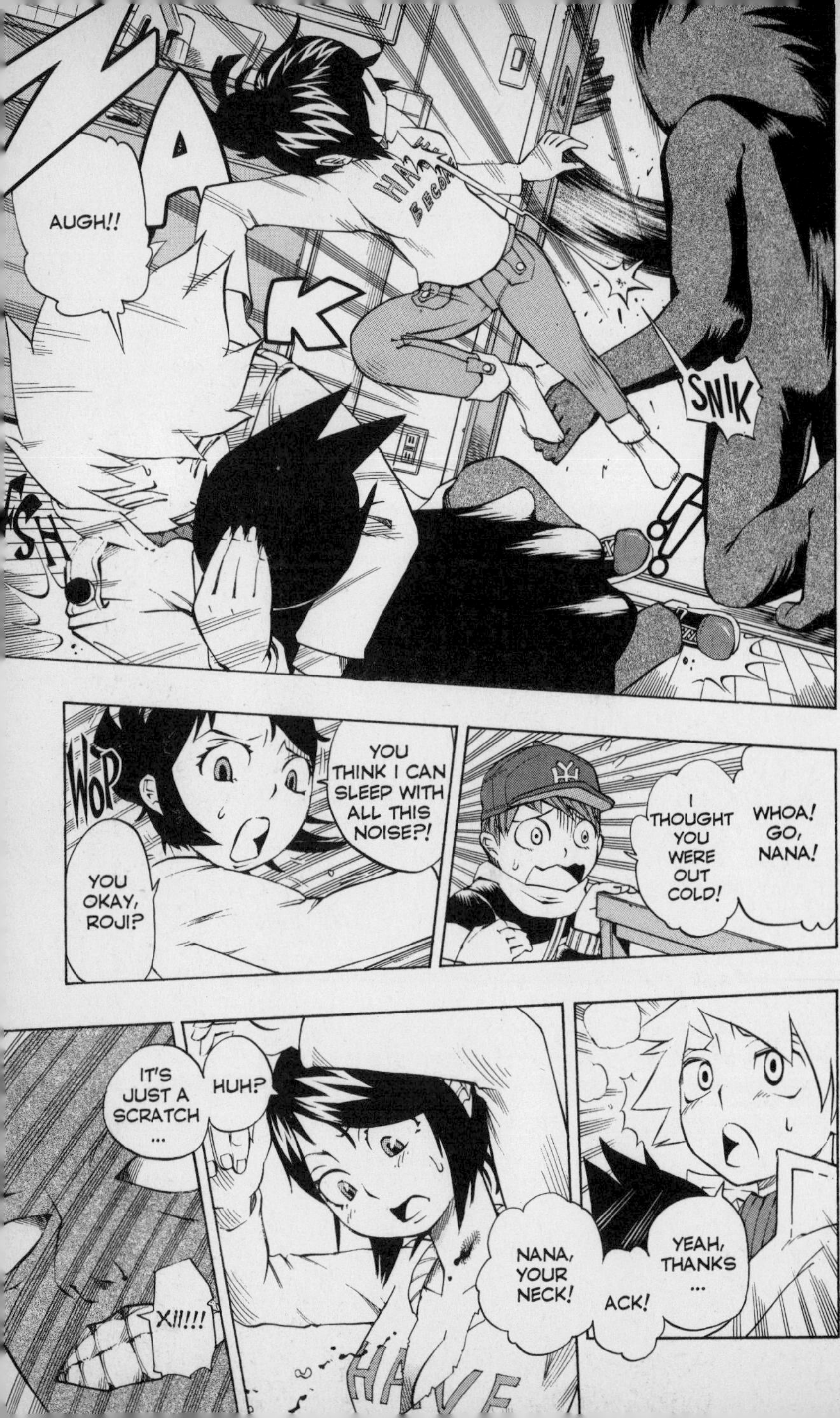
SNIK
ZAK
AUGH!!
WHOA! GO, NANA!
I THOUGHT YOU WERE OUT COLD!
YOU THINK I CAN SLEEP WITH ALL THIS NOISE?!
WOP
YOU OKAY, ROJI?
YEAH, THANKS ...
ACK!
NANA, YOUR NECK!
HUH?
IT'S JUST A SCRATCH ...
XII!!!

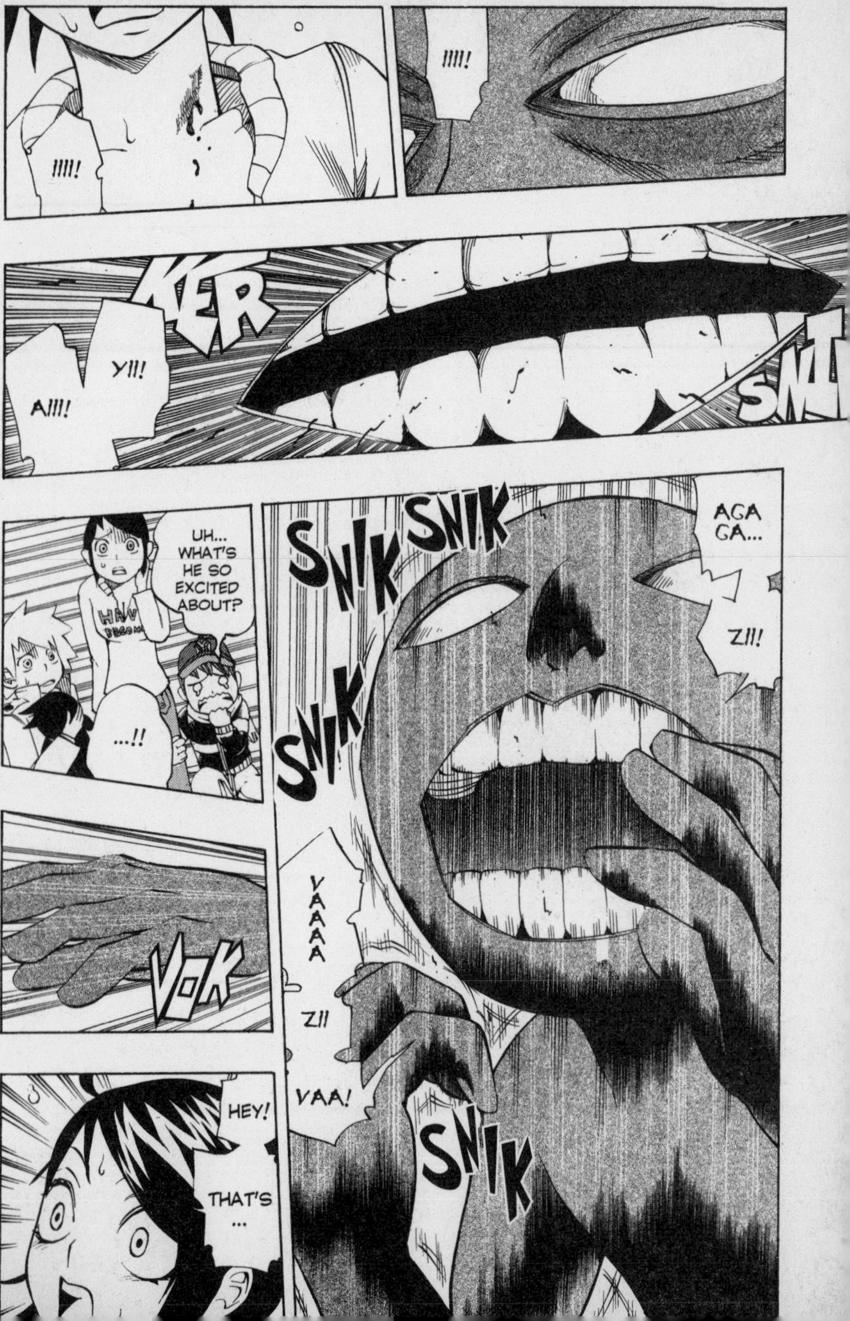

!!!!!
!!!!!
SNI
KER
YII!
AIII!
AGA GA...
ZII!
SNIK
SNIK
SNIK
VAAAA
ZII
VAA!
SNIK
UH... WHAT'S HE SO EXCITED ABOUT?
...!!
VOK
HEY!
THAT'S ...

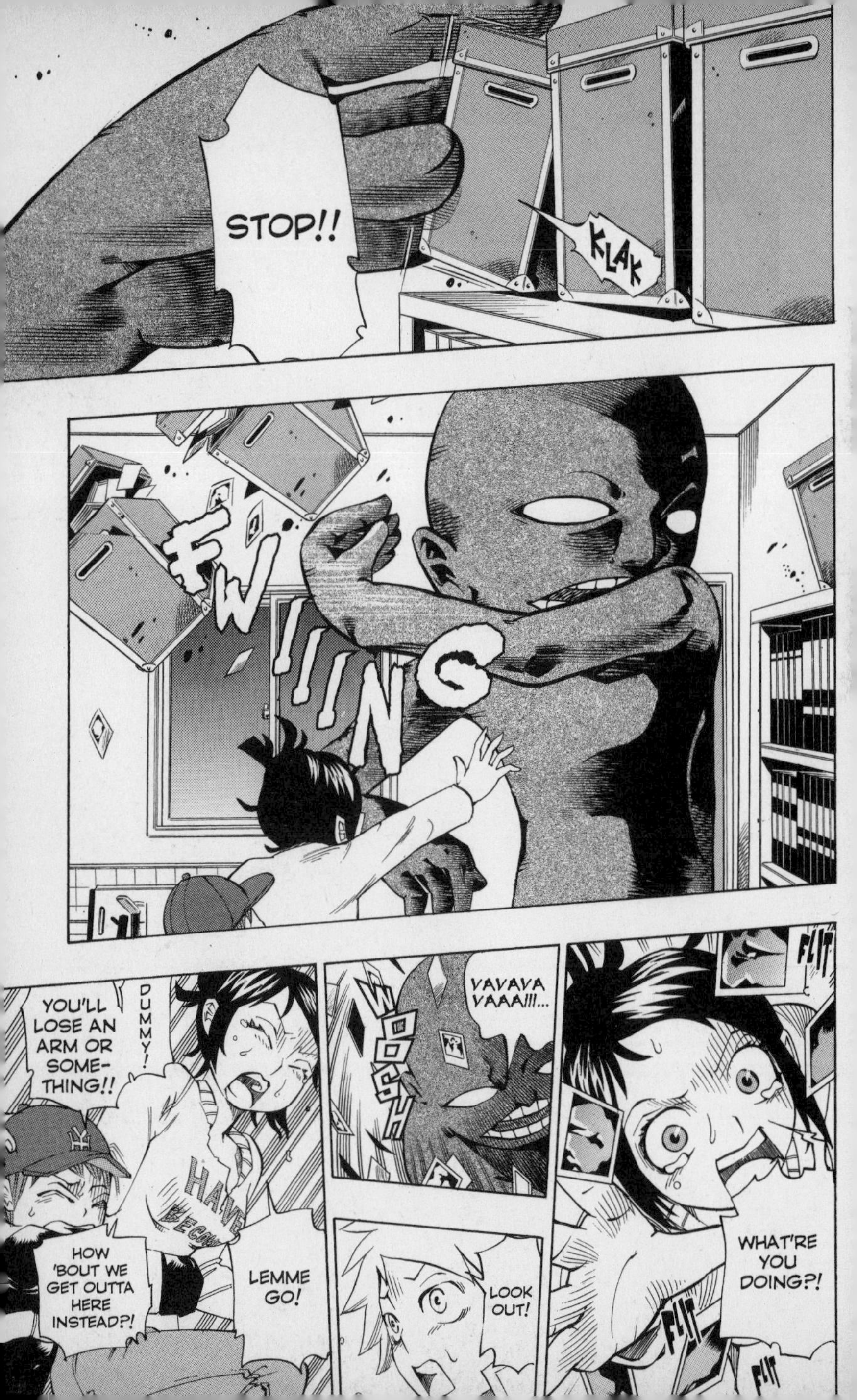
KLAK
STOP!!
FWING
FLIT
WHAT'RE YOU DOING?!
FLIT
FLIT
VAVAVA VAAA!!!...
WOOSH
LOOK OUT!
DUMMY!
YOU'LL LOSE AN ARM OR SOME-THING!!
LEMME GO!
HOW 'BOUT WE GET OUTTA HERE INSTEAD?!

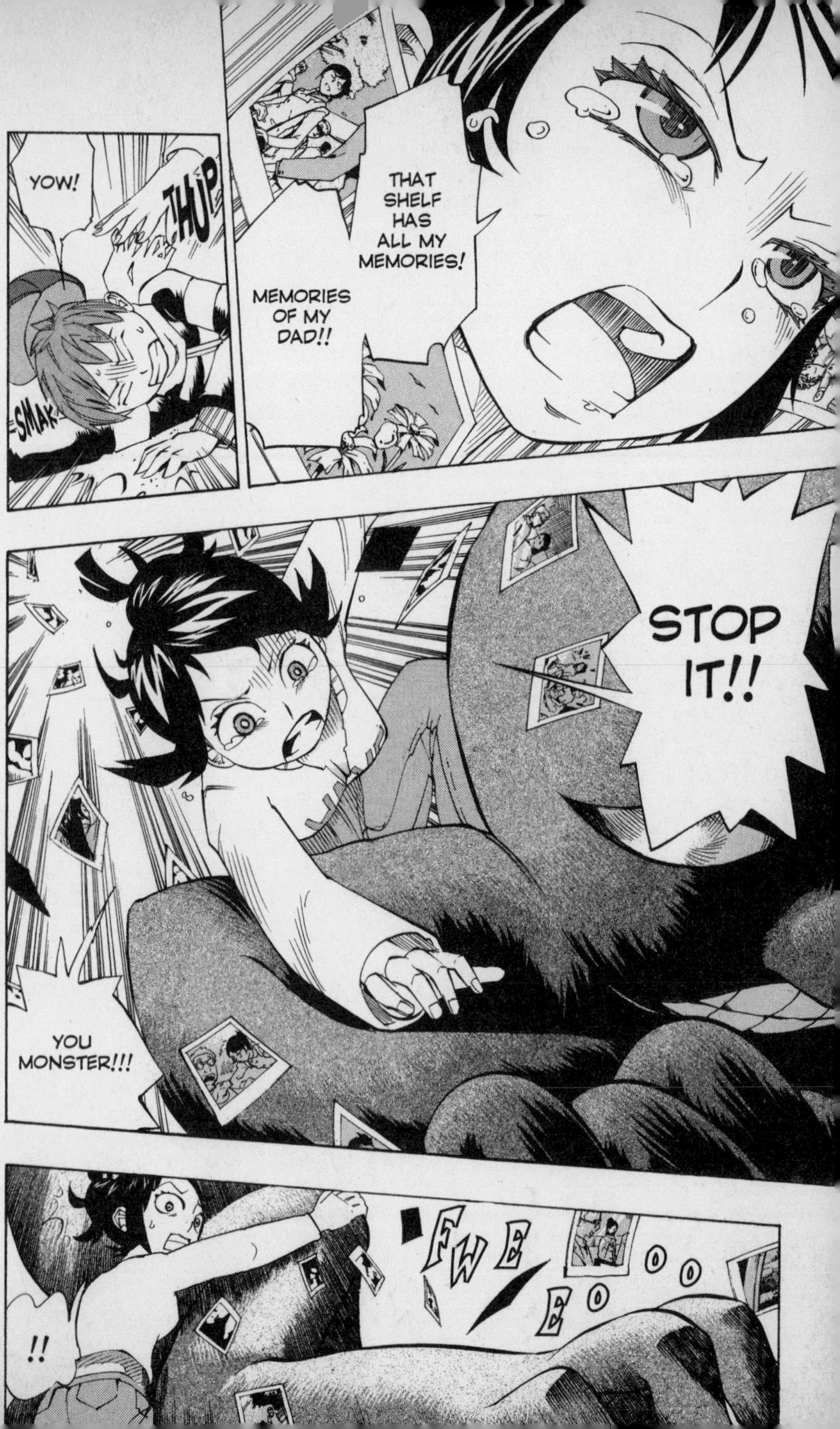
THAT SHELF HAS ALL MY MEMORIES!
MEMORIES OF MY DAD!!
YOW!
THUP
SMAK
STOP IT!!
YOU MONSTER!!!
FWEEOOO
!!

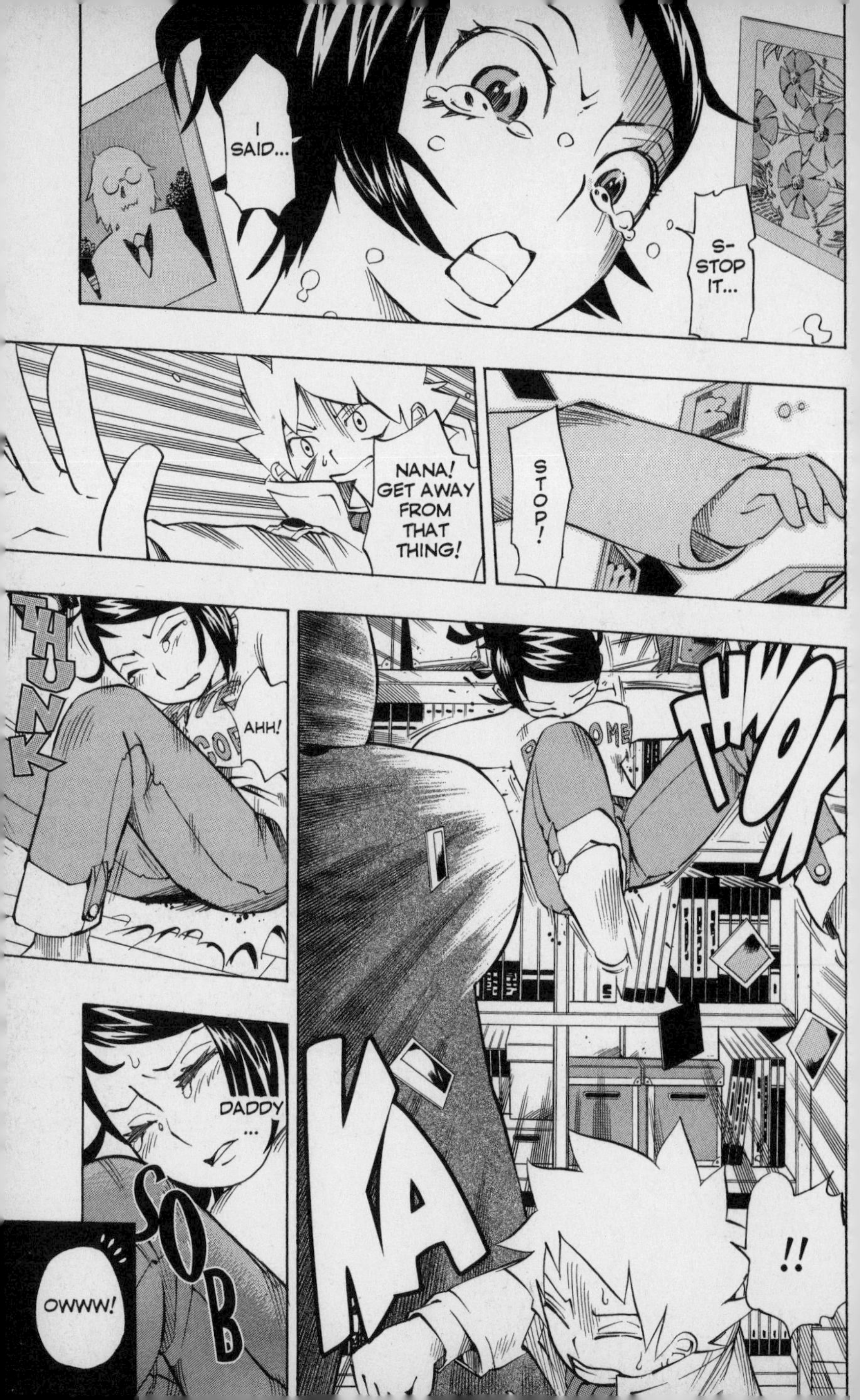
S-STOP IT...
I SAID...
STOP!
NANA! GET AWAY FROM THAT THING!
THWOK
!!
KA
THUNK
AHH!
DADDY...
SOB
OWWW!

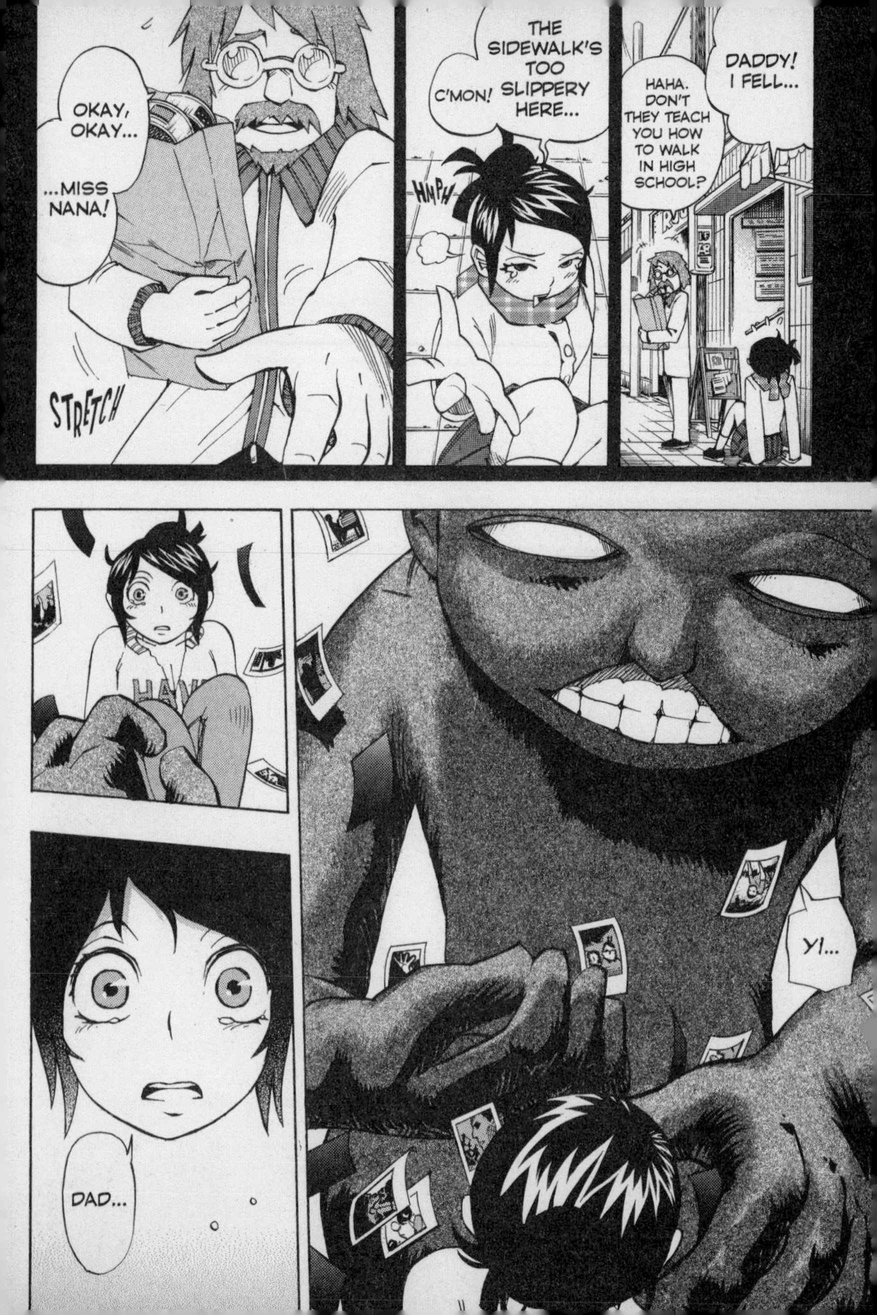
DADDY! I FELL...
HAHA. DON'T THEY TEACH YOU HOW TO WALK IN HIGH SCHOOL?
THE SIDEWALK'S TOO SLIPPERY HERE...
C'MON!
HMPH
OKAY, OKAY...
...MISS NANA!
STRETCH
YI...
DAD...

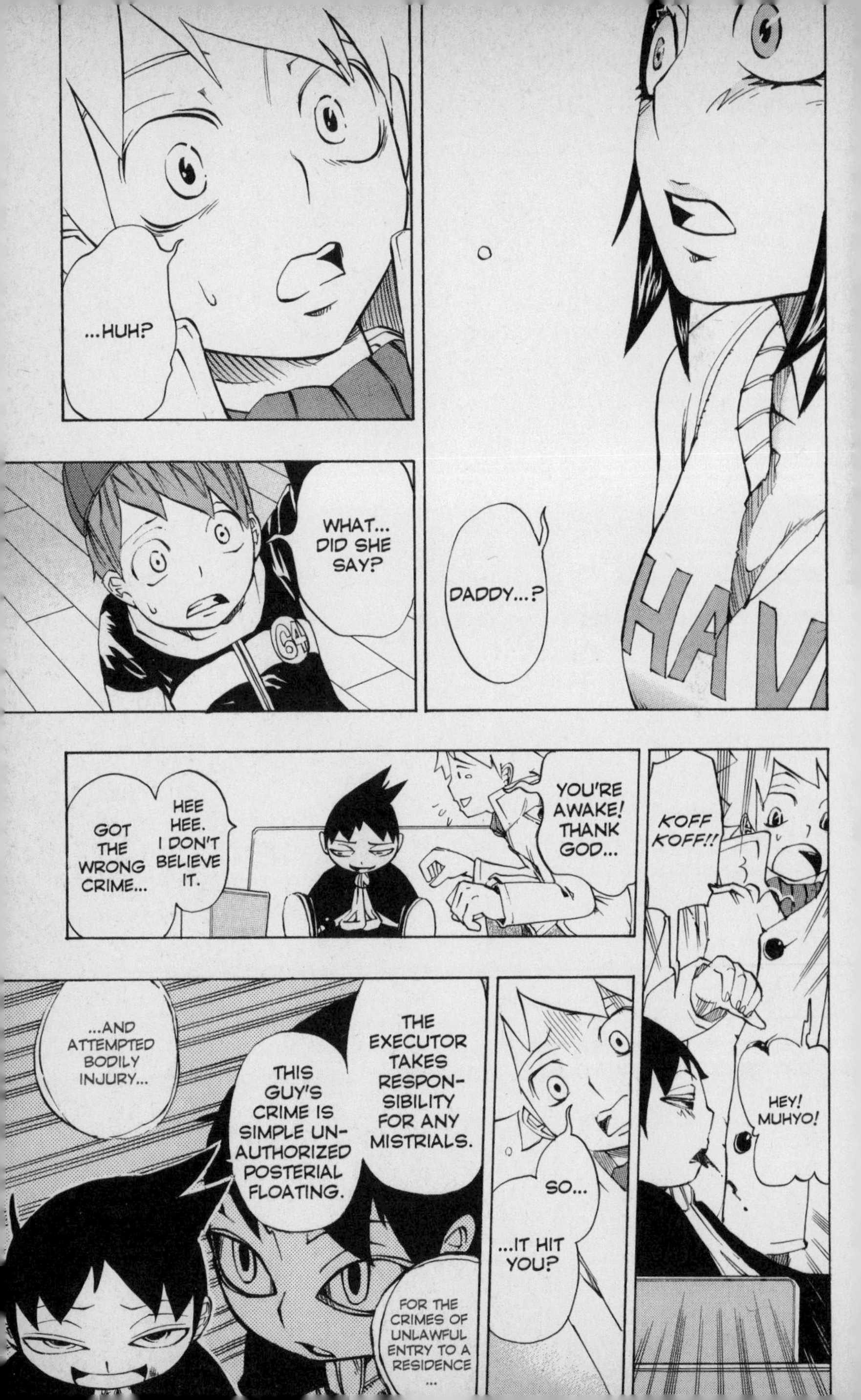
DADDY...?
...HUH?
WHAT... DID SHE SAY?
KOFF KOFF!!
HEY! MUHYO!
YOU'RE AWAKE! THANK GOD...
HEE HEE. I DON'T BELIEVE IT.
GOT THE WRONG CRIME...
SO...
...IT HIT YOU?
THE EXECUTOR TAKES RESPON-SIBILITY FOR ANY MISTRIALS.
THIS GUY'S CRIME IS SIMPLE UN-AUTHORIZED POSTERIAL FLOATING.
FOR THE CRIMES OF UNLAWFUL ENTRY TO A RESIDENCE ...
...AND ATTEMPTED BODILY INJURY...

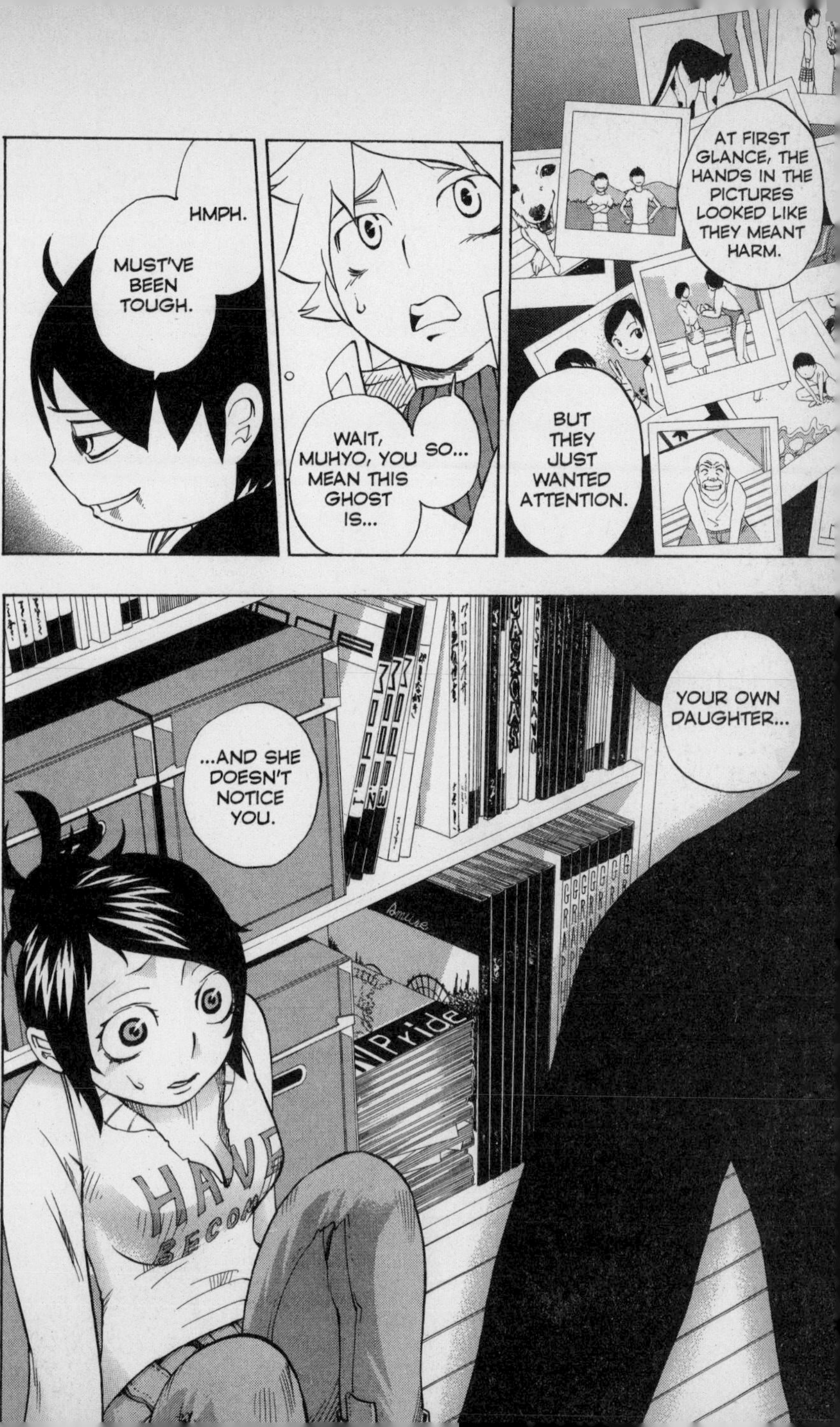
AT FIRST GLANCE, THE HANDS IN THE PICTURES LOOKED LIKE THEY MEANT HARM.
BUT THEY JUST WANTED ATTENTION.
SO...
WAIT, MUHYO, YOU MEAN THIS GHOST IS...
HMPH.
MUST'VE BEEN TOUGH.
YOUR OWN DAUGHTER...
...AND SHE DOESN'T NOTICE YOU.

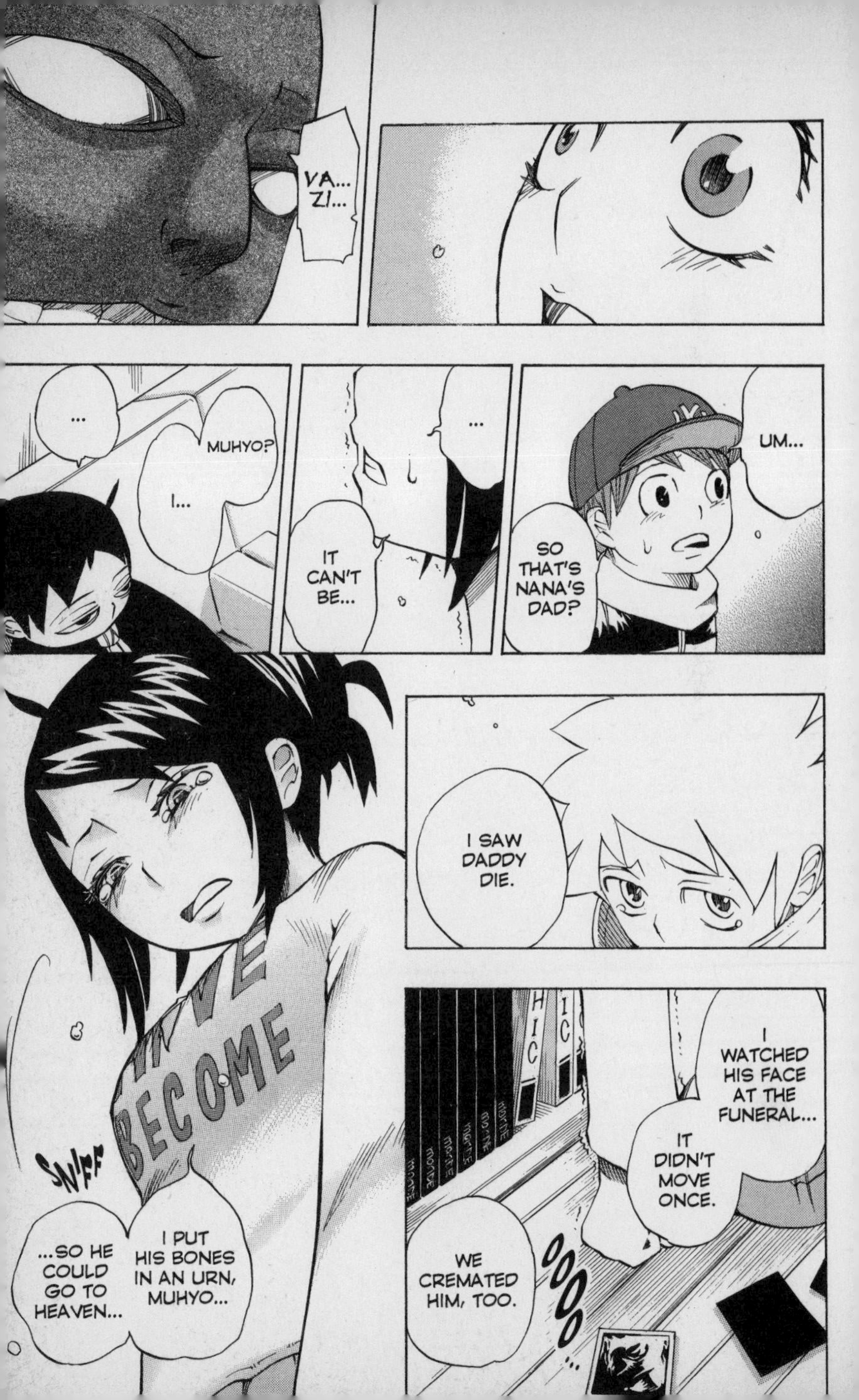
VA... ZI...
UM...
SO THAT'S NANA'S DAD?
...
IT CAN'T BE...
...
MUHYO?
I...
I SAW DADDY DIE.
I WATCHED HIS FACE AT THE FUNERAL...
IT DIDN'T MOVE ONCE.
WE CREMATED HIM, TOO.
OOOO...
BECOME
SNIFF
I PUT HIS BONES IN AN URN, MUHYO...
...SO HE COULD GO TO HEAVEN...

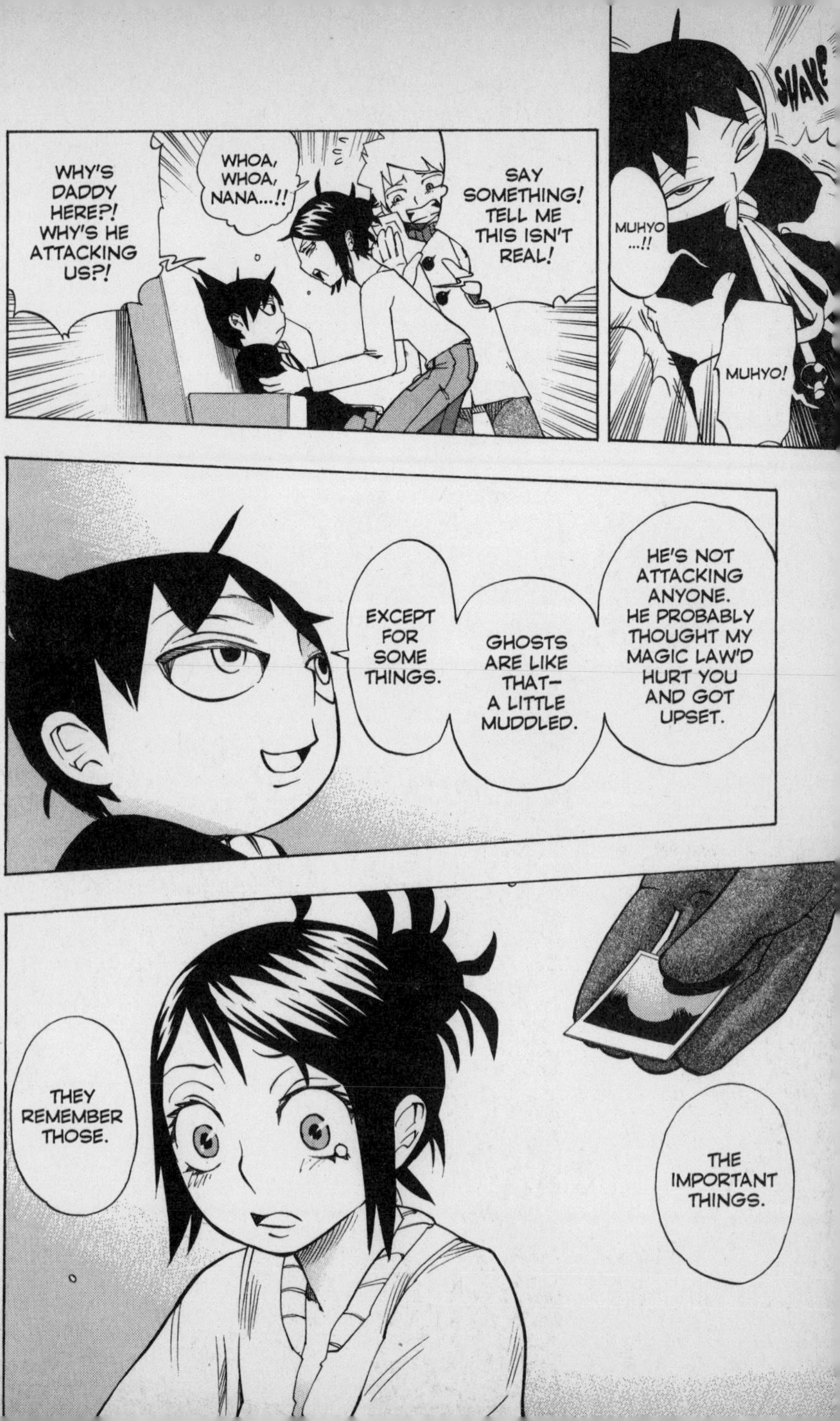
SHAKE
MUHYO ...!!
MUHYO!
SAY SOMETHING! TELL ME THIS ISN'T REAL!
WHOA, WHOA, NANA...!!
WHY'S DADDY HERE?! WHY'S HE ATTACKING US?!
HE'S NOT ATTACKING ANYONE. HE PROBABLY THOUGHT MY MAGIC LAW'D HURT YOU AND GOT UPSET.
GHOSTS ARE LIKE THAT— A LITTLE MUDDLED.
EXCEPT FOR SOME THINGS.
THEY REMEMBER THOSE.
THE IMPORTANT THINGS.

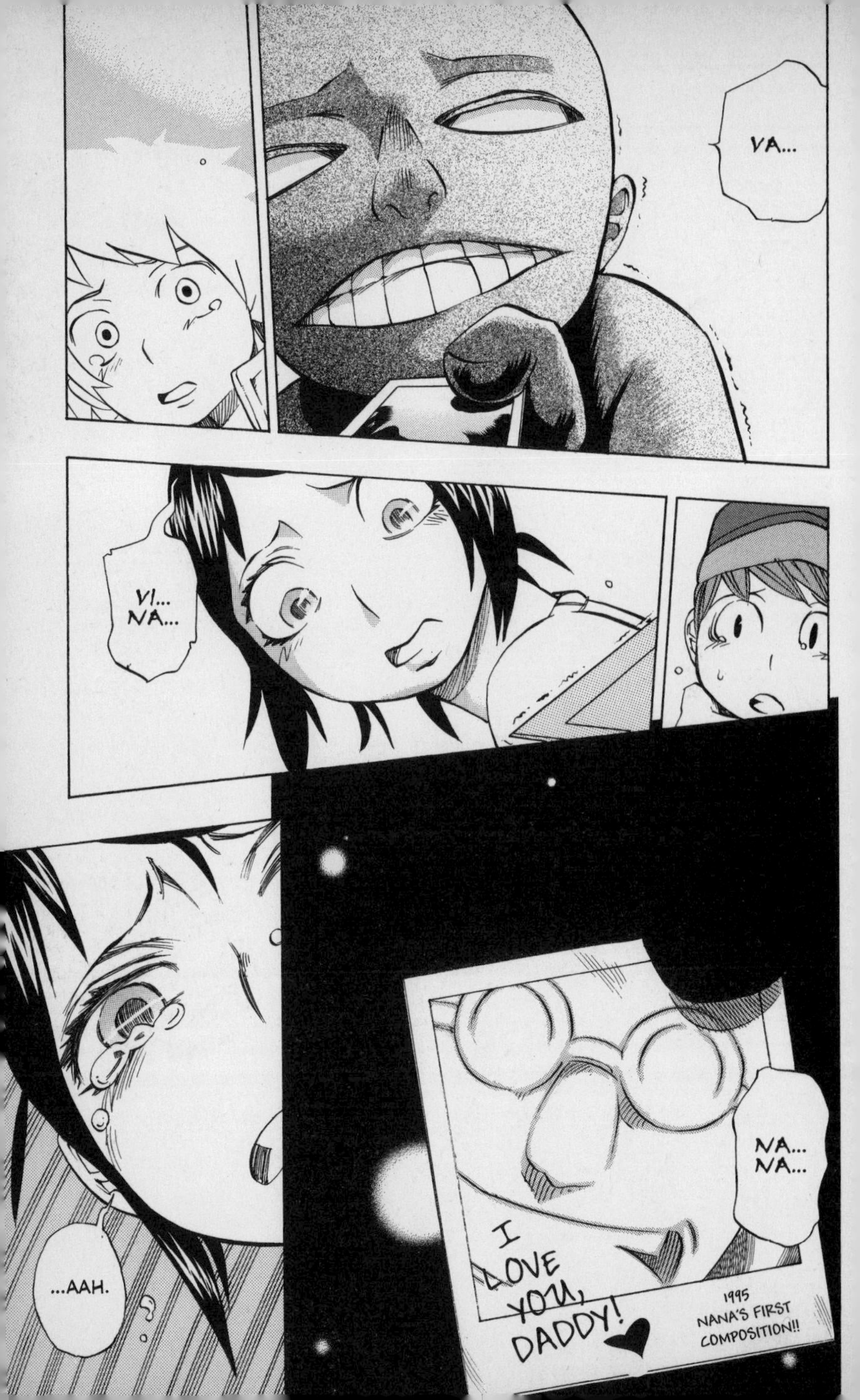

VA...
VI... NA...
NA... NA...
I LOVE YOU, DADDY!
1995 NANA'S FIRST COMPOSITION!!
...AAH.

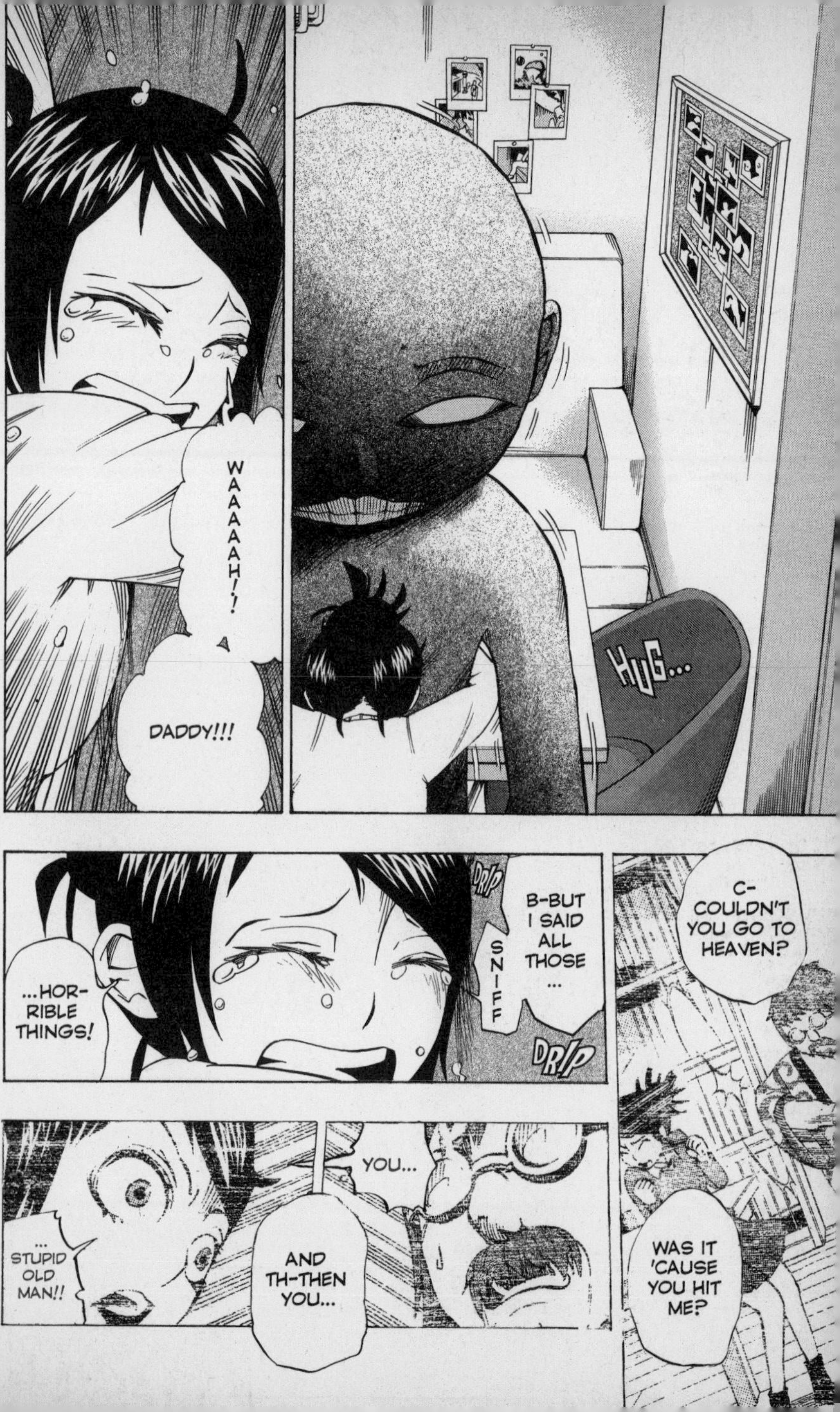
HUG...
WAAAAAAH!!
DADDY!!!
C-COULDN'T YOU GO TO HEAVEN?
WAS IT 'CAUSE YOU HIT ME?
DRIP
B-BUT I SAID ALL THOSE ...
SNIFF
DRIP
...HOR-RIBLE THINGS!
YOU...
AND TH-THEN YOU...
...STUPID OLD MAN!!

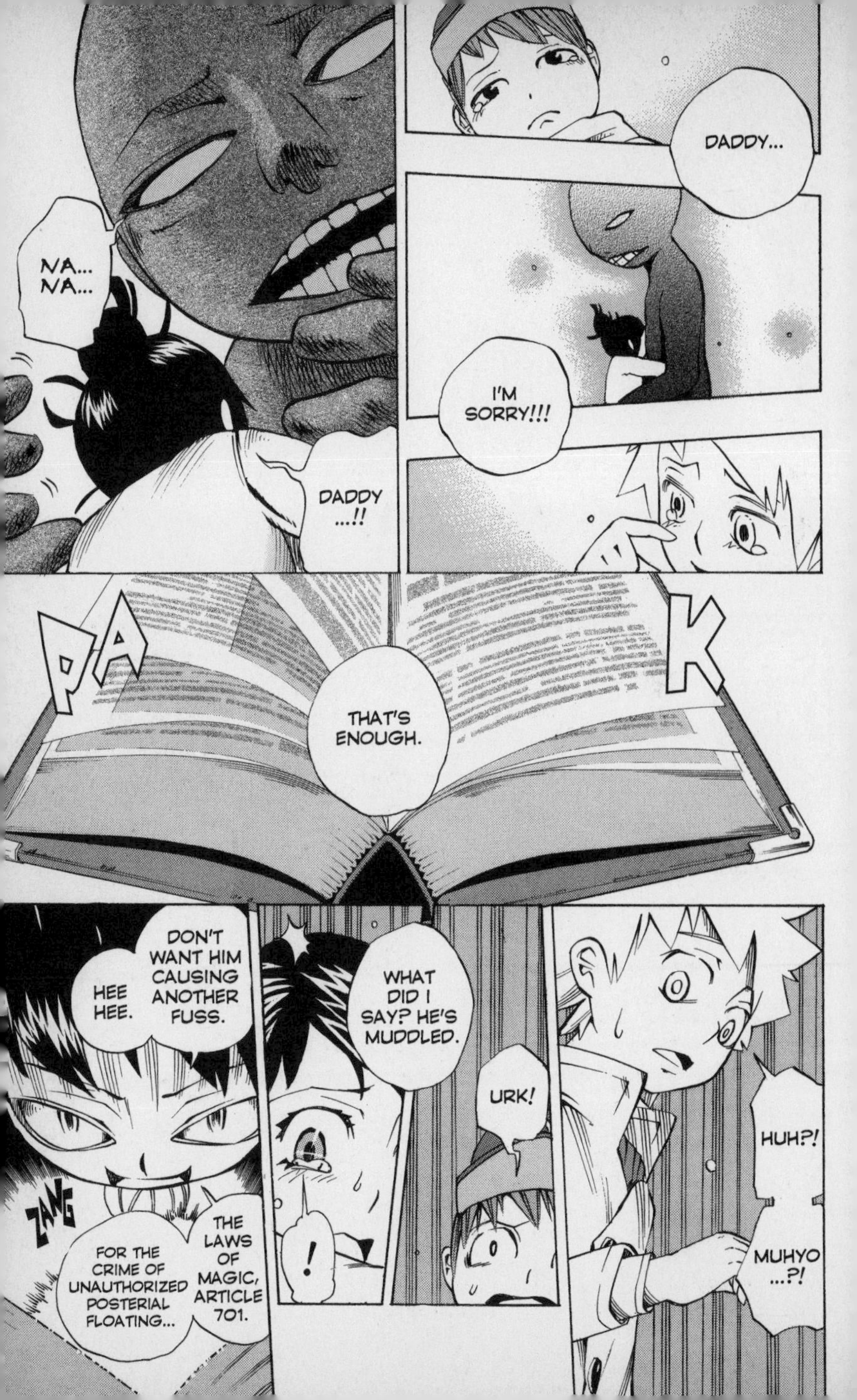
DADDY...
I'M SORRY!!!
NA... NA...
DADDY ...!!
PA
K
THAT'S ENOUGH.
HUH?!
MUHYO ...?!
URK!
WHAT DID I SAY? HE'S MUDDLED.
!
DON'T WANT HIM CAUSING ANOTHER FUSS.
HEE HEE.
THE LAWS OF MAGIC, ARTICLE 701.
FOR THE CRIME OF UNAUTHORIZED POSTERIAL FLOATING...
ZANG

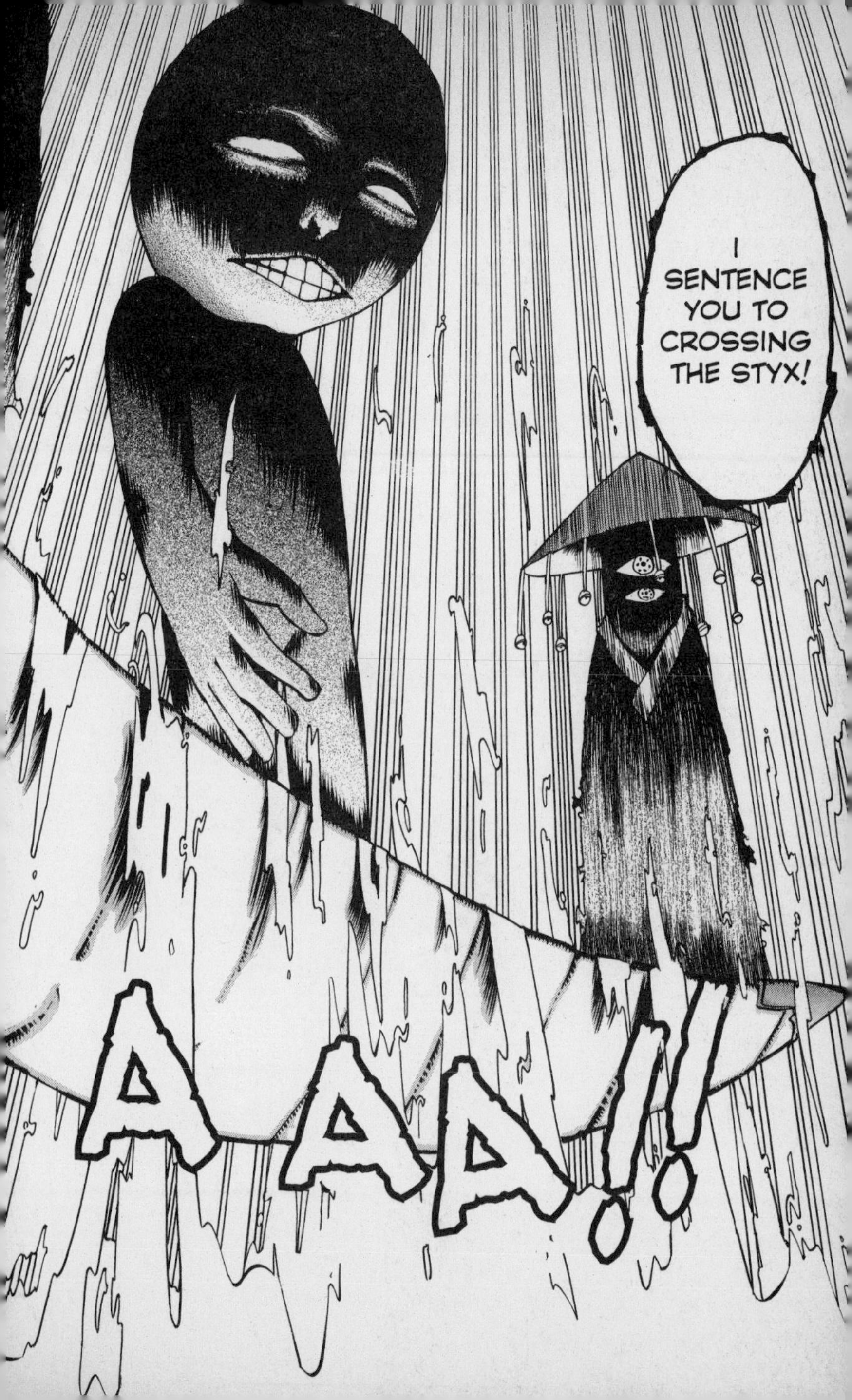
I SENTENCE YOU TO CROSSING THE STYX!
AAA!!

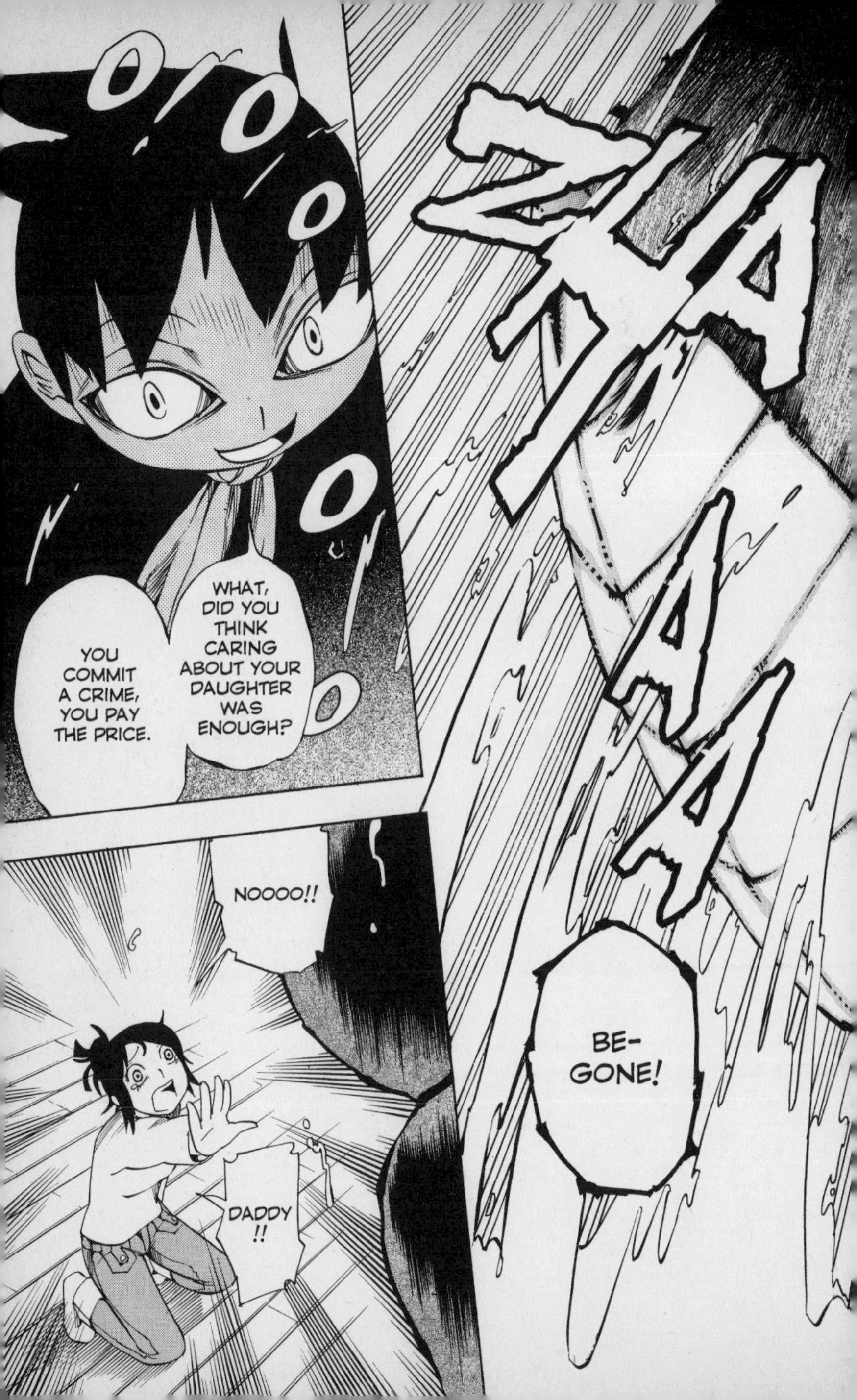
ZAAAA
BE-GONE!
WHAT, DID YOU THINK CARING ABOUT YOUR DAUGHTER WAS ENOUGH?
YOU COMMIT A CRIME, YOU PAY THE PRICE.
NOOOO!!
DADDY !!

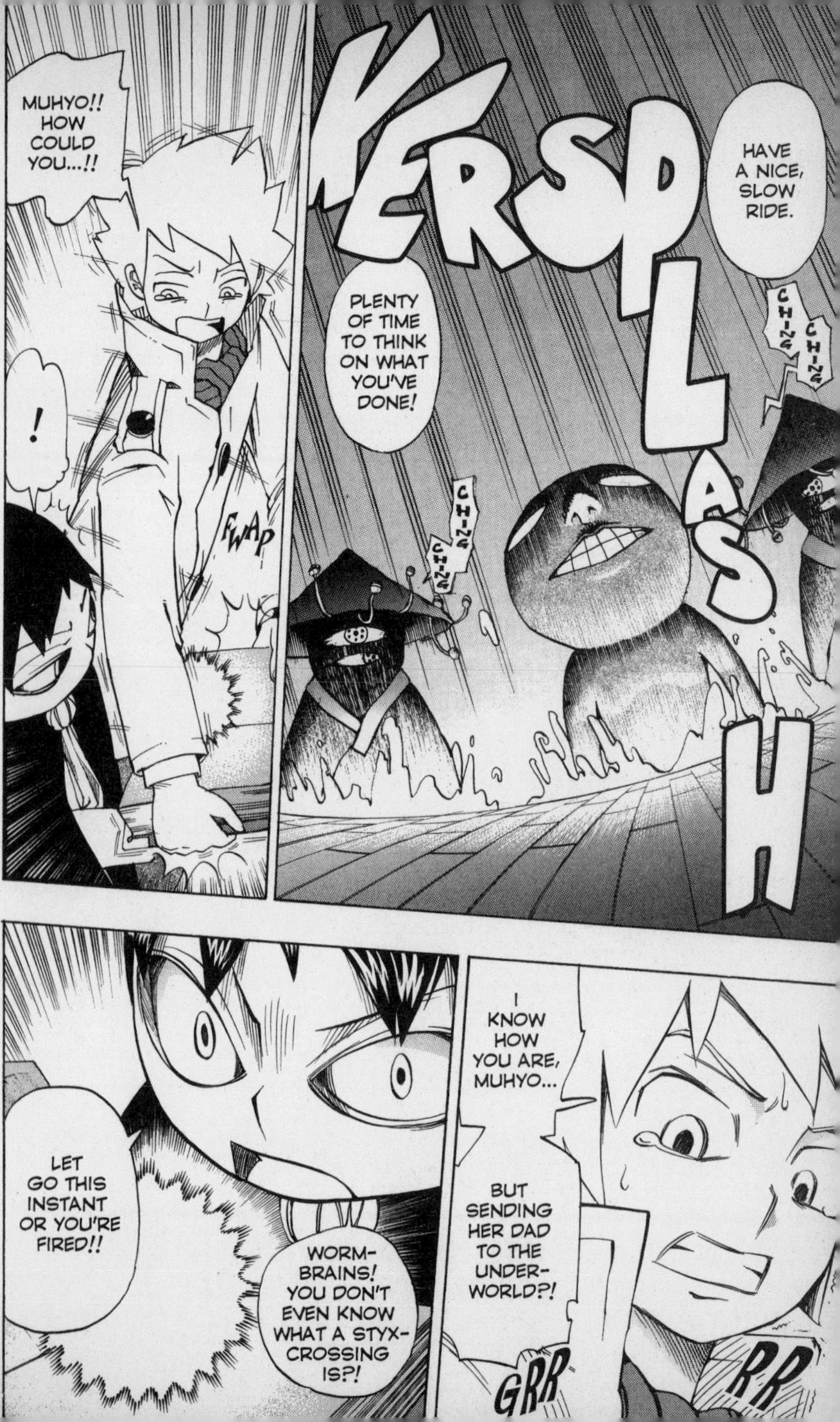
HAVE A NICE, SLOW RIDE.
PLENTY OF TIME TO THINK ON WHAT YOU'VE DONE!
KERSPLASH
CHING CHING
CHING CHING
MUHYO!! HOW COULD YOU...!!
!
FWAP
I KNOW HOW YOU ARE, MUHYO...
BUT SENDING HER DAD TO THE UNDER-WORLD?!
GRR
RR
LET GO THIS INSTANT OR YOU'RE FIRED!!
WORM-BRAINS! YOU DON'T EVEN KNOW WHAT A STYX-CROSSING IS?!

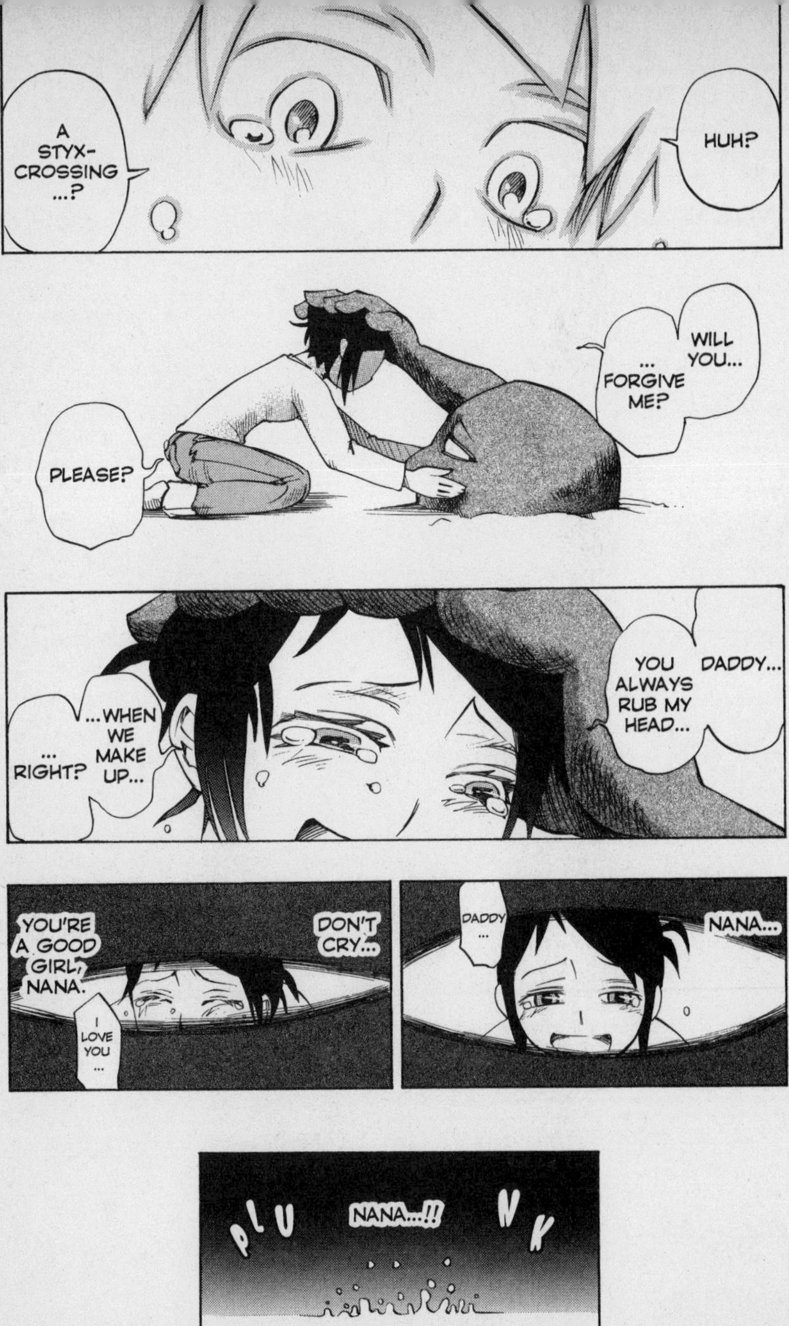
HUH?
A STYX-CROSSING ...?
WILL YOU... ...FORGIVE ME?
PLEASE?
DADDY...
YOU ALWAYS RUB MY HEAD...
...WHEN WE MAKE UP...
...RIGHT?
NANA...
DADDY...
DON'T CRY...
YOU'RE A GOOD GIRL, NANA.
I LOVE YOU...
PLU NK
NANA...!!

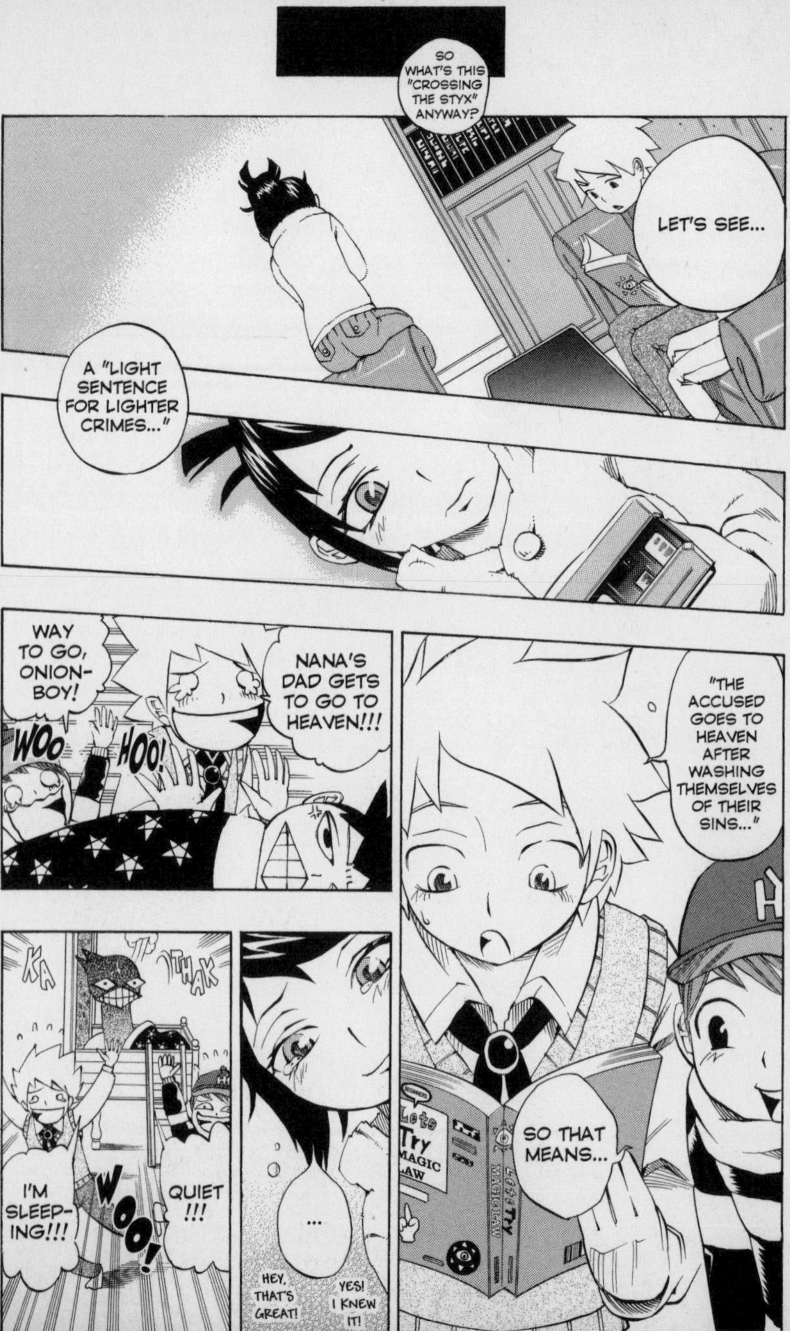
SO WHAT'S THIS "CROSSING THE STYX" ANYWAY?
LET'S SEE...
A "LIGHT SENTENCE FOR LIGHTER CRIMES..."
"THE ACCUSED GOES TO HEAVEN AFTER WASHING THEMSELVES OF THEIR SINS..."
SO THAT MEANS...
NANA'S DAD GETS TO GO TO HEAVEN!!!
WAY TO GO, ONION-BOY!
WOO
HOO!
...
YES! I KNEW IT!
HEY, THAT'S GREAT!
THAK
KA
QUIET!!!
WOO!
I'M SLEEPING!!!

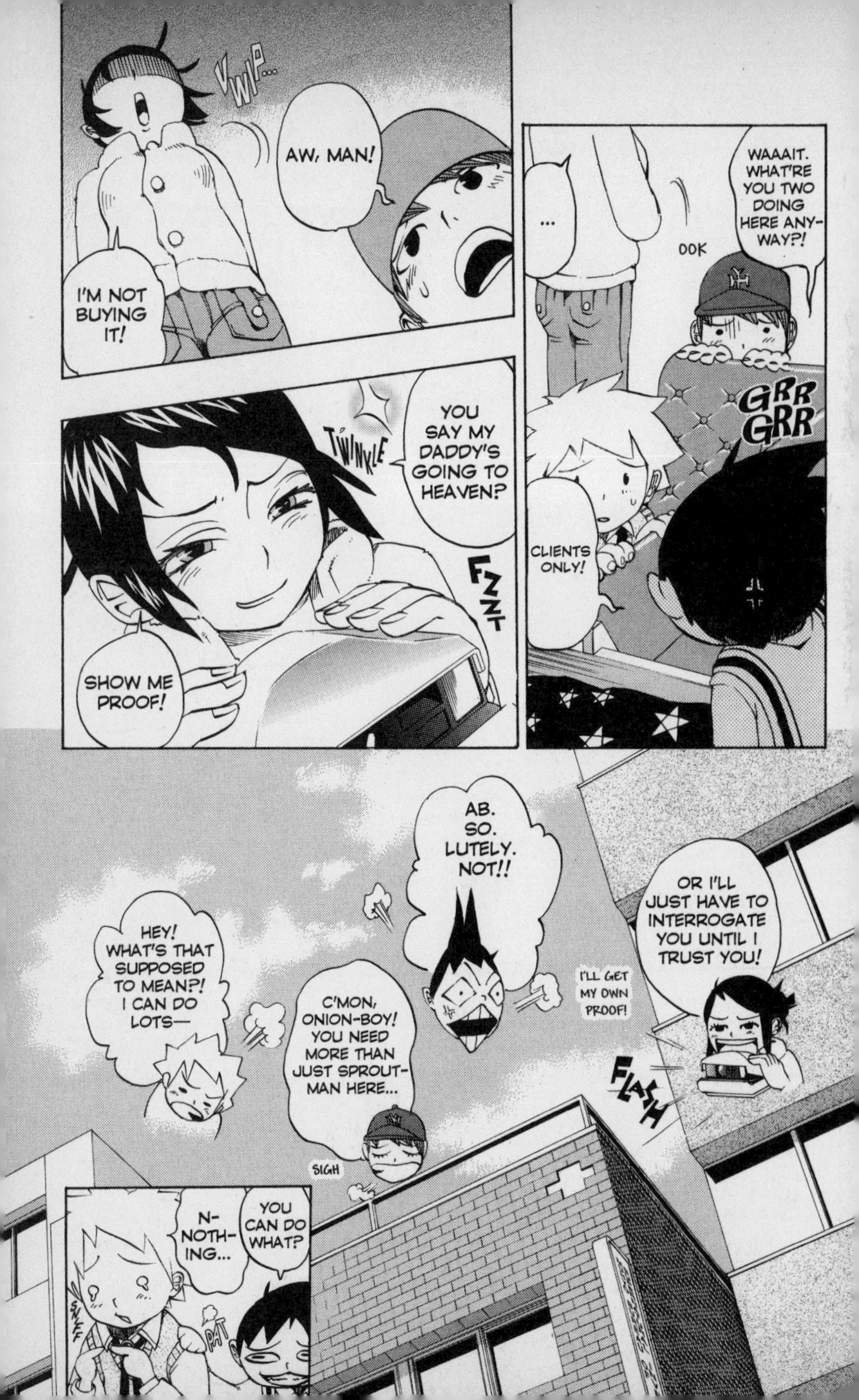
WAAAIT. WHAT'RE YOU TWO DOING HERE ANY-WAY?!
...
OOK
GRR GRR
CLIENTS ONLY!
VWIP...
AW, MAN!
I'M NOT BUYING IT!
YOU SAY MY DADDY'S GOING TO HEAVEN?
TWINKLE
FZZZT
SHOW ME PROOF!
OR I'LL JUST HAVE TO INTERROGATE YOU UNTIL I TRUST YOU!
I'LL GET MY OWN PROOF!
FLASH
AB. SO. LUTELY. NOT!!
C'MON, ONION-BOY! YOU NEED MORE THAN JUST SPROUT-MAN HERE...
SIGH
HEY! WHAT'S THAT SUPPOSED TO MEAN?! I CAN DO LOTS—
YOU CAN DO WHAT?
N-NOTH-ING...
PAT
SNIFF

THE ODD COUPLE

UH OH. ANGRY!

ARTICLE 9
ROJI'S PEN

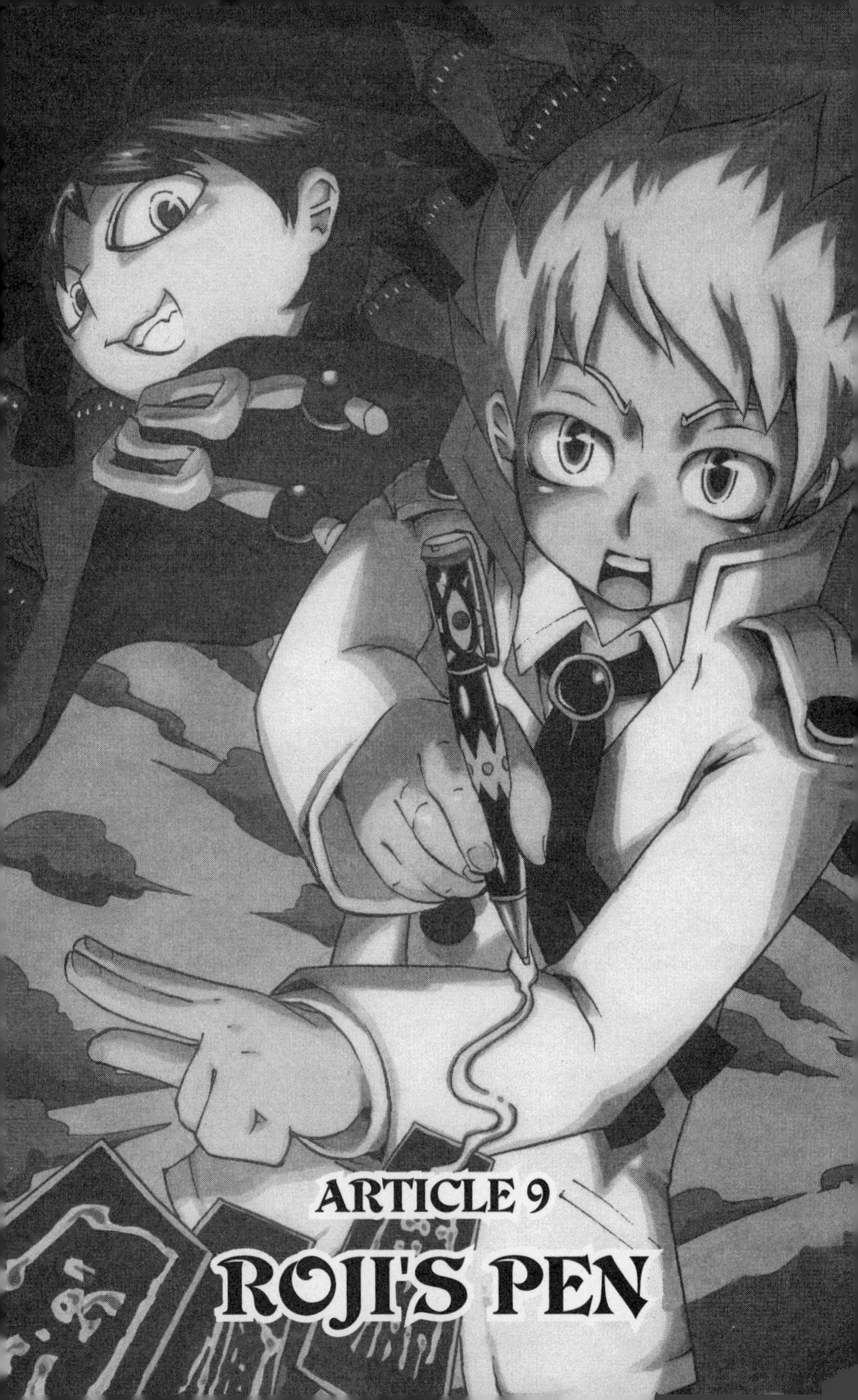

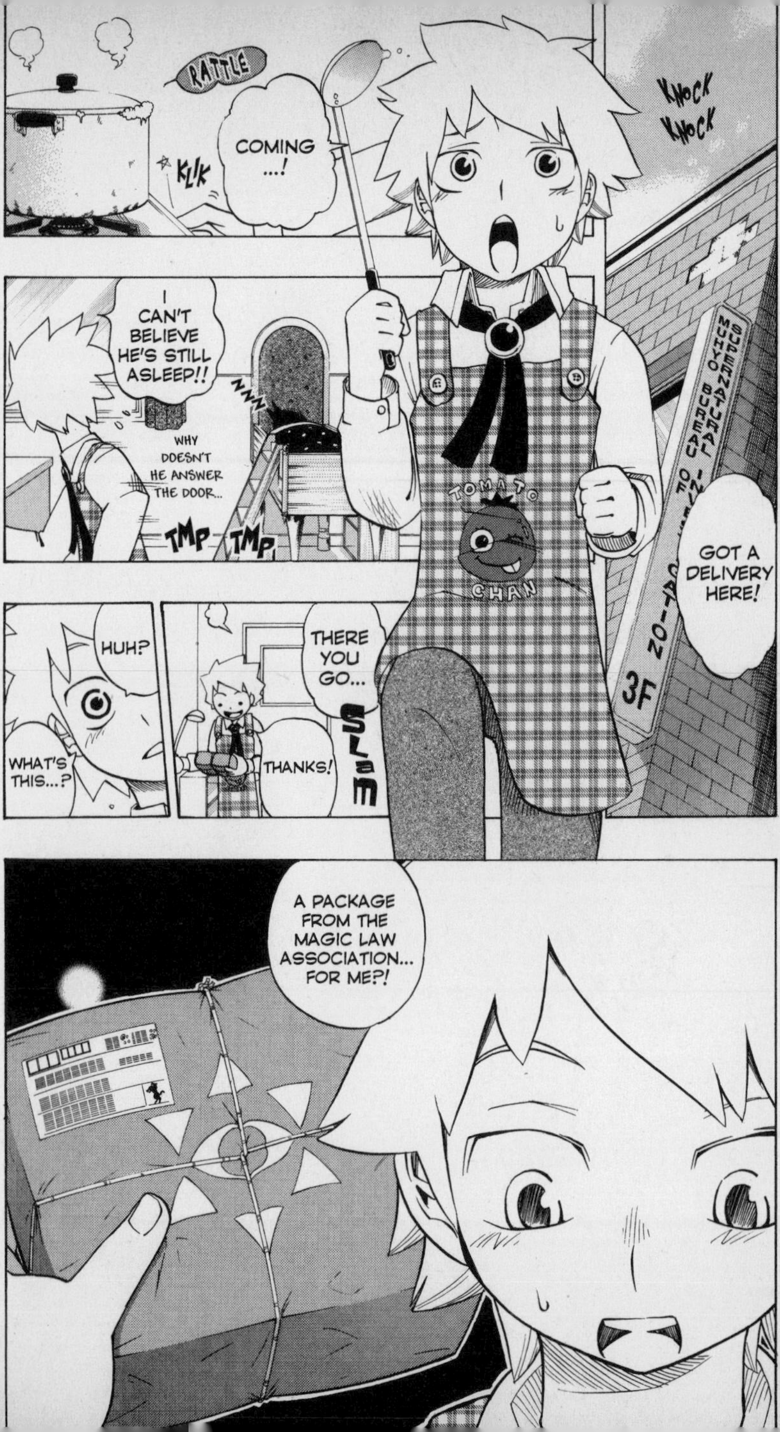
KNOCK KNOCK
GOT A DELIVERY HERE!
3F
RATTLE
COMING ...!
KLIK
I CAN'T BELIEVE HE'S STILL ASLEEP!!
ZZZ
WHY DOESN'T HE ANSWER THE DOOR..
TMP TMP
THERE YOU GO...
SLAM
THANKS!
HUH?
WHAT'S THIS...?
A PACKAGE FROM THE MAGIC LAW ASSOCIATION... FOR ME?!

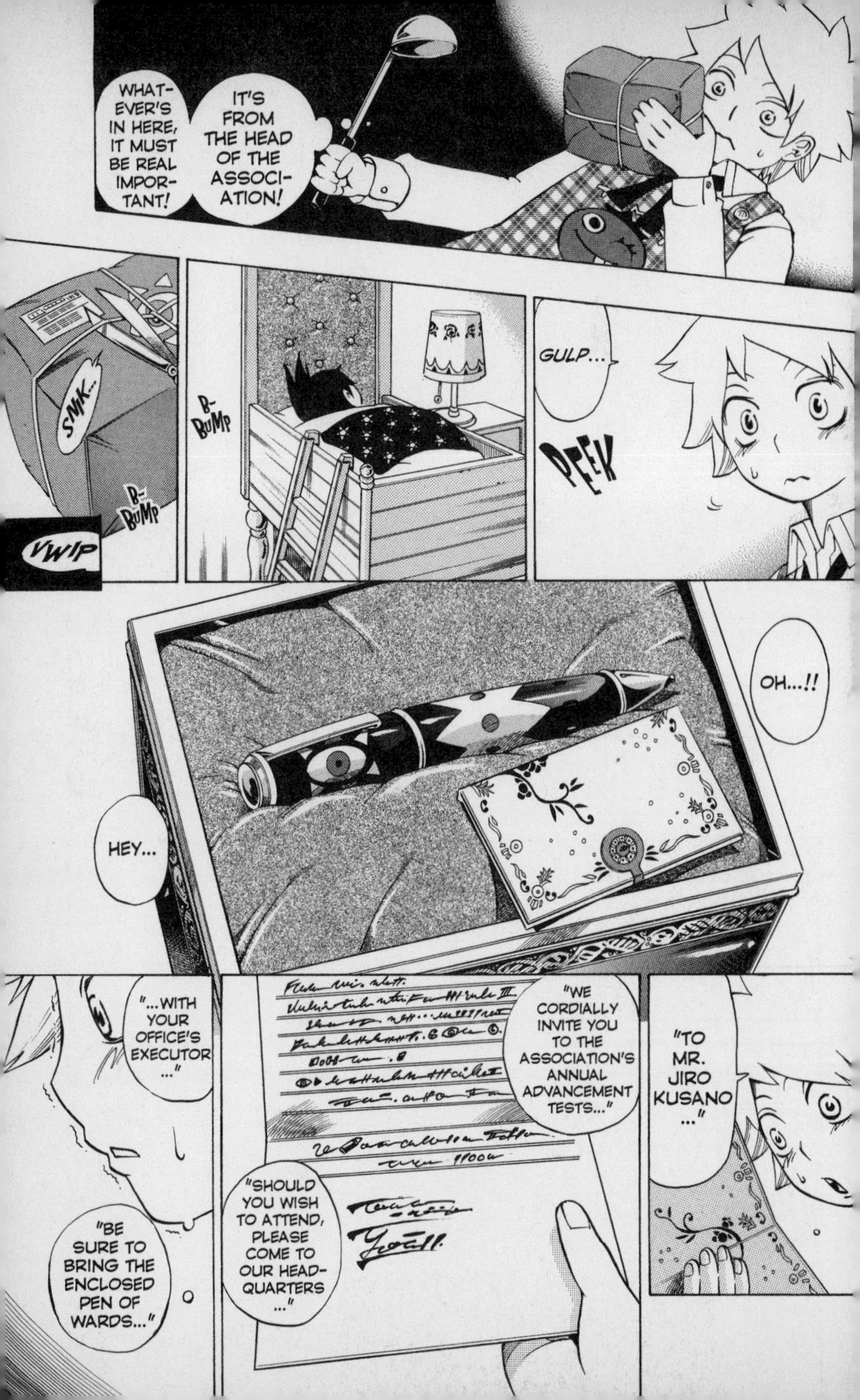
IT'S FROM THE HEAD OF THE ASSOCIATION!
WHAT-EVER'S IN HERE, IT MUST BE REAL IMPOR-TANT!
GULP...
PEEK
B-BUMP
SNIK...
B-BUMP
VWIP
OH...!!
HEY...
"TO MR. JIRO KUSANO..."
"WE CORDIALLY INVITE YOU TO THE ASSOCIATION'S ANNUAL ADVANCEMENT TESTS..."
"SHOULD YOU WISH TO ATTEND, PLEASE COME TO OUR HEAD-QUARTERS..."
"...WITH YOUR OFFICE'S EXECUTOR..."
"BE SURE TO BRING THE ENCLOSED PEN OF WARDS..."

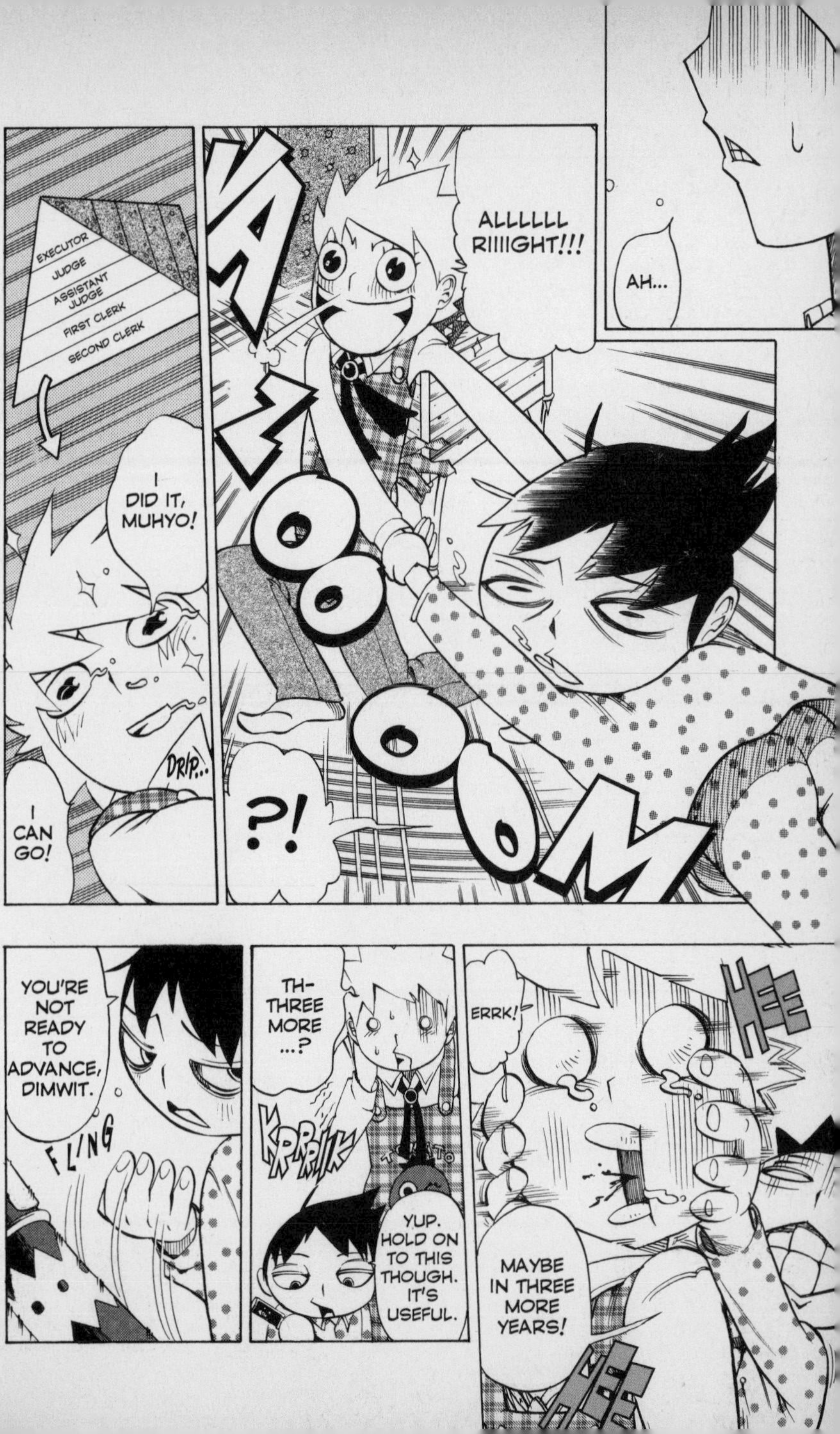
AH...
ALLLLLL RIIIIGHT!!!
VAZOOOOM
?!
EXECUTOR
JUDGE
ASSISTANT JUDGE
FIRST CLERK
SECOND CLERK
I DID IT, MUHYO!
DRIP...
I CAN GO!
ERRK!
HEE
MAYBE IN THREE MORE YEARS!
HEE
TH- THREE MORE ...?
KRRRIIK
YUP. HOLD ON TO THIS THOUGH. IT'S USEFUL.
YOU'RE NOT READY TO ADVANCE, DIMWIT.
FLING

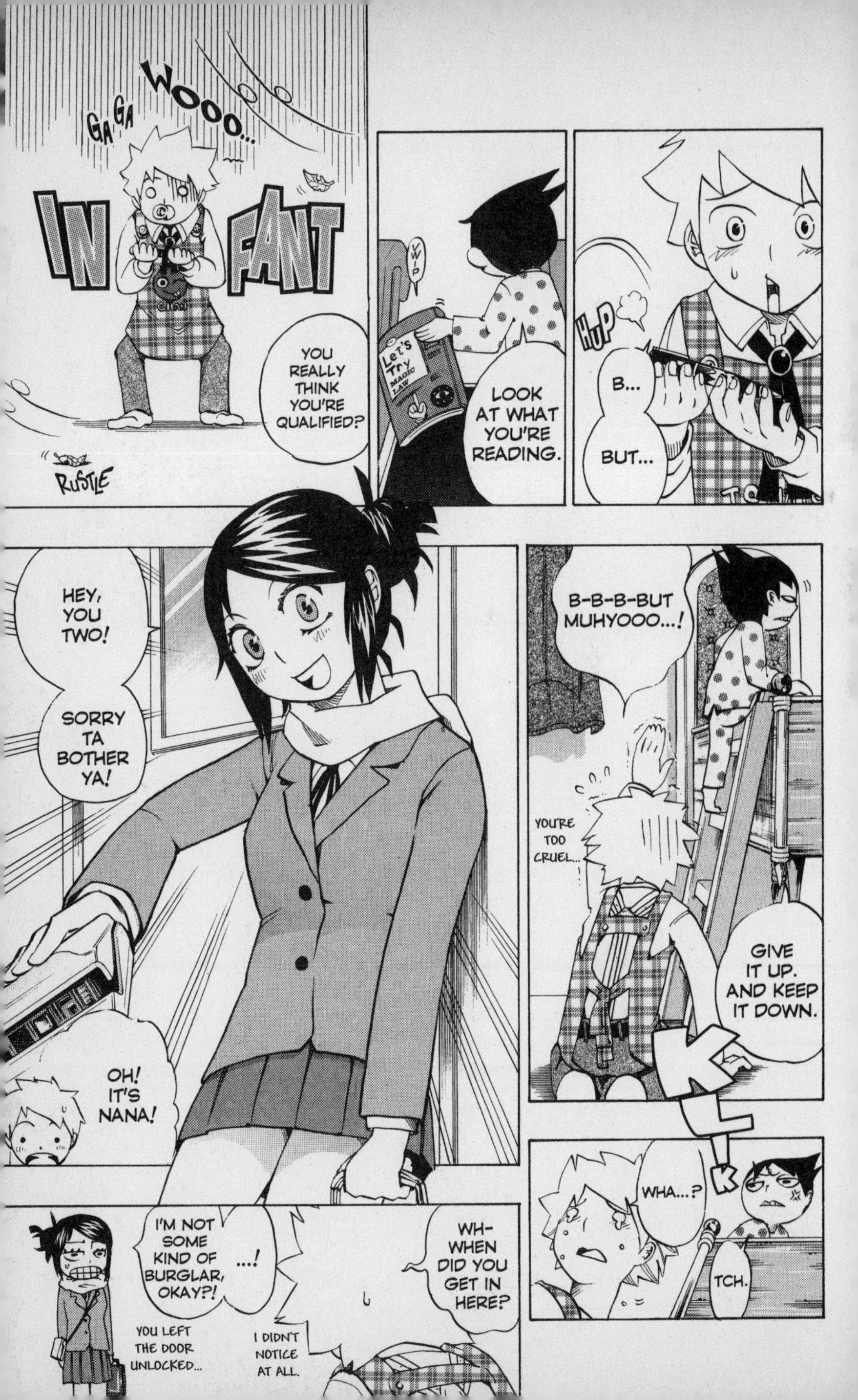
HUP
B...
BUT...
VWIP
Let's Try MAGIC LAW
LOOK AT WHAT YOU'RE READING.
GA GA
WOOO...
IN FANT
YOU REALLY THINK YOU'RE QUALIFIED?
RUSTLE
B-B-B-BUT MUHYOOO...!
YOU'RE TOO CRUEL...
GIVE IT UP. AND KEEP IT DOWN.
KLK
WHA...?
TCH.
HEY, YOU TWO!
SORRY TA BOTHER YA!
OH! IT'S NANA!
WH- WHEN DID YOU GET IN HERE?
I DIDN'T NOTICE AT ALL.
...!
I'M NOT SOME KIND OF BURGLAR, OKAY?!
YOU LEFT THE DOOR UNLOCKED...

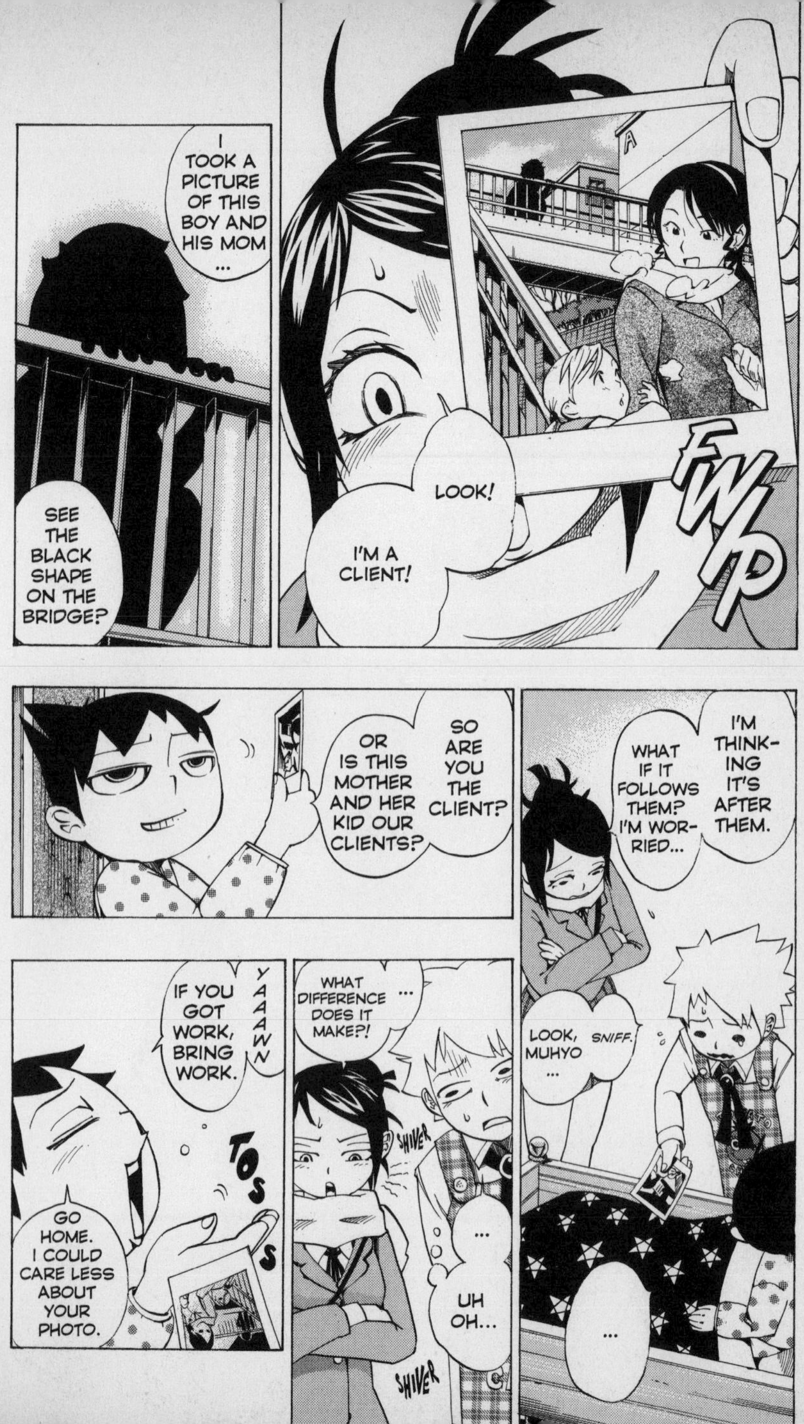
LOOK!
I'M A CLIENT!
FWIP
I TOOK A PICTURE OF THIS BOY AND HIS MOM ...
SEE THE BLACK SHAPE ON THE BRIDGE?
I'M THINKING IT'S AFTER THEM.
WHAT IF IT FOLLOWS THEM? I'M WORRIED...
LOOK, MUHYO ...
SNIFF.
...
SO ARE YOU THE CLIENT?
OR IS THIS MOTHER AND HER KID OUR CLIENTS?
WHAT DIFFERENCE DOES IT MAKE?!
...
SHIVER
...
UH OH...
SHIVER
YAAAWN
IF YOU GOT WORK, BRING WORK.
TOSS
GO HOME. I COULD CARE LESS ABOUT YOUR PHOTO.

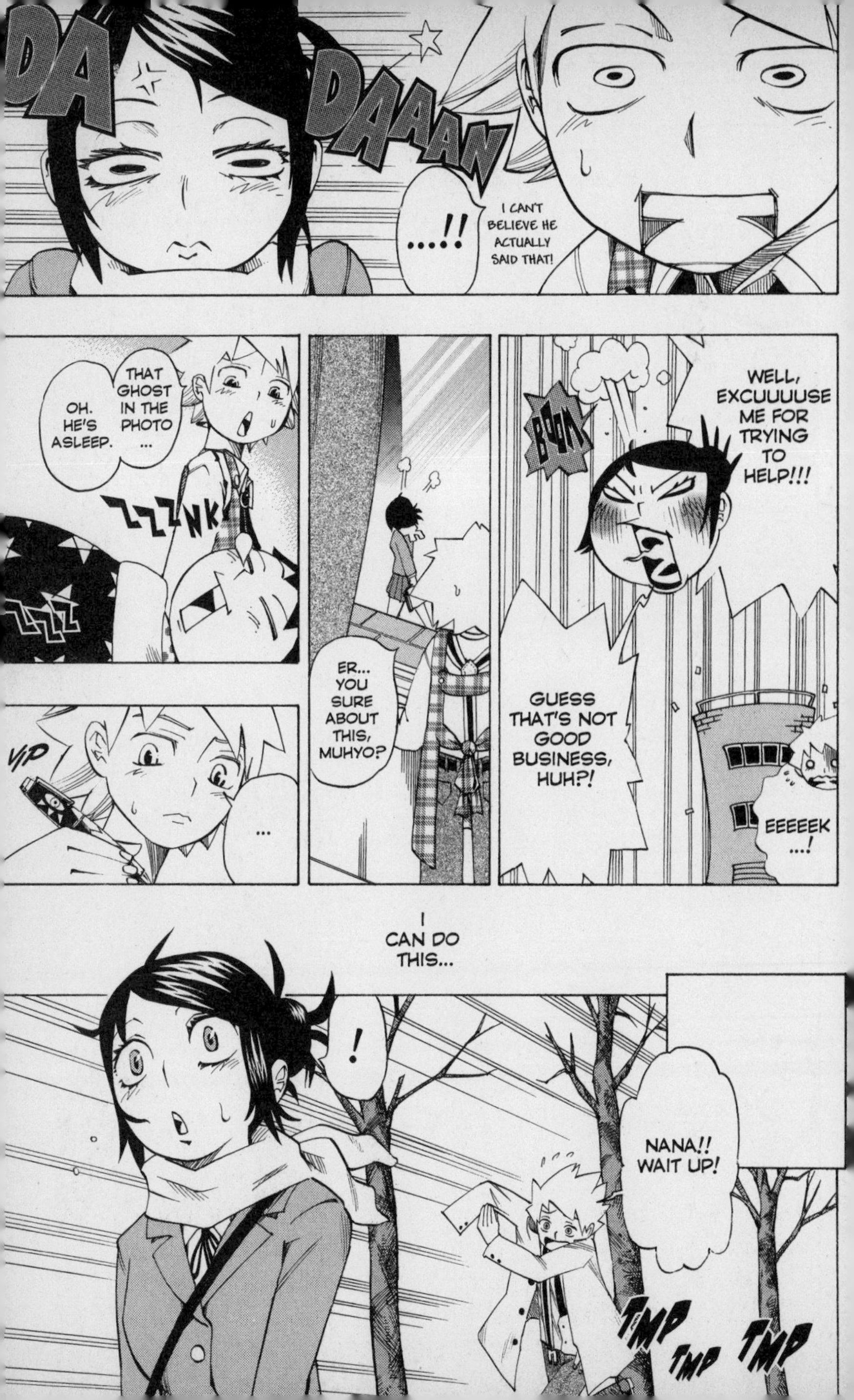
I CAN'T BELIEVE HE ACTUALLY SAID THAT!
....!!
DA DAAAN
WELL, EXCUUUUSE ME FOR TRYING TO HELP!!!
BOOM
GUESS THAT'S NOT GOOD BUSINESS, HUH?!
EEEEEK...!
ER... YOU SURE ABOUT THIS, MUHYO?
THAT GHOST IN THE PHOTO...
OH. HE'S ASLEEP.
ZZZZNK
ZZZZ
VIP
...
I CAN DO THIS...
NANA!! WAIT UP!
!
TMP TMP TMP

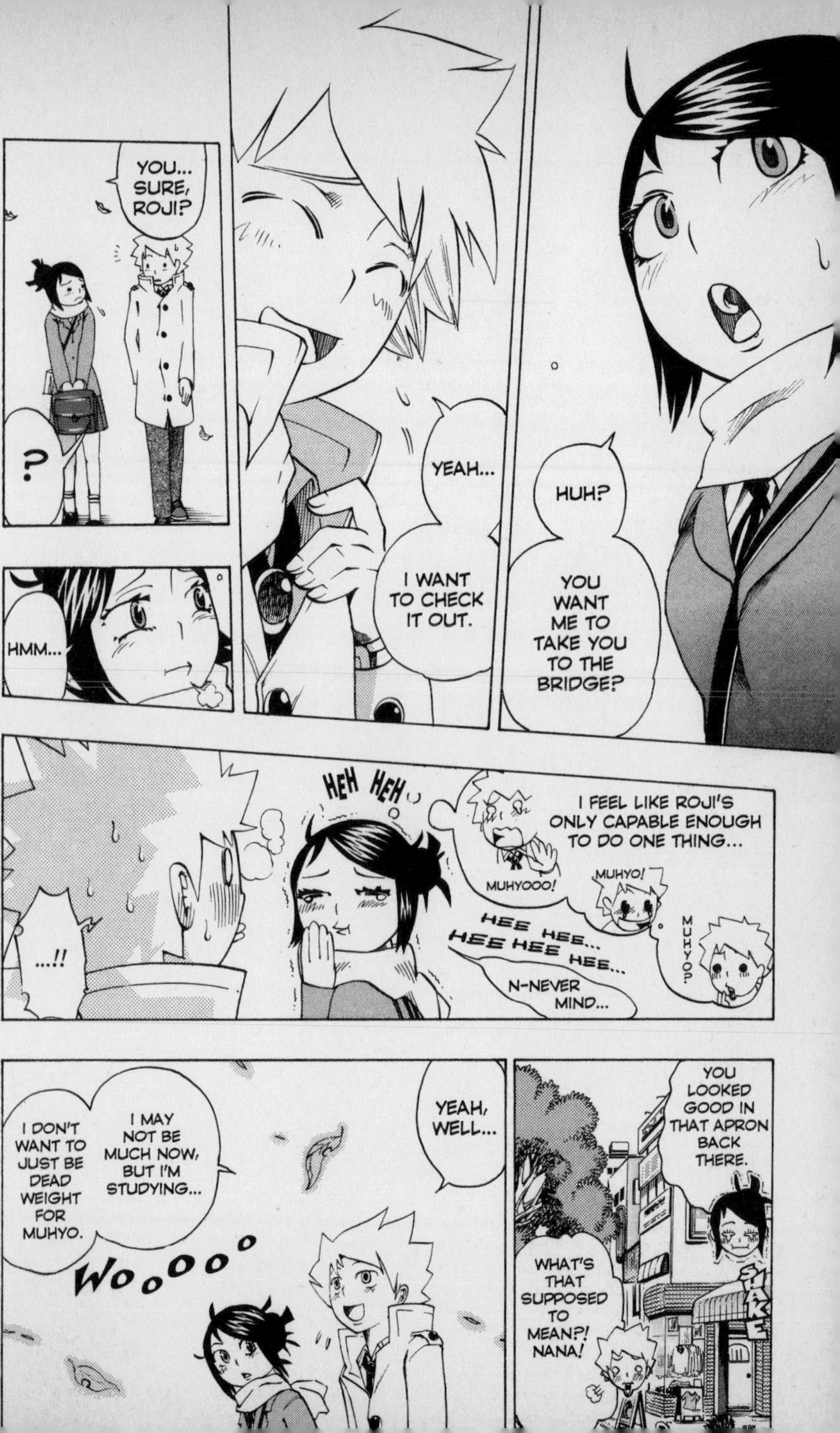
HUH?
YOU WANT ME TO TAKE YOU TO THE BRIDGE?
YEAH...
I WANT TO CHECK IT OUT.
YOU... SURE, ROJI?
?
HMM...
HEH HEH
I FEEL LIKE ROJI'S ONLY CAPABLE ENOUGH TO DO ONE THING...
MUHYOOO!
MUHYO!
MUHYO?
HEE HEE... HEE HEE HEE...
N-NEVER MIND...
...!!
YOU LOOKED GOOD IN THAT APRON BACK THERE.
SHAKE
WHAT'S THAT SUPPOSED TO MEAN?! NANA!
YEAH, WELL...
I MAY NOT BE MUCH NOW, BUT I'M STUDYING...
I DON'T WANT TO JUST BE DEAD WEIGHT FOR MUHYO.
WOOOOO

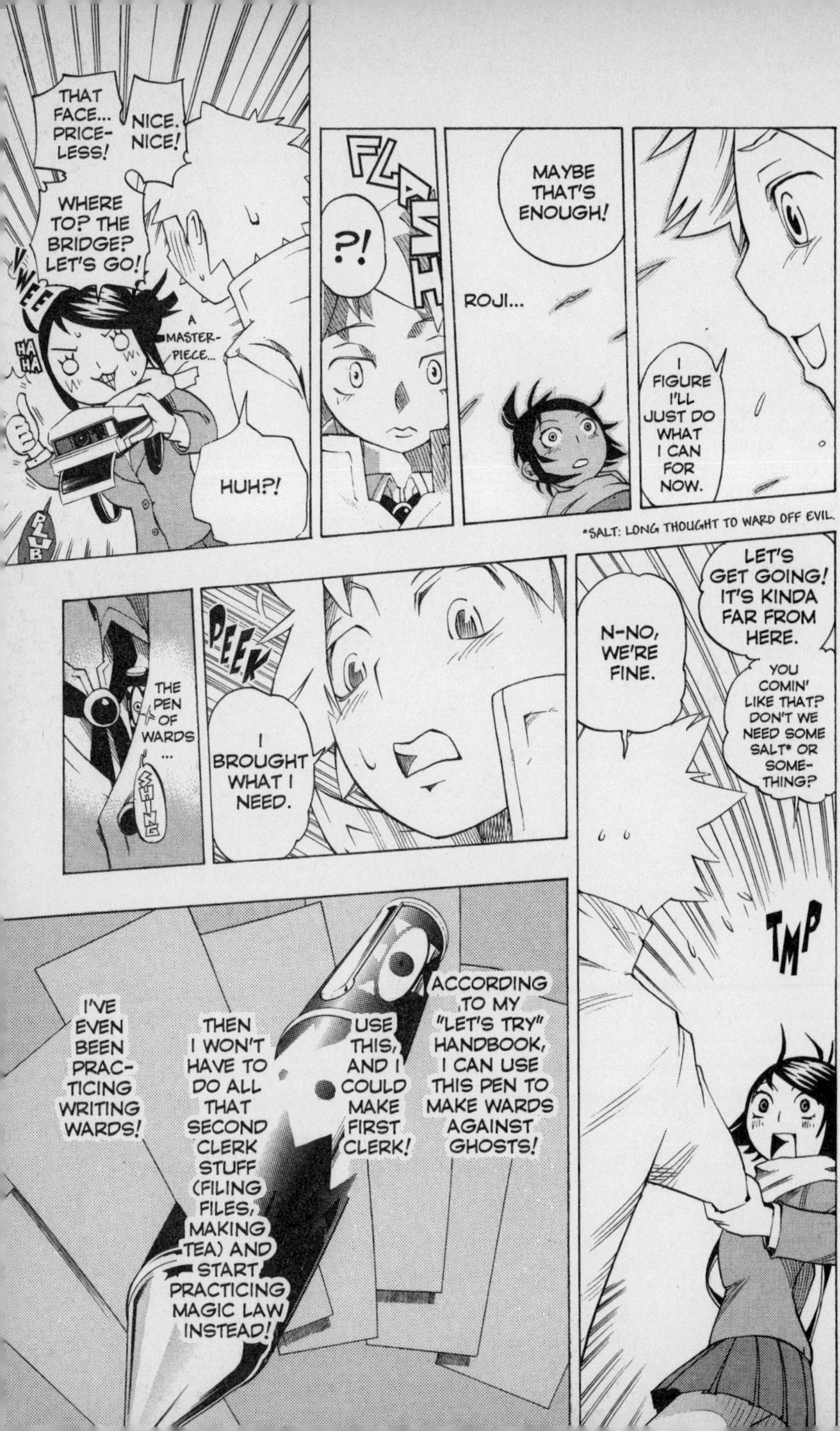
I FIGURE I'LL JUST DO WHAT I CAN FOR NOW.
MAYBE THAT'S ENOUGH!
ROJI...
FLASH
?!
NICE. NICE!
THAT FACE... PRICE-LESS!
WHERE TO? THE BRIDGE? LET'S GO!
VWEE
A MASTER-PIECE...
HA HA
HUH?!
PLUB
LET'S GET GOING! IT'S KINDA FAR FROM HERE.
YOU COMIN' LIKE THAT? DON'T WE NEED SOME SALT* OR SOME-THING?
N-NO, WE'RE FINE.
TMP
PEEK
I BROUGHT WHAT I NEED.
THE PEN OF WARDS...
SHING
ACCORDING TO MY "LET'S TRY" HANDBOOK, I CAN USE THIS PEN TO MAKE WARDS AGAINST GHOSTS!
USE THIS, AND I COULD MAKE FIRST CLERK!
THEN I WON'T HAVE TO DO ALL THAT SECOND CLERK STUFF (FILING FILES, MAKING TEA) AND START PRACTICING MAGIC LAW INSTEAD!
I'VE EVEN BEEN PRAC-TICING WRITING WARDS!

*SALT: LONG THOUGHT TO WARD OFF EVIL.

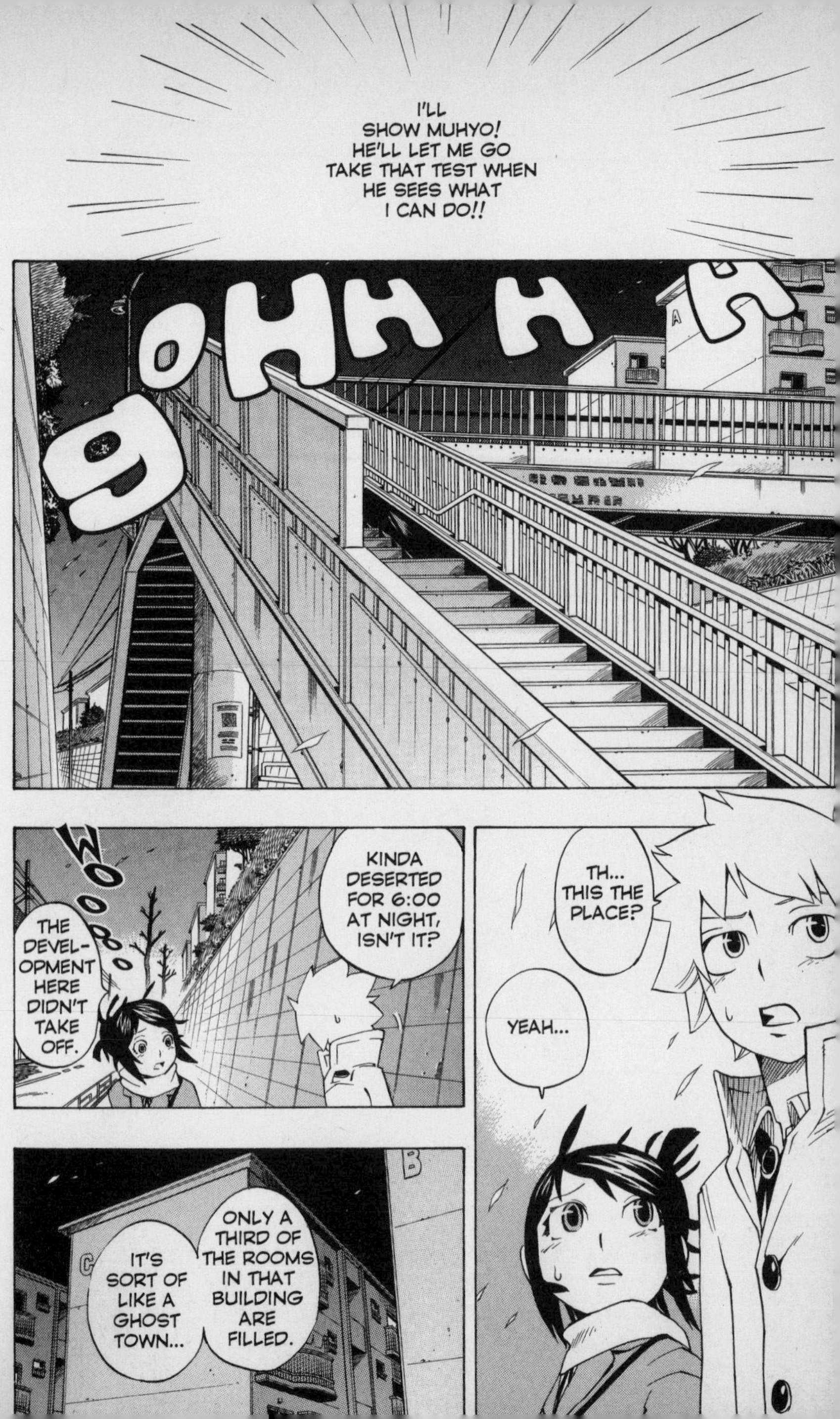
I'LL SHOW MUHYO! HE'LL LET ME GO TAKE THAT TEST WHEN HE SEES WHAT I CAN DO!!
GOHHHH
TH... THIS THE PLACE?
YEAH...
KINDA DESERTED FOR 6:00 AT NIGHT, ISN'T IT?
WOOOOO
THE DEVELOPMENT HERE DIDN'T TAKE OFF.
ONLY A THIRD OF THE ROOMS IN THAT BUILDING ARE FILLED.
IT'S SORT OF LIKE A GHOST TOWN...

READ THIS WAY

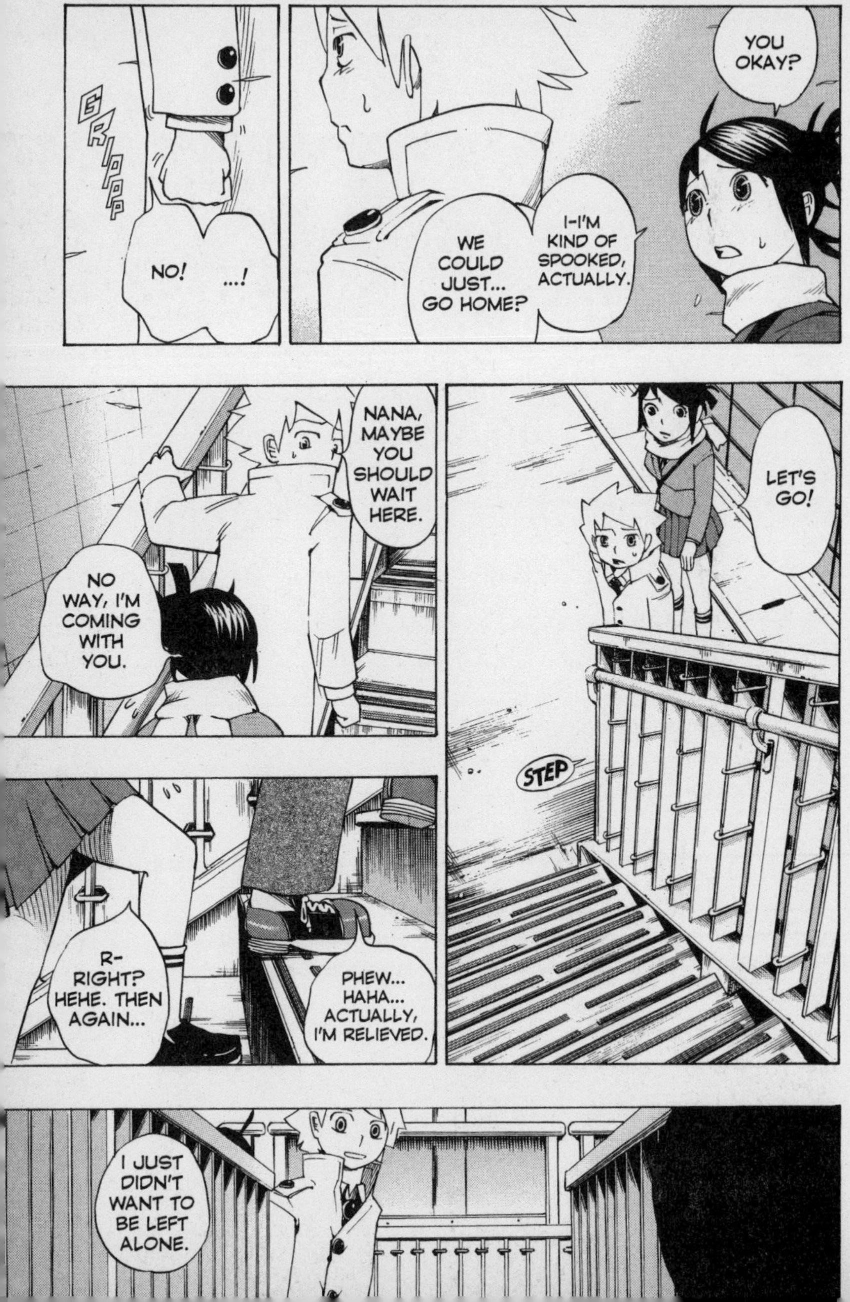
YOU OKAY?
I-I'M KIND OF SPOOKED, ACTUALLY.
WE COULD JUST... GO HOME?
GRIPPP
NO! ...!
LET'S GO!
STEP
NANA, MAYBE YOU SHOULD WAIT HERE.
NO WAY, I'M COMING WITH YOU.
PHEW... HAHA... ACTUALLY, I'M RELIEVED.
R-RIGHT? HEHE. THEN AGAIN...
I JUST DIDN'T WANT TO BE LEFT ALONE.

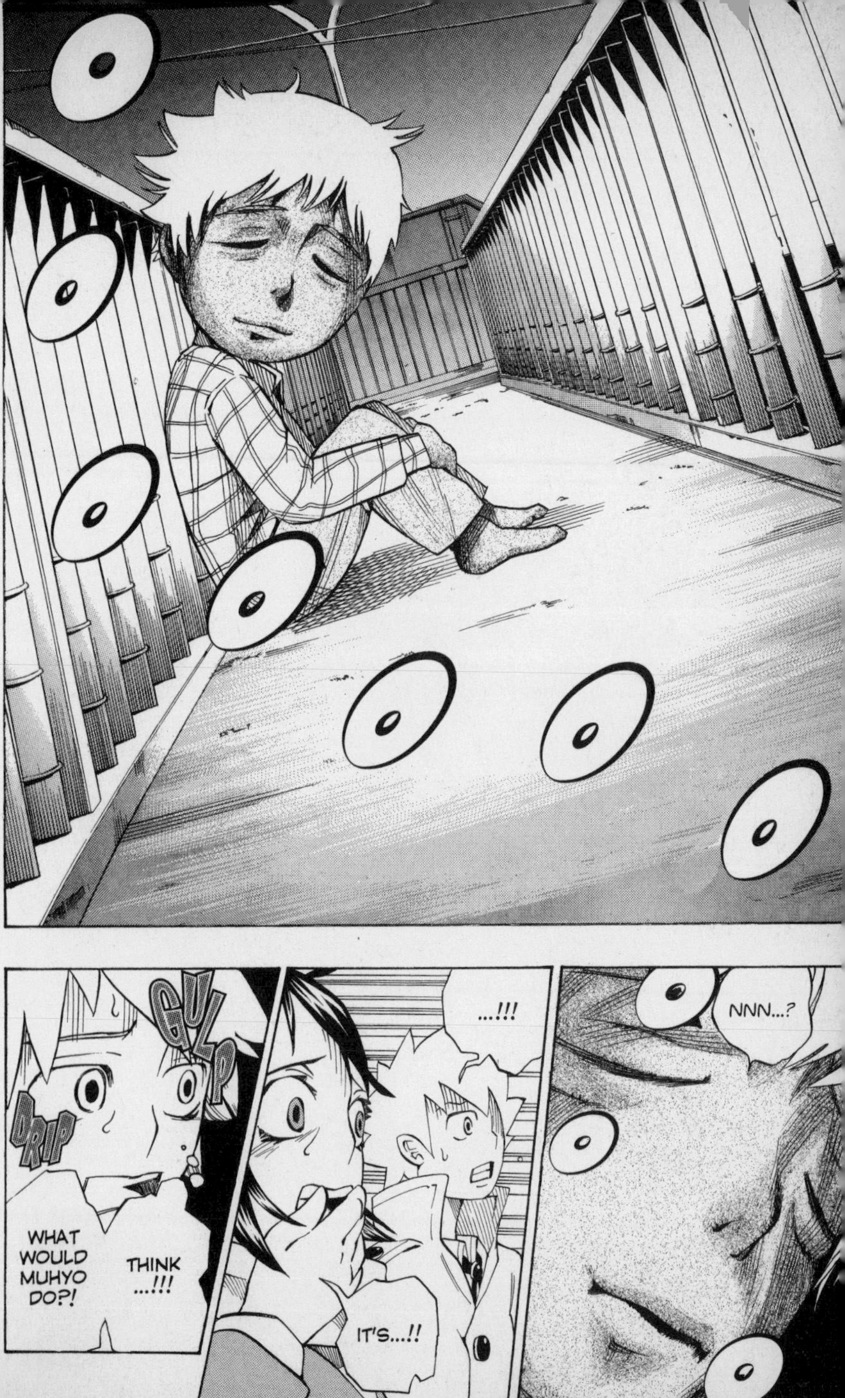
NNN...?
...!!!
IT'S...!!
GULP
DRIP
WHAT WOULD MUHYO DO?!
THINK ...!!!

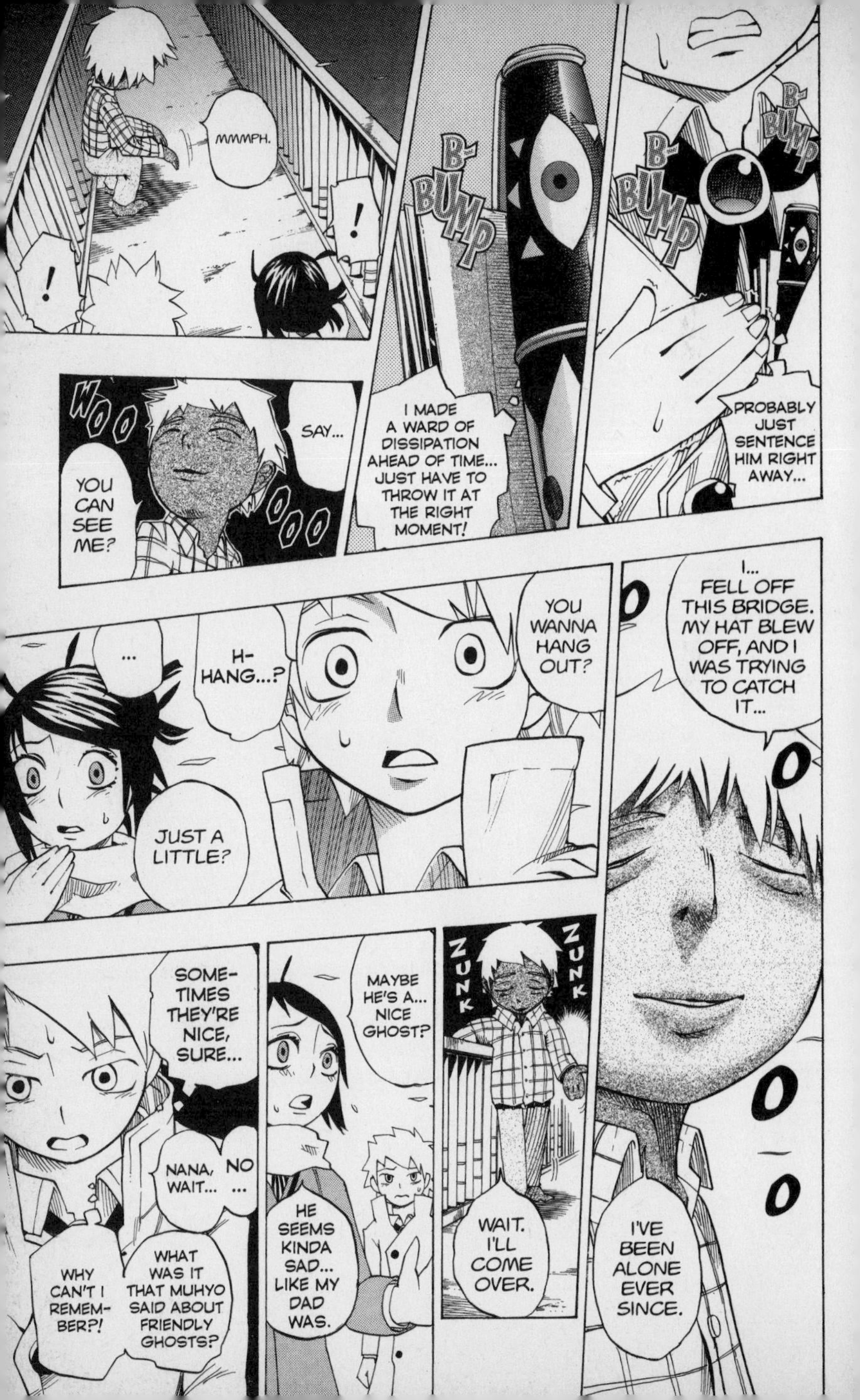
B-BUMP
B-BUMP
PROBABLY JUST SENTENCE HIM RIGHT AWAY...
B-BUMP
I MADE A WARD OF DISSIPATION AHEAD OF TIME... JUST HAVE TO THROW IT AT THE RIGHT MOMENT!
MMMPH.
!
!
SAY...
WOO
YOU CAN SEE ME?
OOO
I... FELL OFF THIS BRIDGE. MY HAT BLEW OFF, AND I WAS TRYING TO CATCH IT...
I'VE BEEN ALONE EVER SINCE.
YOU WANNA HANG OUT?
H-HANG...?
...
JUST A LITTLE?
ZUNK ZUNK
WAIT. I'LL COME OVER.
MAYBE HE'S A... NICE GHOST?
HE SEEMS KINDA SAD... LIKE MY DAD WAS.
SOME-TIMES THEY'RE NICE, SURE...
NO...
NANA, WAIT...
WHAT WAS IT THAT MUHYO SAID ABOUT FRIENDLY GHOSTS?
WHY CAN'T I REMEM-BER?!

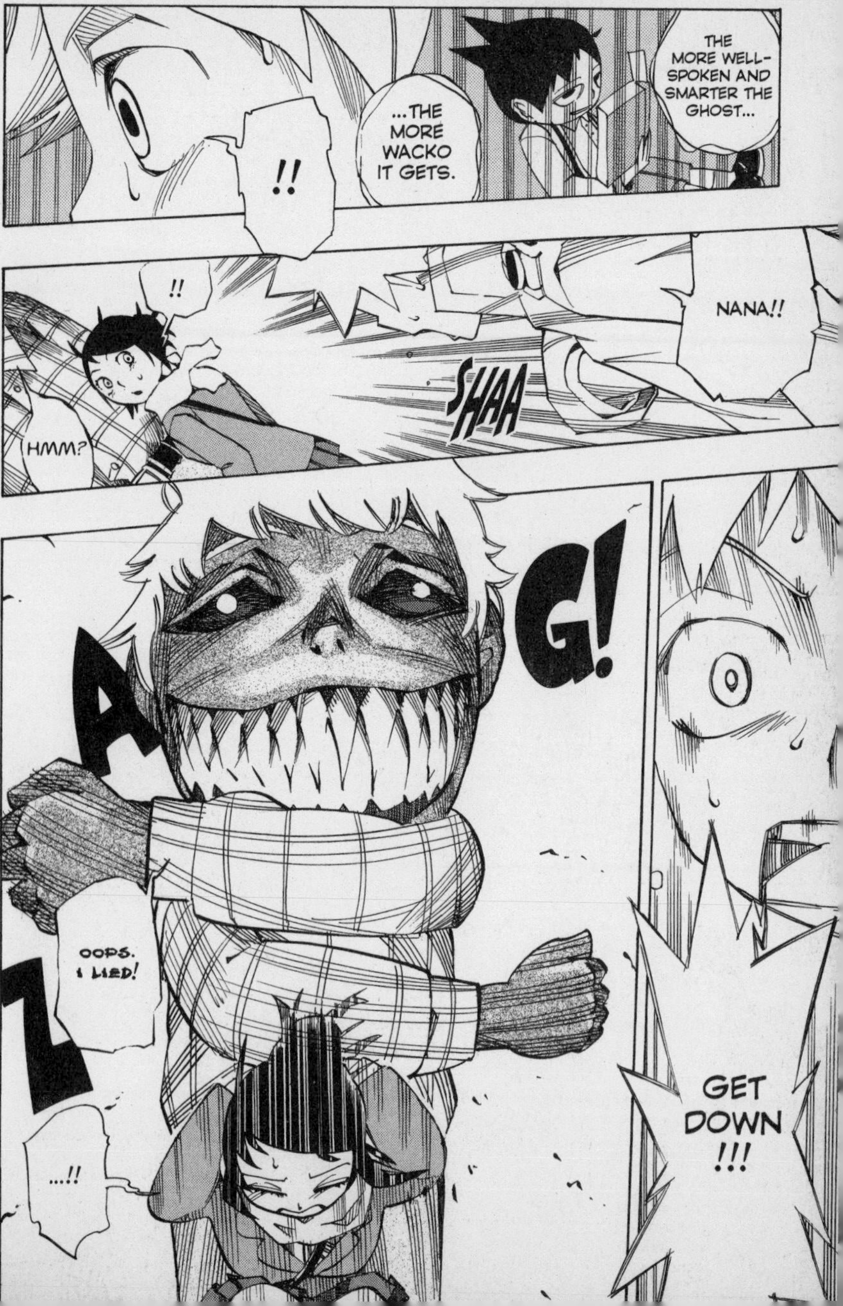
THE MORE WELL-SPOKEN AND SMARTER THE GHOST...
...THE MORE WACKO IT GETS.
!!
NANA!!
SHAA
!!
HMM?
GET DOWN!!!
A
G!
Z
OOPS. I LIED!
...!!

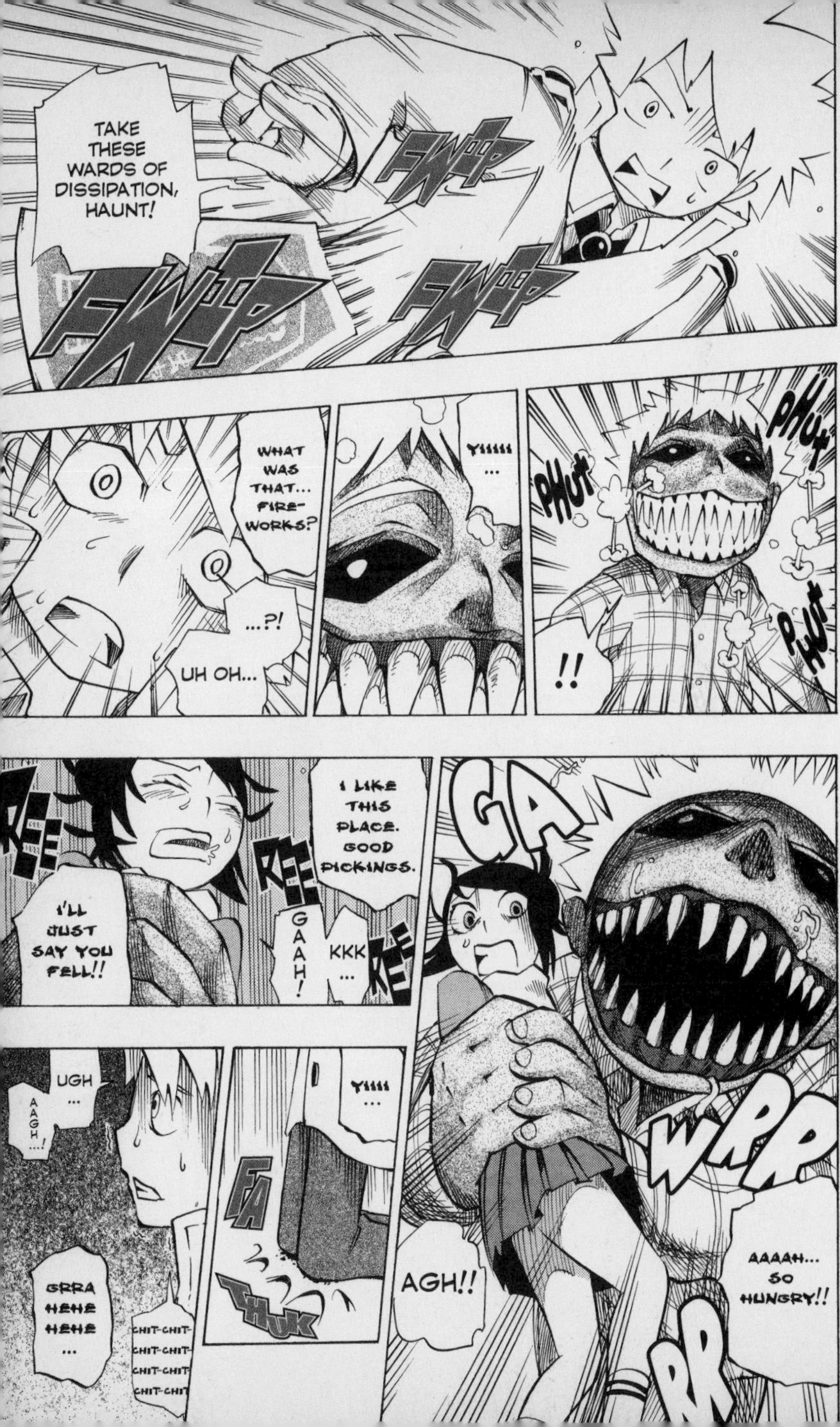
TAKE THESE WARDS OF DISSIPATION, HAUNT!
FWIP
FWIP
FWIP
PHUT
PHUT
PHUT
!!
YIIIII...
WHAT WAS THAT... FIRE-WORKS?
...?!
UH OH...
GA
AAAAH... SO HUNGRY!!
AGH!!
WRRRR
I LIKE THIS PLACE. GOOD PICKINGS.
REE
REE
GAAH!
KKK...
REE
I'LL JUST SAY YOU FELL!!
YIIII...
FA
THUK
UGH...
AAGH...!
GRRA HEHE HEHE...
CHIT-CHIT-
CHIT-CHIT-
CHIT-CHIT-
CHIT-CHIT-

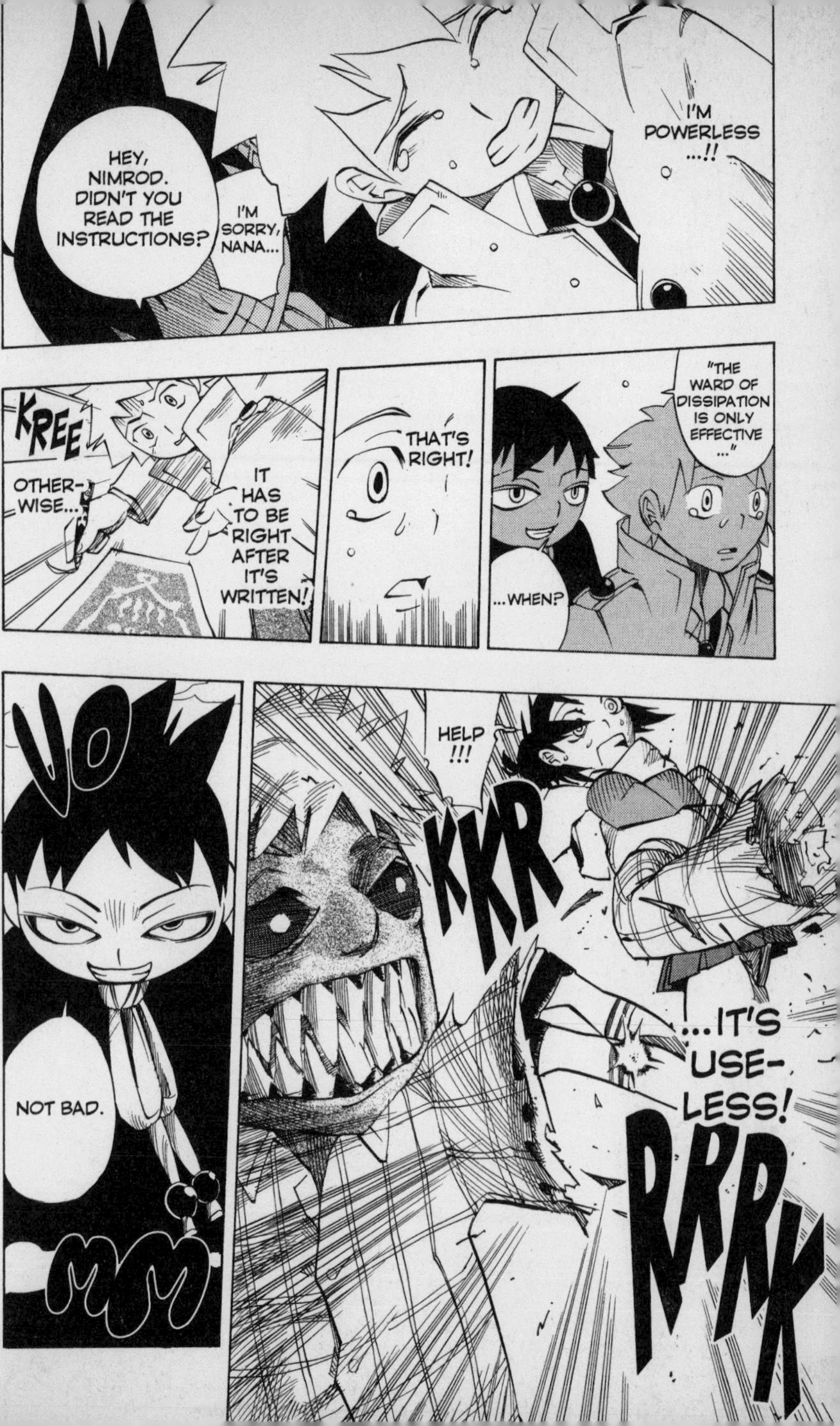

I'M POWERLESS ...!!
I'M SORRY, NANA...
HEY, NIMROD. DIDN'T YOU READ THE INSTRUCTIONS?
"THE WARD OF DISSIPATION IS ONLY EFFECTIVE ..."
...WHEN?
THAT'S RIGHT!
IT HAS TO BE RIGHT AFTER IT'S WRITTEN!
KREE
OTHER-WISE...
HELP !!!
KKR
...IT'S USE-LESS!
RRRK
VO
NOT BAD.
MM

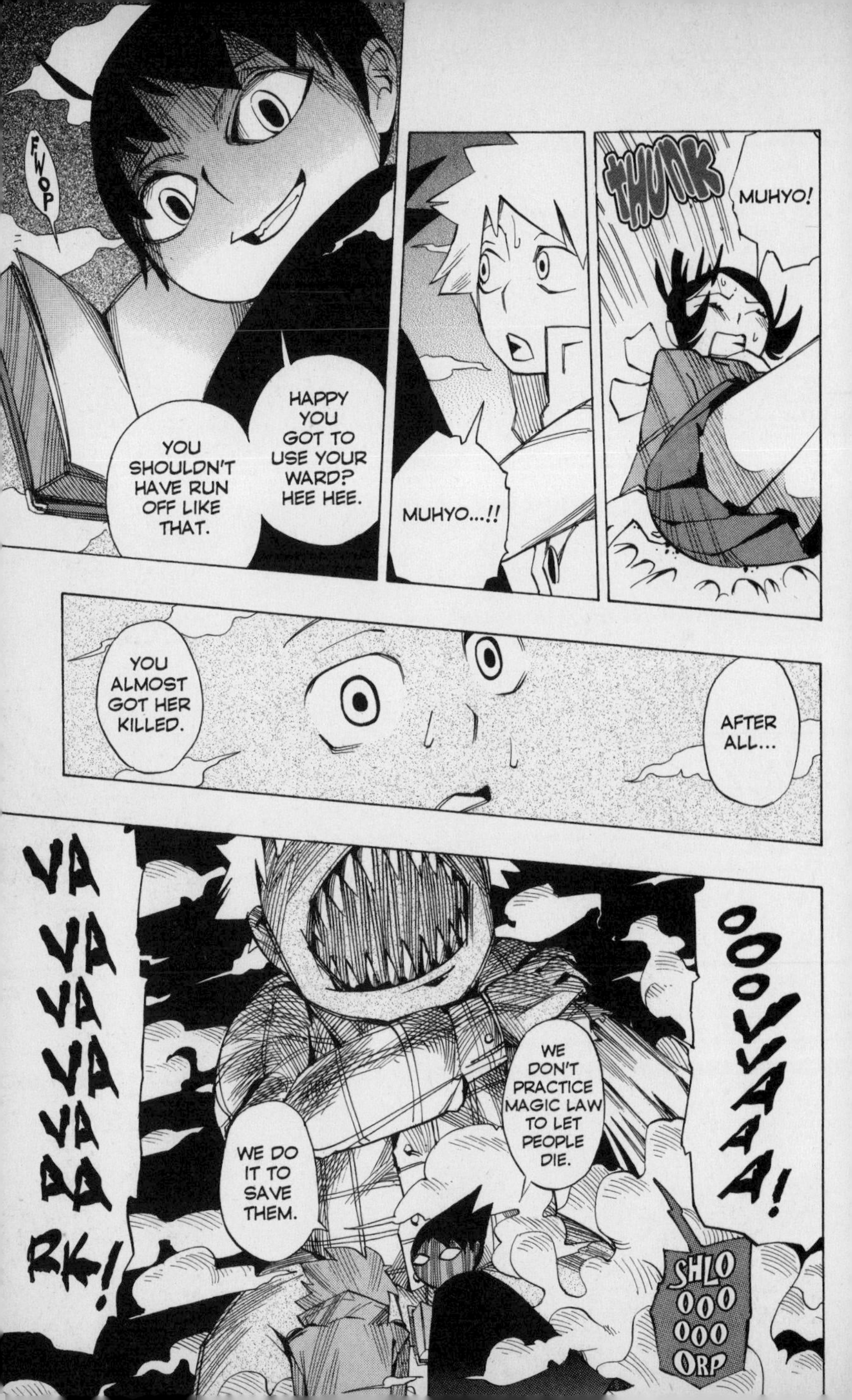
THUNK
MUHYO!
MUHYO...!!
HAPPY YOU GOT TO USE YOUR WARD? HEE HEE.
FWOP
YOU SHOULDN'T HAVE RUN OFF LIKE THAT.
AFTER ALL...
YOU ALMOST GOT HER KILLED.
OOOVAAAA!
SHLOOOOOOOORP
WE DON'T PRACTICE MAGIC LAW TO LET PEOPLE DIE.
WE DO IT TO SAVE THEM.
VAVAVAVAVAVAAARK!

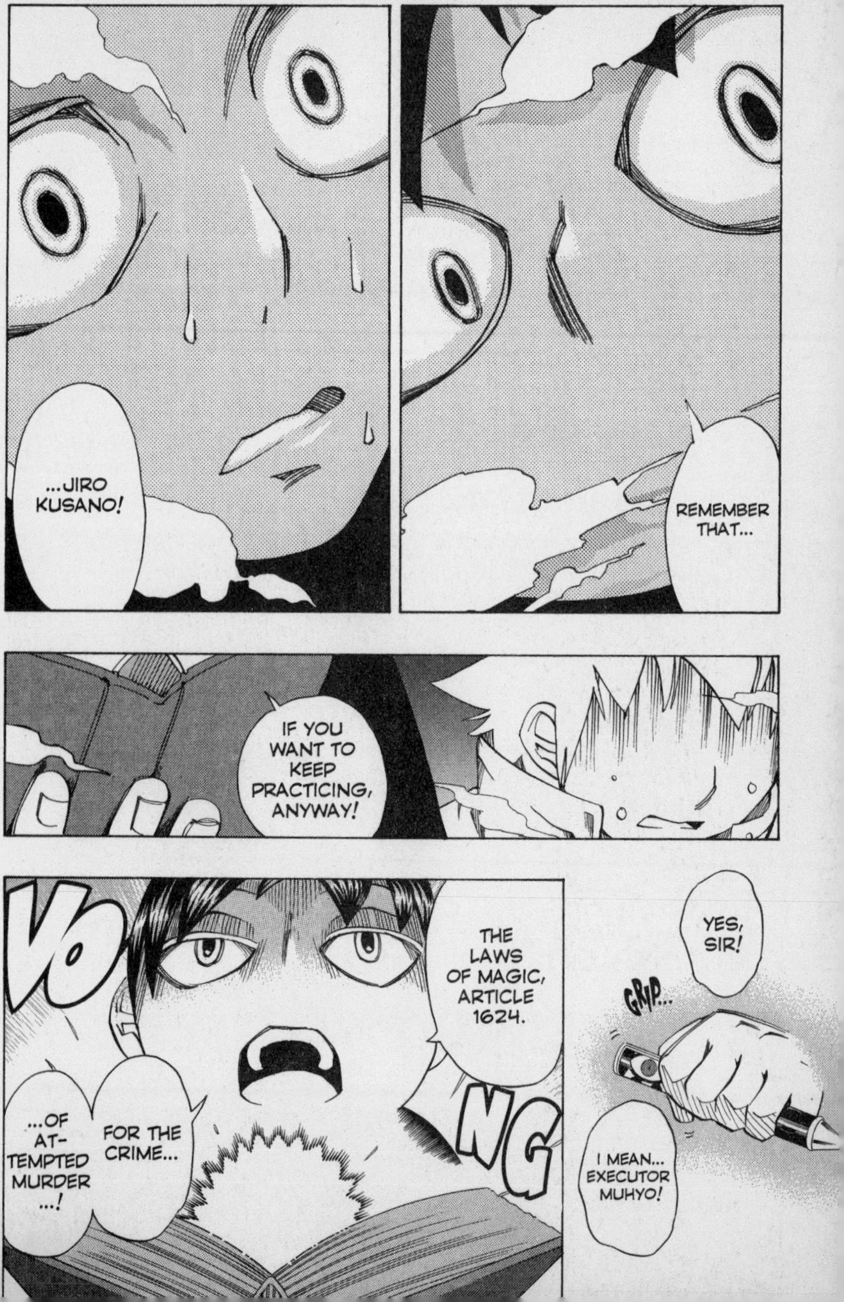
REMEMBER THAT...
...JIRO KUSANO!
IF YOU WANT TO KEEP PRACTICING, ANYWAY!
YES, SIR!
GRIP...
I MEAN... EXECUTOR MUHYO!
VO
THE LAWS OF MAGIC, ARTICLE 1624.
NG
FOR THE CRIME...
...OF AT-TEMPTED MURDER ...!

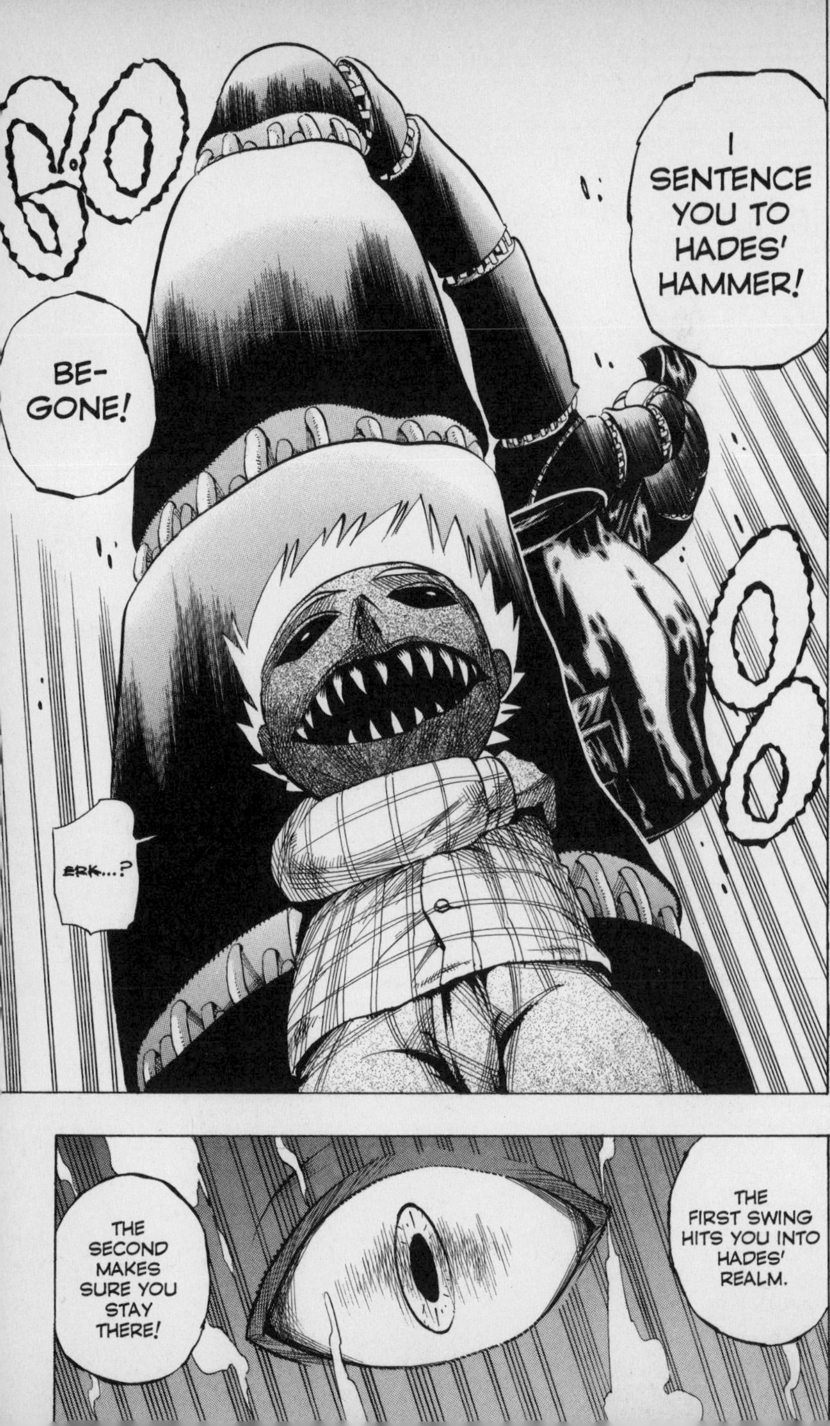
I SENTENCE YOU TO HADES' HAMMER!
BE-GONE!
ERK...?
THE FIRST SWING HITS YOU INTO HADES' REALM.
THE SECOND MAKES SURE YOU STAY THERE!

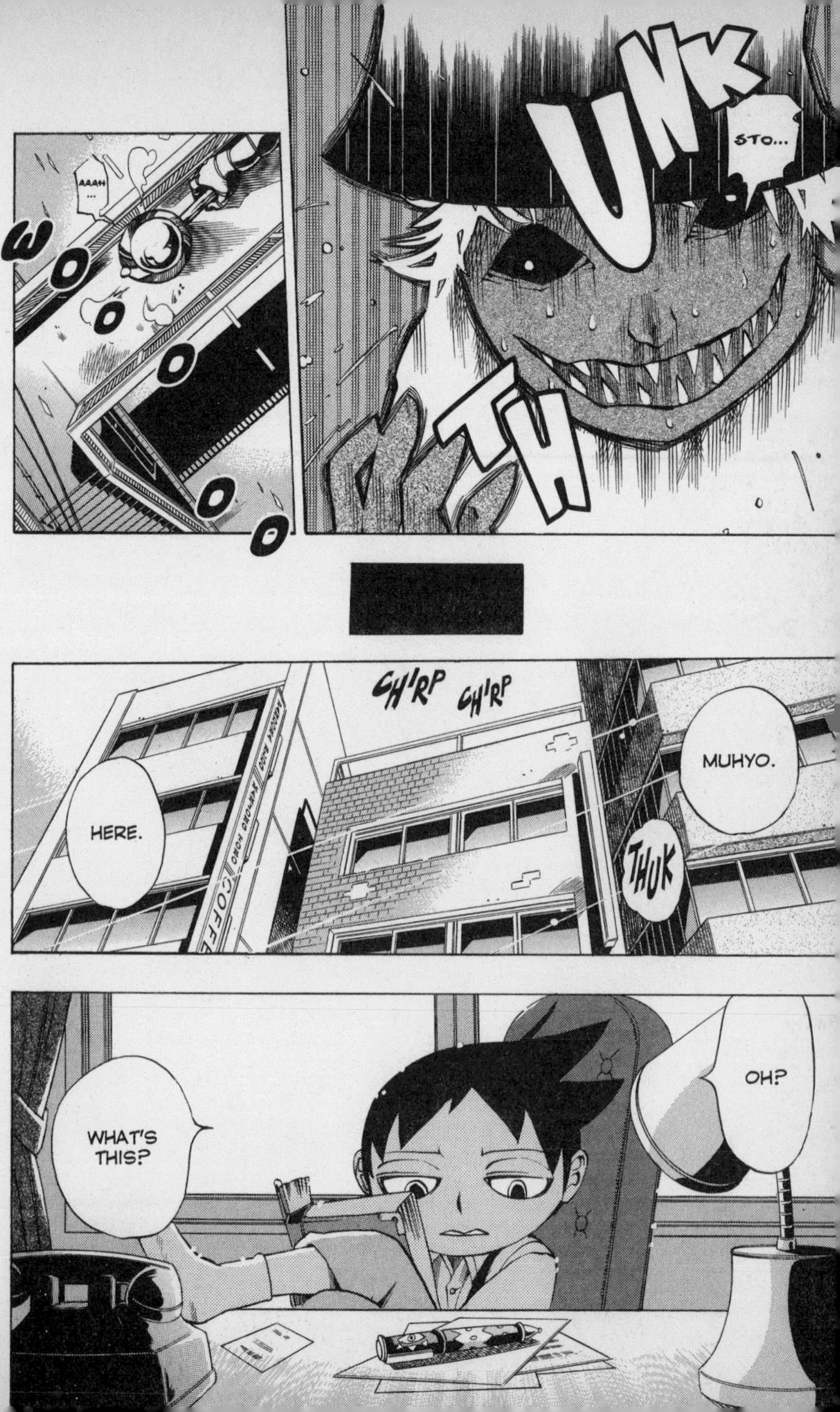
UNK
STO...
TH
AAAH...
WOOOOOO
CHIRP CHIRP
MUHYO.
THUK
HERE.
COFFE
OH?
WHAT'S THIS?

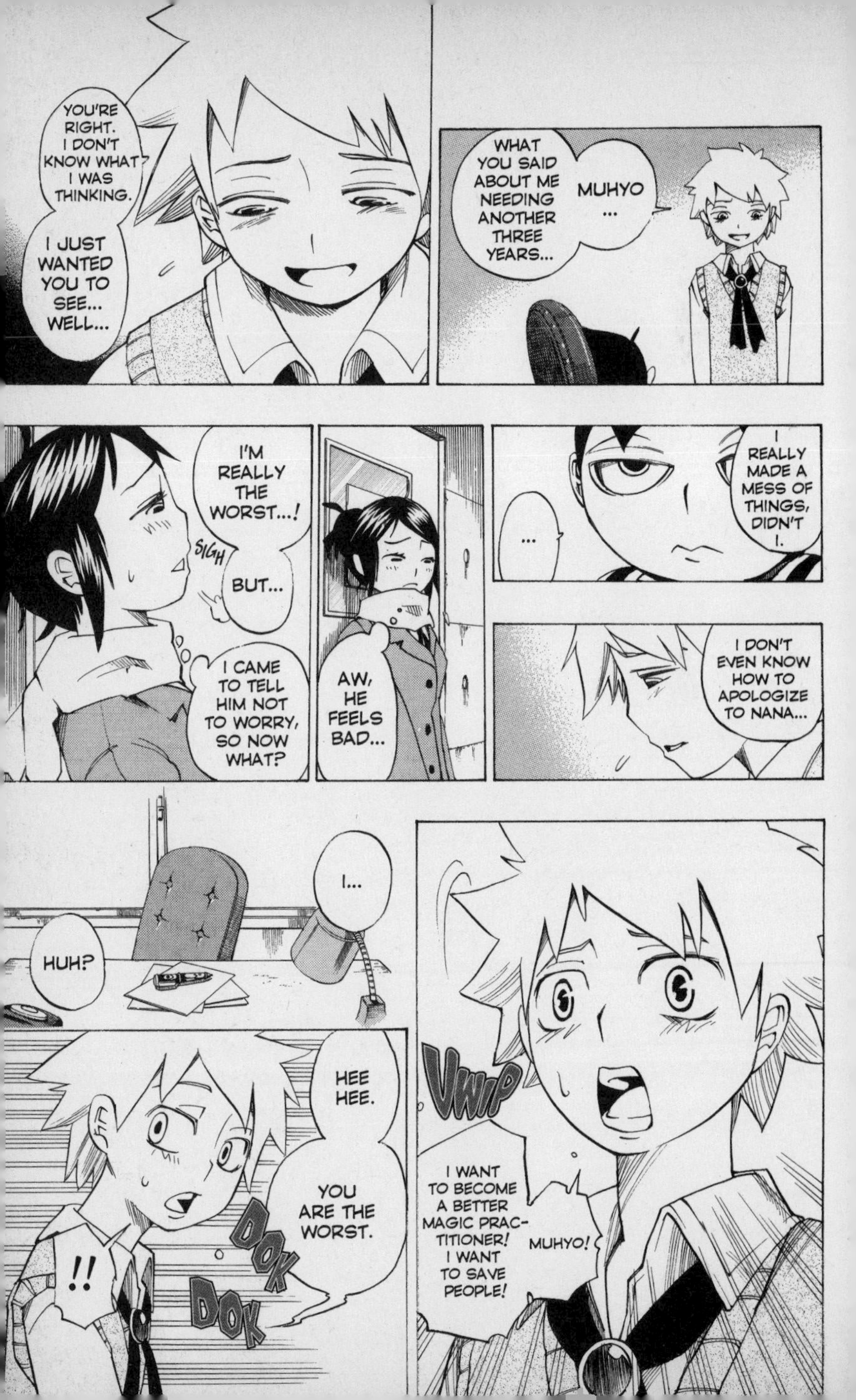
MUHYO...
WHAT YOU SAID ABOUT ME NEEDING ANOTHER THREE YEARS...
YOU'RE RIGHT. I DON'T KNOW WHAT I WAS THINKING.
I JUST WANTED YOU TO SEE... WELL...
I REALLY MADE A MESS OF THINGS, DIDN'T I.
...
I DON'T EVEN KNOW HOW TO APOLOGIZE TO NANA...
AW, HE FEELS BAD...
I'M REALLY THE WORST...!
SIGH
BUT...
I CAME TO TELL HIM NOT TO WORRY, SO NOW WHAT?
VWIP
MUHYO!
I WANT TO BECOME A BETTER MAGIC PRAC-TITIONER! I WANT TO SAVE PEOPLE!
I...
HUH?
HEE HEE.
YOU ARE THE WORST.
DOK
DOK
!!

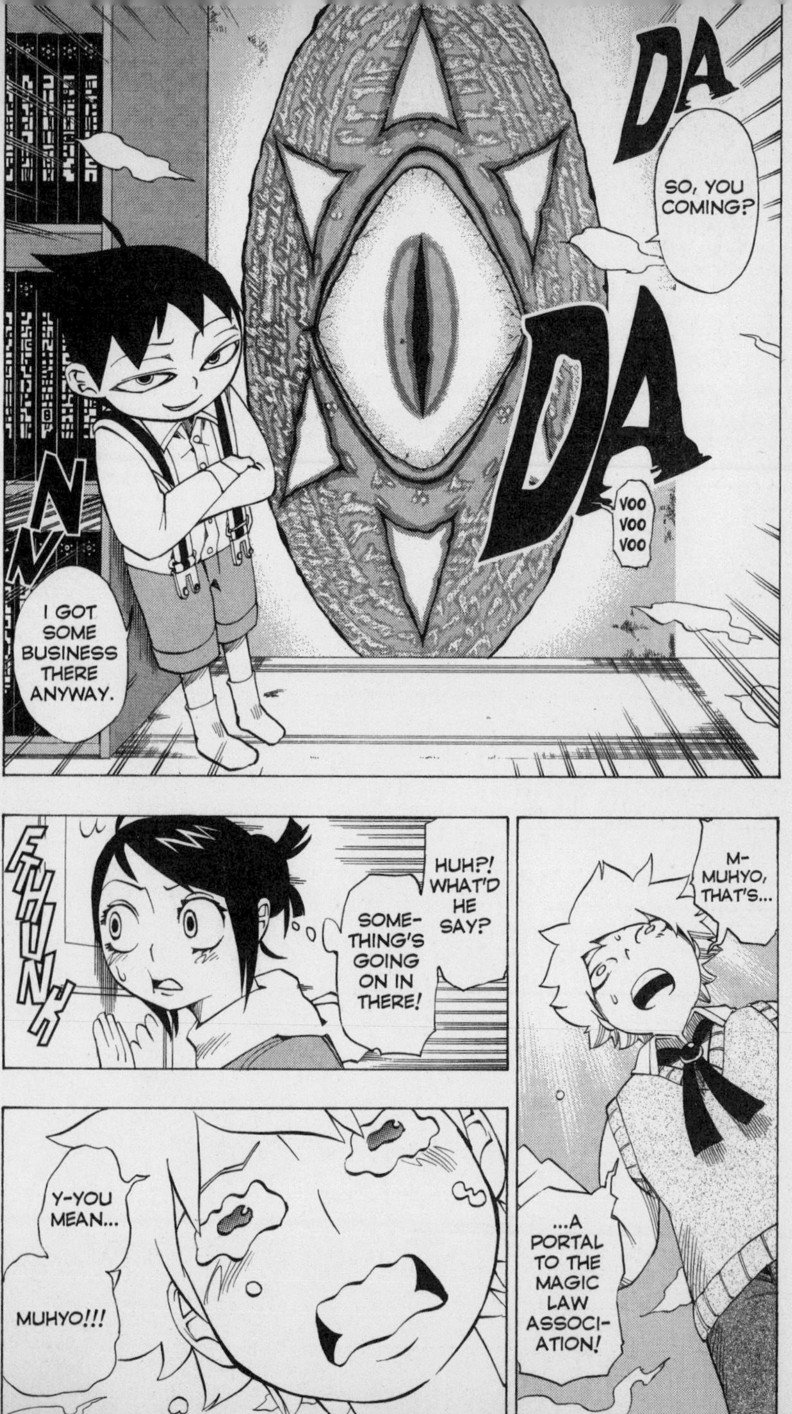
DA
SO, YOU COMING?
DA
DA
VOO VOO VOO
N N
I GOT SOME BUSINESS THERE ANYWAY.
M-MUHYO, THAT'S...
...A PORTAL TO THE MAGIC LAW ASSOCIATION!
HUH?! WHAT'D HE SAY?
SOME-THING'S GOING ON IN THERE!
FTHUNK
Y-YOU MEAN...
MUHYO!!!

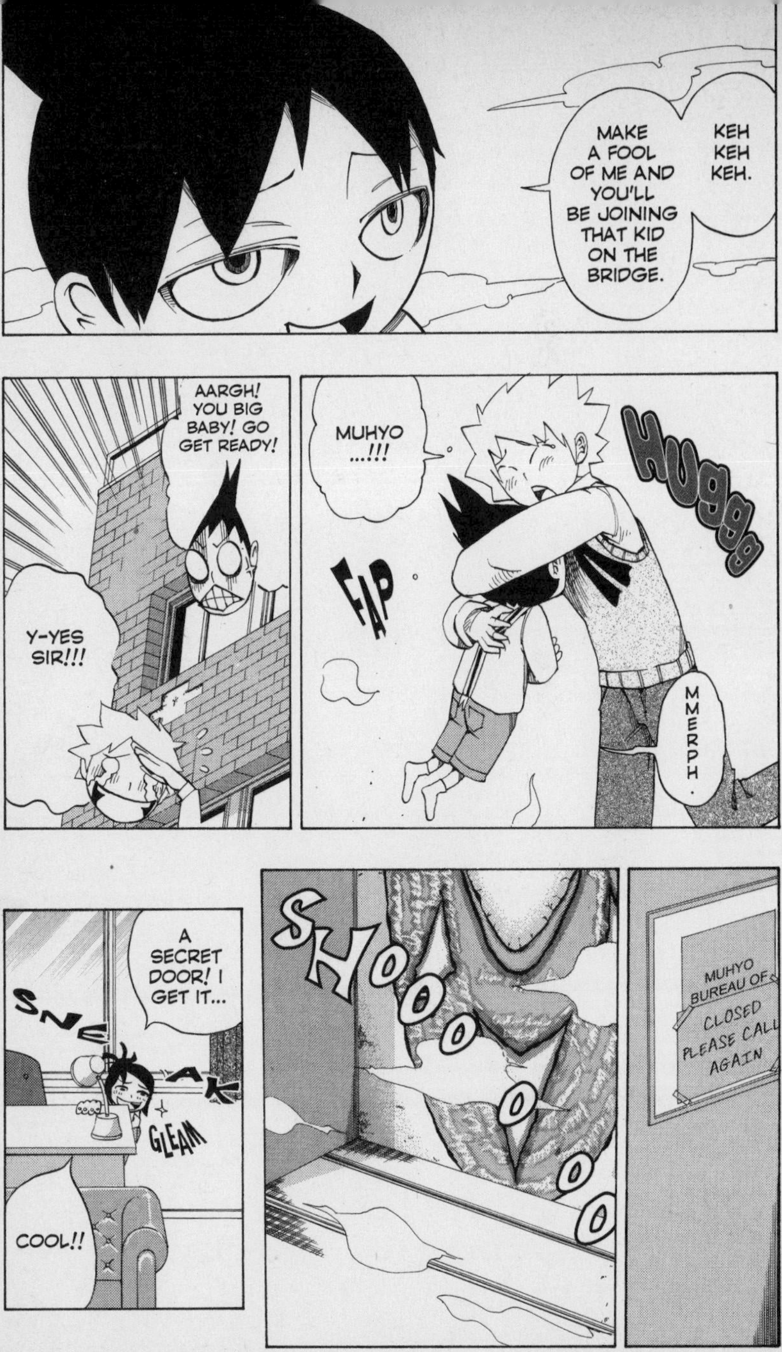
KEH KEH KEH.
MAKE A FOOL OF ME AND YOU'LL BE JOINING THAT KID ON THE BRIDGE.
HUGGG
MUHYO ...!!!
FAP
MMERPH.
AARGH! YOU BIG BABY! GO GET READY!
Y-YES SIR!!!
MUHYO BUREAU OF
CLOSED PLEASE CALL AGAIN
SHOOOOOOOO
A SECRET DOOR! I GET IT...
SNEAK
GLEAM
COOL!!

THOUGHT MAGIC CIRCLES WERE MORE LIKE...

IS THIS...?

ARTICLE 10
PRESENCE

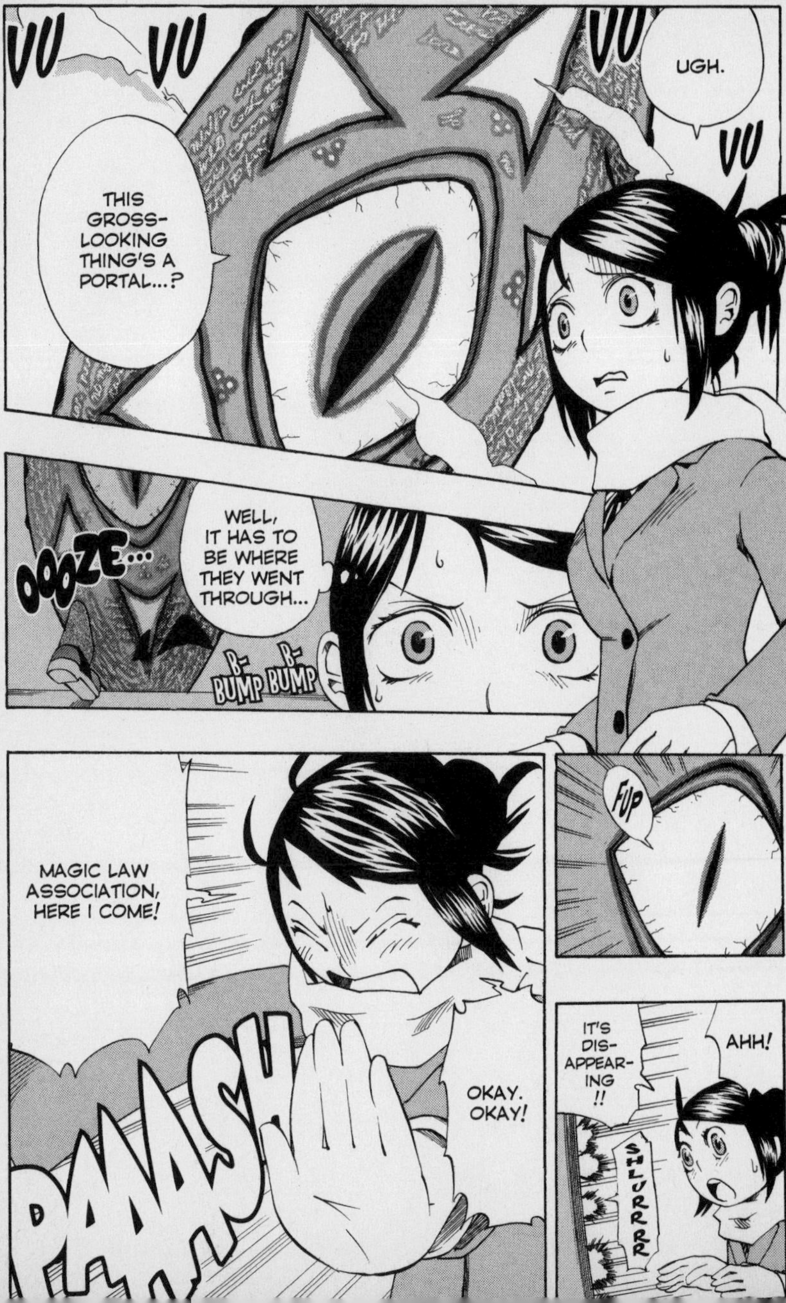
VU
UGH.
VU
VU
VU
THIS GROSS-LOOKING THING'S A PORTAL...?
WELL, IT HAS TO BE WHERE THEY WENT THROUGH...
OOOZE...
B-BUMP B-BUMP
FUP
AHH!
IT'S DIS-APPEAR-ING!!
SHLURRR
OKAY. OKAY!
MAGIC LAW ASSOCIATION, HERE I COME!
PAAASH

ARTICLE 10
PRESENCE

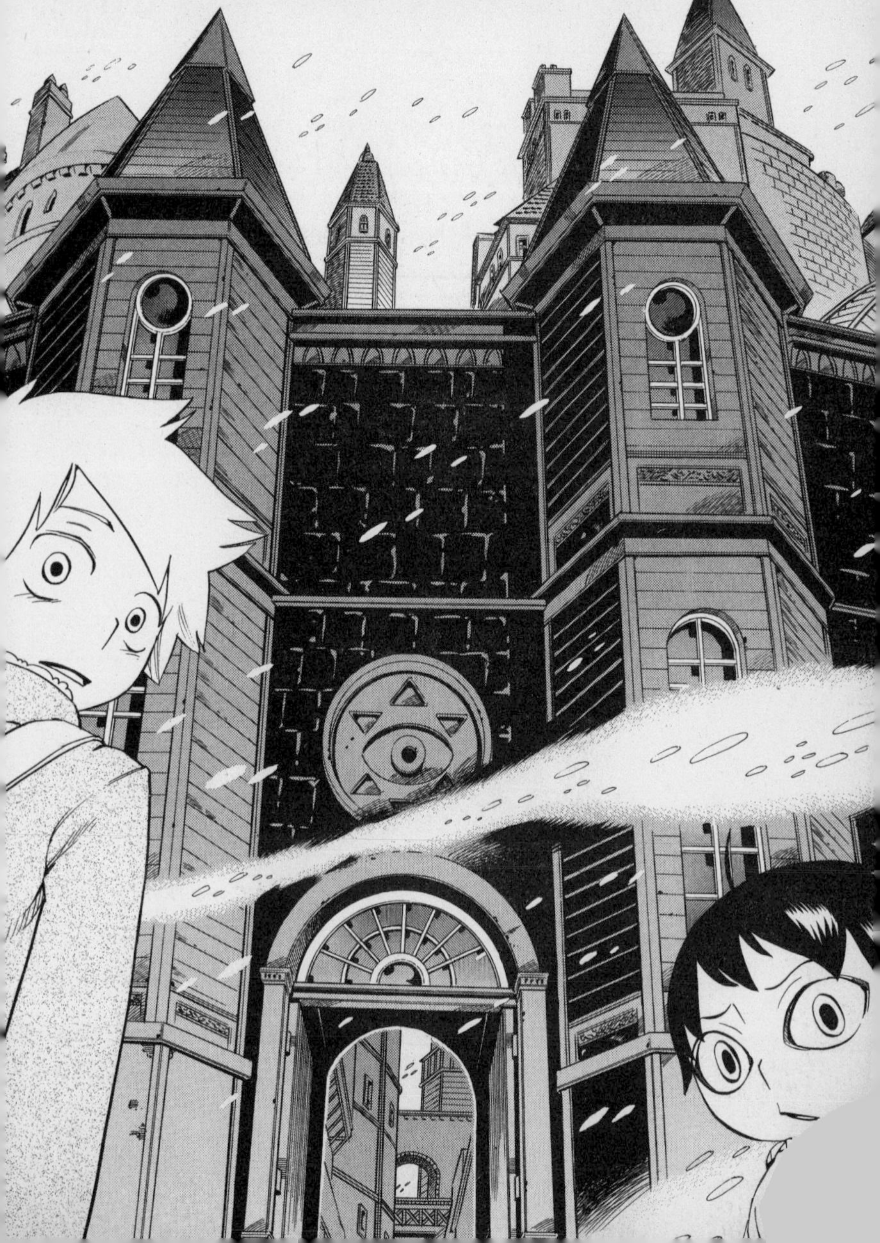

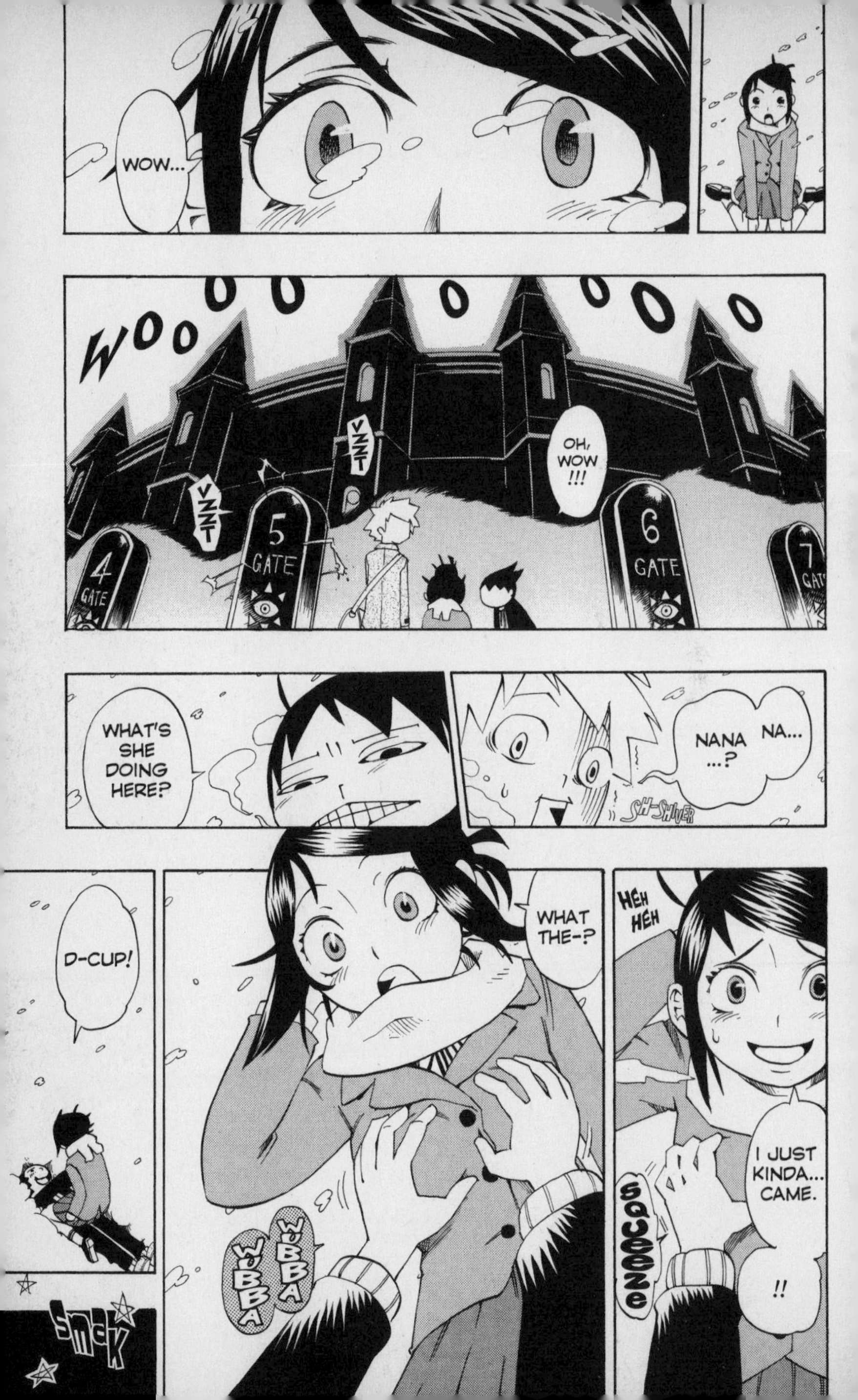
WOW...
WOOOOOOOO
OH, WOW !!!
VZZT
VZZT
4 GATE
5 GATE
6 GATE
7
NANA ...?
NA...
SH-SHIVER
WHAT'S SHE DOING HERE?
HEH HEH
I JUST KINDA... CAME.
!!
SQUEEZE
WHAT THE-?
WUBBA
WUBBA
D-CUP!
SMACK

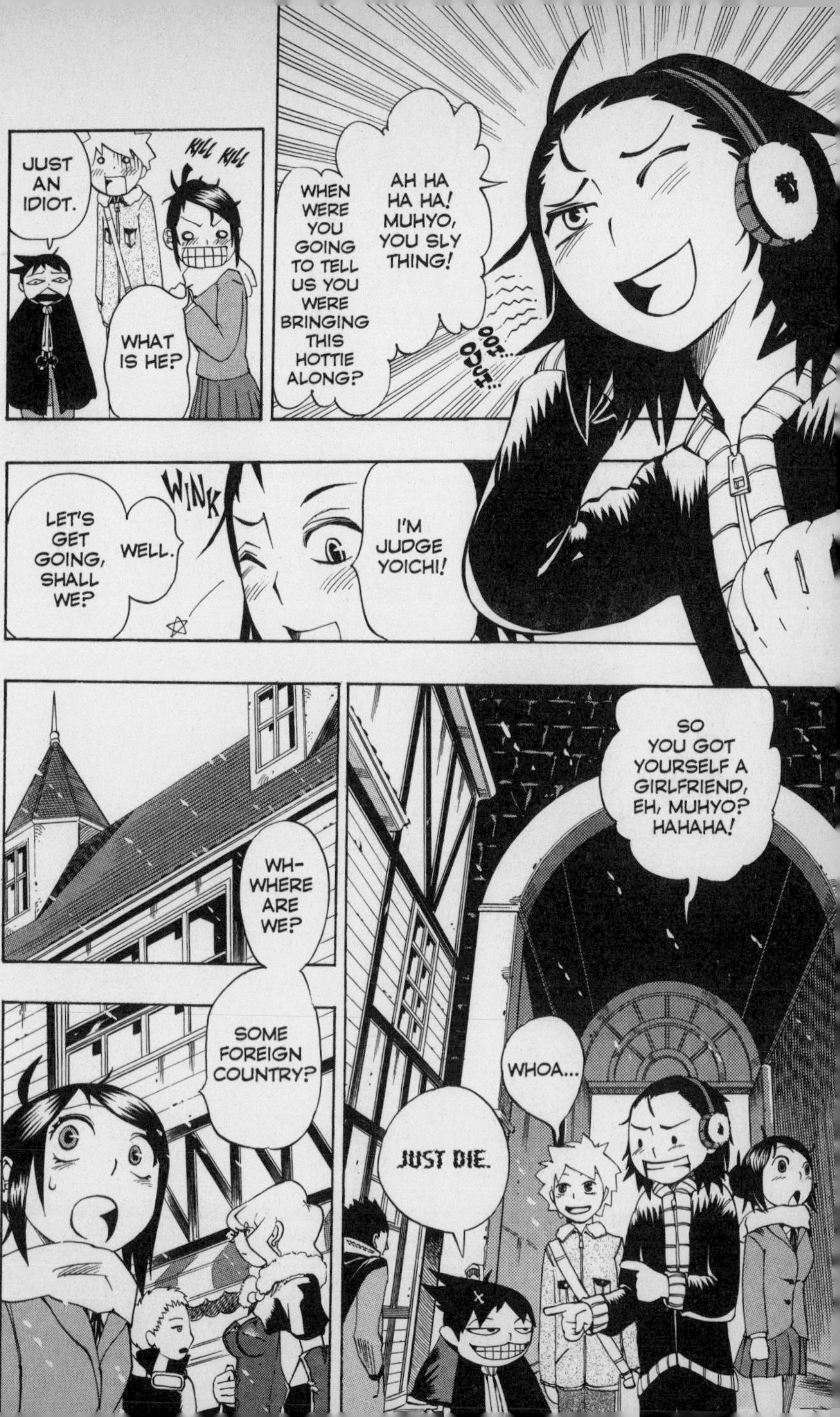
AH HA HA HA! MUHYO, YOU SLY THING!
WHEN WERE YOU GOING TO TELL US YOU WERE BRINGING THIS HOTTIE ALONG?
OOF... OUCH...
KILL KILL
WHAT IS HE?
JUST AN IDIOT.
I'M JUDGE YOICHI!
WINK
WELL.
LET'S GET GOING, SHALL WE?
SO YOU GOT YOURSELF A GIRLFRIEND, EH, MUHYO? HAHAHA!
WHOA...
JUST DIE.
WH- WHERE ARE WE?
SOME FOREIGN COUNTRY?

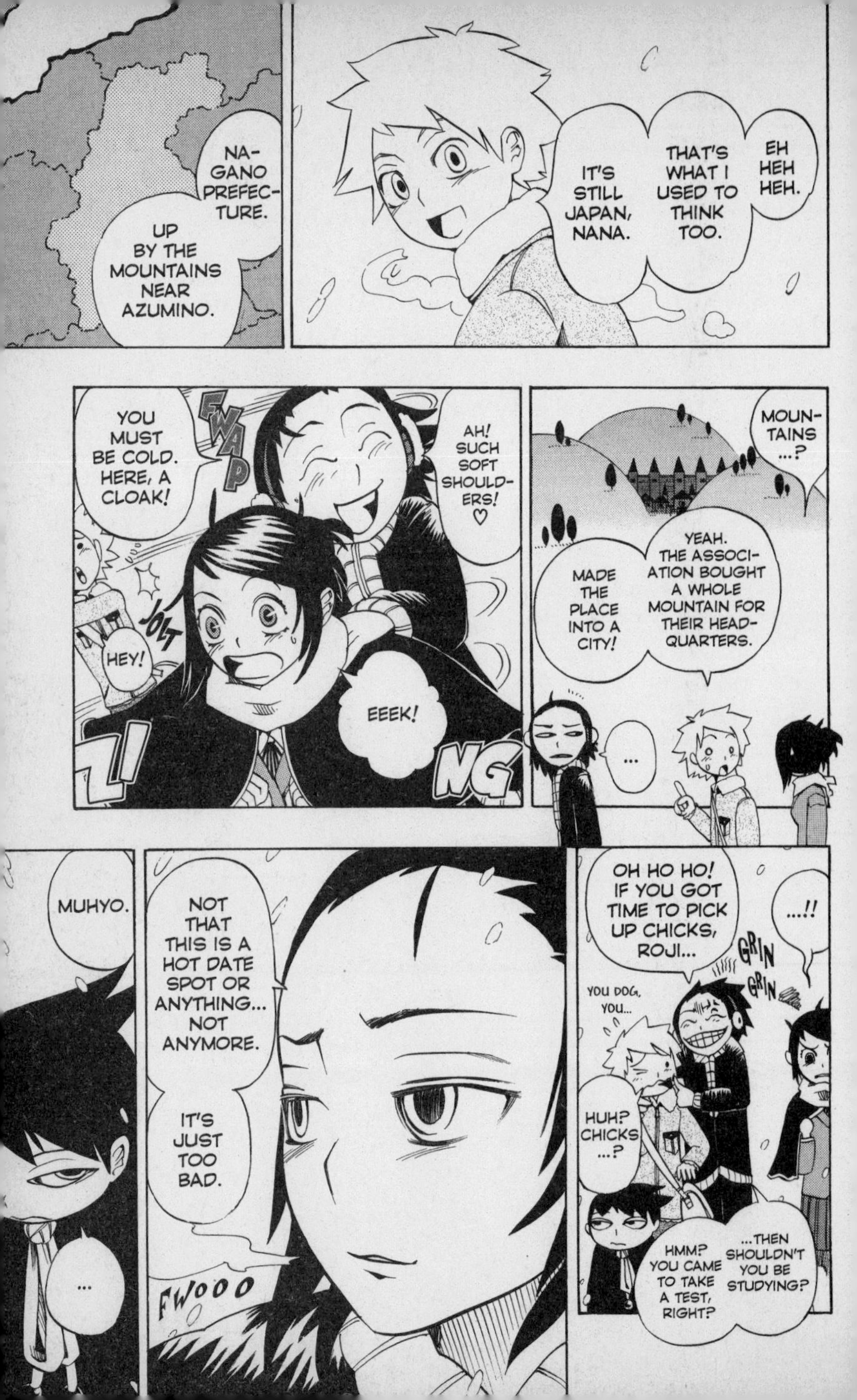
EH HEH HEH.
THAT'S WHAT I USED TO THINK TOO.
IT'S STILL JAPAN, NANA.
NAGANO PREFECTURE.
UP BY THE MOUNTAINS NEAR AZUMINO.
MOUNTAINS ...?
YEAH. THE ASSOCIATION BOUGHT A WHOLE MOUNTAIN FOR THEIR HEADQUARTERS.
MADE THE PLACE INTO A CITY!
...
AH! SUCH SOFT SHOULDERS! ♡
FWAP
YOU MUST BE COLD. HERE, A CLOAK!
JOLT
HEY!
EEEK!
ZING
...!!
OH HO HO! IF YOU GOT TIME TO PICK UP CHICKS, ROJI...
GRIN GRIN
YOU DOG, YOU...
HUH? CHICKS ...?
...THEN SHOULDN'T YOU BE STUDYING?
HMM? YOU CAME TO TAKE A TEST, RIGHT?
NOT THAT THIS IS A HOT DATE SPOT OR ANYTHING... NOT ANYMORE.
IT'S JUST TOO BAD.
FWOOO
MUHYO.
...

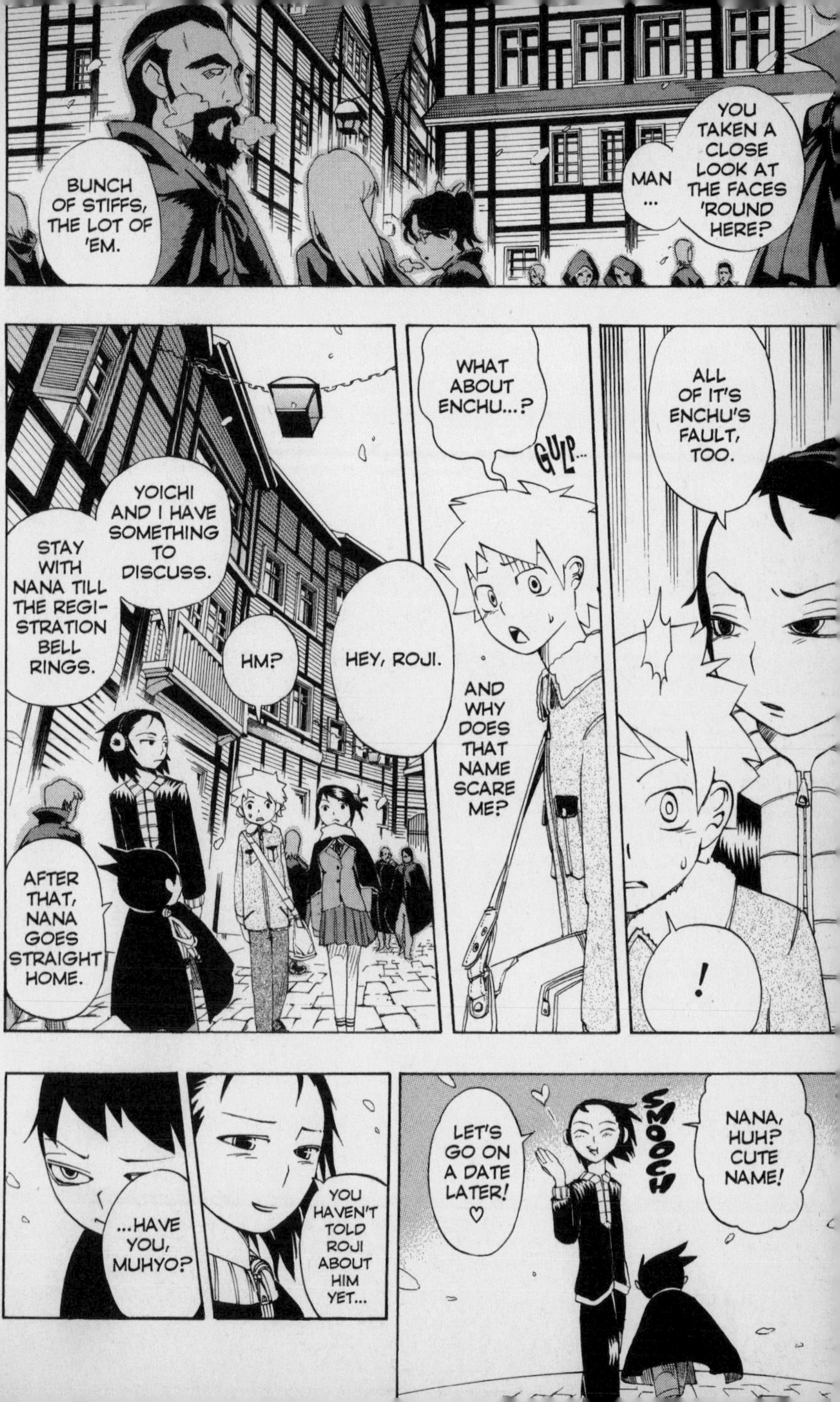
YOU TAKEN A CLOSE LOOK AT THE FACES 'ROUND HERE?
MAN ...
BUNCH OF STIFFS, THE LOT OF 'EM.
ALL OF IT'S ENCHU'S FAULT, TOO.
!
WHAT ABOUT ENCHU...?
GULP...
AND WHY DOES THAT NAME SCARE ME?
HEY, ROJI.
HM?
YOICHI AND I HAVE SOMETHING TO DISCUSS.
STAY WITH NANA TILL THE REGI-STRATION BELL RINGS.
AFTER THAT, NANA GOES STRAIGHT HOME.
NANA, HUH? CUTE NAME!
SMOOCH
LET'S GO ON A DATE LATER! ♡
YOU HAVEN'T TOLD ROJI ABOUT HIM YET...
...HAVE YOU, MUHYO?

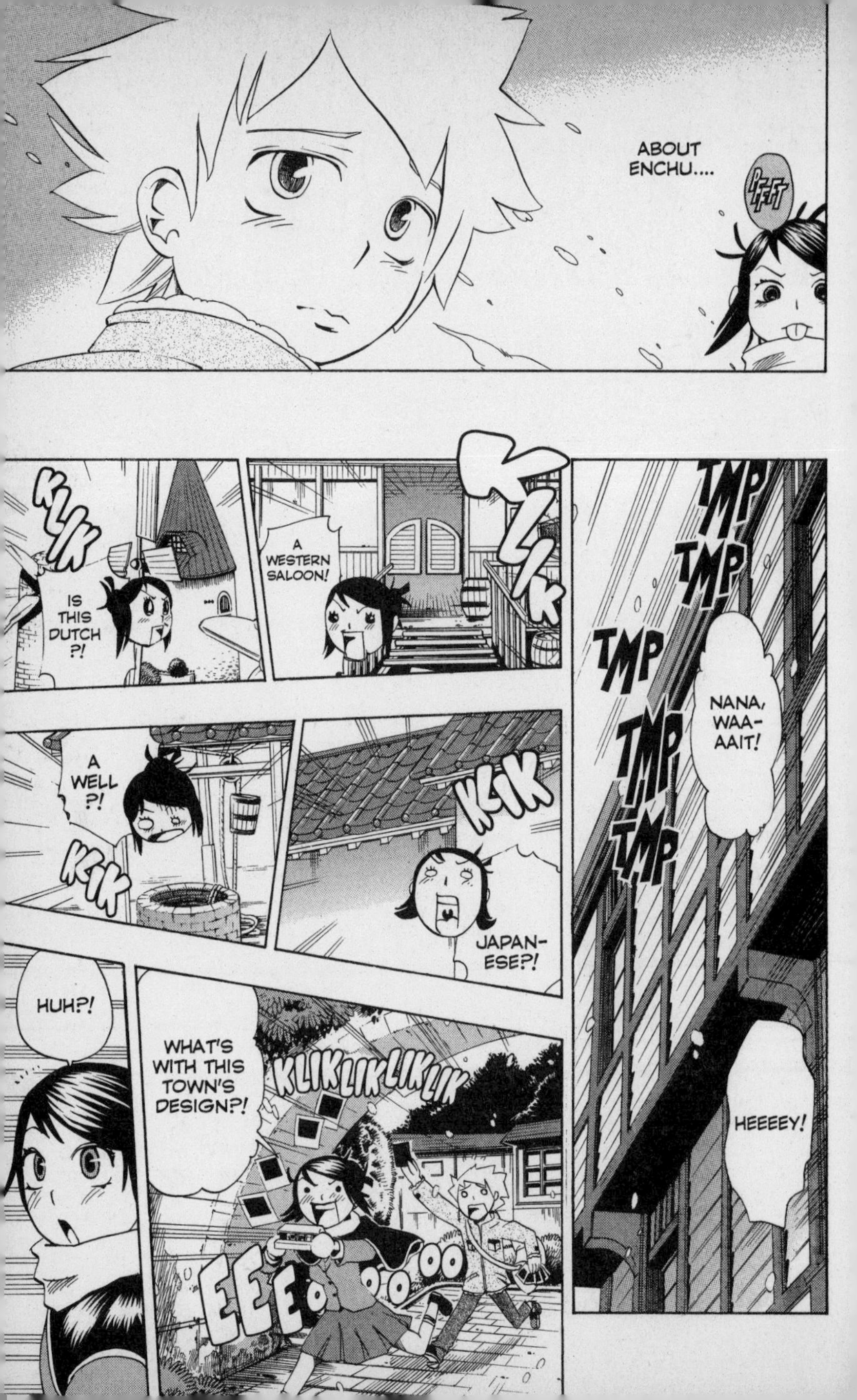
ABOUT ENCHU....
PFFFT
TMP
TMP
TMP
TMP
TMP
TMP
NANA, WAA-AAIT!
HEEEEY!
KLIK
A WESTERN SALOON!
KLIK
IS THIS DUTCH?!
KLIK
JAPAN-ESE?!
A WELL?!
KLIK
WHAT'S WITH THIS TOWN'S DESIGN?!
KLIKLIKLIKLIK
EEEoooooo
HUH?!

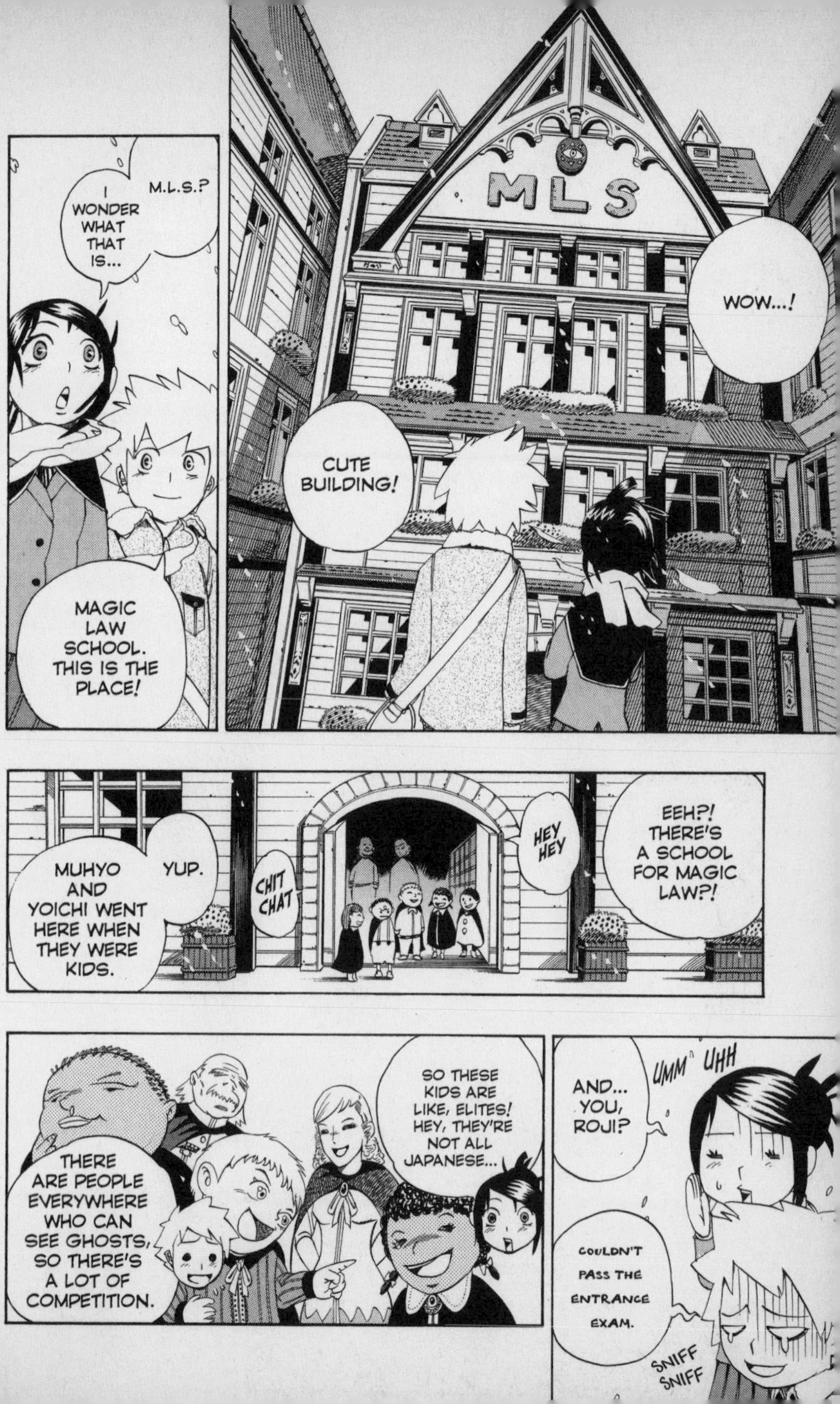
MLS
WOW...!
CUTE BUILDING!
M.L.S.?
I WONDER WHAT THAT IS...
MAGIC LAW SCHOOL. THIS IS THE PLACE!
EEH?! THERE'S A SCHOOL FOR MAGIC LAW?!
HEY HEY
CHIT CHAT
YUP.
MUHYO AND YOICHI WENT HERE WHEN THEY WERE KIDS.
UMM UHH
AND... YOU, ROJI?
COULDN'T PASS THE ENTRANCE EXAM.
SNIFF SNIFF
SO THESE KIDS ARE LIKE, ELITES! HEY, THEY'RE NOT ALL JAPANESE...
THERE ARE PEOPLE EVERYWHERE WHO CAN SEE GHOSTS, SO THERE'S A LOT OF COMPETITION.

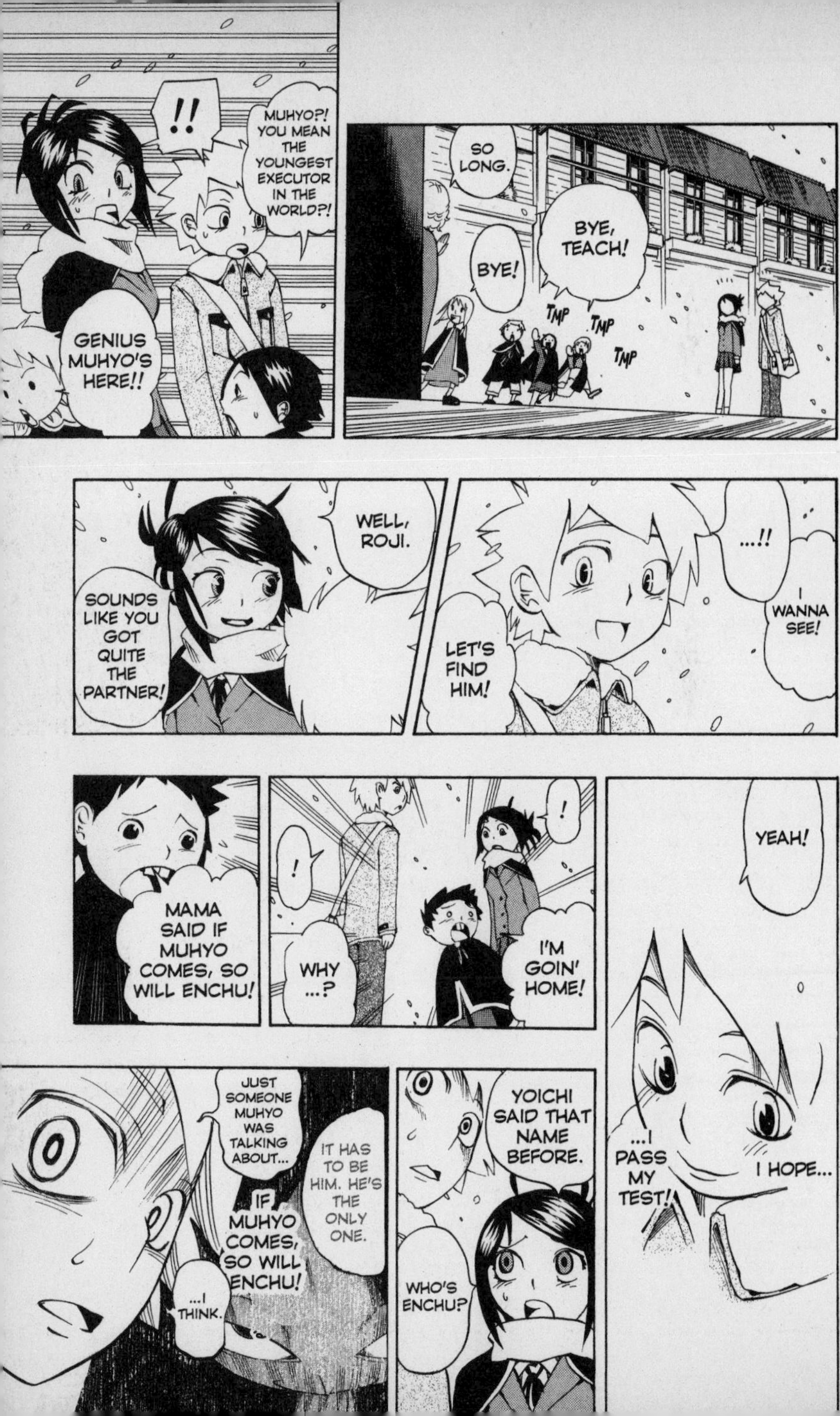
SO LONG.
BYE, TEACH!
BYE!
TMP
TMP
TMP
!!
MUHYO?! YOU MEAN THE YOUNGEST EXECUTOR IN THE WORLD?!
GENIUS MUHYO'S HERE!!
...!!
I WANNA SEE!
LET'S FIND HIM!
WELL, ROJI.
SOUNDS LIKE YOU GOT QUITE THE PARTNER!
YEAH!
I HOPE...
...I PASS MY TEST!
!
!
I'M GOIN' HOME!
WHY ...?
MAMA SAID IF MUHYO COMES, SO WILL ENCHU!
YOICHI SAID THAT NAME BEFORE.
WHO'S ENCHU?
JUST SOMEONE MUHYO WAS TALKING ABOUT...
IT HAS TO BE HIM. HE'S THE ONLY ONE.
IF MUHYO COMES, SO WILL ENCHU!
...I THINK.

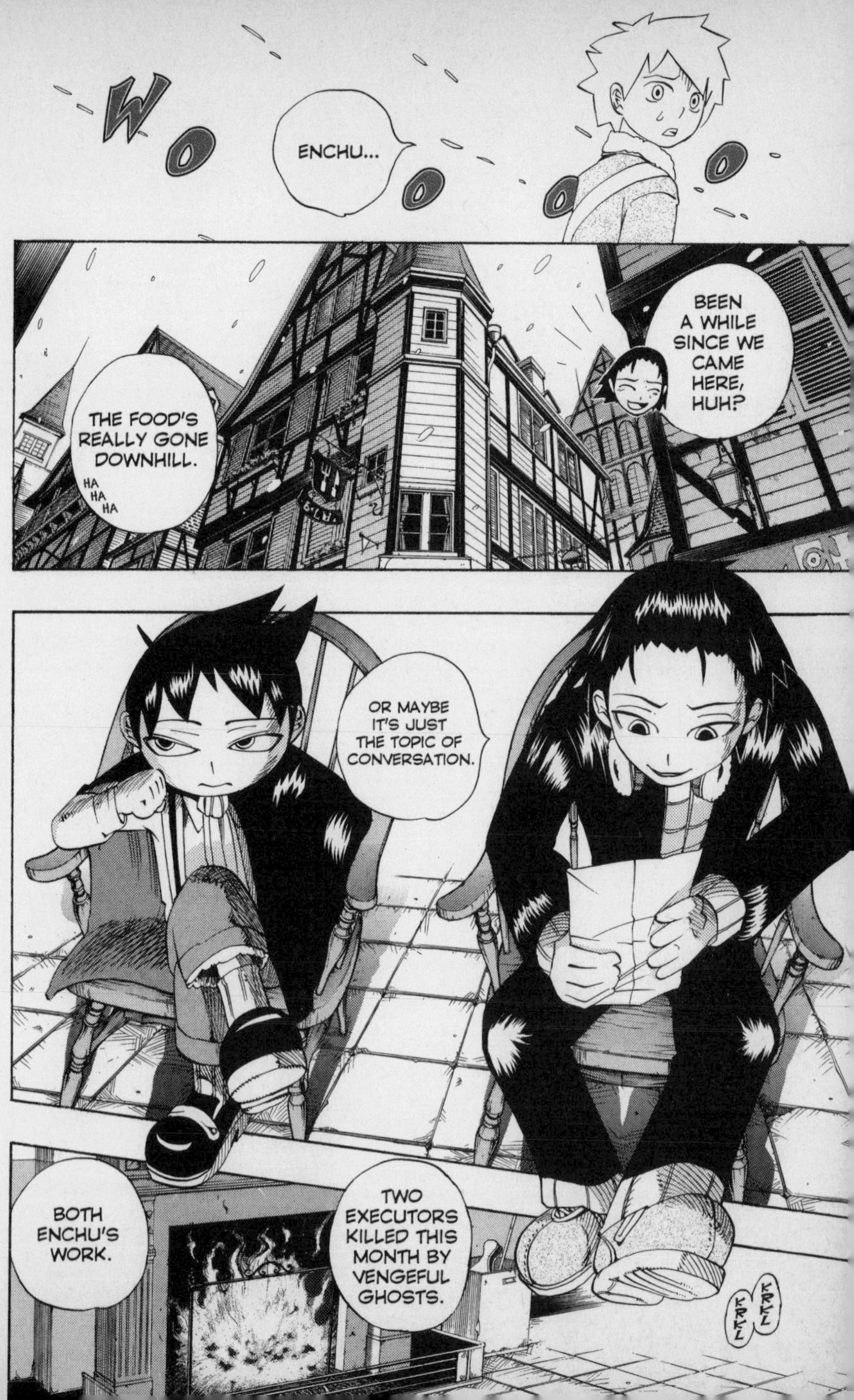
WOOOO
ENCHU...
BEEN A WHILE SINCE WE CAME HERE, HUH?
THE FOOD'S REALLY GONE DOWNHILL.
HA HA HA
OR MAYBE IT'S JUST THE TOPIC OF CONVERSATION.
KRKL KRKL
TWO EXECUTORS KILLED THIS MONTH BY VENGEFUL GHOSTS.
BOTH ENCHU'S WORK.

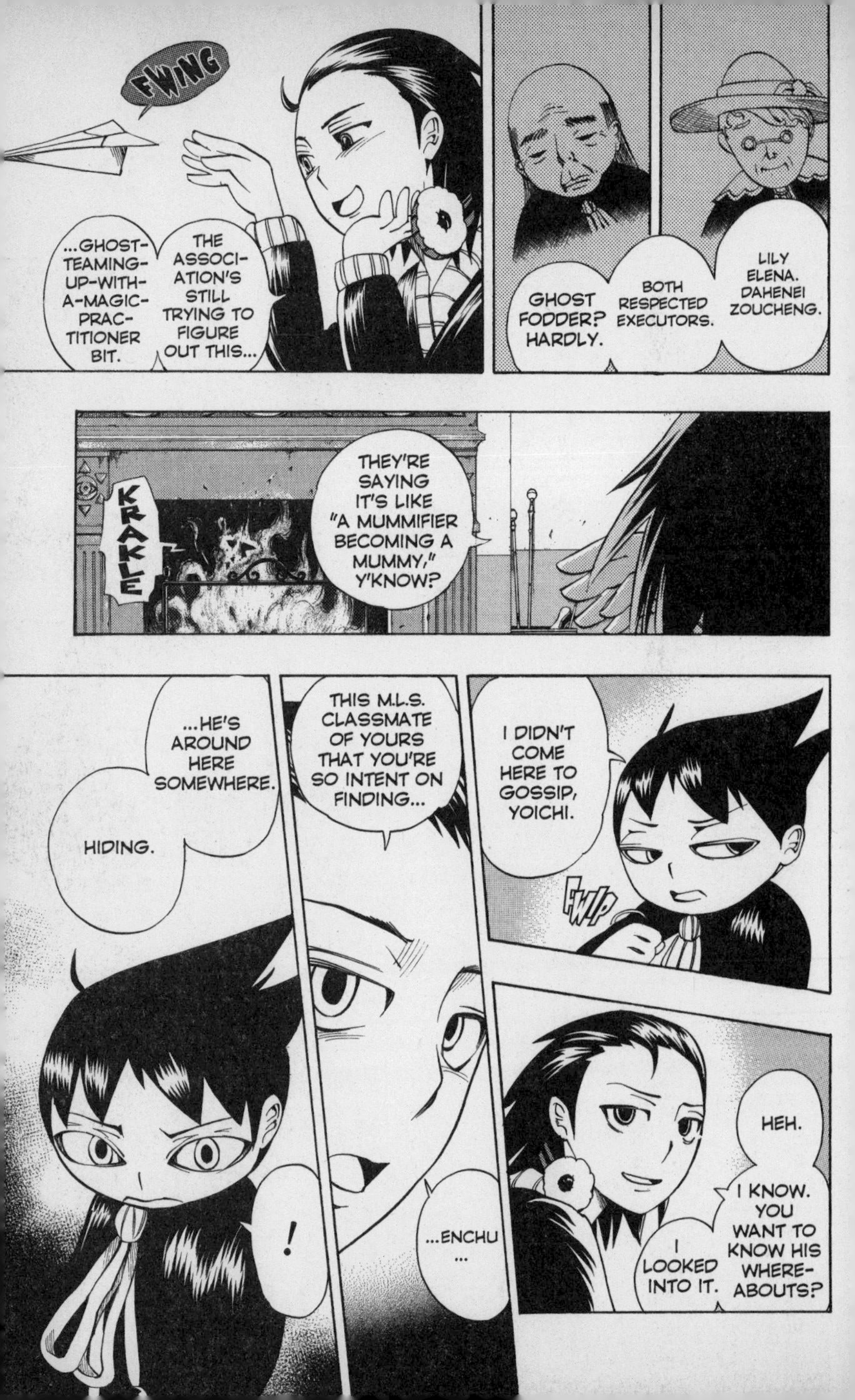
LILY ELENA. DAHENEI ZOUCHENG.
BOTH RESPECTED EXECUTORS.
GHOST FODDER? HARDLY.
FWING
THE ASSOCIATION'S STILL TRYING TO FIGURE OUT THIS...
...GHOST-TEAMING-UP-WITH-A-MAGIC-PRACTITIONER BIT.
THEY'RE SAYING IT'S LIKE "A MUMMIFIER BECOMING A MUMMY," Y'KNOW?
KRAKLE
I DIDN'T COME HERE TO GOSSIP, YOICHI.
FWIP
HEH.
I KNOW. YOU WANT TO KNOW HIS WHEREABOUTS?
I LOOKED INTO IT.
THIS M.L.S. CLASSMATE OF YOURS THAT YOU'RE SO INTENT ON FINDING...
...ENCHU ...
...HE'S AROUND HERE SOMEWHERE.
HIDING.
!

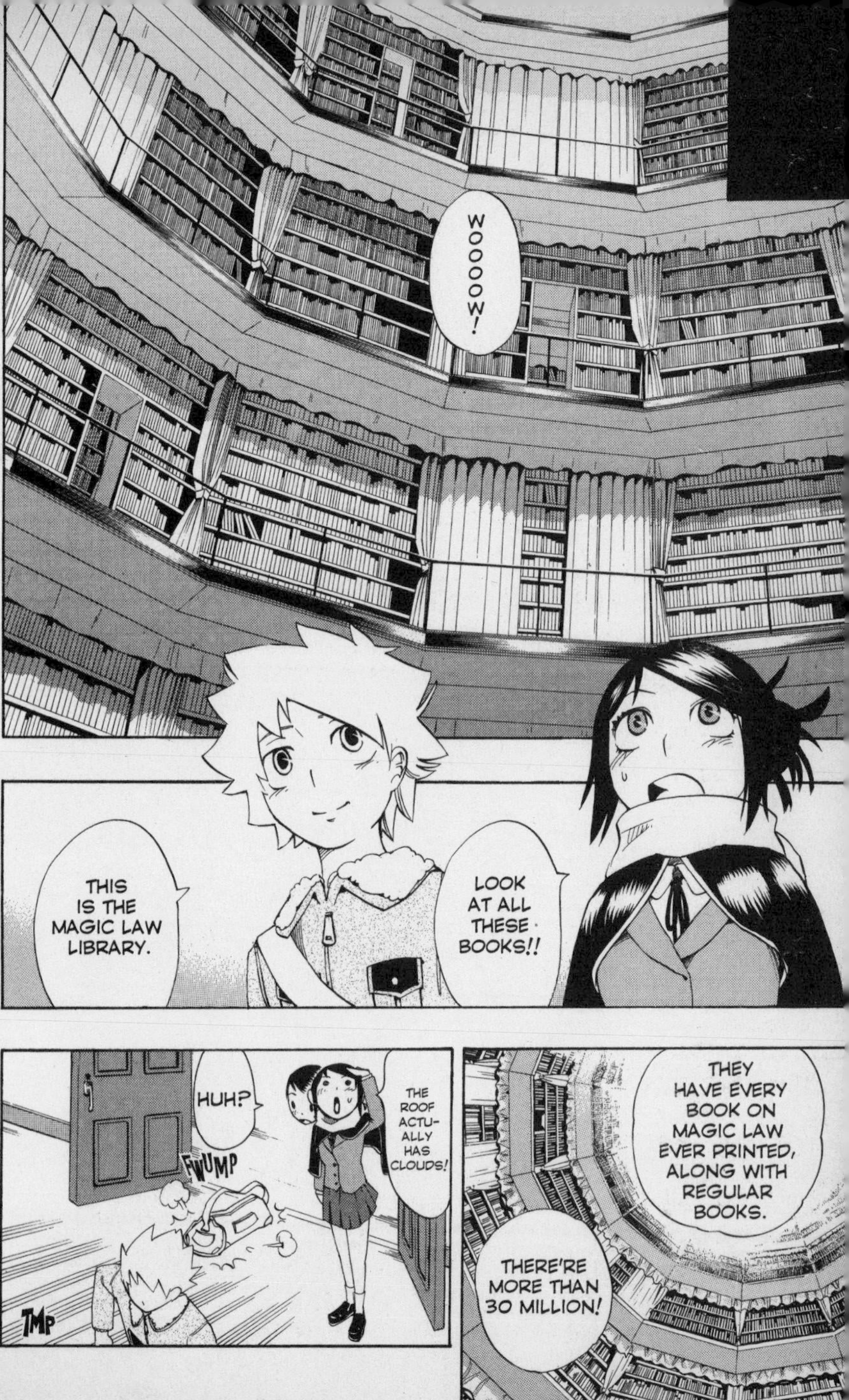
WOOOOW!
LOOK AT ALL THESE BOOKS!!
THIS IS THE MAGIC LAW LIBRARY.
THEY HAVE EVERY BOOK ON MAGIC LAW EVER PRINTED, ALONG WITH REGULAR BOOKS.
THERE'RE MORE THAN 30 MILLION!
THE ROOF ACTU-ALLY HAS CLOUDS!
HUH?
FWUMP
TMP

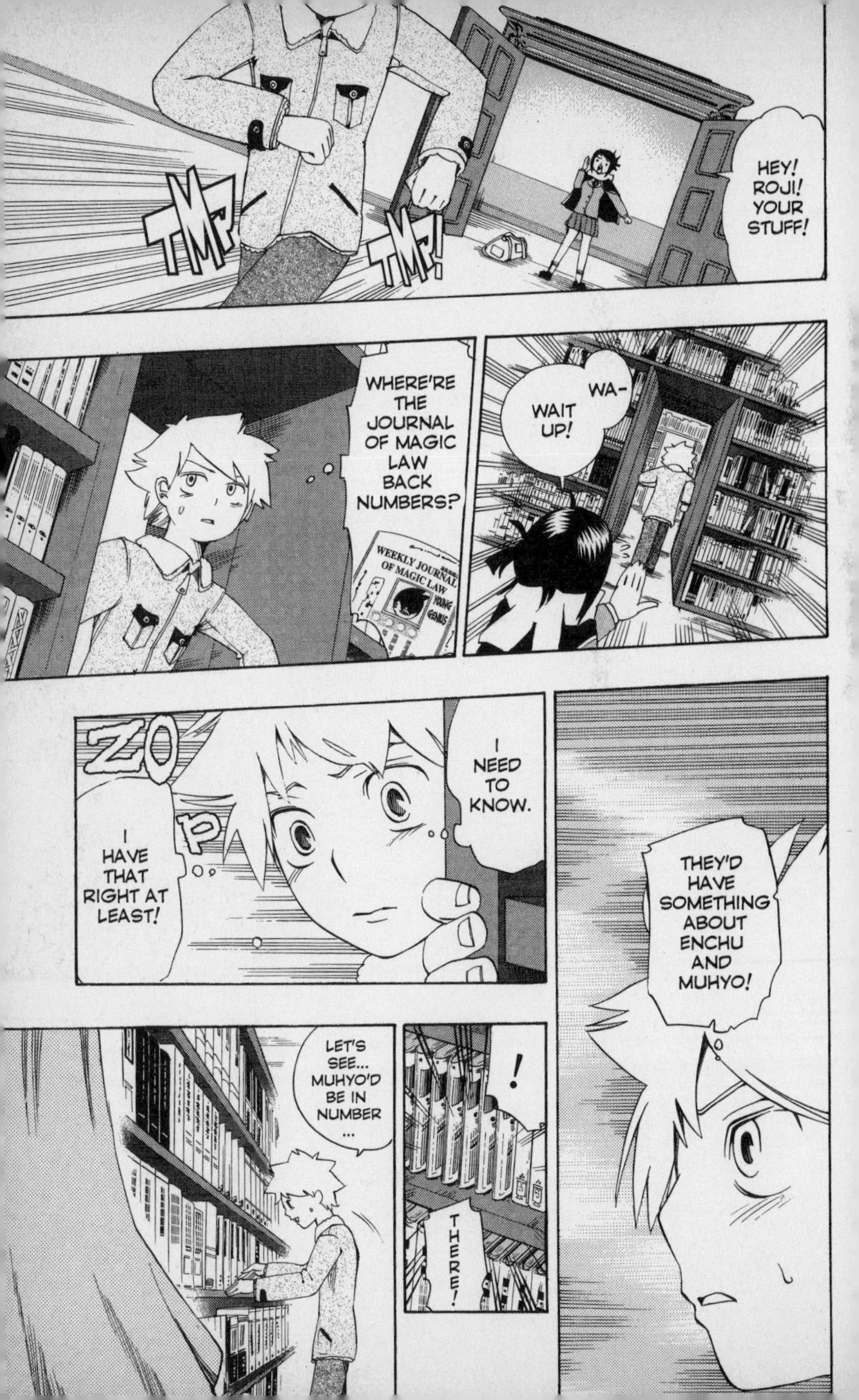
TMP
TMP!
HEY! ROJI! YOUR STUFF!
WA- WAIT UP!
WHERE'RE THE JOURNAL OF MAGIC LAW BACK NUMBERS?
WEEKLY JOURNAL OF MAGIC LAW
YOUNG GENIUS
THEY'D HAVE SOMETHING ABOUT ENCHU AND MUHYO!
I NEED TO KNOW.
ZOP
I HAVE THAT RIGHT AT LEAST!
!
THERE!
LET'S SEE... MUHYO'D BE IN NUMBER...

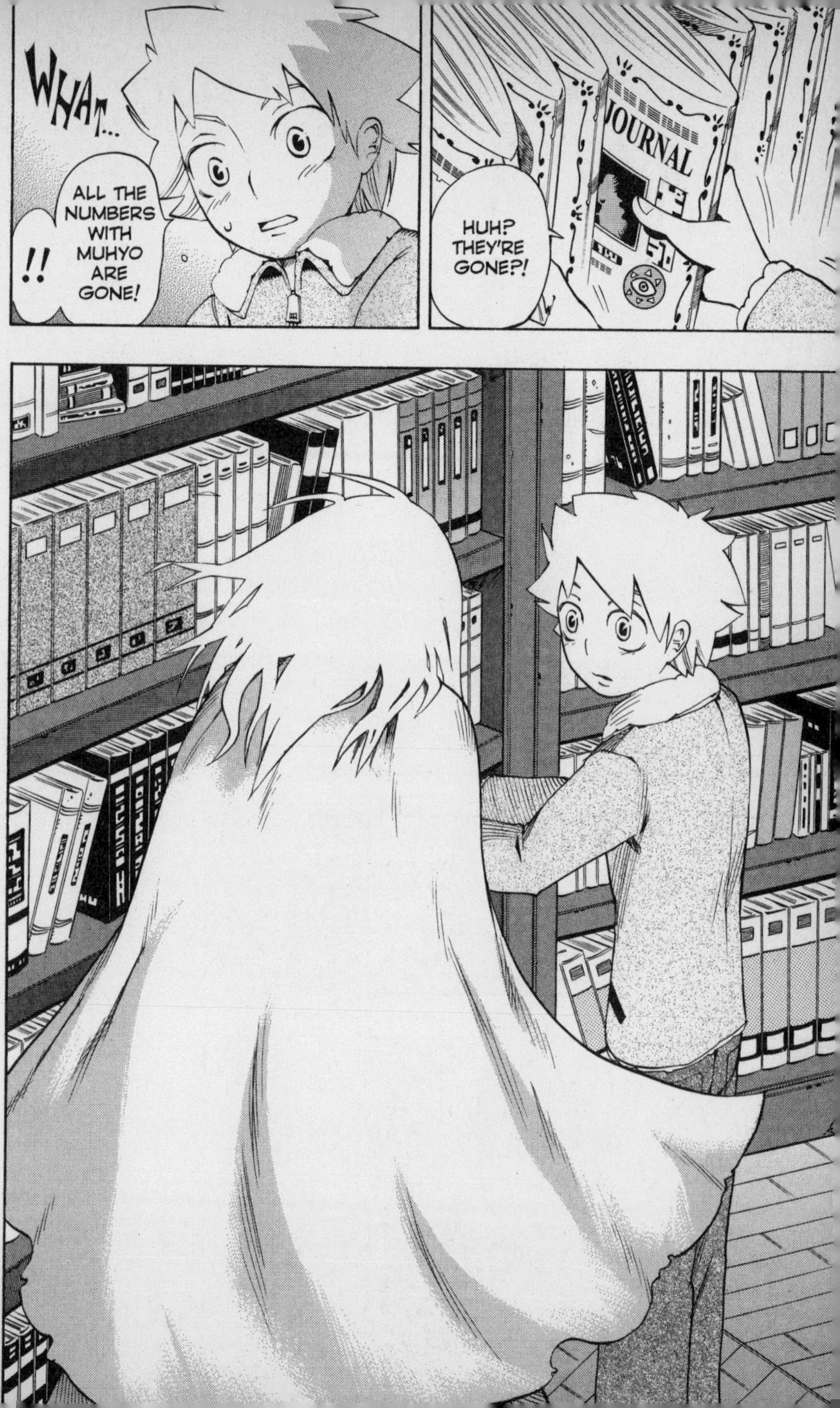
JOURNAL
HUH? THEY'RE GONE?!
WHAT...
ALL THE NUMBERS WITH MUHYO ARE GONE!
!!

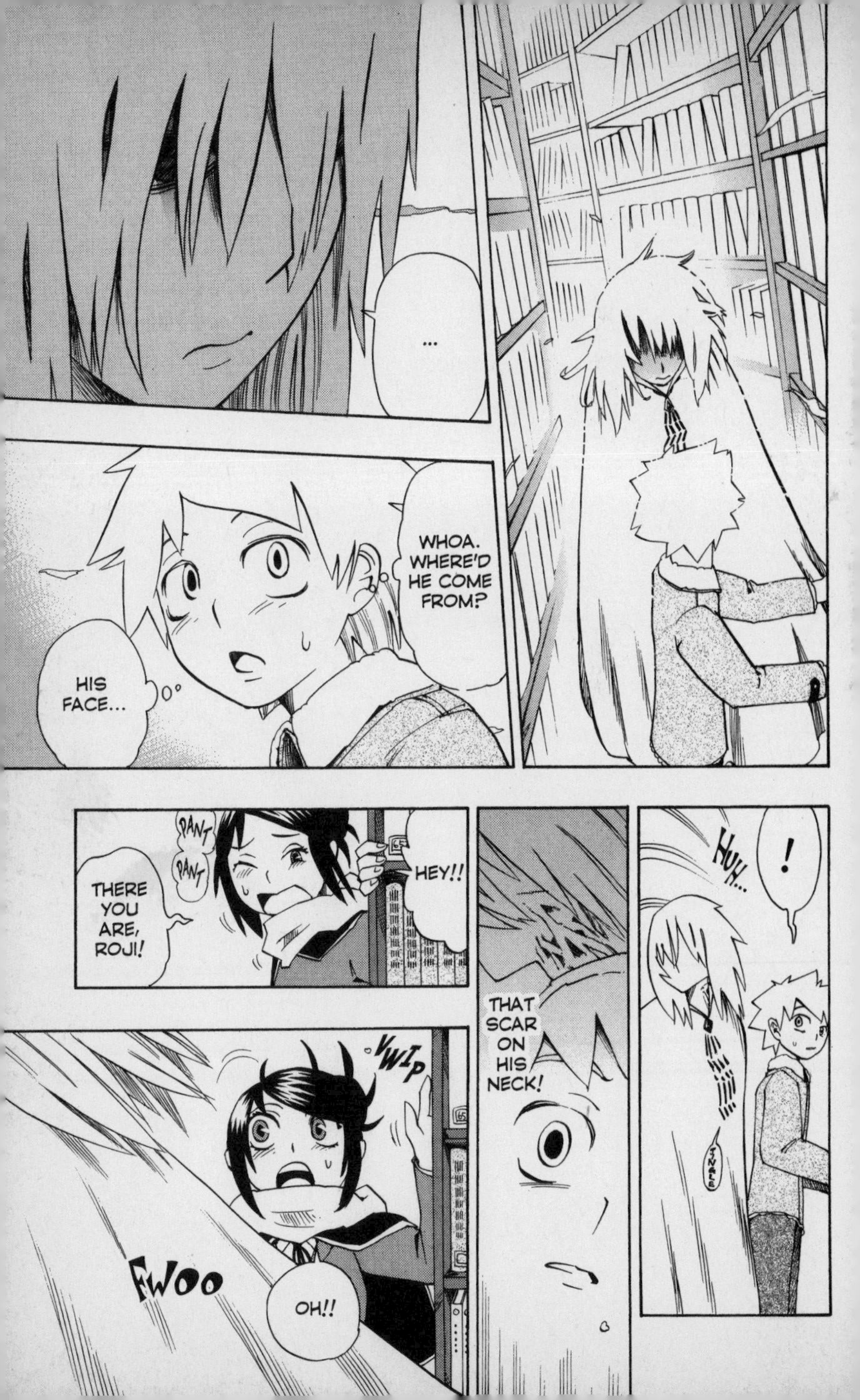
...
WHOA. WHERE'D HE COME FROM?
HIS FACE...
!
HUH...
JINGLE
THAT SCAR ON HIS NECK!
HEY!!
PANT PANT
THERE YOU ARE, ROJI!
VWIP
FWOO
OH!!

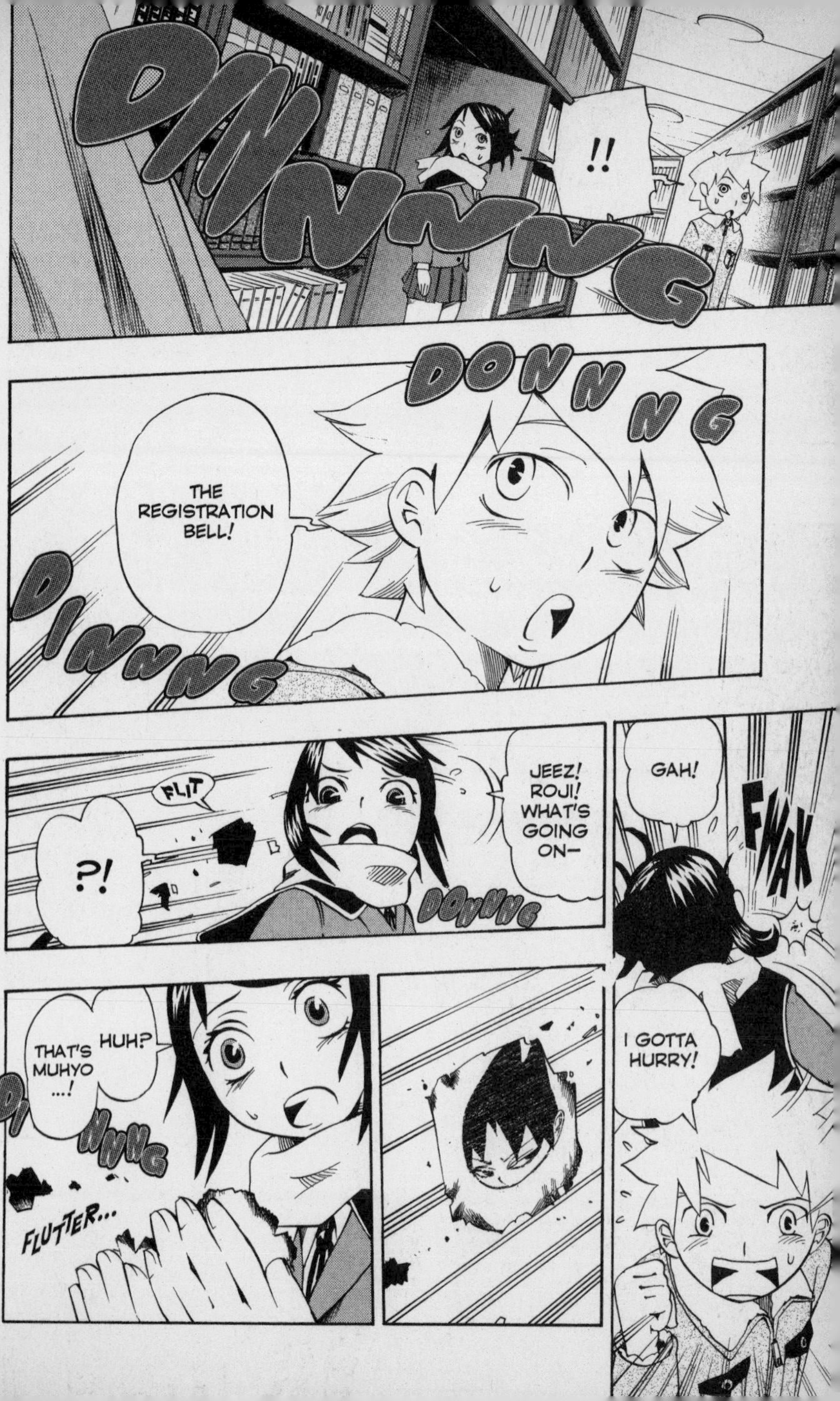
DINNNNG
!!
DONNNG
THE REGISTRATION BELL!
DINNNG
GAH!
FWAK
I GOTTA HURRY!
JEEZ! ROJI! WHAT'S GOING ON—
DONNNG
FLIT
?!
HUH?
THAT'S MUHYO ...!
DINNNG
FLUTTER...

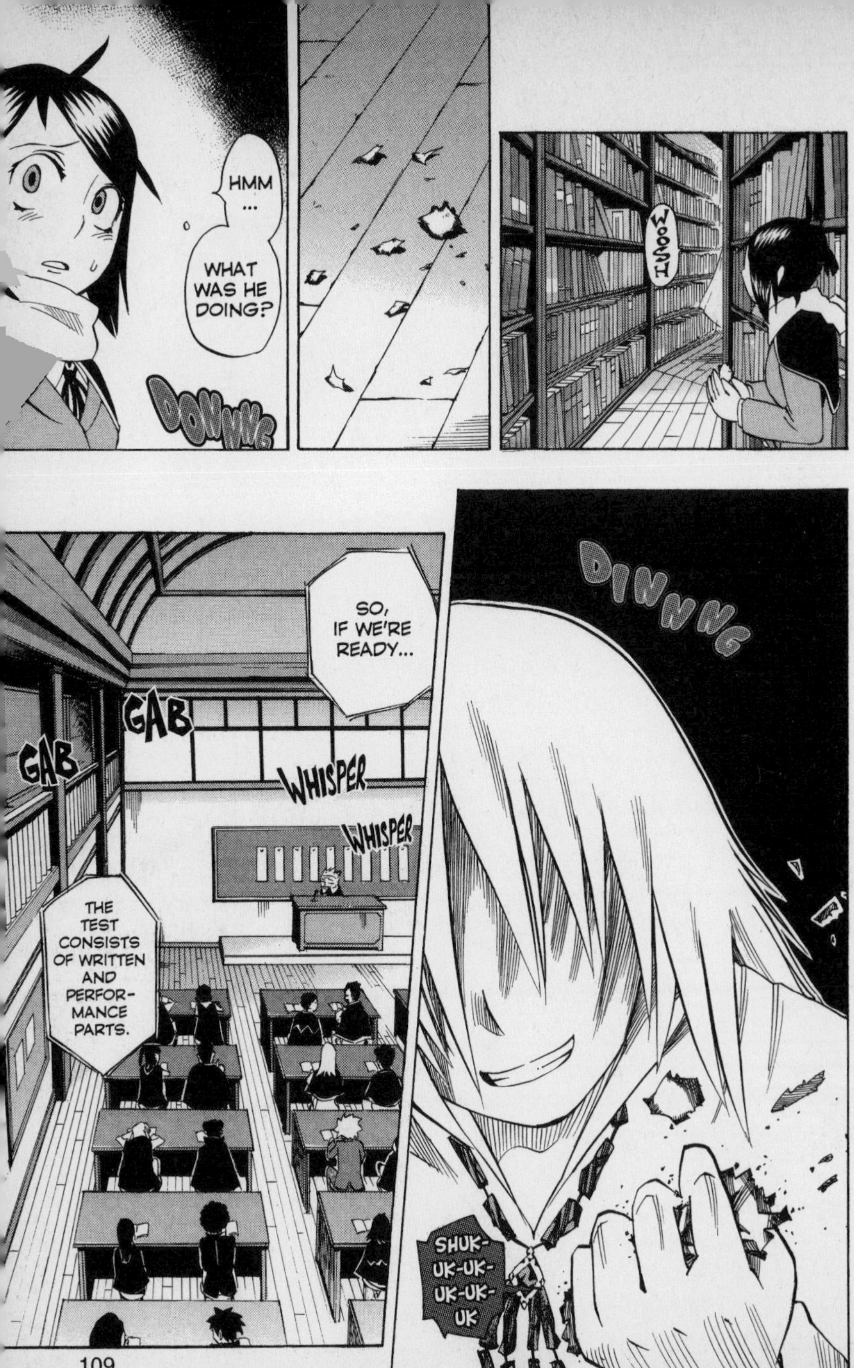
WOOSH
HMM ...
WHAT WAS HE DOING?
DONNNG
DINNNG
SHUK-UK-UK-UK-UK-UK
SO, IF WE'RE READY...
GAB
GAB
WHISPER
WHISPER
THE TEST CONSISTS OF WRITTEN AND PERFORMANCE PARTS.

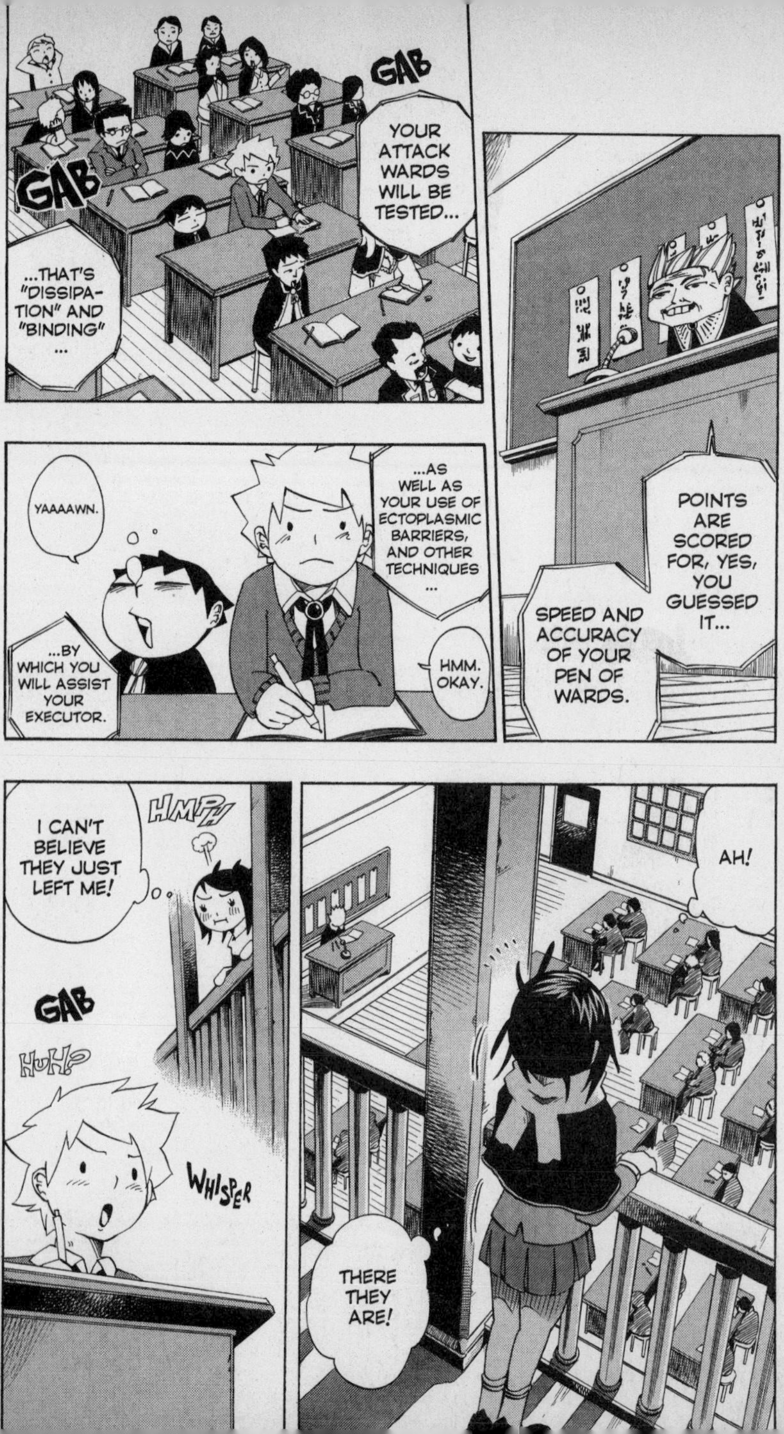
GAB
YOUR ATTACK WARDS WILL BE TESTED...
GAB
...THAT'S "DISSIPATION" AND "BINDING"...
POINTS ARE SCORED FOR, YES, YOU GUESSED IT...
SPEED AND ACCURACY OF YOUR PEN OF WARDS.
...AS WELL AS YOUR USE OF ECTOPLASMIC BARRIERS, AND OTHER TECHNIQUES...
YAAAAWN.
HMM. OKAY.
...BY WHICH YOU WILL ASSIST YOUR EXECUTOR.
AH!
THERE THEY ARE!
HMPH
I CAN'T BELIEVE THEY JUST LEFT ME!
GAB
HUH?
WHISPER

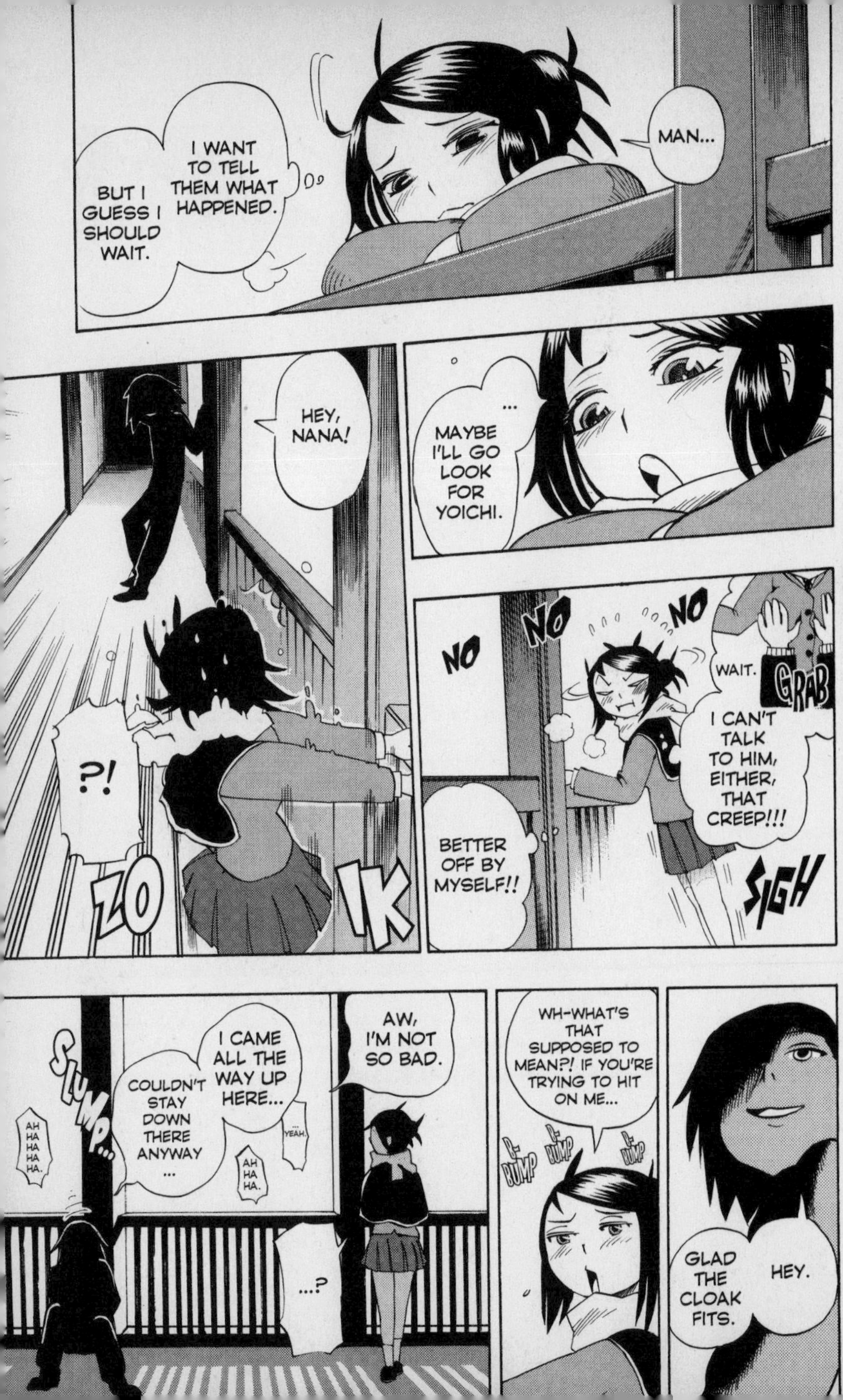
MAN...
I WANT TO TELL THEM WHAT HAPPENED.
BUT I GUESS I SHOULD WAIT.
... MAYBE I'LL GO LOOK FOR YOICHI.
NO
NO
NO
NO
WAIT.
GRAB
I CAN'T TALK TO HIM, EITHER, THAT CREEP!!!
BETTER OFF BY MYSELF!!
SIGH
HEY, NANA!
?!
ZO
IK
HEY.
GLAD THE CLOAK FITS.
WH-WHAT'S THAT SUPPOSED TO MEAN?! IF YOU'RE TRYING TO HIT ON ME...
D-BUMP
D-BUMP
D-BUMP
AW, I'M NOT SO BAD.
...?
... YEAH.
AH HA HA.
I CAME ALL THE WAY UP HERE...
COULDN'T STAY DOWN THERE ANYWAY ...
SLUMP...
AH HA HA HA HA.

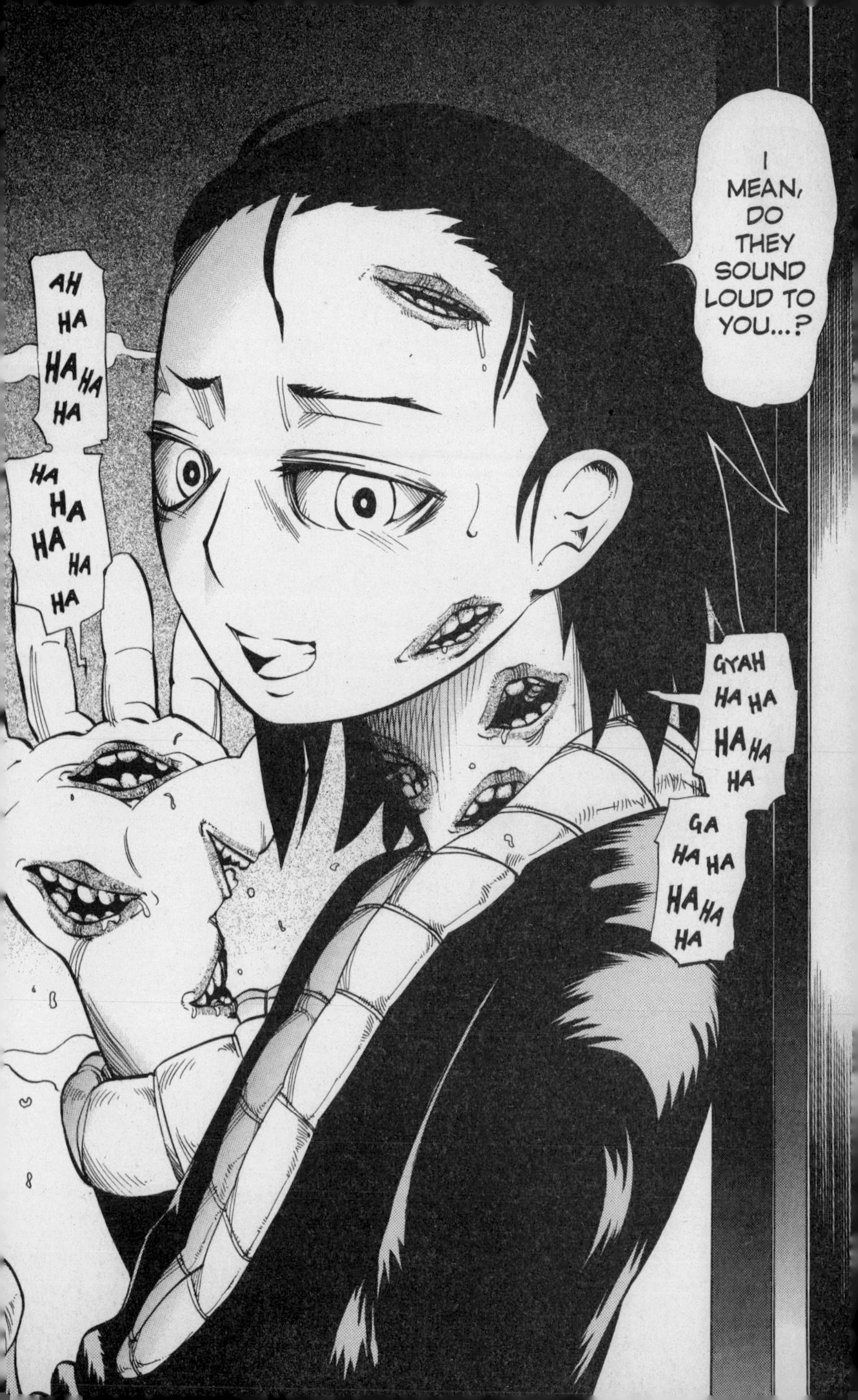
I MEAN, DO THEY SOUND LOUD TO YOU...?
GYAH HA HA HA HA HA
GA HA HA HA HA HA
AH HA HA HA HA
HA HA HA HA HA HA

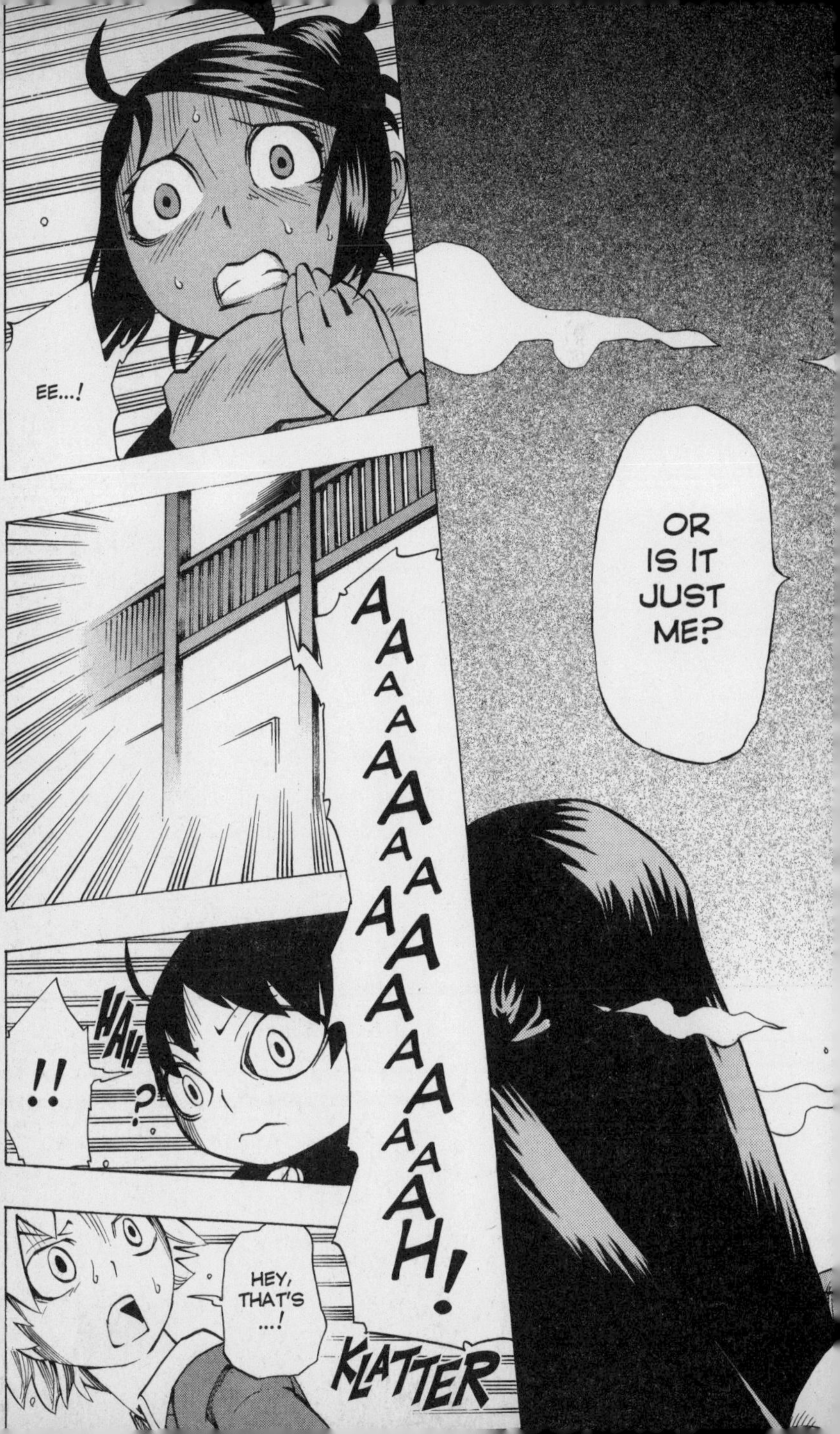
OR IS IT JUST ME?
AAAAAAAAAAAAAAAAAAH!
KLATTER
EE...!
HAH
!!
?
HEY, THAT'S ....!

IF YOU'RE GOING TO WORK...

STAFF ROLL

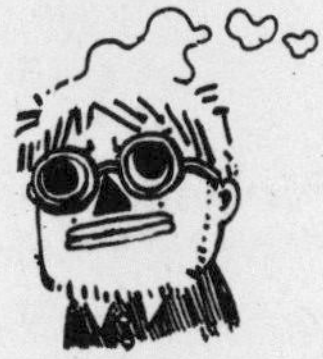

AUTHOR

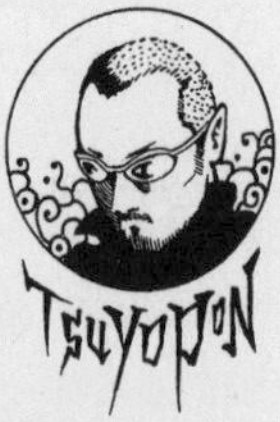
TSUYOPON

CHIEF #1

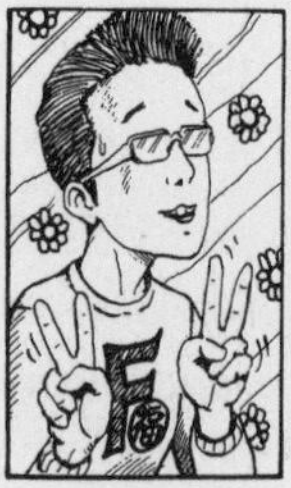

CHIEF #2

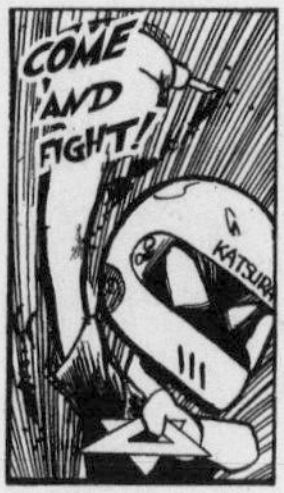
COME AND FIGHT!
KATSURA

ASSISTANT STAFF MEMBER

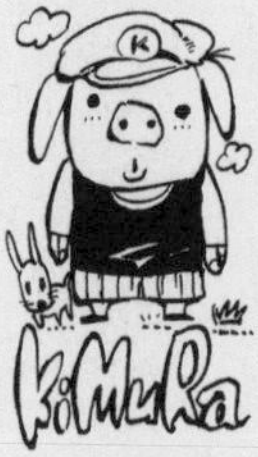
KIMURA

STAFF MEMBER

SUPER ASSISTANTS:

TAKAHIRO HIRAISHI
TATSUYA ENDO
SATOKO NAKAMURA
HIGO-NO-KAMI

...HAVE FUN DOING IT!

ARTICLE 11
PREMONITION

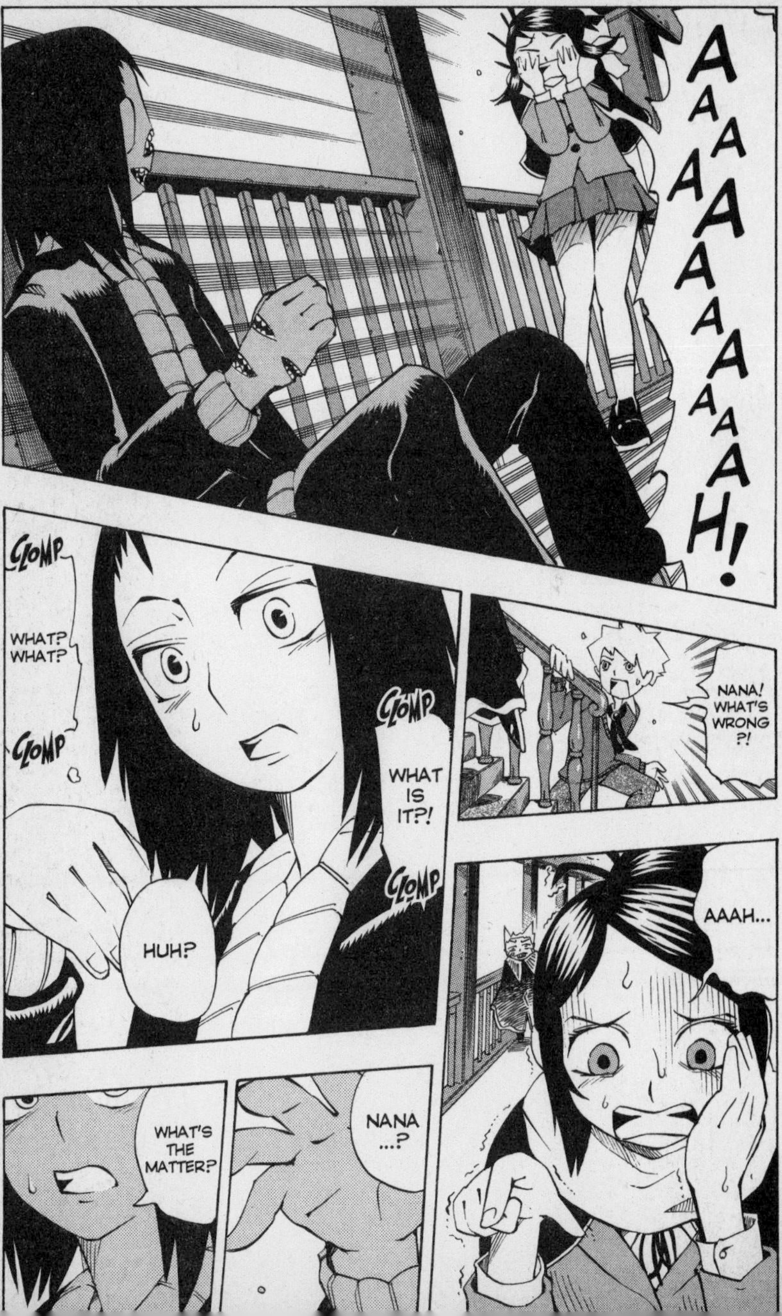

AAAAAAAAAAAAH!
NANA! WHAT'S WRONG ?!
CLOMP
WHAT IS IT?!
CLOMP
CLOMP
WHAT? WHAT?
CLOMP
HUH?
AAAH...
NANA ...?
WHAT'S THE MATTER?

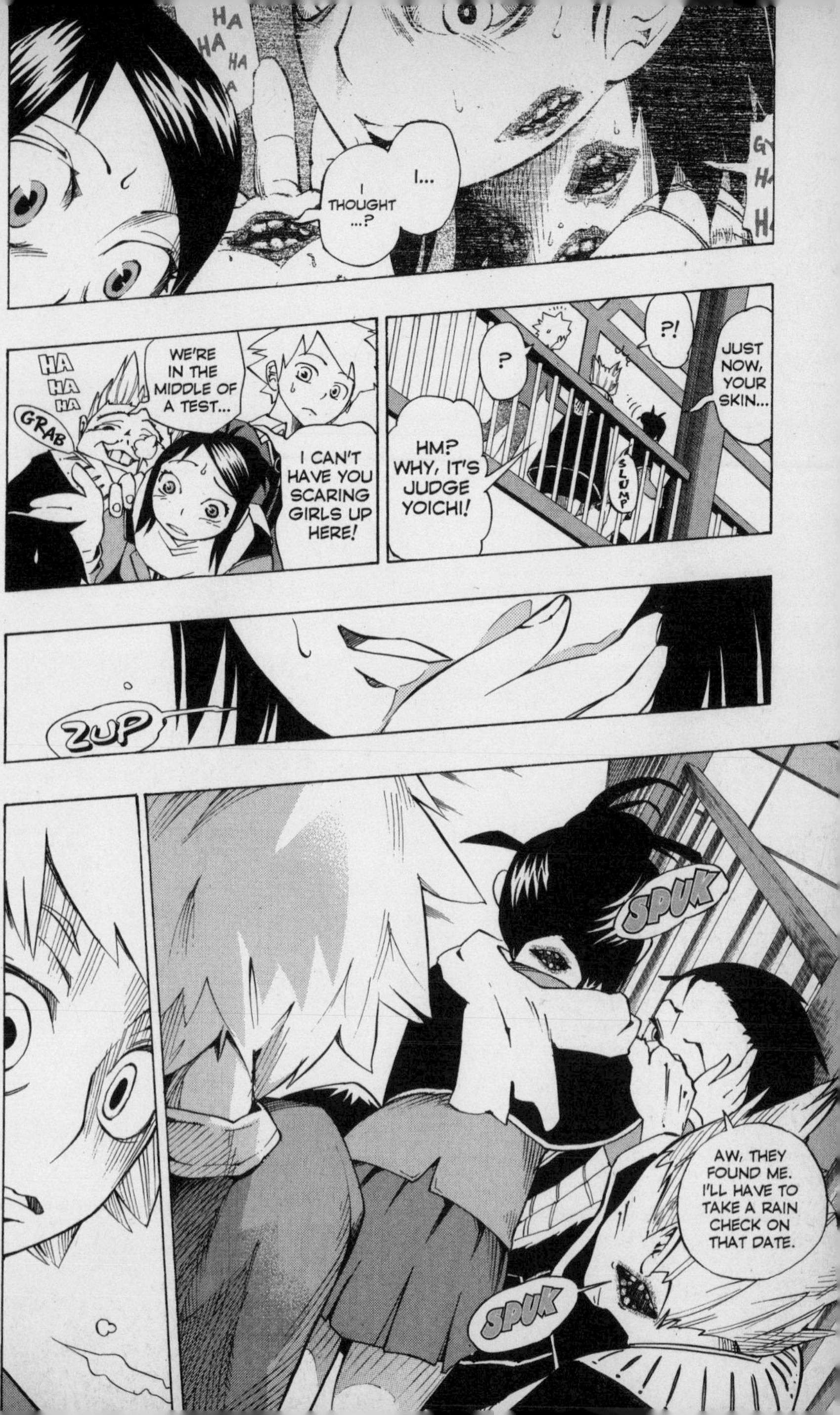
HA HA
I...
I THOUGHT ...?
HA HA HA HA
JUST NOW, YOUR SKIN...
?!
?
HM? WHY, IT'S JUDGE YOICHI!
SLUMP
WE'RE IN THE MIDDLE OF A TEST...
I CAN'T HAVE YOU SCARING GIRLS UP HERE!
HA HA HA
GRAB
ZUP
SPUK
AW, THEY FOUND ME. I'LL HAVE TO TAKE A RAIN CHECK ON THAT DATE.
SPUK

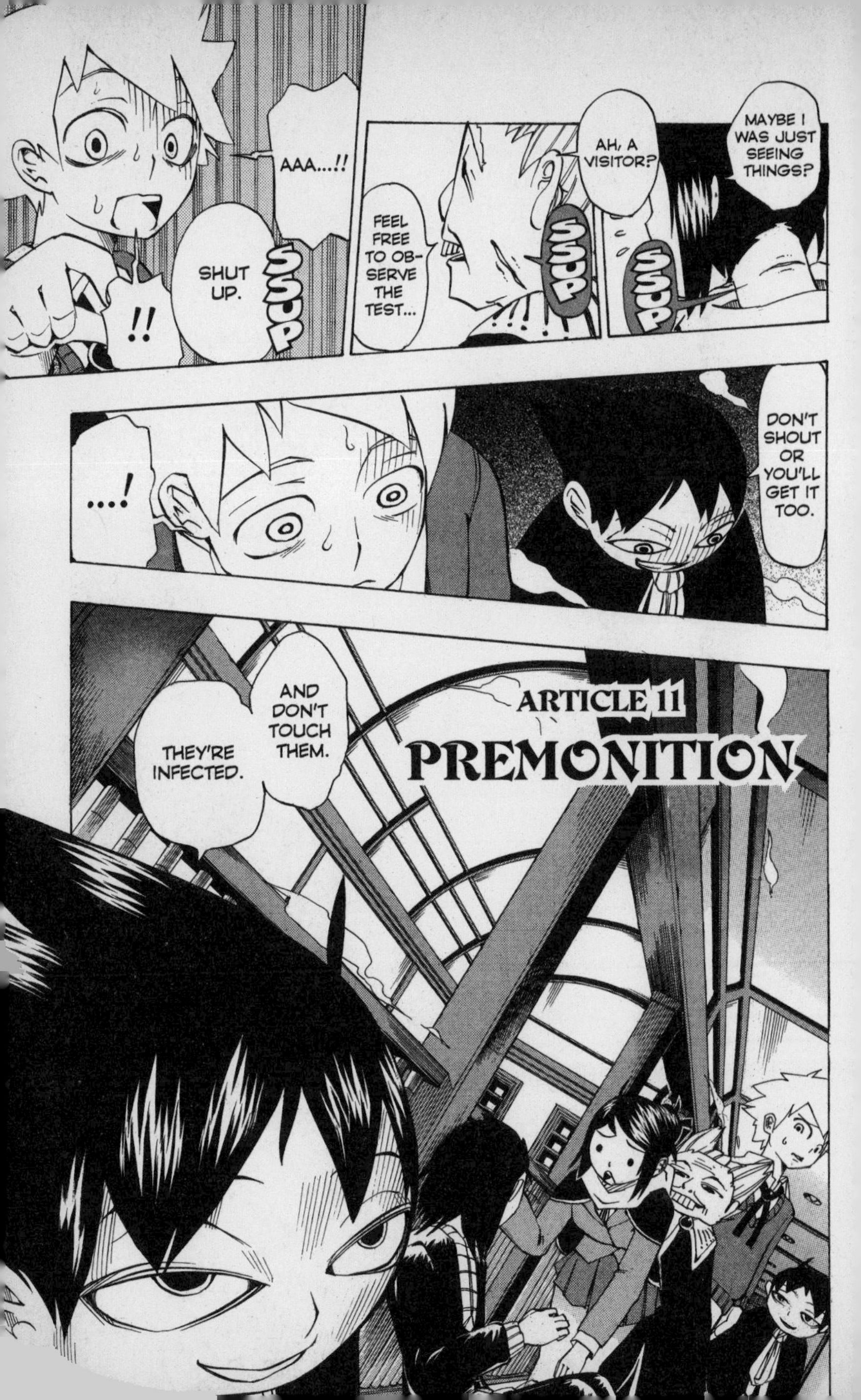
MAYBE I WAS JUST SEEING THINGS?
SSUP
AH, A VISITOR?
SSUP
FEEL FREE TO OB-SERVE THE TEST...
!!!
AAA...!!
SHUT UP.
SSUP
!!
DON'T SHOUT OR YOU'LL GET IT TOO.
...!
AND DON'T TOUCH THEM.
THEY'RE INFECTED.
ARTICLE 11
PREMONITION

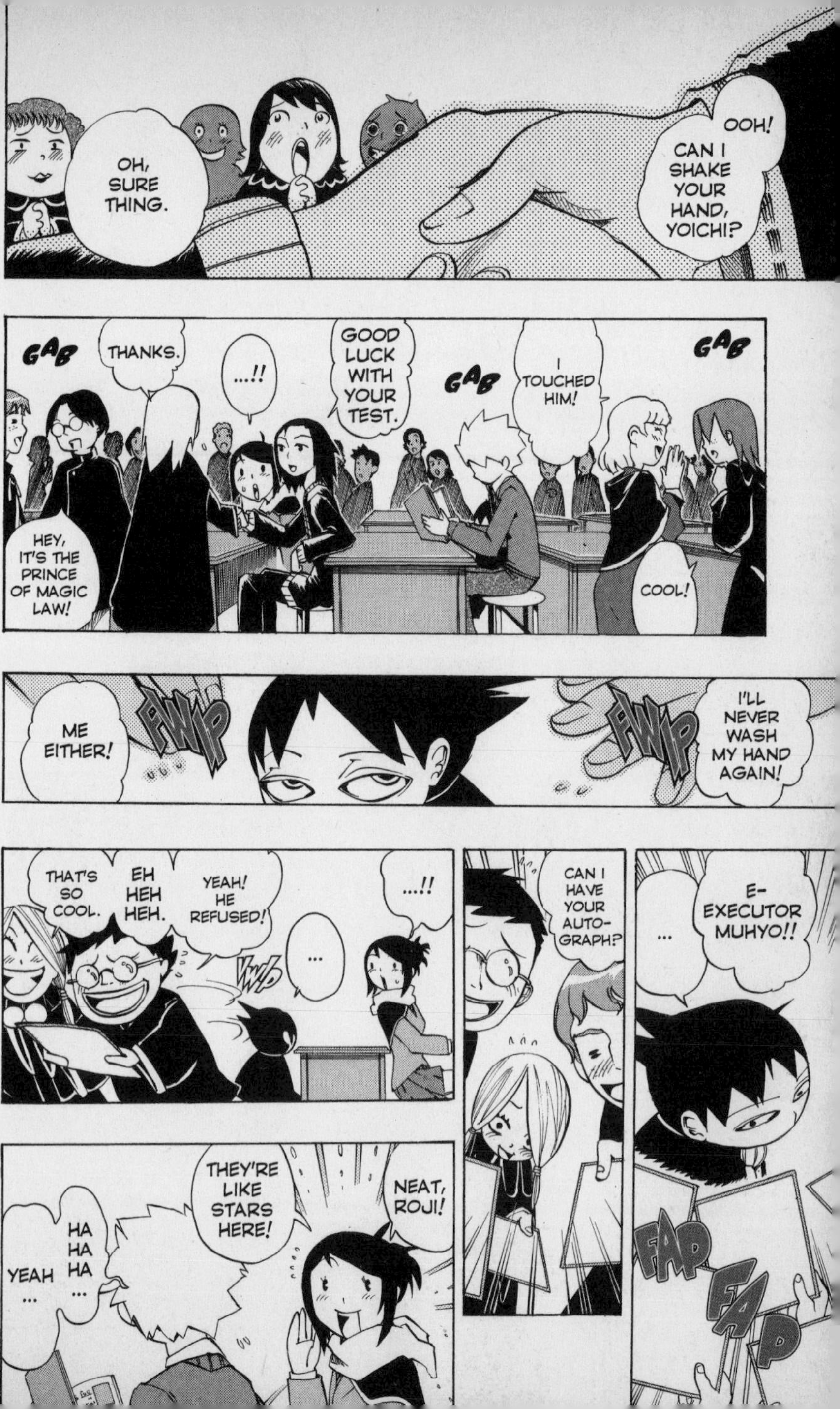
OOH! CAN I SHAKE YOUR HAND, YOICHI?
OH, SURE THING.
GAB
I TOUCHED HIM!
GAB
GOOD LUCK WITH YOUR TEST.
...!!
THANKS.
GAB
COOL!
HEY, IT'S THE PRINCE OF MAGIC LAW!
I'LL NEVER WASH MY HAND AGAIN!
FWIP
FWIP
ME EITHER!
E-EXECUTOR MUHYO!!
...
FAP
FAP
FAP
CAN I HAVE YOUR AUTO-GRAPH?
...!!
...
YEAH! HE REFUSED!
VWIP
EH HEH HEH.
THAT'S SO COOL.
NEAT, ROJI!
THEY'RE LIKE STARS HERE!
HA HA HA ...
YEAH ...

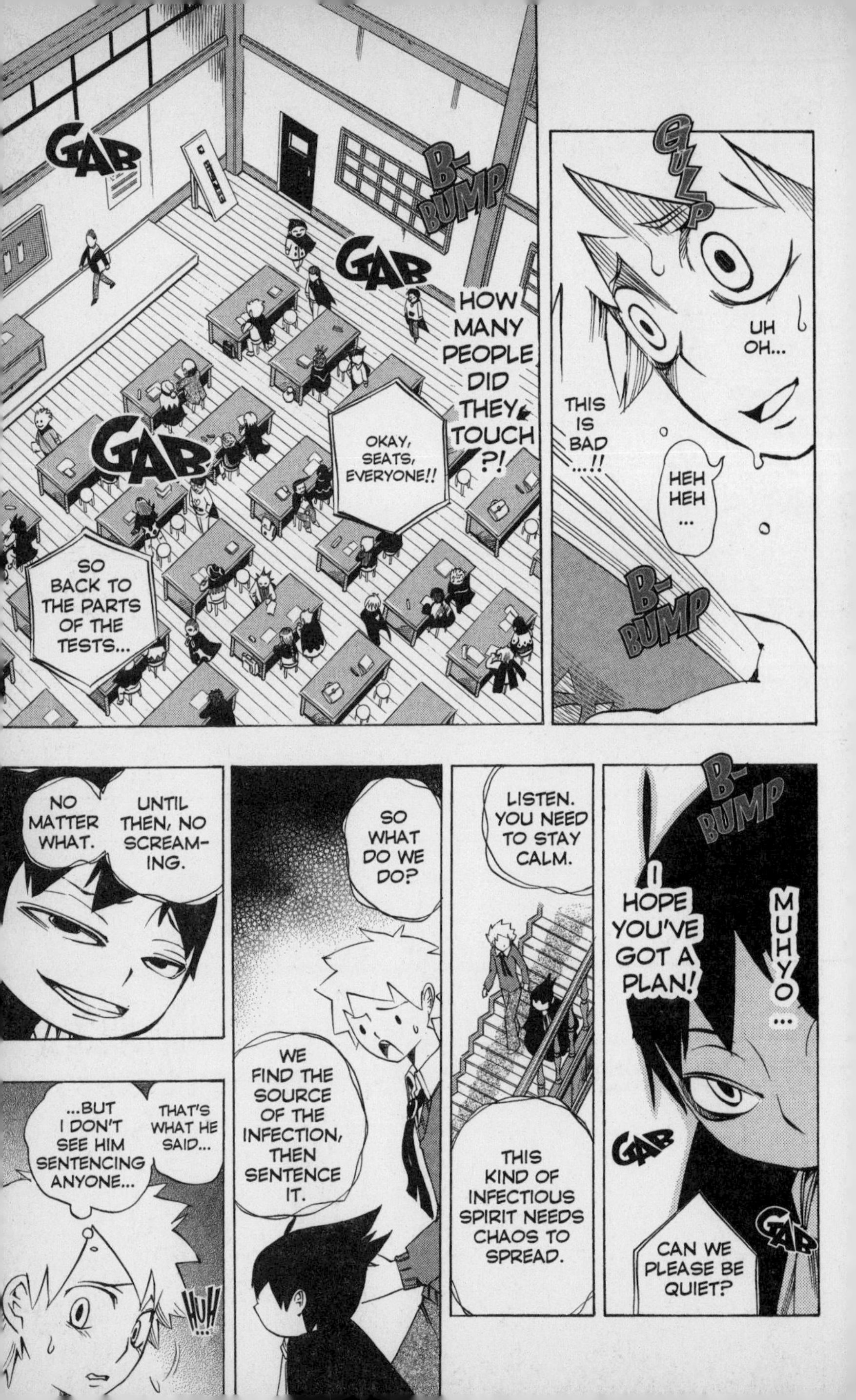
GULP
UH OH...
THIS IS BAD...!!
HEH HEH...
B-BUMP
GAB
B-BUMP
GAB
HOW MANY PEOPLE DID THEY TOUCH?!
OKAY, SEATS, EVERYONE!!
GAB
SO BACK TO THE PARTS OF THE TESTS...
B-BUMP
MUHYO...
I HOPE YOU'VE GOT A PLAN!
GAB
GAB
CAN WE PLEASE BE QUIET?
LISTEN. YOU NEED TO STAY CALM.
THIS KIND OF INFECTIOUS SPIRIT NEEDS CHAOS TO SPREAD.
SO WHAT DO WE DO?
WE FIND THE SOURCE OF THE INFECTION, THEN SENTENCE IT.
UNTIL THEN, NO SCREAMING.
NO MATTER WHAT.
THAT'S WHAT HE SAID...
...BUT I DON'T SEE HIM SENTENCING ANYONE...
HUH!?

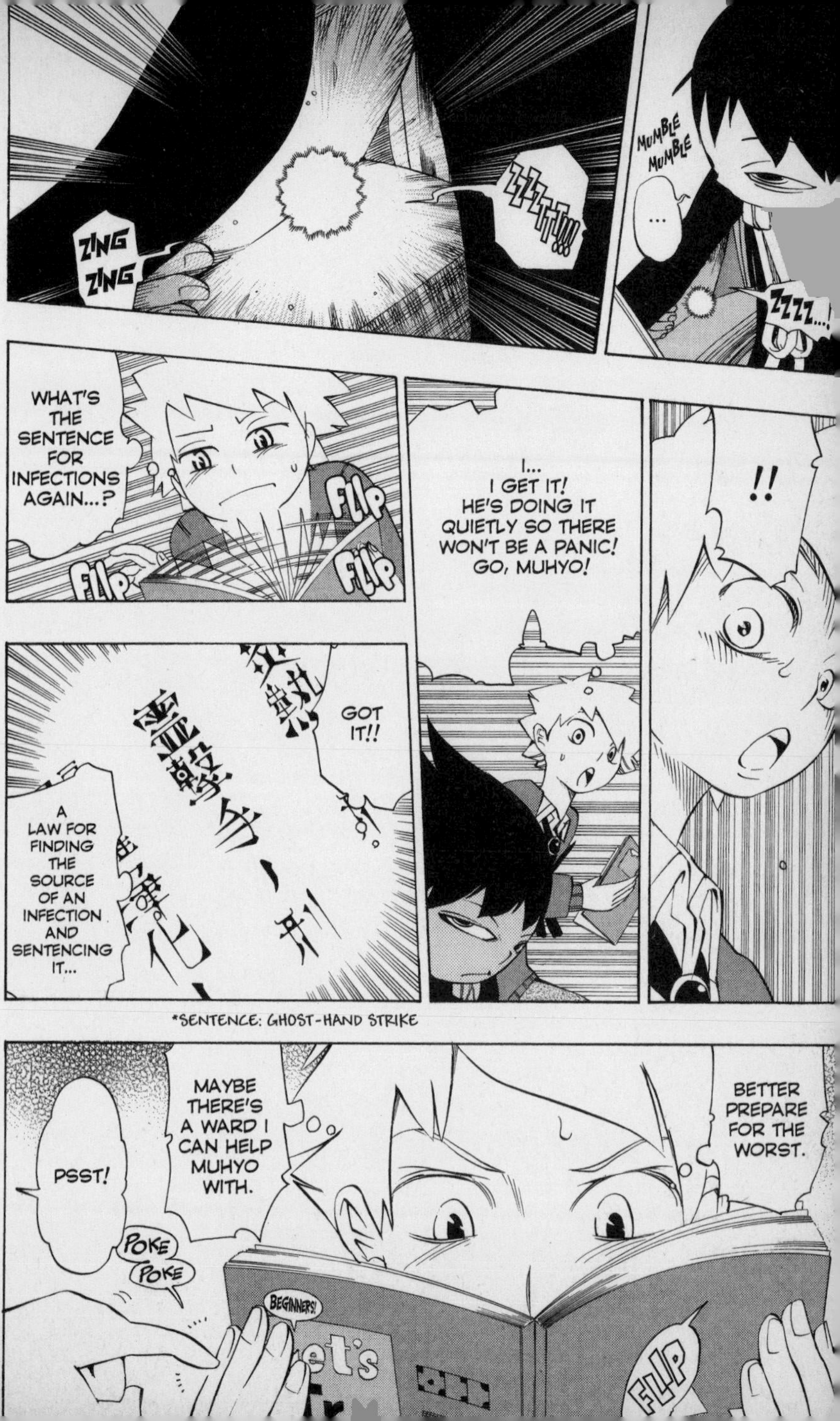
MUMBLE MUMBLE
...
ZZZZ...!
ZZZTTT!!!
ZING ZING
!!
I... I GET IT! HE'S DOING IT QUIETLY SO THERE WON'T BE A PANIC! GO, MUHYO!
WHAT'S THE SENTENCE FOR INFECTIONS AGAIN...?
FLIP
FLIP
FLIP
GOT IT!!
A LAW FOR FINDING THE SOURCE OF AN INFECTION AND SENTENCING IT...
BETTER PREPARE FOR THE WORST.
MAYBE THERE'S A WARD I CAN HELP MUHYO WITH.
PSST!
POKE POKE
...
BEGINNERS!
FLIP
*SENTENCE: GHOST-HAND STRIKE

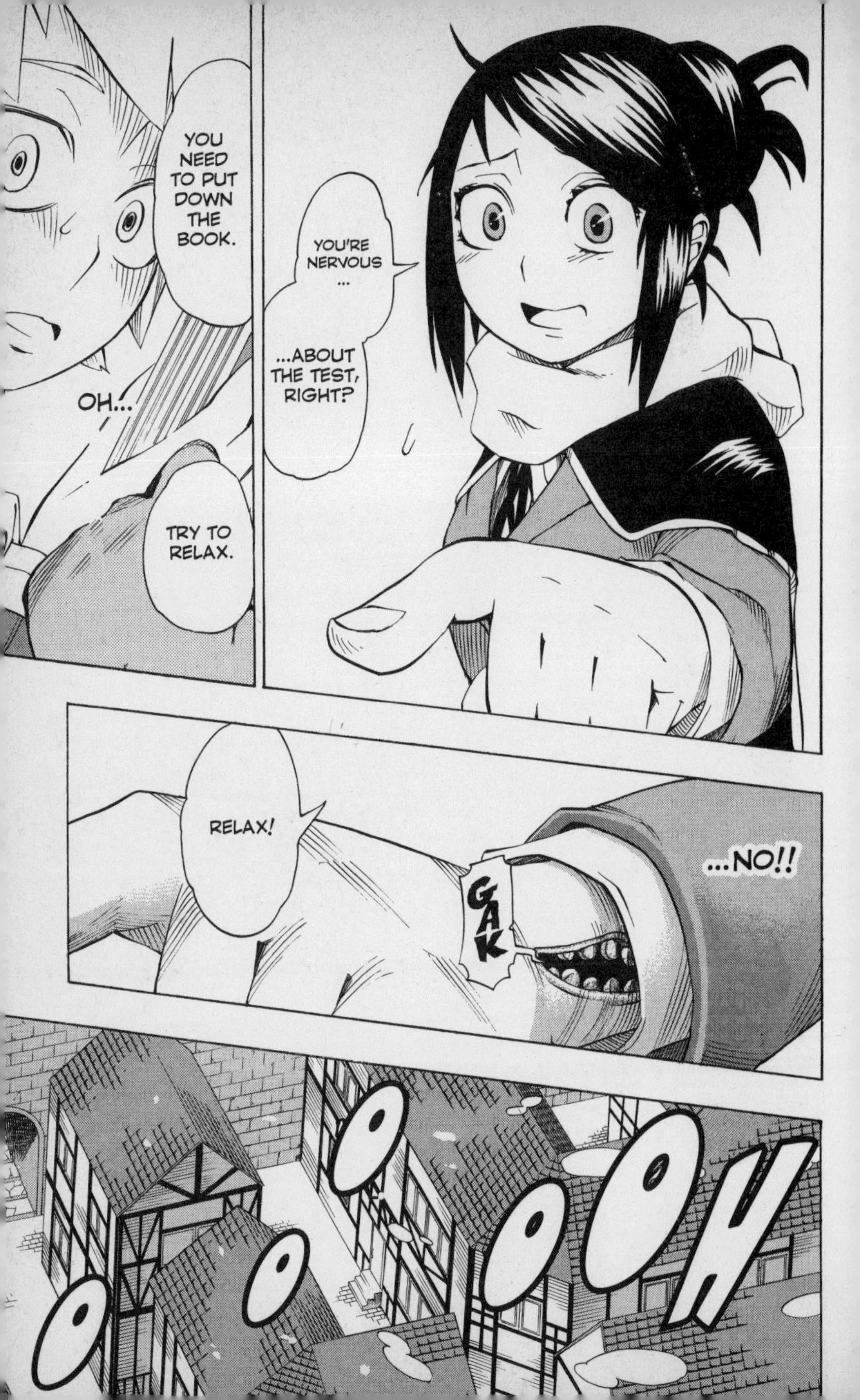
YOU'RE NERVOUS ...
...ABOUT THE TEST, RIGHT?
YOU NEED TO PUT DOWN THE BOOK.
OH...
TRY TO RELAX.
...NO!!
GAK
RELAX!
OOOOOH

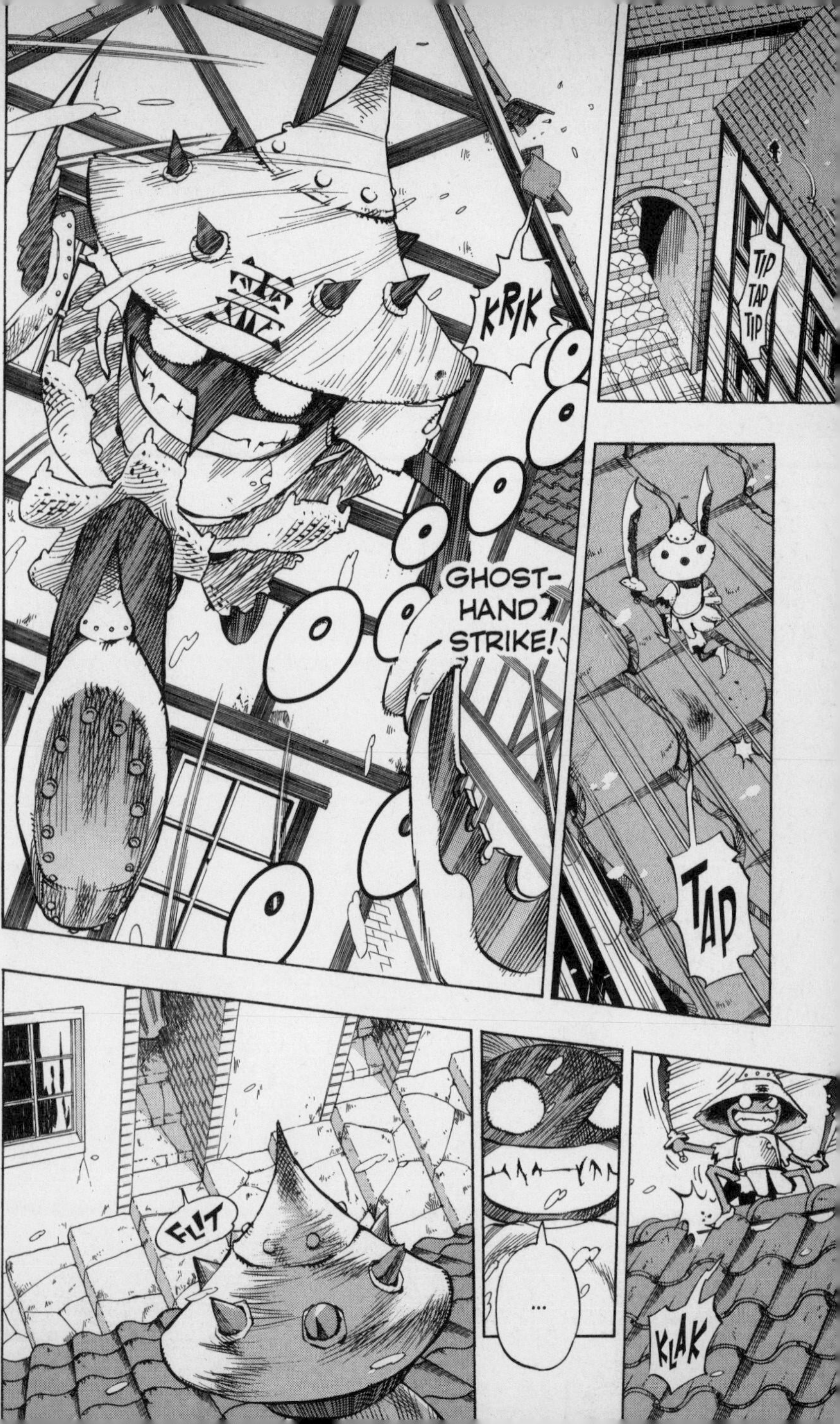
TIP
TAP
TIP
TAP
KRIK
GHOST-HAND STRIKE!
KLAK
...
FLIT

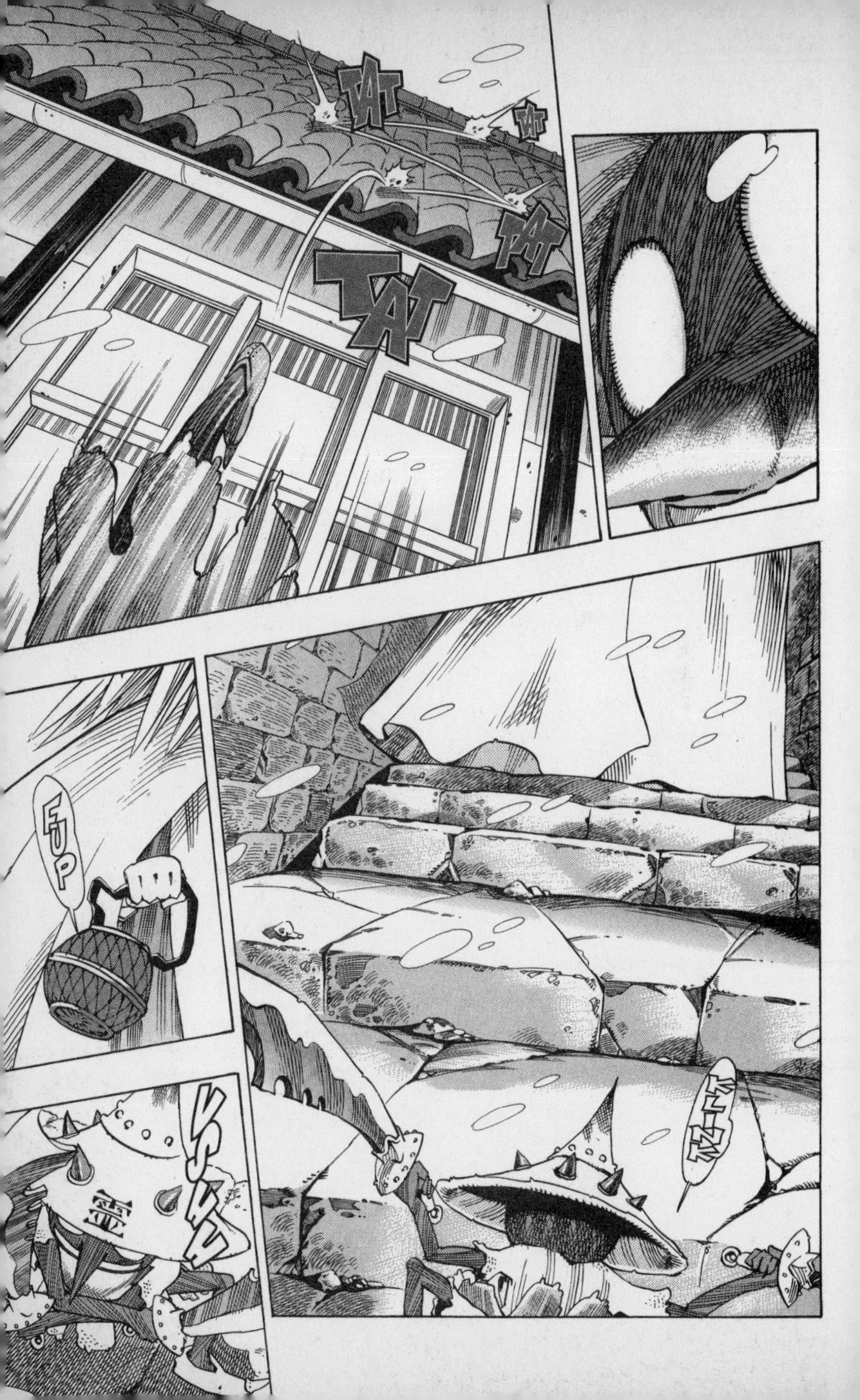
TAT
TAT
TAT
TAT
KLINK
FUP
VS!!

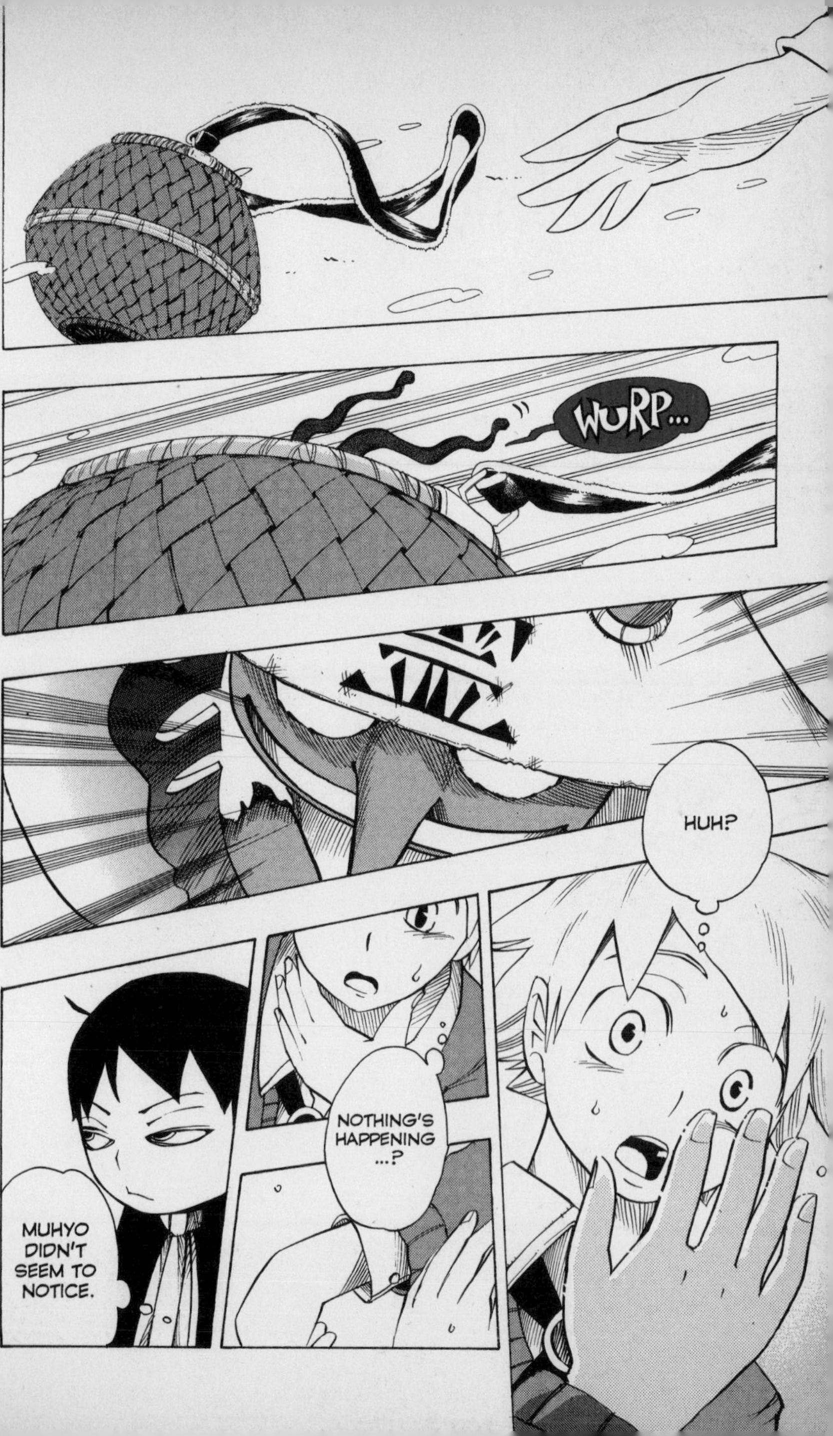
WURP...
HUH?
NOTHING'S HAPPENING ...?
MUHYO DIDN'T SEEM TO NOTICE.

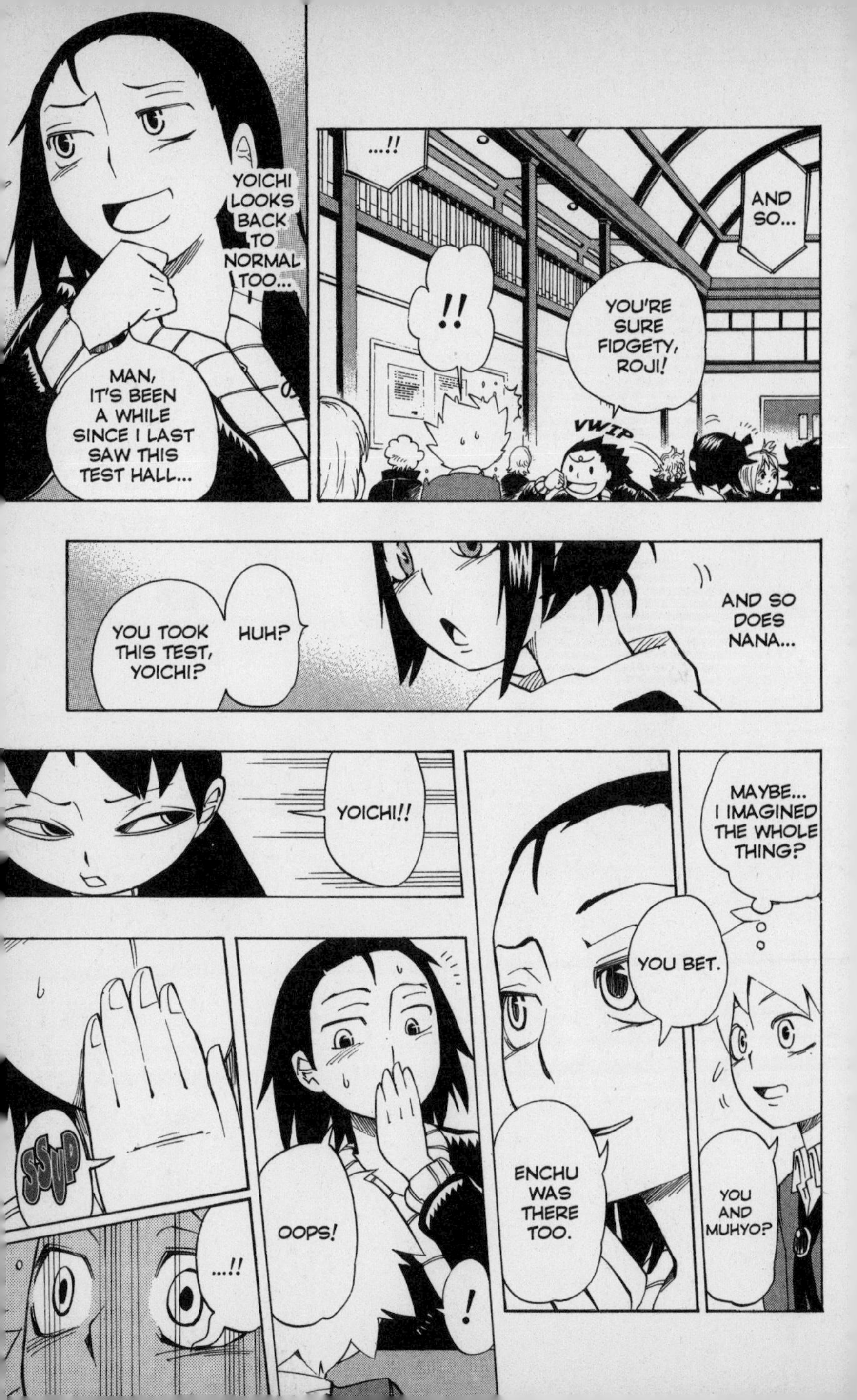
AND SO...
...!!
YOU'RE SURE FIDGETY, ROJI!
!!
VWIP
YOICHI LOOKS BACK TO NORMAL TOO...
MAN, IT'S BEEN A WHILE SINCE I LAST SAW THIS TEST HALL...
AND SO DOES NANA...
HUH?
YOU TOOK THIS TEST, YOICHI?
MAYBE... I IMAGINED THE WHOLE THING?
YOU AND MUHYO?
YOU BET.
ENCHU WAS THERE TOO.
YOICHI!!
OOPS!
!
SSUP
...!!

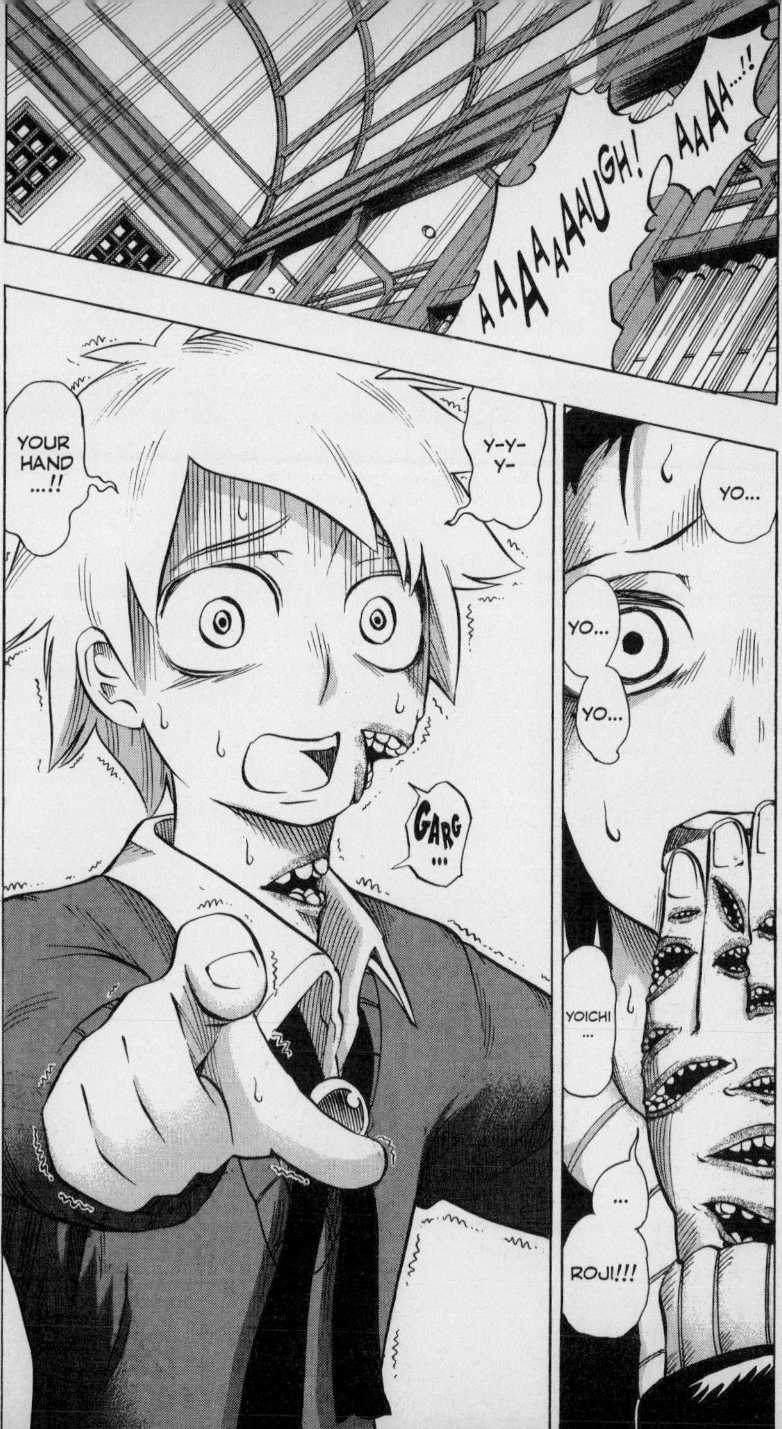
AAAAAAAAUGH! AAAA...!!
YO...
YO...
YO...
YOICHI...
...
ROJI!!!
Y-Y-Y-
YOUR HAND ...!!
GARG ...

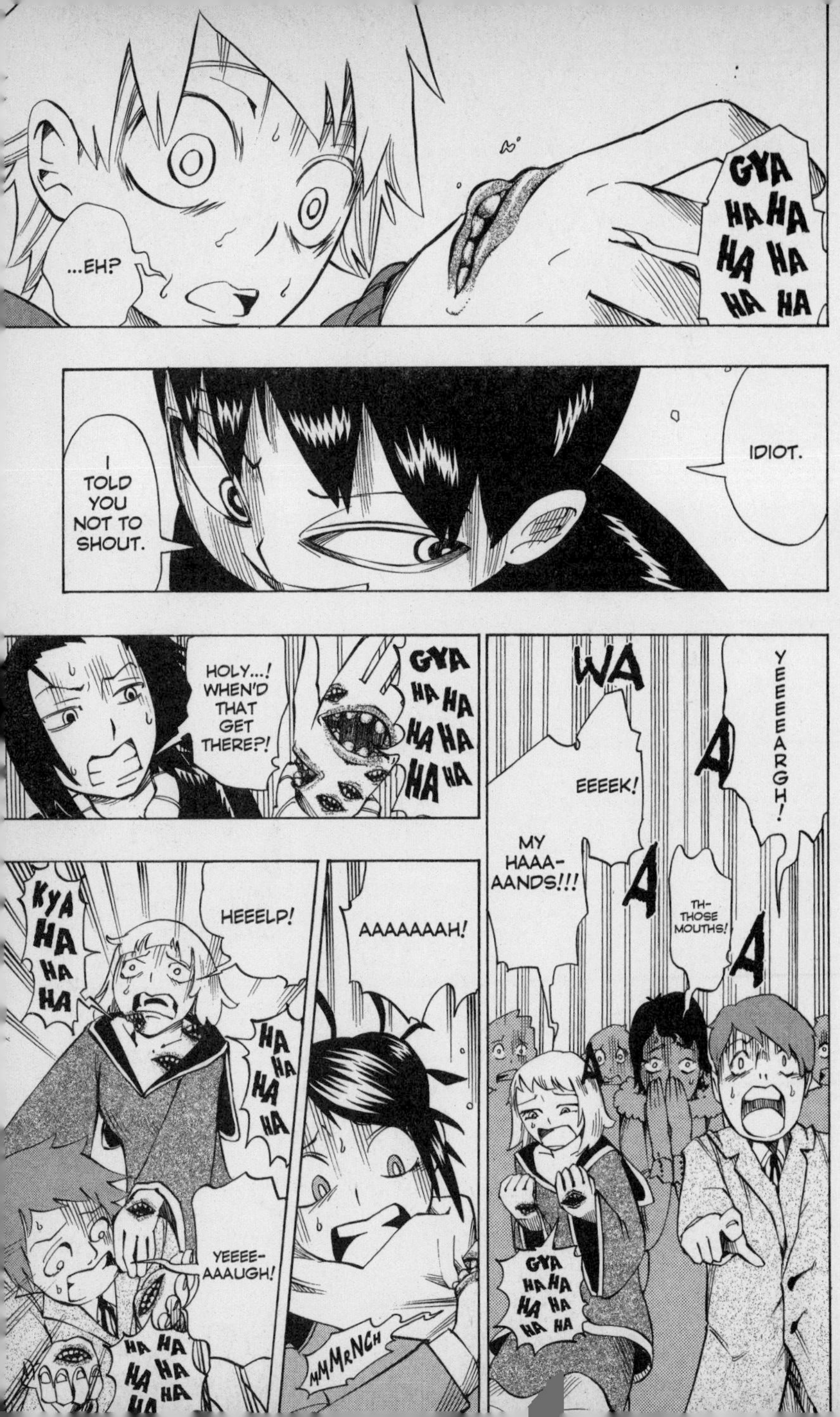
GYA HA HA HA HA HA HA
...EH?
IDIOT.
I TOLD YOU NOT TO SHOUT.
YEEEEARGH!
WA A A A A
EEEEK!
MY HAAA-AANDS!!!
TH-THOSE MOUTHS!
GYA HA HA HA HA HA HA HA HA
GYA HA HA HA HA HA HA HA HA
HOLY...! WHEN'D THAT GET THERE?!
AAAAAAAH!
MMMRNCH
HEEELP!
KYA HA HA HA HA
HA HA HA HA HA
YEEEE-AAAUGH!
HA HA HA HA HA HA

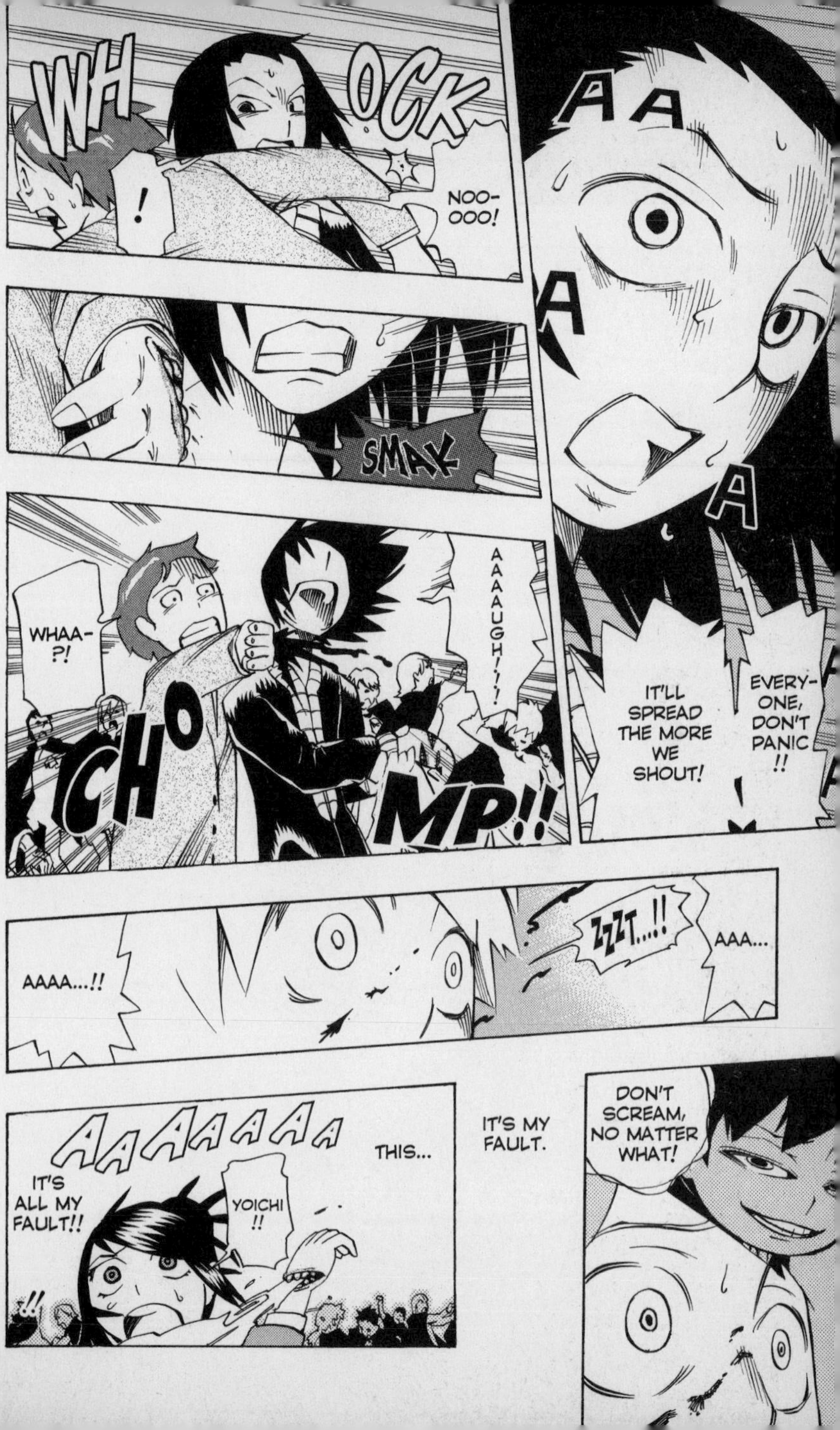
AAAAA
EVERY-ONE, DON'T PANIC!!
IT'LL SPREAD THE MORE WE SHOUT!
WHOCK
NOO-OOO!
!
SMAK
AAAAUGH!!?!
WHAA-?!
CHOMP!!
AAA...
ZZZT...!!
AAAA...!!
DON'T SCREAM, NO MATTER WHAT!
IT'S MY FAULT.
THIS...
AAAAAAA
YOICHI!!
IT'S ALL MY FAULT!!

READ THIS WAY

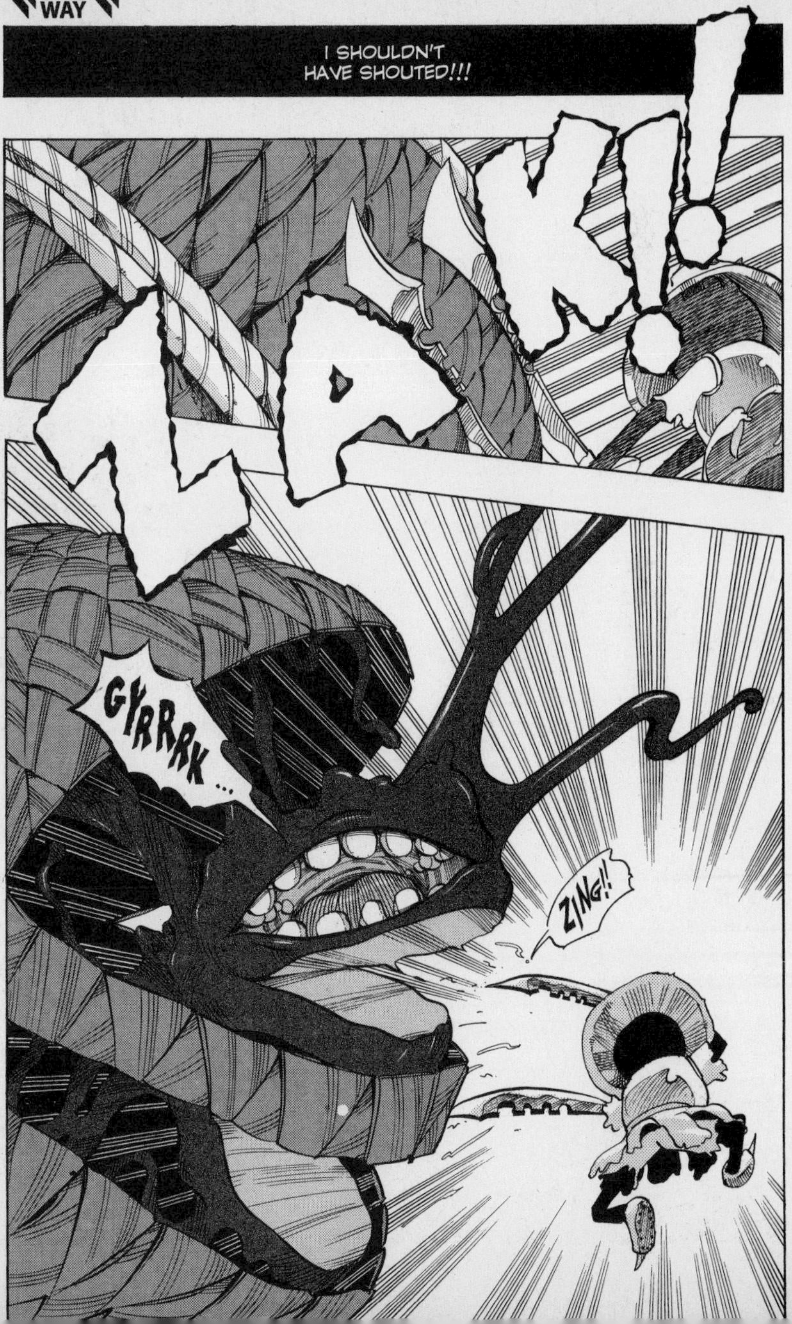
I SHOULDN'T HAVE SHOUTED!!!
GYRRRK...
ZING!!

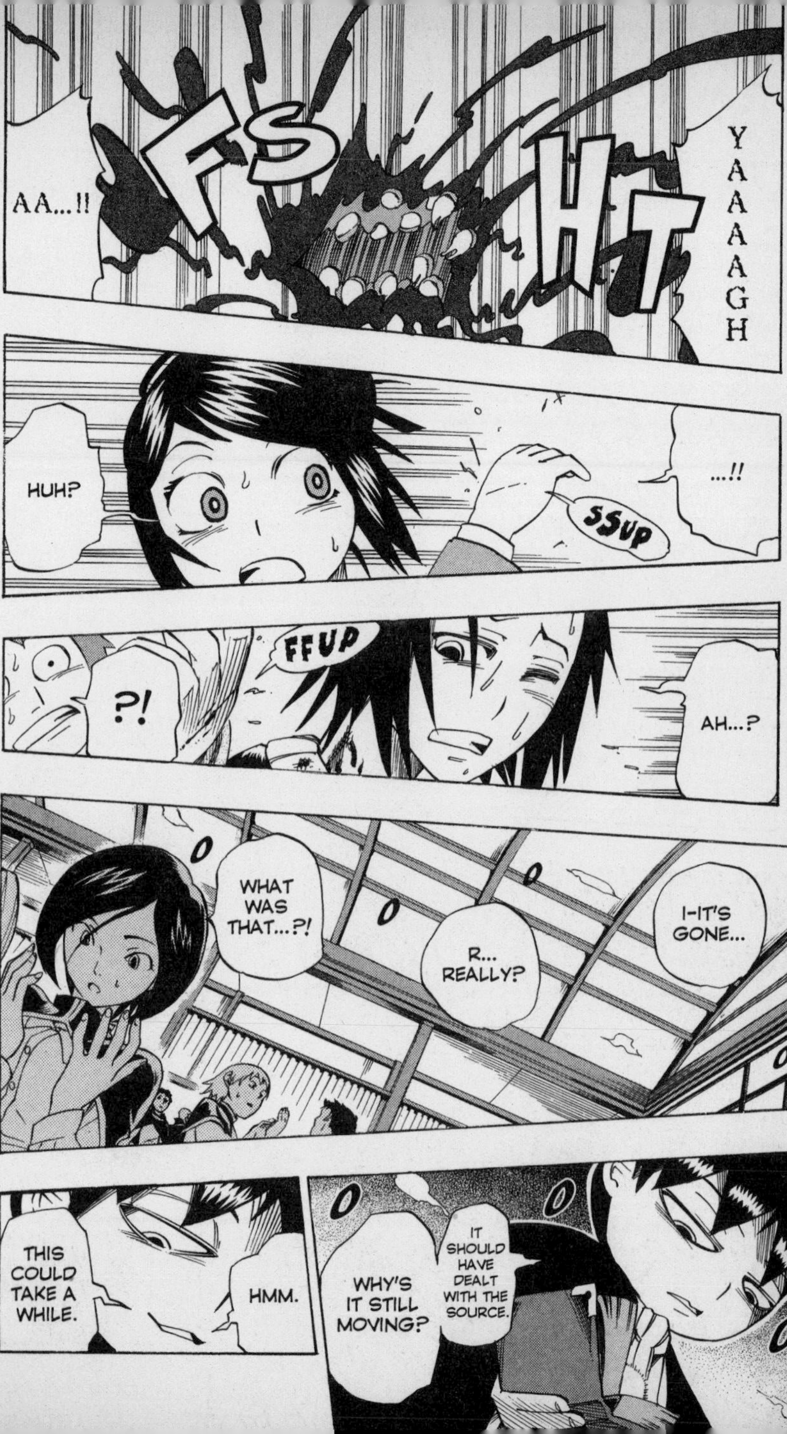
YAAAAGH
FSHT
AA...!!
...!!
SSUP
HUH?
AH...?
FFUP
?!
I-IT'S GONE...
R... REALLY?
WHAT WAS THAT...?!
IT SHOULD HAVE DEALT WITH THE SOURCE.
WHY'S IT STILL MOVING?
HMM.
THIS COULD TAKE A WHILE.

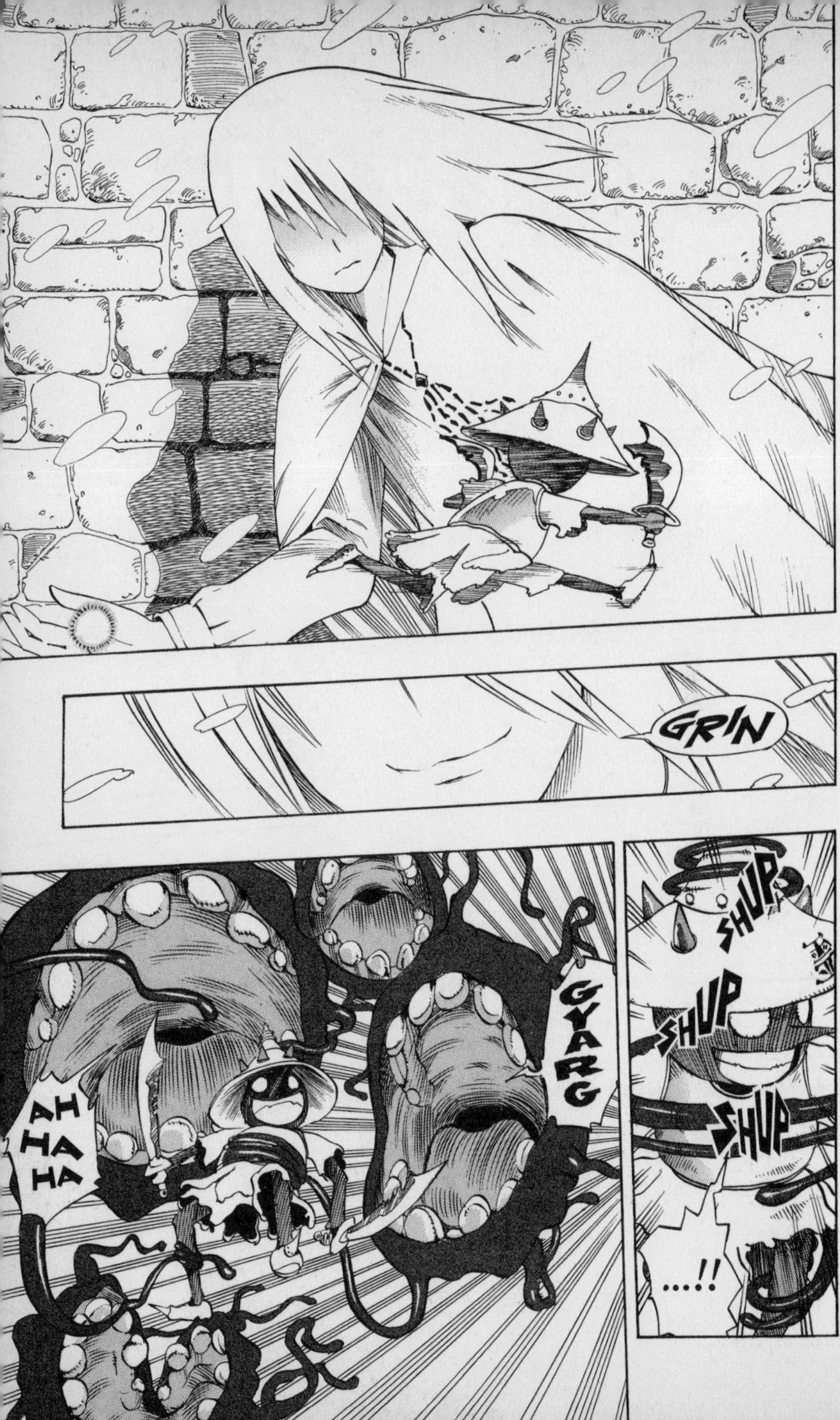
GRIN
SHUP
SHUP
SHUP
....!!
GYARG
AH HA HA HA

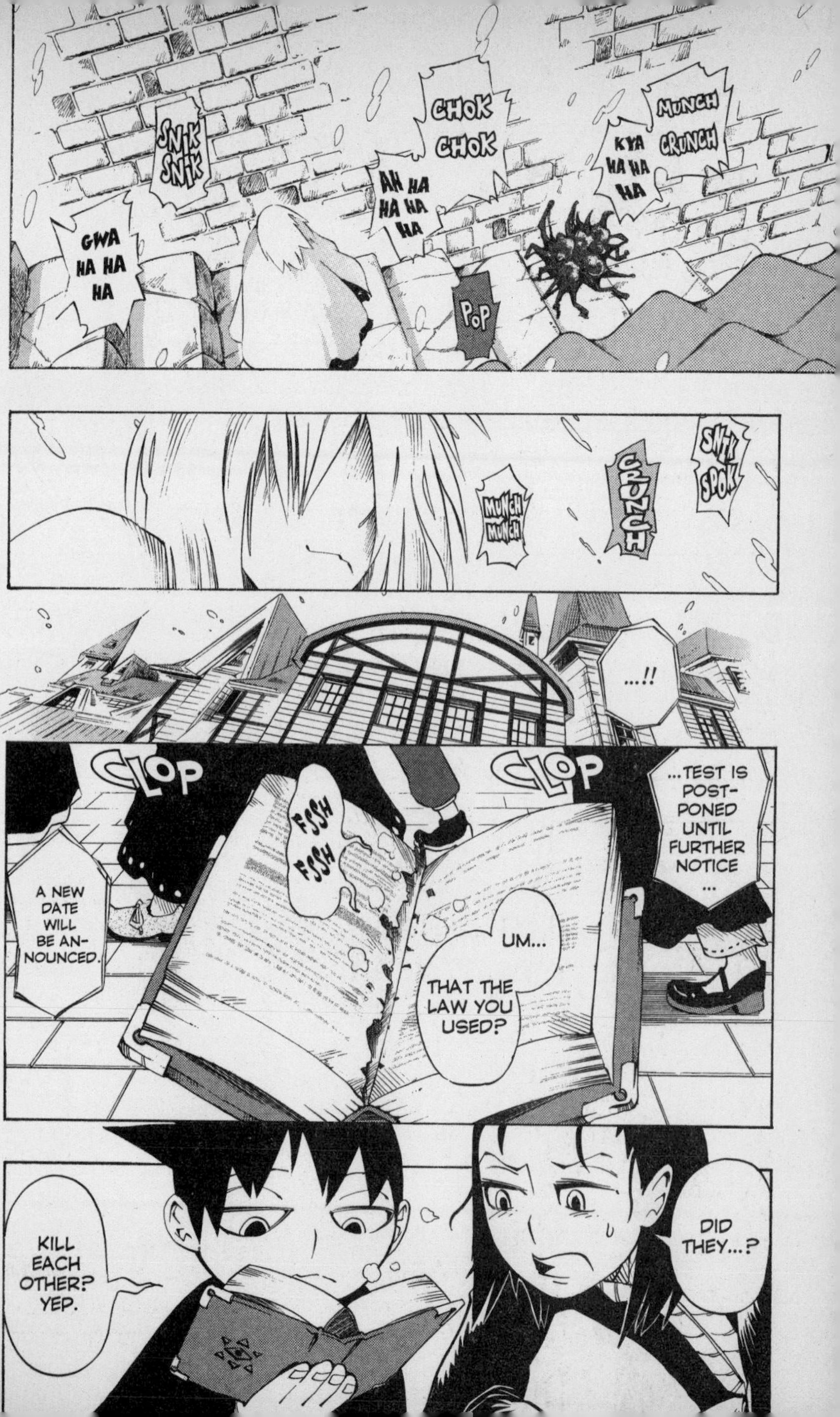
MUNCH CRUNCH
KYA HA HA HA
CHOK CHOK
AH HA HA HA HA
POP
SNIK SNIK
GWA HA HA HA
SNIK SPOK
CRUNCH
MUNCH MUNCH
...!!
CLOP
...TEST IS POST-PONED UNTIL FURTHER NOTICE ...
CLOP
FSSH FSSH
A NEW DATE WILL BE AN-NOUNCED.
UM...
THAT THE LAW YOU USED?
DID THEY...?
KILL EACH OTHER? YEP.

READ THIS WAY

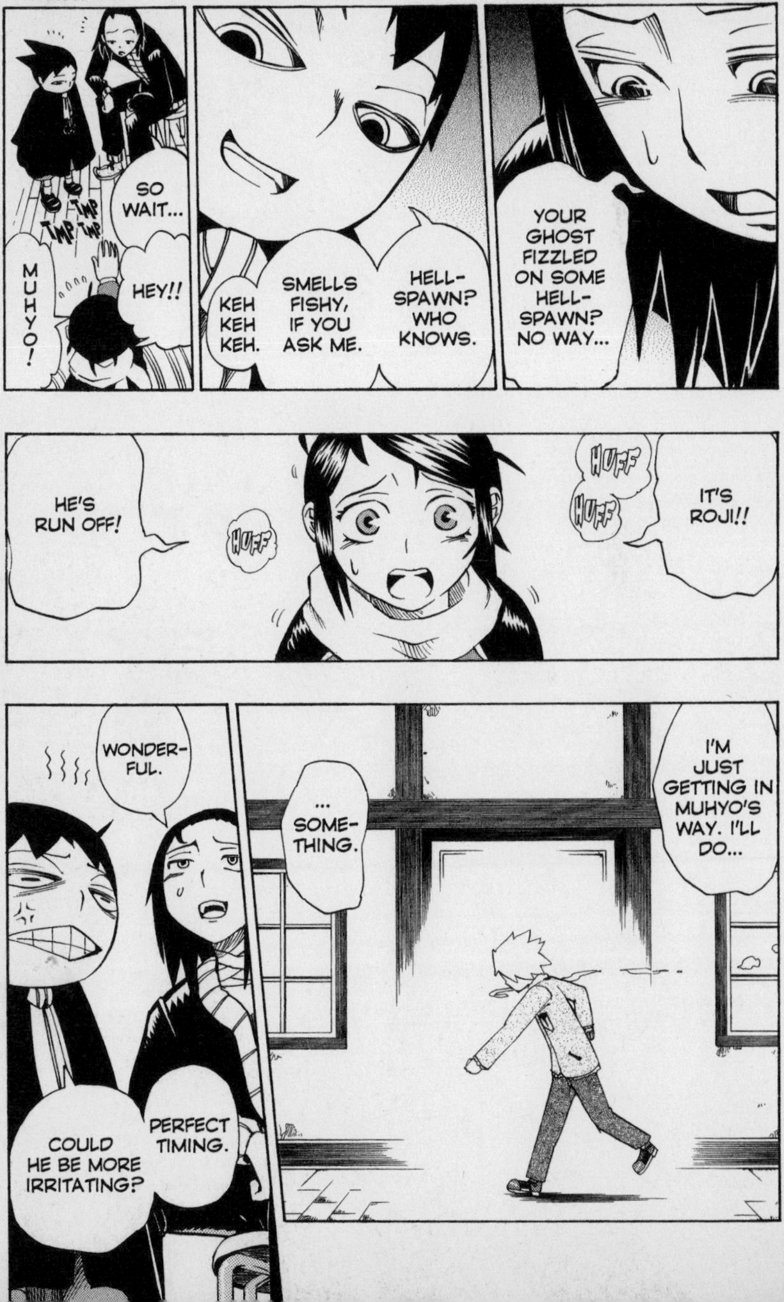
YOUR GHOST FIZZLED ON SOME HELL-SPAWN? NO WAY...
HELL-SPAWN? WHO KNOWS.
SMELLS FISHY, IF YOU ASK ME.
KEH KEH KEH.
SO WAIT...
TMP TMP TMP TMP
HEY!!
MUHYO!
IT'S ROJI!!
HUFF HUFF
HUFF
HE'S RUN OFF!
I'M JUST GETTING IN MUHYO'S WAY. I'LL DO...
... SOME-THING.
WONDER-FUL.
PERFECT TIMING.
COULD HE BE MORE IRRITATING?

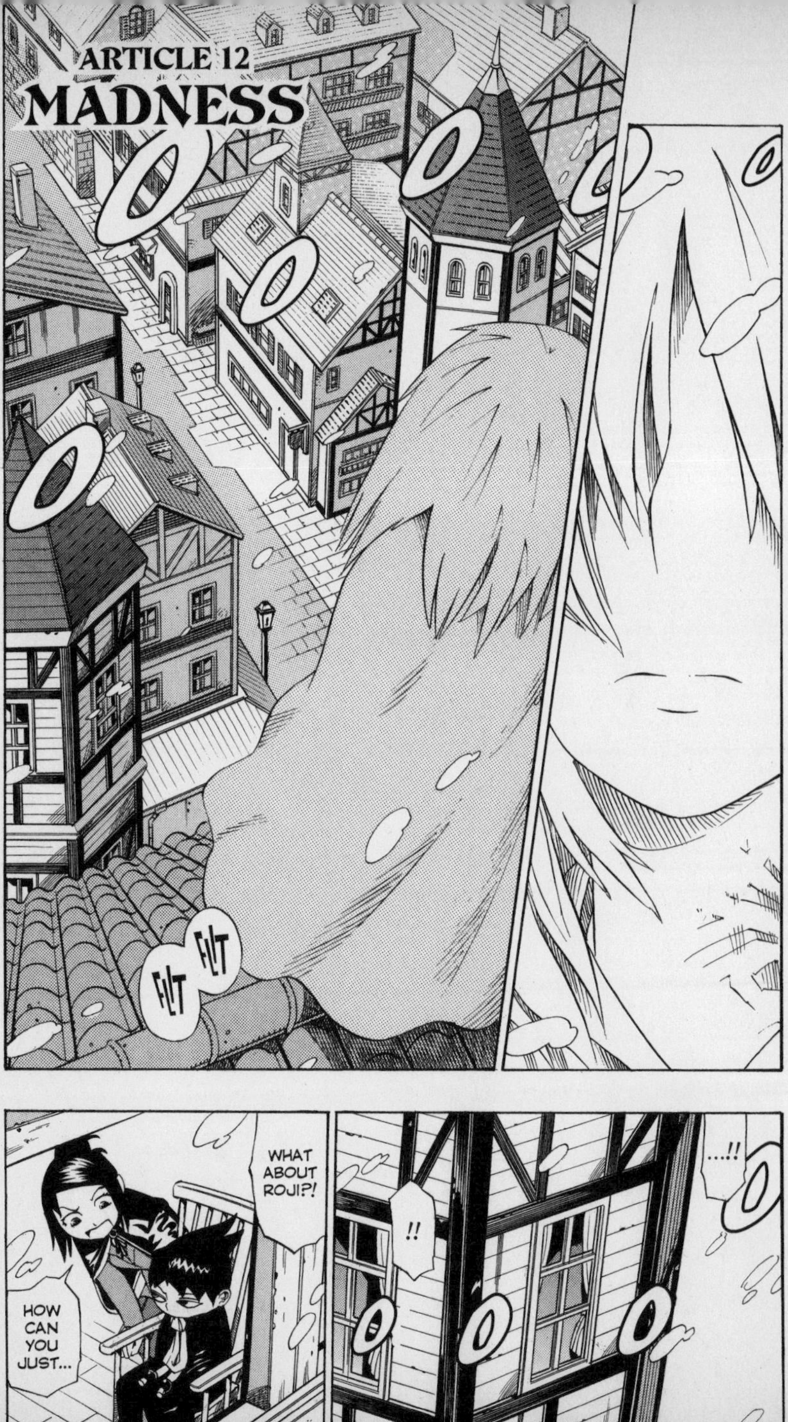

ARTICLE 12
MADNESS
FLIT FLIT
...!!
!!
WHAT ABOUT ROJI?!
HOW CAN YOU JUST...

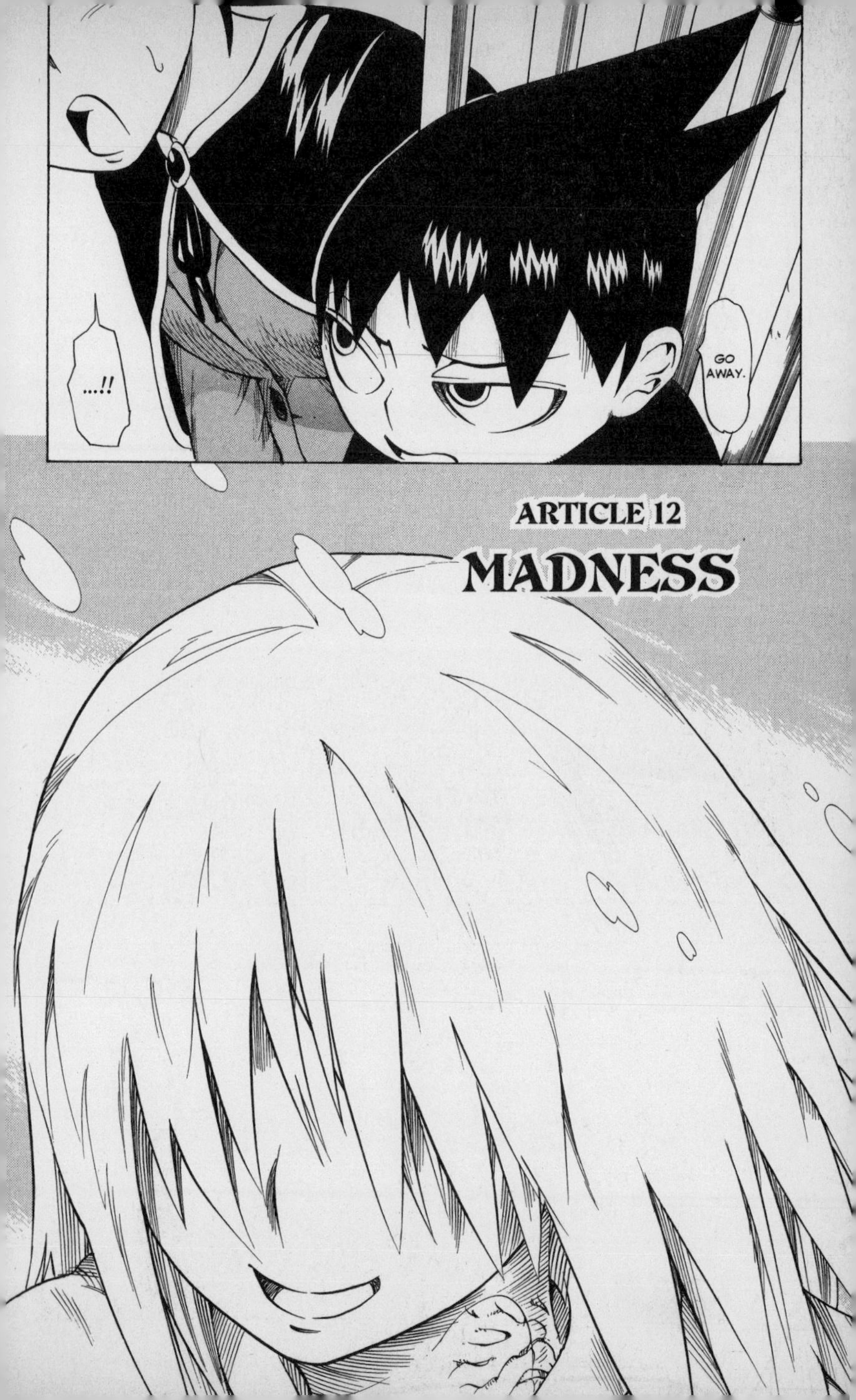
GO AWAY.
...!!
ARTICLE 12
MADNESS

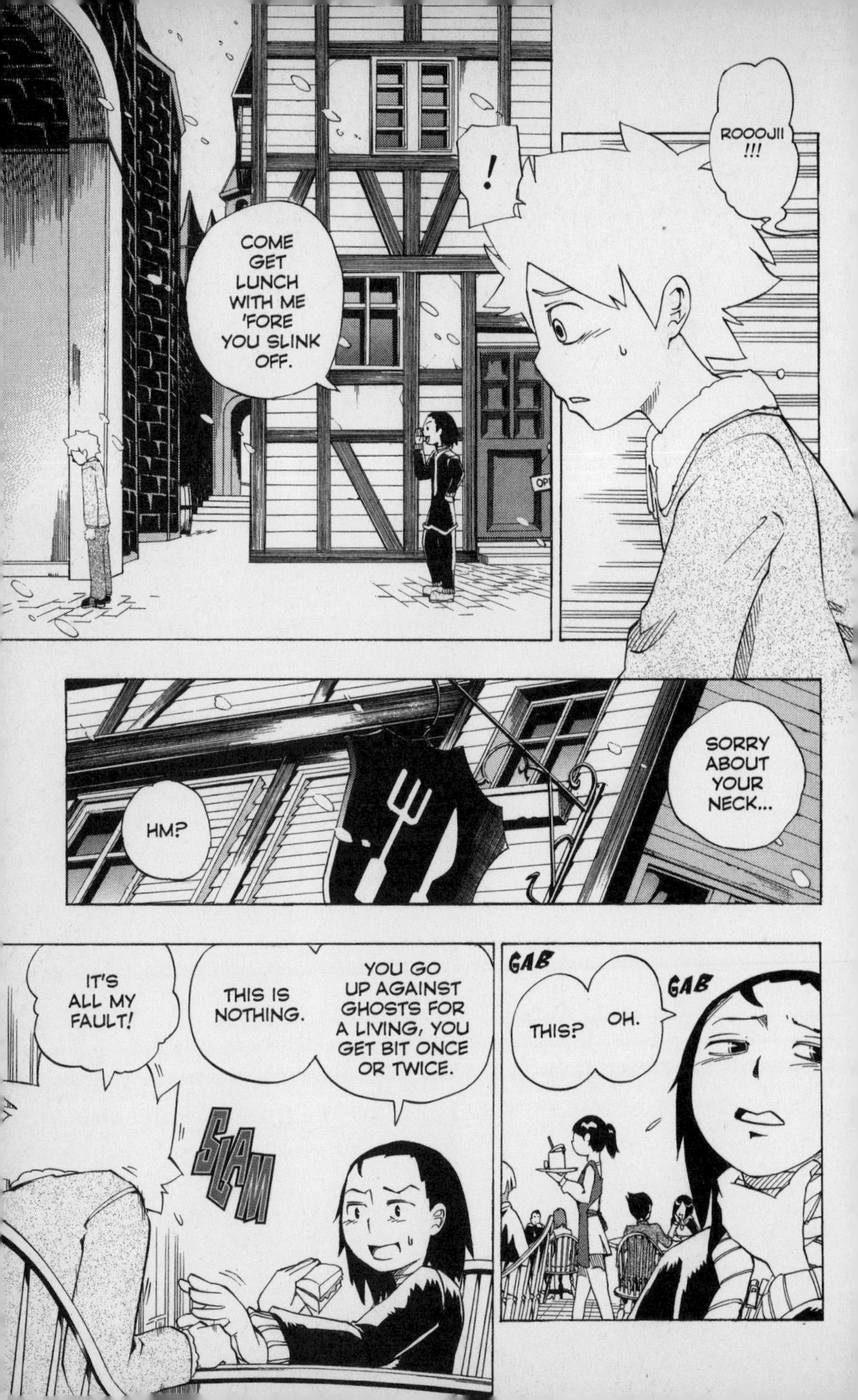
ROOOJII !!!
!
COME GET LUNCH WITH ME 'FORE YOU SLINK OFF.
SORRY ABOUT YOUR NECK...
HM?
GAB
OH.
THIS?
GAB
YOU GO UP AGAINST GHOSTS FOR A LIVING, YOU GET BIT ONCE OR TWICE.
THIS IS NOTHING.
IT'S ALL MY FAULT!
SLAM

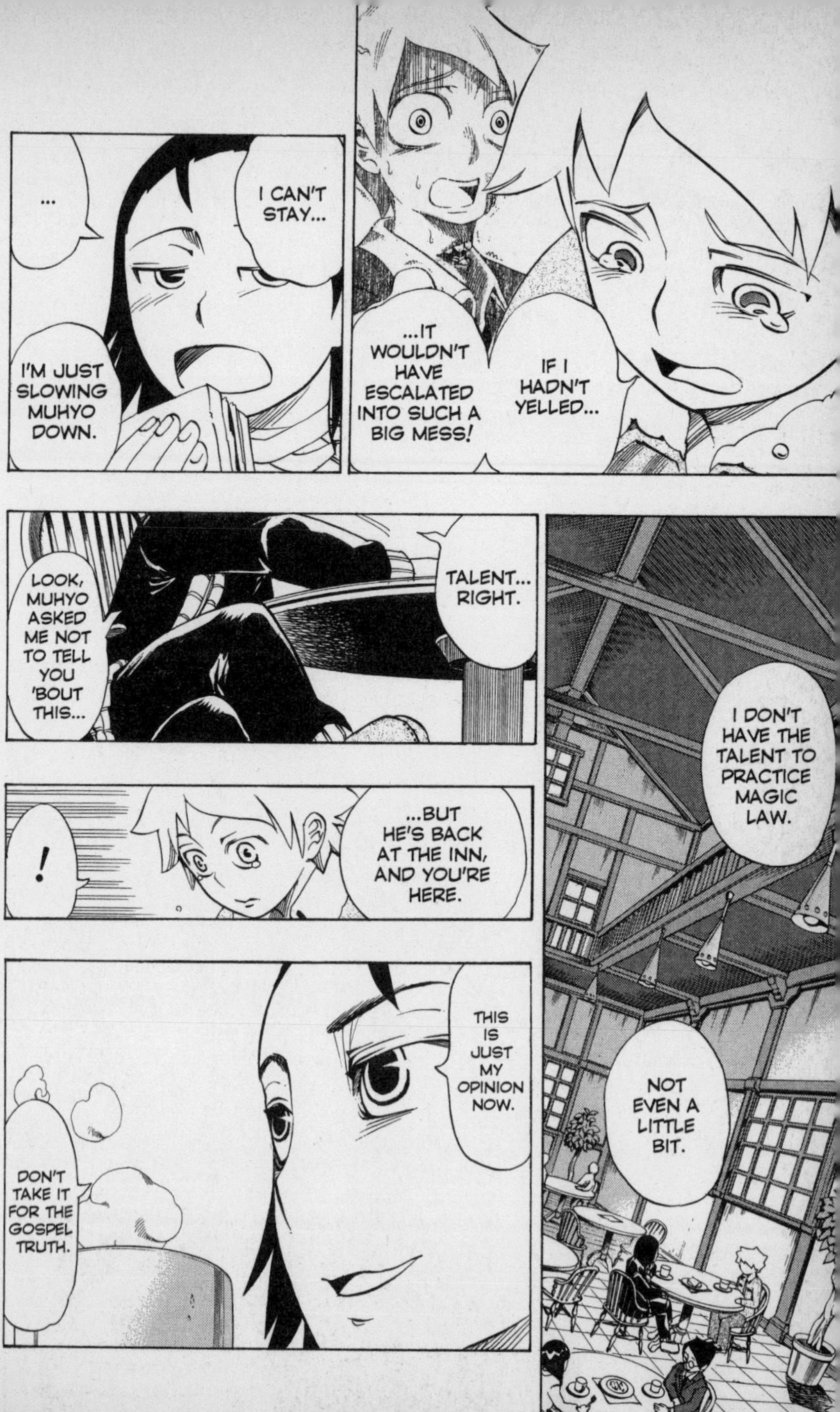
IF I HADN'T YELLED...
...IT WOULDN'T HAVE ESCALATED INTO SUCH A BIG MESS!
I CAN'T STAY...
...
I'M JUST SLOWING MUHYO DOWN.
I DON'T HAVE THE TALENT TO PRACTICE MAGIC LAW.
NOT EVEN A LITTLE BIT.
TALENT... RIGHT.
LOOK, MUHYO ASKED ME NOT TO TELL YOU 'BOUT THIS...
...BUT HE'S BACK AT THE INN, AND YOU'RE HERE.
!
THIS IS JUST MY OPINION NOW.
DON'T TAKE IT FOR THE GOSPEL TRUTH.

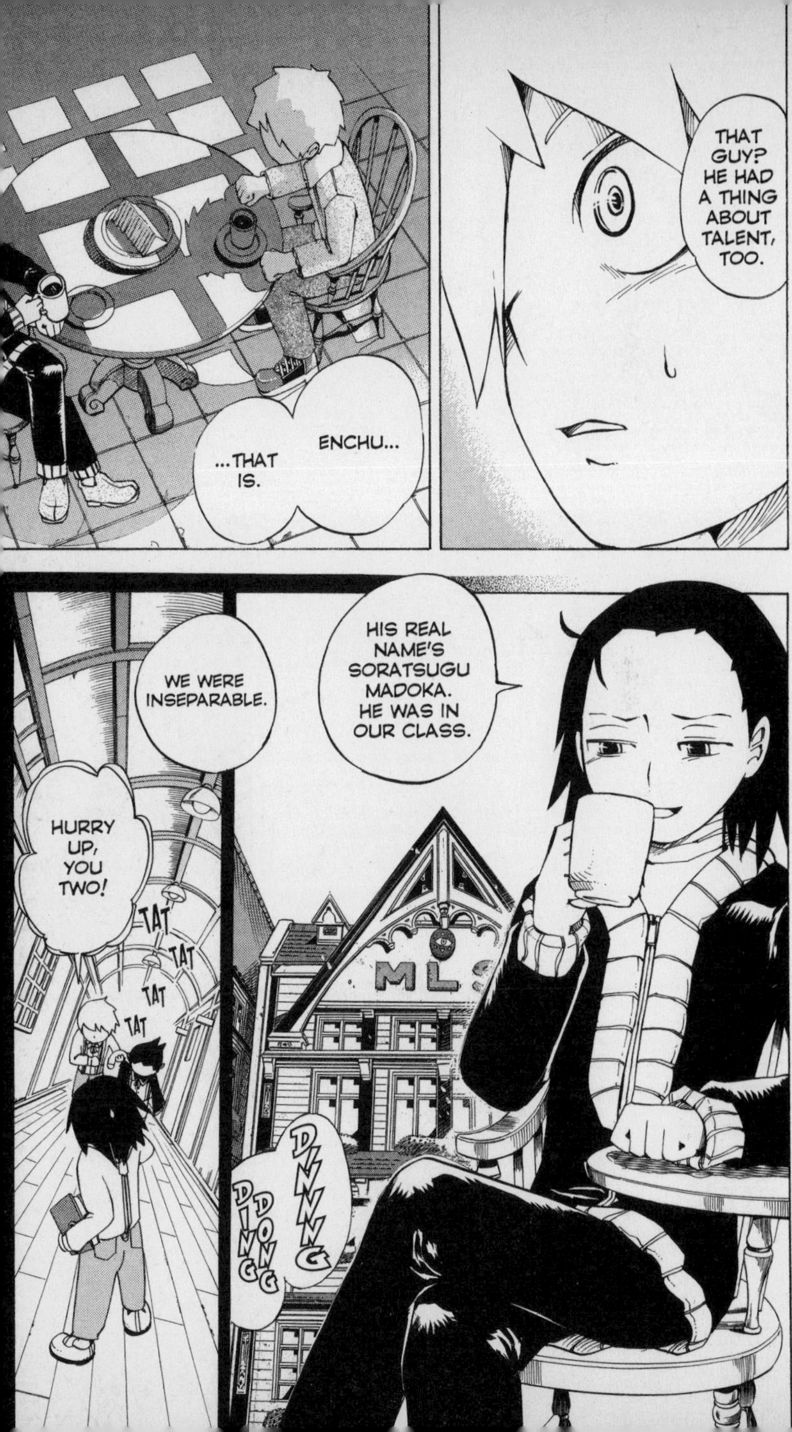
THAT GUY? HE HAD A THING ABOUT TALENT, TOO.
ENCHU...
...THAT IS.
HIS REAL NAME'S SORATSUGU MADOKA. HE WAS IN OUR CLASS.
ML
DINNNG
DING DONG
WE WERE INSEPARABLE.
HURRY UP, YOU TWO!
TAT
TAT
TAT
TAT

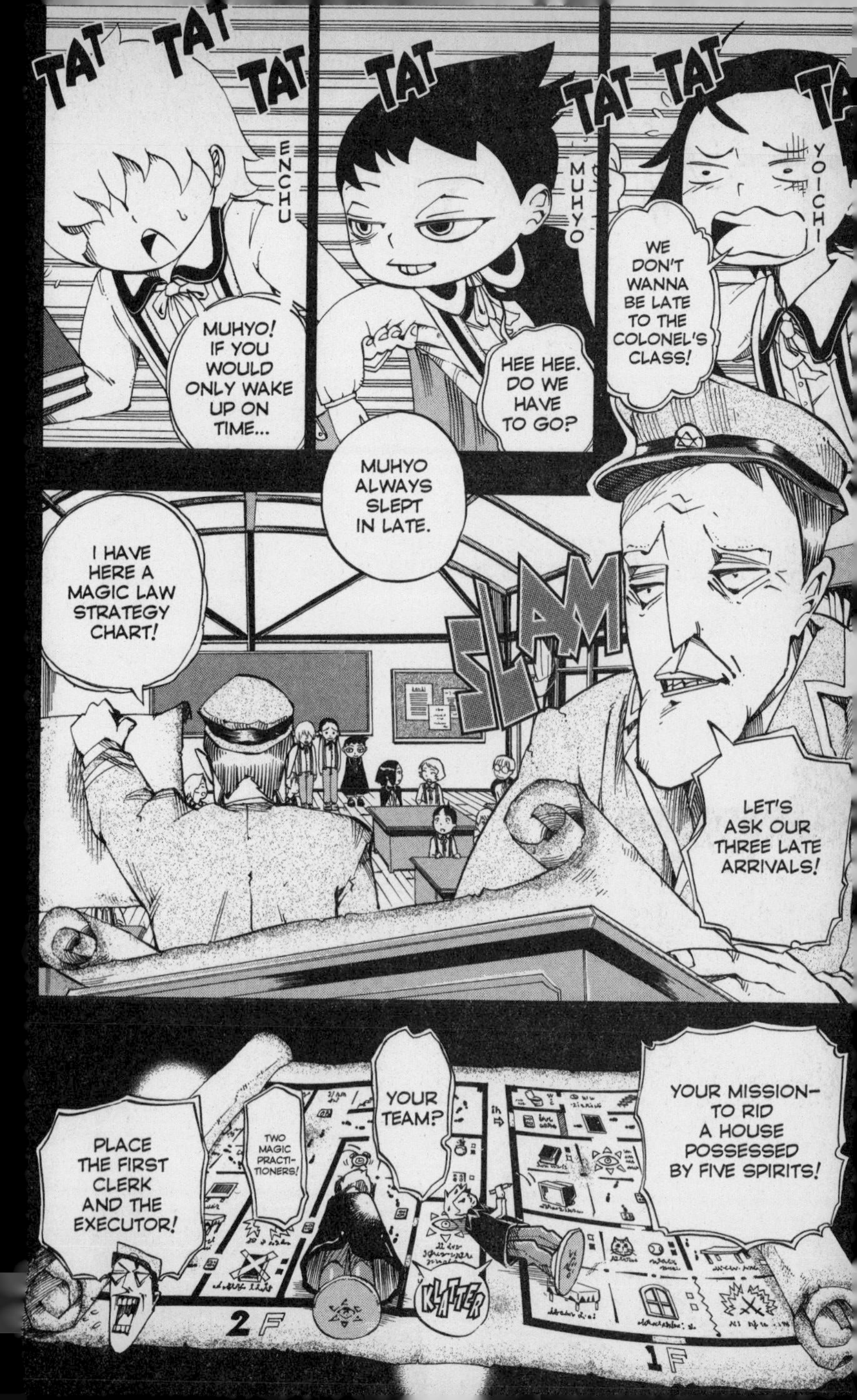
TAT TAT
YOICHI
WE DON'T WANNA BE LATE TO THE COLONEL'S CLASS!
TAT
MUHYO
HEE HEE. DO WE HAVE TO GO?
TAT TAT TAT
ENCHU
MUHYO! IF YOU WOULD ONLY WAKE UP ON TIME...
MUHYO ALWAYS SLEPT IN LATE.
SLAM
I HAVE HERE A MAGIC LAW STRATEGY CHART!
LET'S ASK OUR THREE LATE ARRIVALS!
YOUR MISSION- TO RID A HOUSE POSSESSED BY FIVE SPIRITS!
1F
YOUR TEAM?
TWO MAGIC PRACTI- TIONERS!
KLATTER
PLACE THE FIRST CLERK AND THE EXECUTOR!
2F

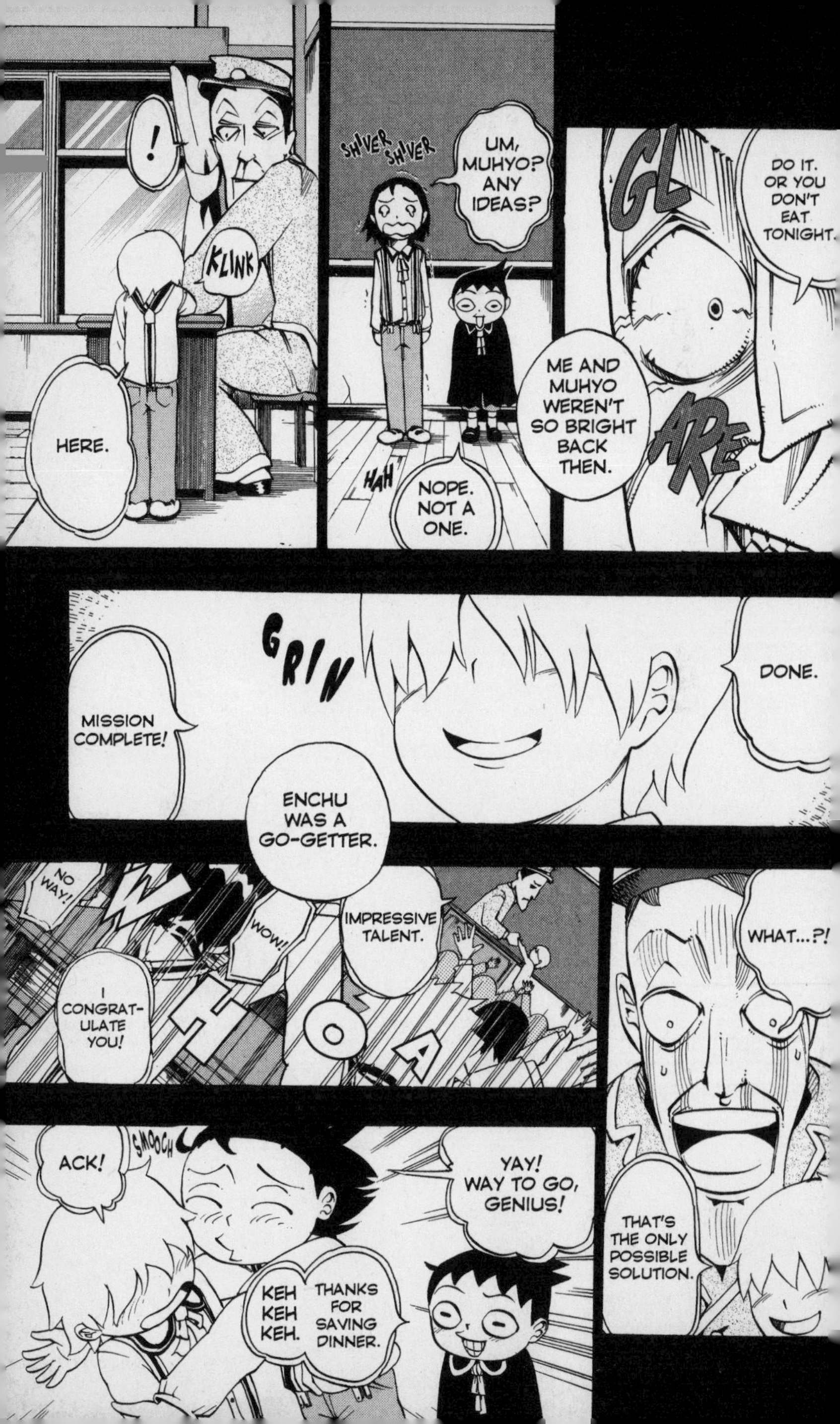
DO IT. OR YOU DON'T EAT TONIGHT.
GL
ARE
ME AND MUHYO WEREN'T SO BRIGHT BACK THEN.
SHIVER SHIVER
UM, MUHYO? ANY IDEAS?
HAH
NOPE. NOT A ONE.
!
KLINK
HERE.
DONE.
GRIN
MISSION COMPLETE!
ENCHU WAS A GO-GETTER.
WHAT...?!
THAT'S THE ONLY POSSIBLE SOLUTION.
IMPRESSIVE TALENT.
WOW!
NO WAY!
WHOA
I CONGRAT-ULATE YOU!
YAY! WAY TO GO, GENIUS!
THANKS FOR SAVING DINNER.
KEH KEH KEH.
SMOOCH
ACK!

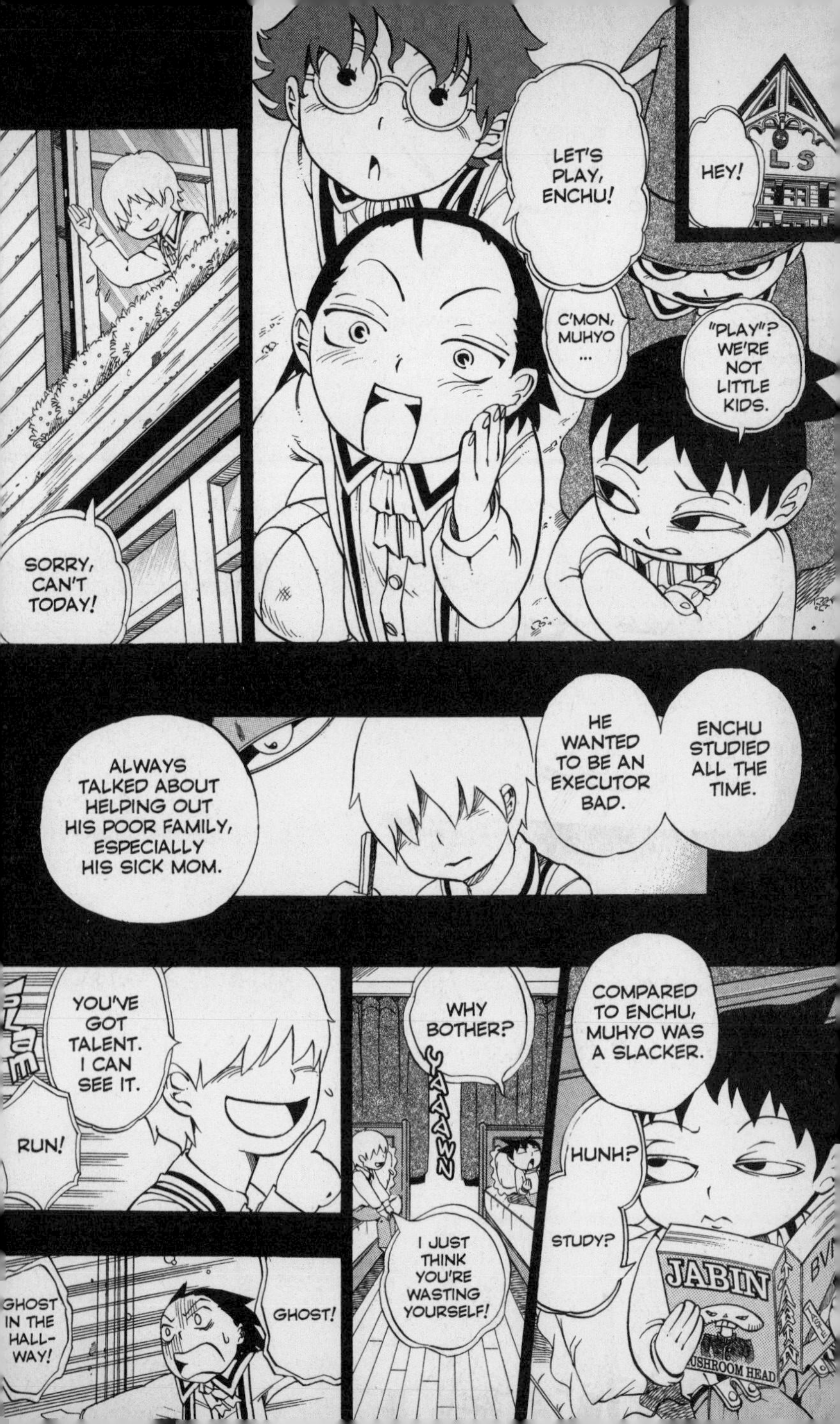
HEY!
LET'S PLAY, ENCHU!
C'MON, MUHYO ...
"PLAY"? WE'RE NOT LITTLE KIDS.
SORRY, CAN'T TODAY!
ENCHU STUDIED ALL THE TIME.
HE WANTED TO BE AN EXECUTOR BAD.
ALWAYS TALKED ABOUT HELPING OUT HIS POOR FAMILY, ESPECIALLY HIS SICK MOM.
COMPARED TO ENCHU, MUHYO WAS A SLACKER.
HUNH?
STUDY?
JABIN
MUSHROOM HEAD
WHY BOTHER?
YAAAAWN
I JUST THINK YOU'RE WASTING YOURSELF!
YOU'VE GOT TALENT. I CAN SEE IT.
RUN!
GHOST!
GHOST IN THE HALL-WAY!

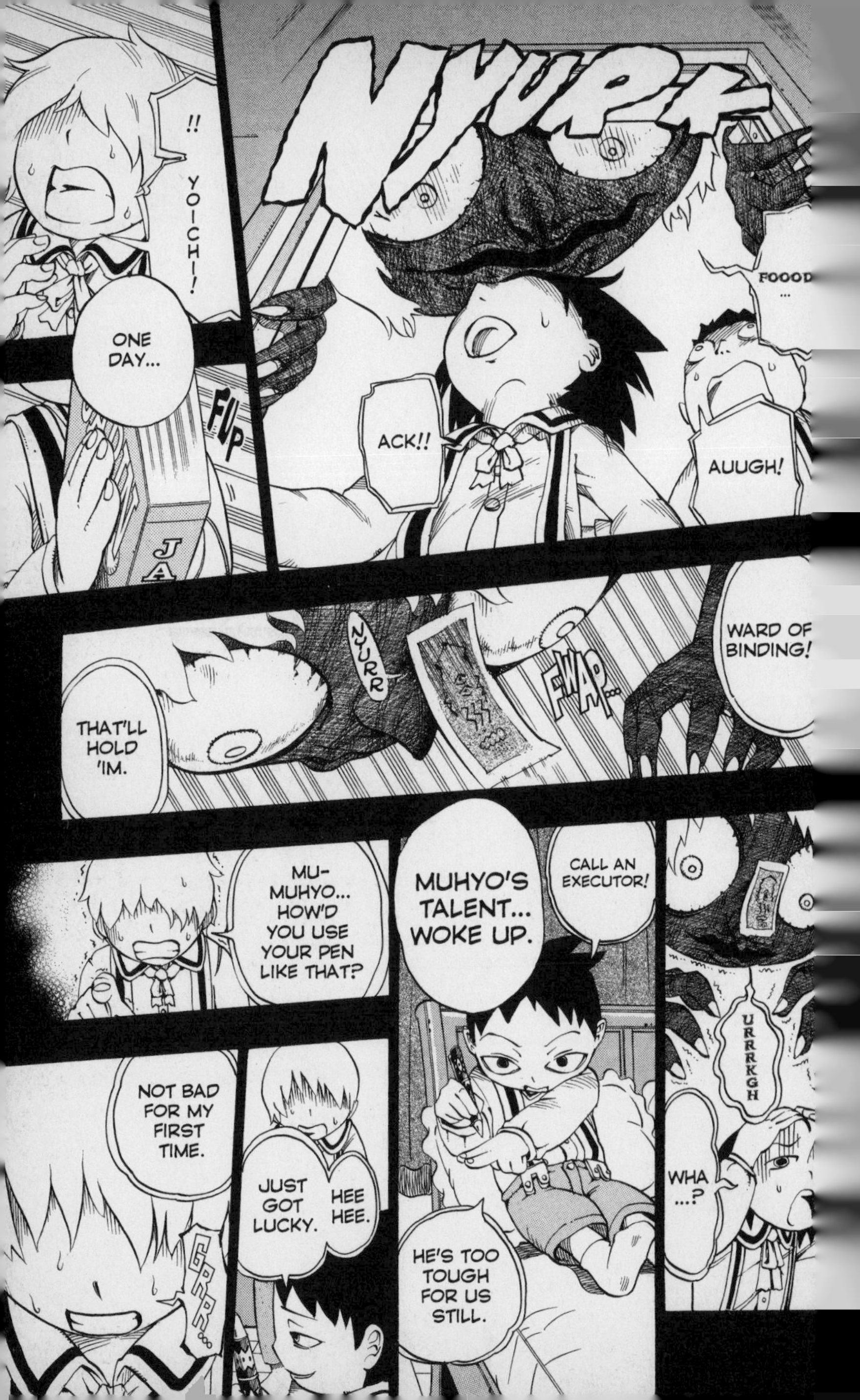
NYUPK
FOOOD...
AUUGH!
ACK!!
!!
YOICHI!
ONE DAY...
FUP
WARD OF BINDING!
FWAP...
NYURR
THAT'LL HOLD 'IM.
URRRKGH
WHA...?
CALL AN EXECUTOR!
MUHYO'S TALENT... WOKE UP.
HE'S TOO TOUGH FOR US STILL.
MU-MUHYO... HOW'D YOU USE YOUR PEN LIKE THAT?
HEE HEE.
JUST GOT LUCKY.
NOT BAD FOR MY FIRST TIME.
GRRR...

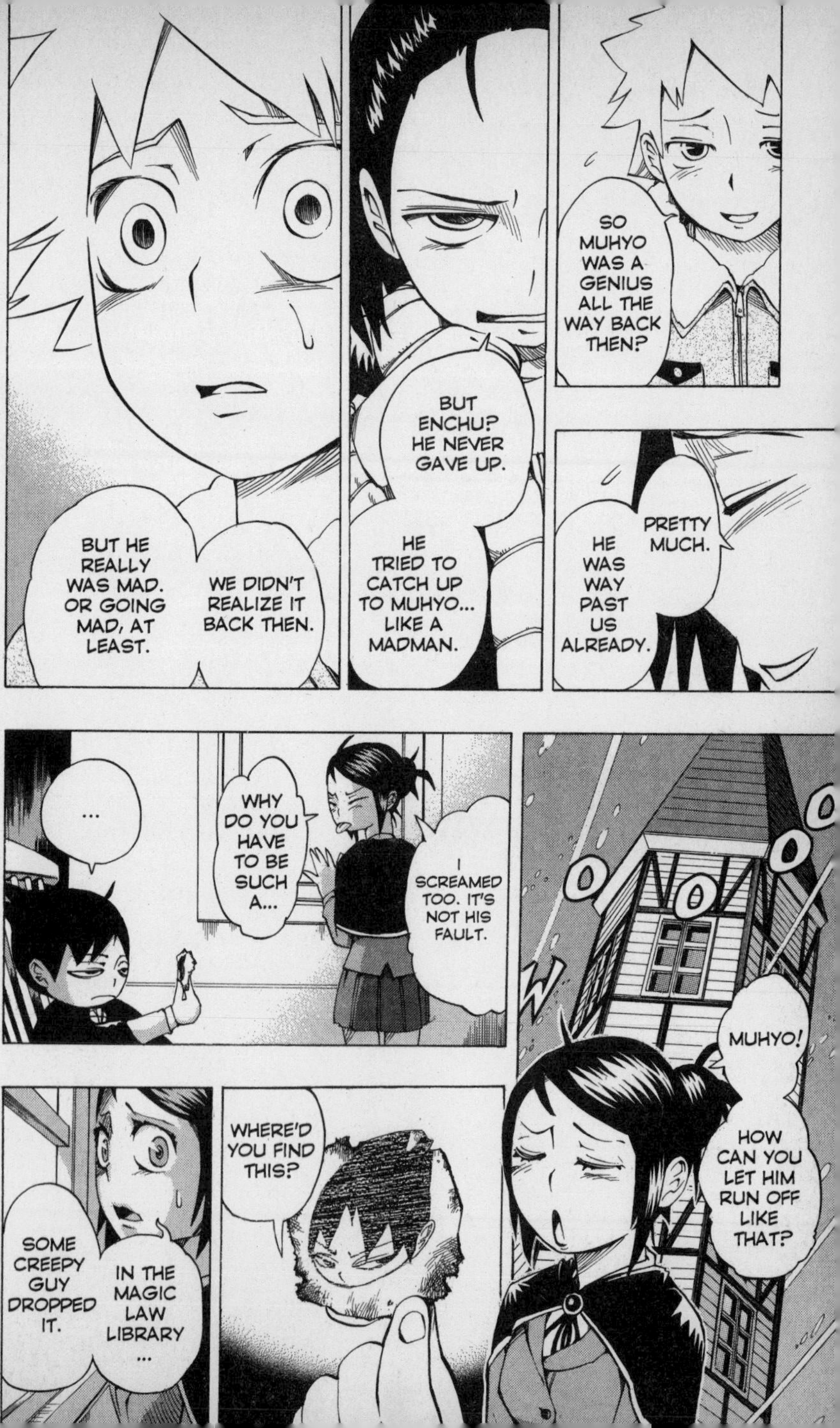
SO MUHYO WAS A GENIUS ALL THE WAY BACK THEN?
PRETTY MUCH.
HE WAS WAY PAST US ALREADY.
BUT ENCHU? HE NEVER GAVE UP.
HE TRIED TO CATCH UP TO MUHYO... LIKE A MADMAN.
WE DIDN'T REALIZE IT BACK THEN.
BUT HE REALLY WAS MAD. OR GOING MAD, AT LEAST.
OOOO
MUHYO!
HOW CAN YOU LET HIM RUN OFF LIKE THAT?
I SCREAMED TOO. IT'S NOT HIS FAULT.
WHY DO YOU HAVE TO BE SUCH A...
...
WHERE'D YOU FIND THIS?
IN THE MAGIC LAW LIBRARY ...
SOME CREEPY GUY DROPPED IT.

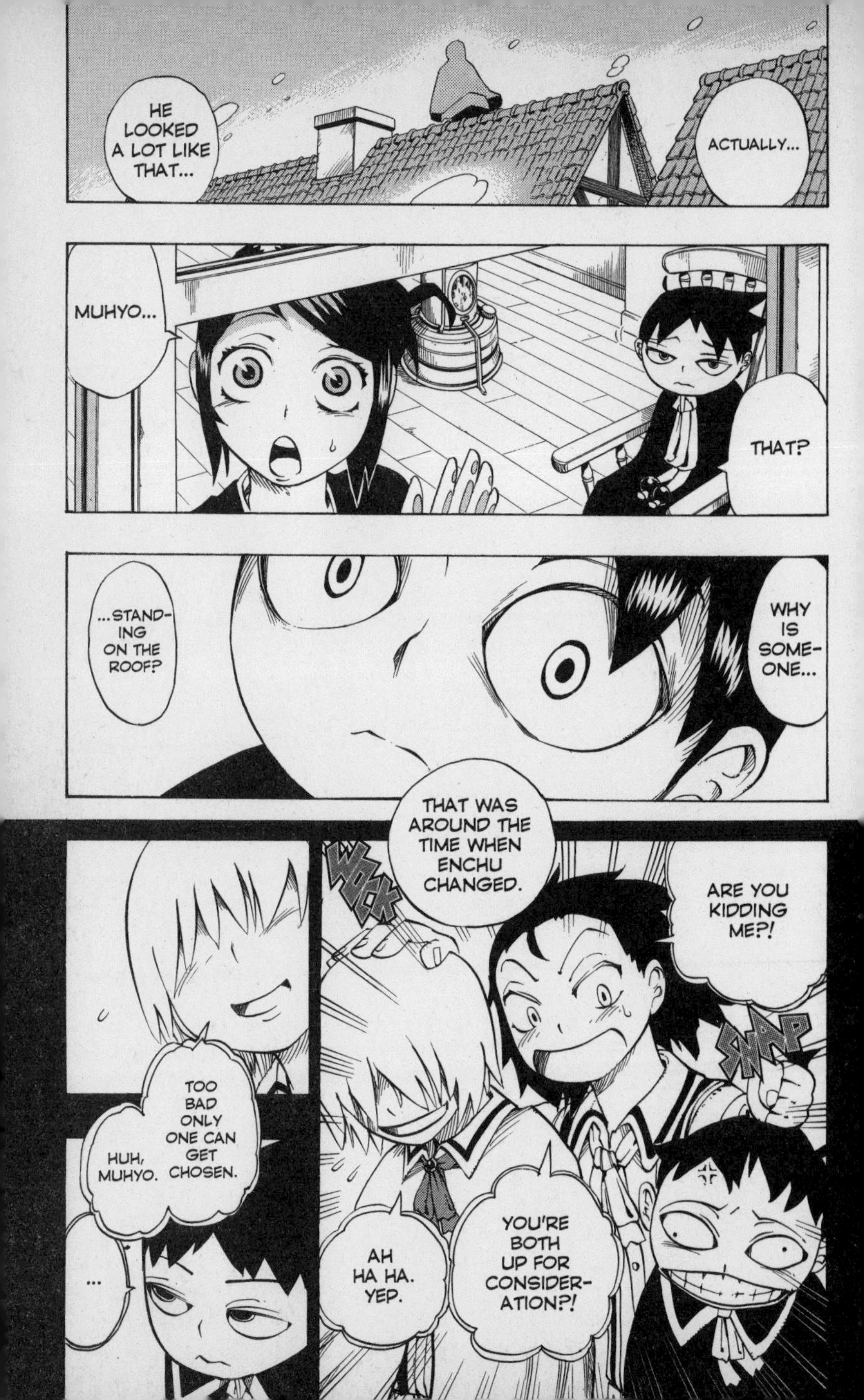
ACTUALLY...
HE LOOKED A LOT LIKE THAT...
THAT?
MUHYO...
WHY IS SOME-ONE...
...STAND-ING ON THE ROOF?
THAT WAS AROUND THE TIME WHEN ENCHU CHANGED.
WOCK
ARE YOU KIDDING ME?!
SNAP
YOU'RE BOTH UP FOR CONSIDER-ATION?!
AH HA HA. YEP.
TOO BAD ONLY ONE CAN GET CHOSEN.
HUH, MUHYO.
...

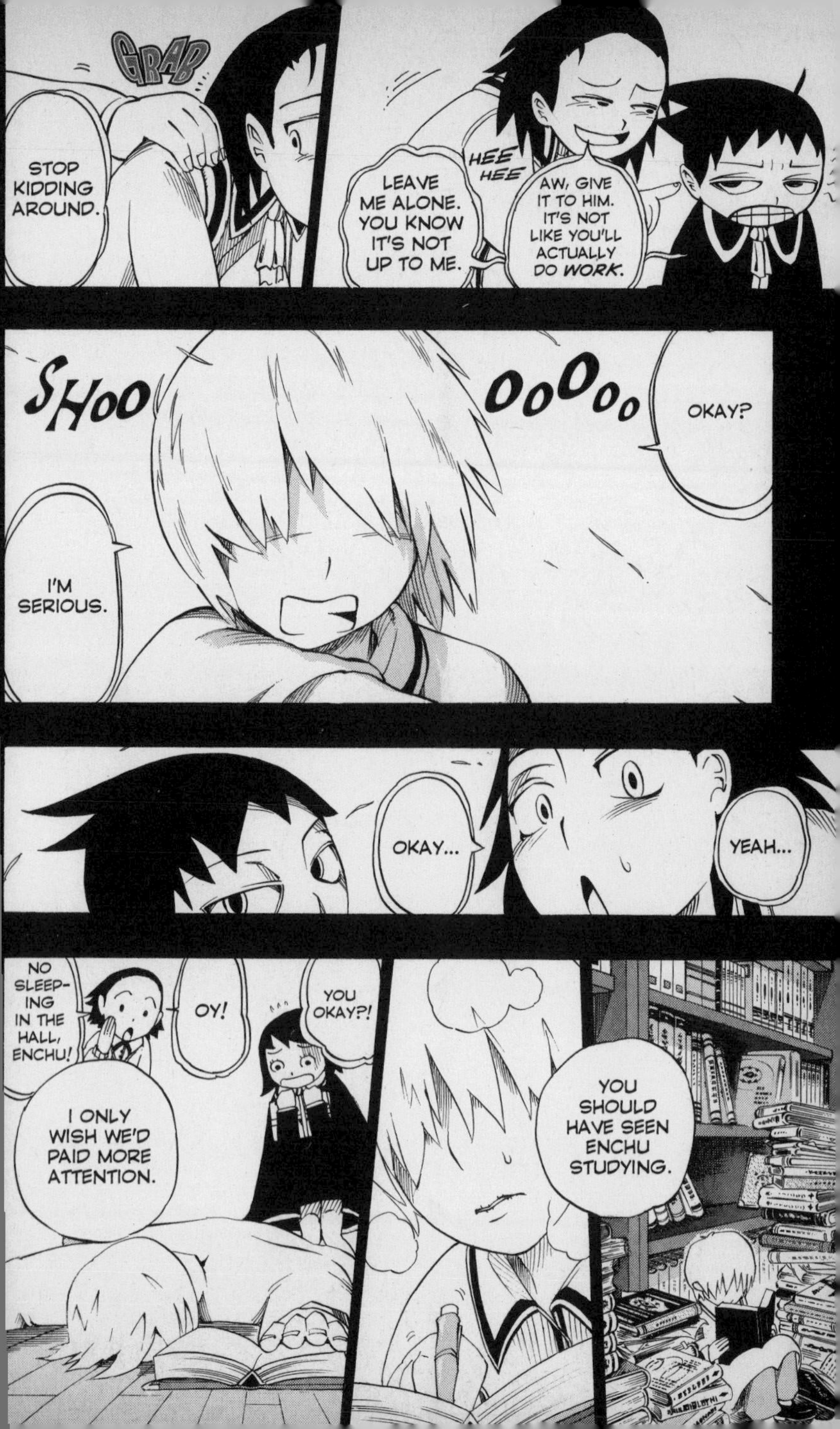
HEE HEE
AW, GIVE IT TO HIM. IT'S NOT LIKE YOU'LL ACTUALLY DO **WORK**.
LEAVE ME ALONE. YOU KNOW IT'S NOT UP TO ME.
GRAB
STOP KIDDING AROUND.
OKAY?
OOOOOO
SHOO
I'M SERIOUS.
YEAH...
OKAY...
YOU SHOULD HAVE SEEN ENCHU STUDYING.
YOU OKAY?!
OY!
NO SLEEP-ING IN THE HALL, ENCHU!
I ONLY WISH WE'D PAID MORE ATTENTION.

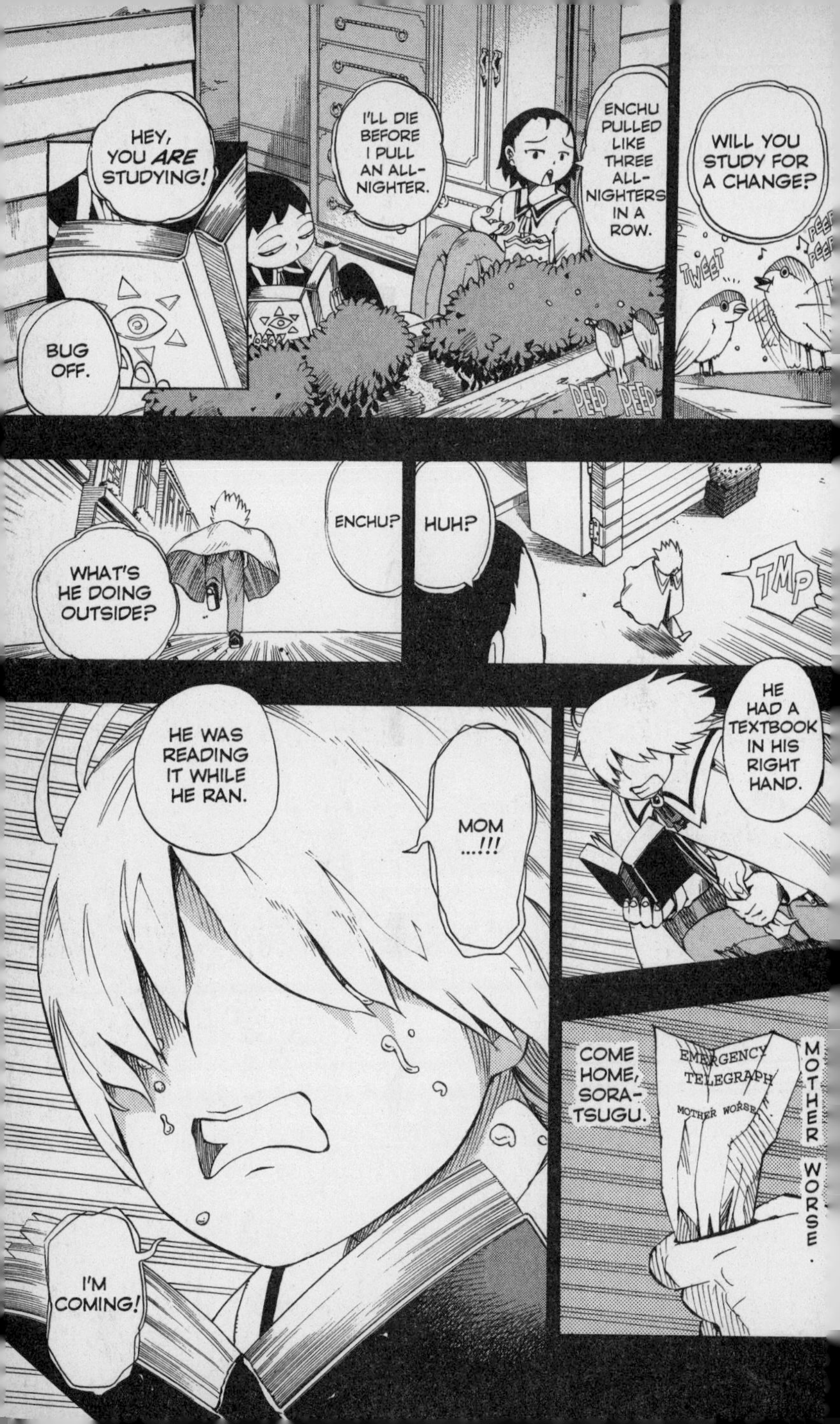

WILL YOU STUDY FOR A CHANGE?
TWEET
PEEP PEEP
ENCHU PULLED LIKE THREE ALL-NIGHTERS IN A ROW.
I'LL DIE BEFORE I PULL AN ALL-NIGHTER.
PEEP PEEP
HEY, YOU ***ARE*** STUDYING!
BUG OFF.
TMP
HUH?
ENCHU?
WHAT'S HE DOING OUTSIDE?
HE HAD A TEXTBOOK IN HIS RIGHT HAND.
MOTHER WORSE.
EMERGENCY TELEGRAPH
MOTHER WORSE
COME HOME, SORA-TSUGU.
HE WAS READING IT WHILE HE RAN.
MOM ...!!!
I'M COMING!

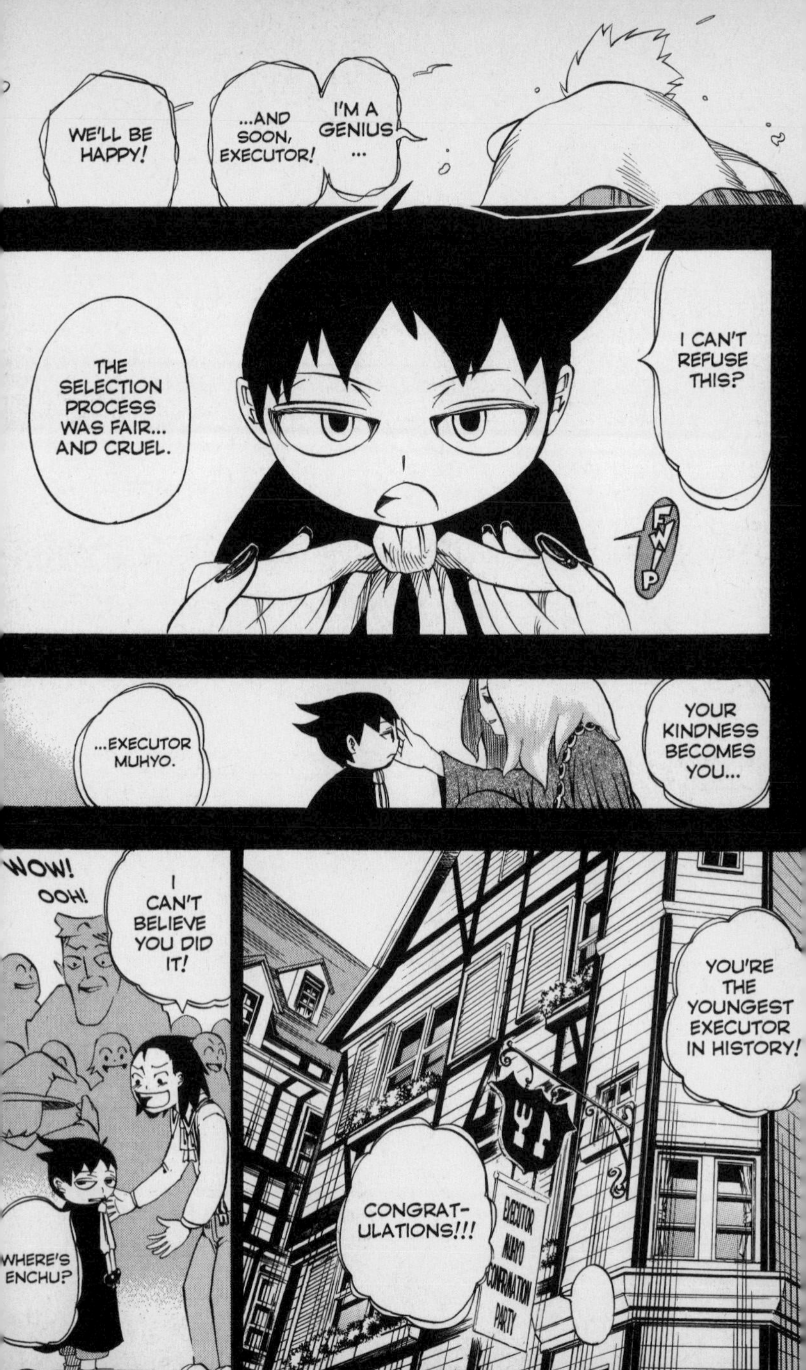
I'M A GENIUS...
...AND SOON, EXECUTOR!
WE'LL BE HAPPY!
I CAN'T REFUSE THIS?
FWIP
THE SELECTION PROCESS WAS FAIR... AND CRUEL.
YOUR KINDNESS BECOMES YOU...
...EXECUTOR MUHYO.
YOU'RE THE YOUNGEST EXECUTOR IN HISTORY!
EXECUTOR MUHYO CONFIRMATION PARTY
CONGRAT-ULATIONS!!!
WOW!
OOH!
I CAN'T BELIEVE YOU DID IT!
WHERE'S ENCHU?

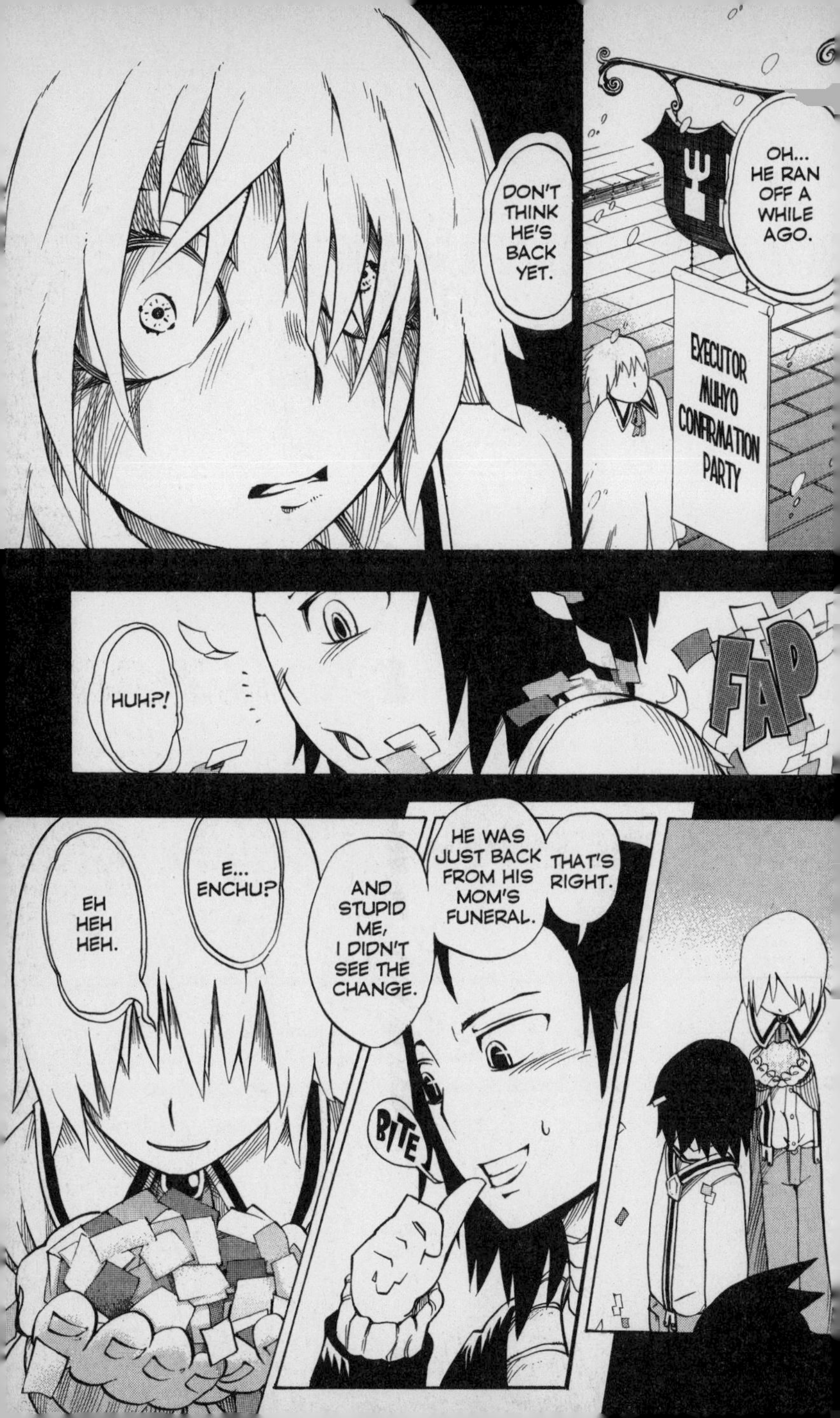
OH... HE RAN OFF A WHILE AGO.
EXECUTOR MUHYO CONFIRMATION PARTY
DON'T THINK HE'S BACK YET.
FAP
HUH?!
THAT'S RIGHT.
HE WAS JUST BACK FROM HIS MOM'S FUNERAL.
AND STUPID ME, I DIDN'T SEE THE CHANGE.
BITE
E... ENCHU?
EH HEH HEH.

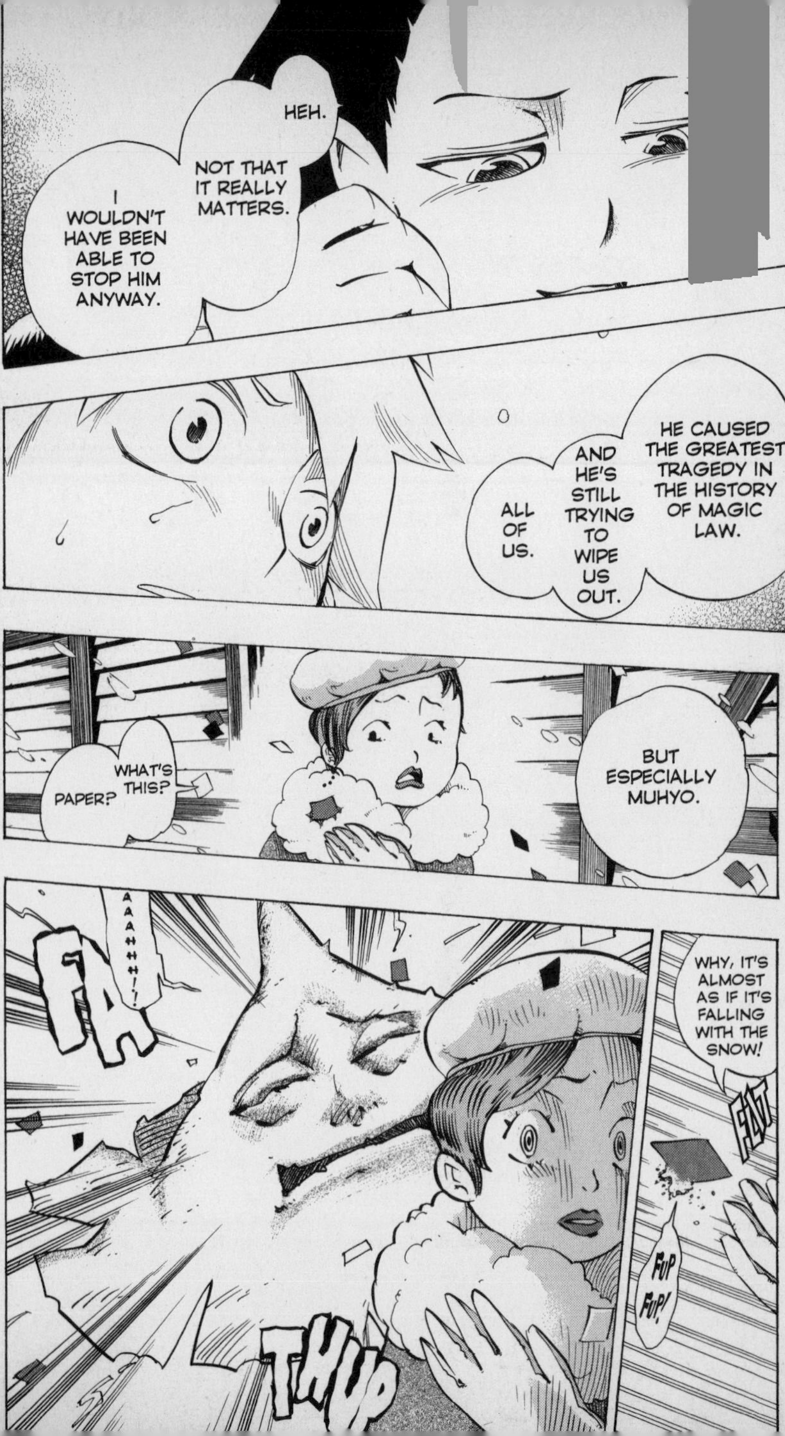
HEH.
NOT THAT IT REALLY MATTERS.
I WOULDN'T HAVE BEEN ABLE TO STOP HIM ANYWAY.
HE CAUSED THE GREATEST TRAGEDY IN THE HISTORY OF MAGIC LAW.
AND HE'S STILL TRYING TO WIPE US OUT.
ALL OF US.
BUT ESPECIALLY MUHYO.
WHAT'S THIS?
PAPER?
WHY, IT'S ALMOST AS IF IT'S FALLING WITH THE SNOW!
FLIT
FUP FUP!
AAAAHHHH!!
FA
THUMP

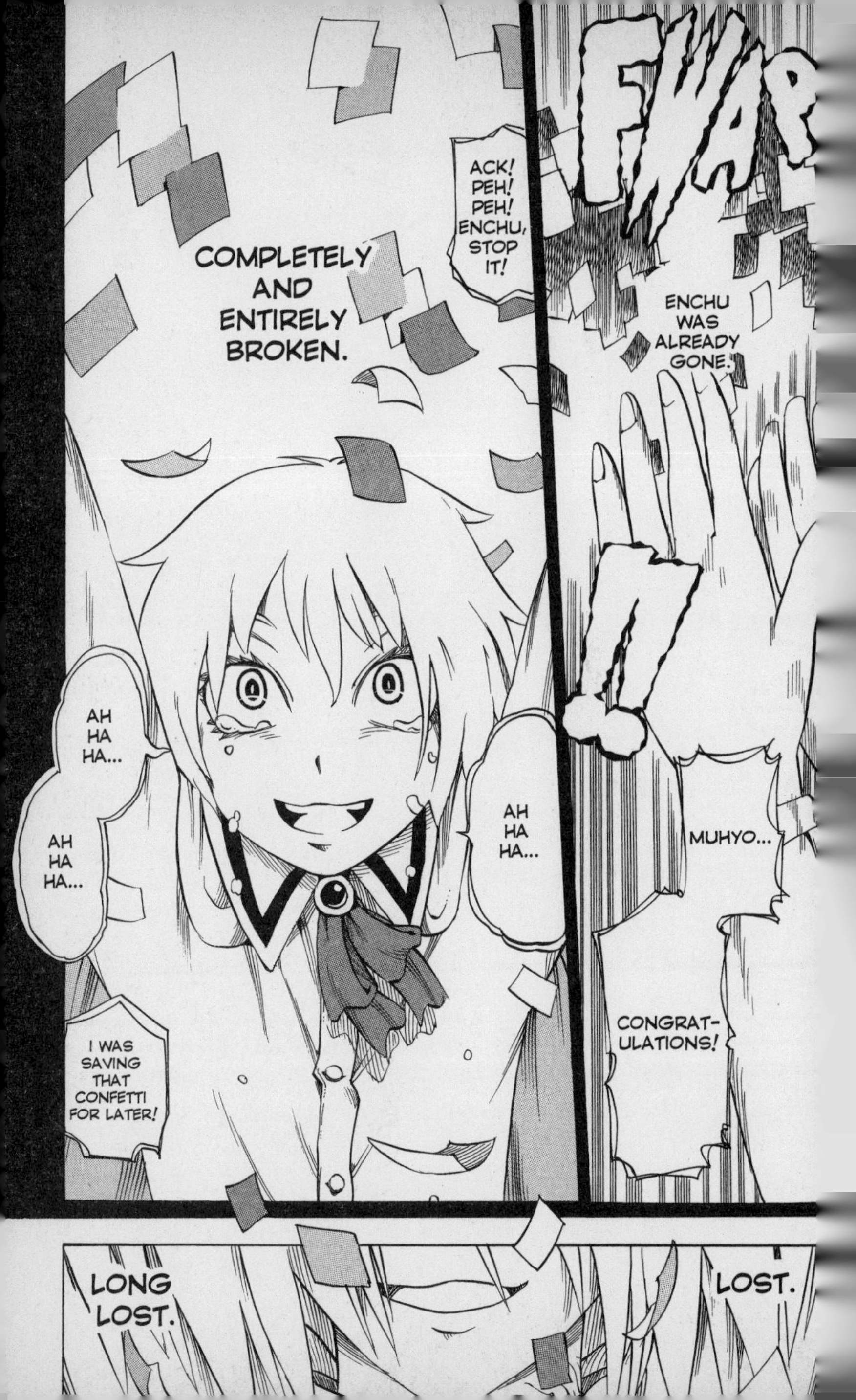
FWA
ENCHU WAS ALREADY GONE.
!
MUHYO...
CONGRAT-ULATIONS!
ACK! PEH! PEH! ENCHU, STOP IT!
COMPLETELY AND ENTIRELY BROKEN.
AH HA HA...
AH HA HA...
AH HA HA...
I WAS SAVING THAT CONFETTI FOR LATER!
LOST.
LONG LOST.

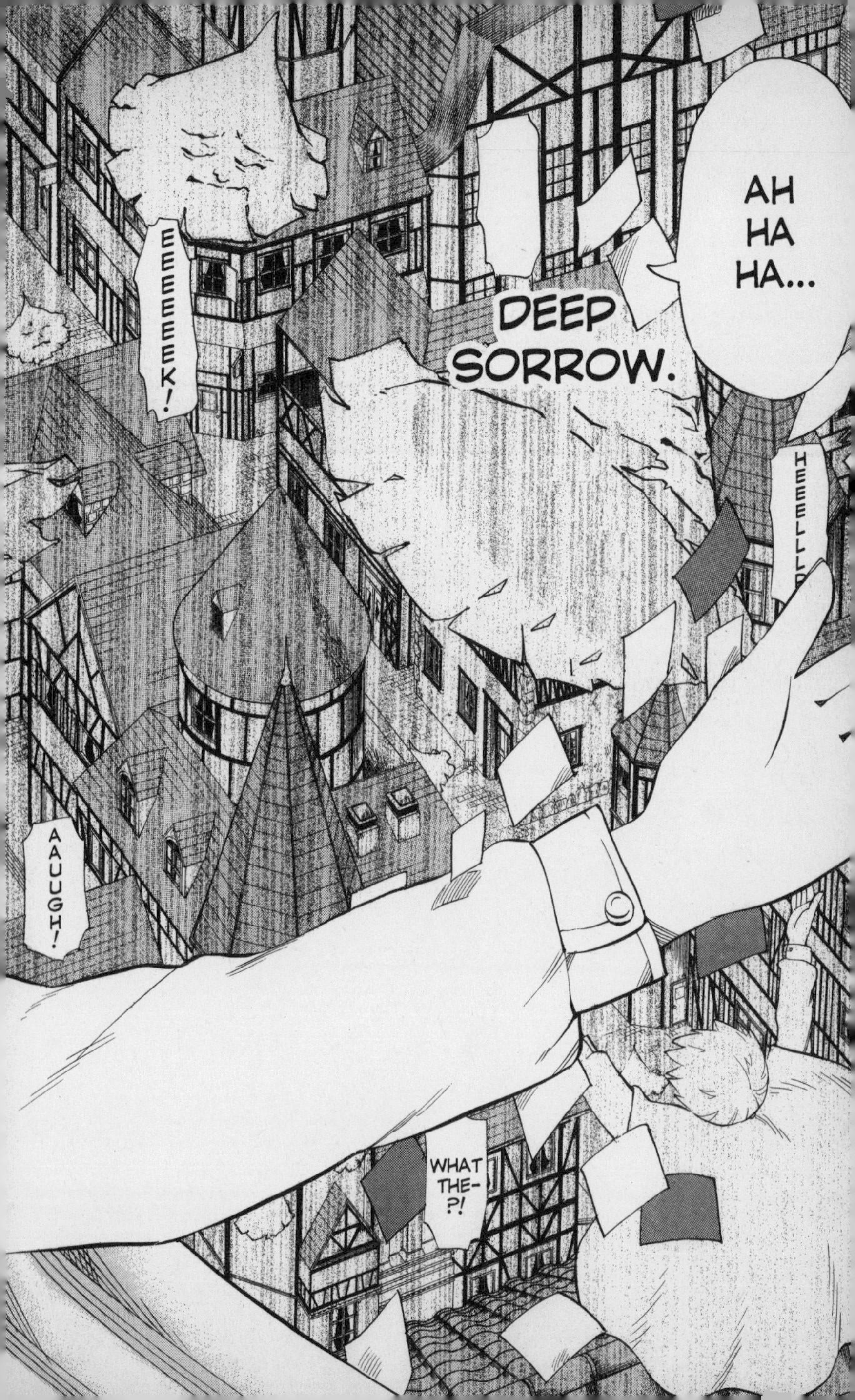
AH HA HA...
DEEP SORROW.
HEEELLL
EEEEEEEK!
AAUUGH!
WHAT THE-?!

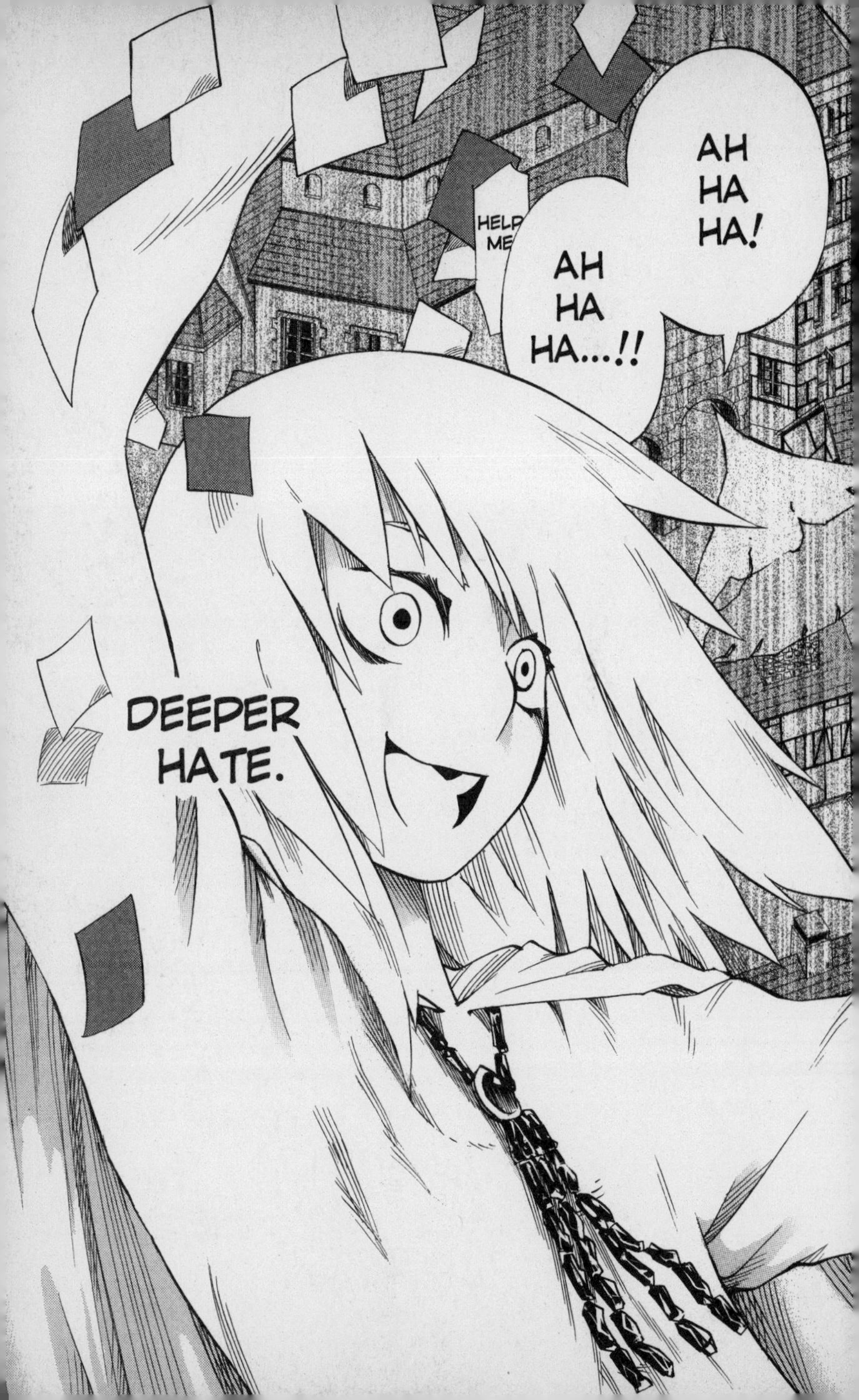
AH HA HA!
AH HA HA...!!
HELP ME
DEEPER HATE.

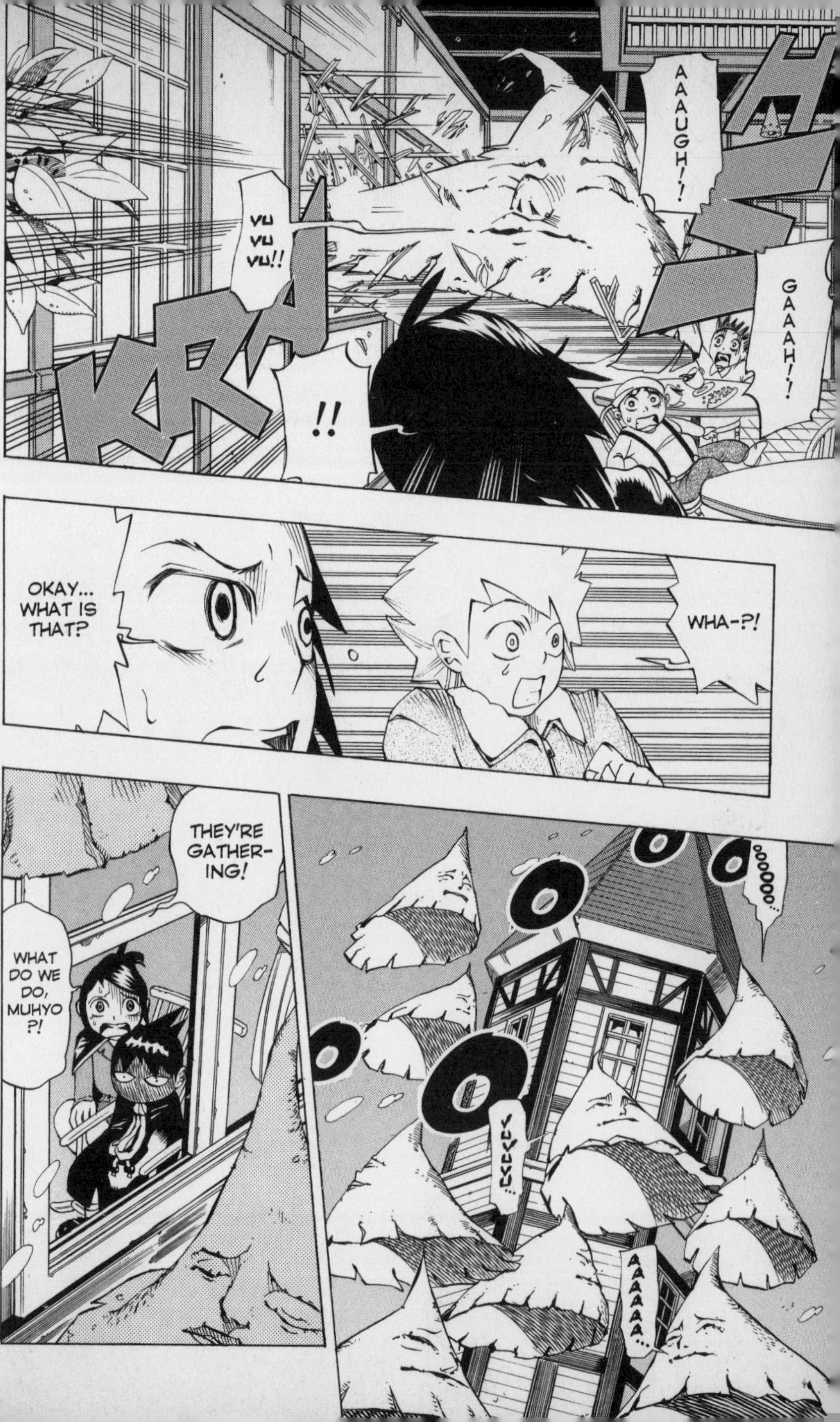
AAAUGH!!
GAAAH!!
VU VU VU!!
!!
WHA-?!
OKAY... WHAT IS THAT?
OOOOOO...
VVVVVV...
AAAAAA...
THEY'RE GATHER-ING!
WHAT DO WE DO, MUHYO?!

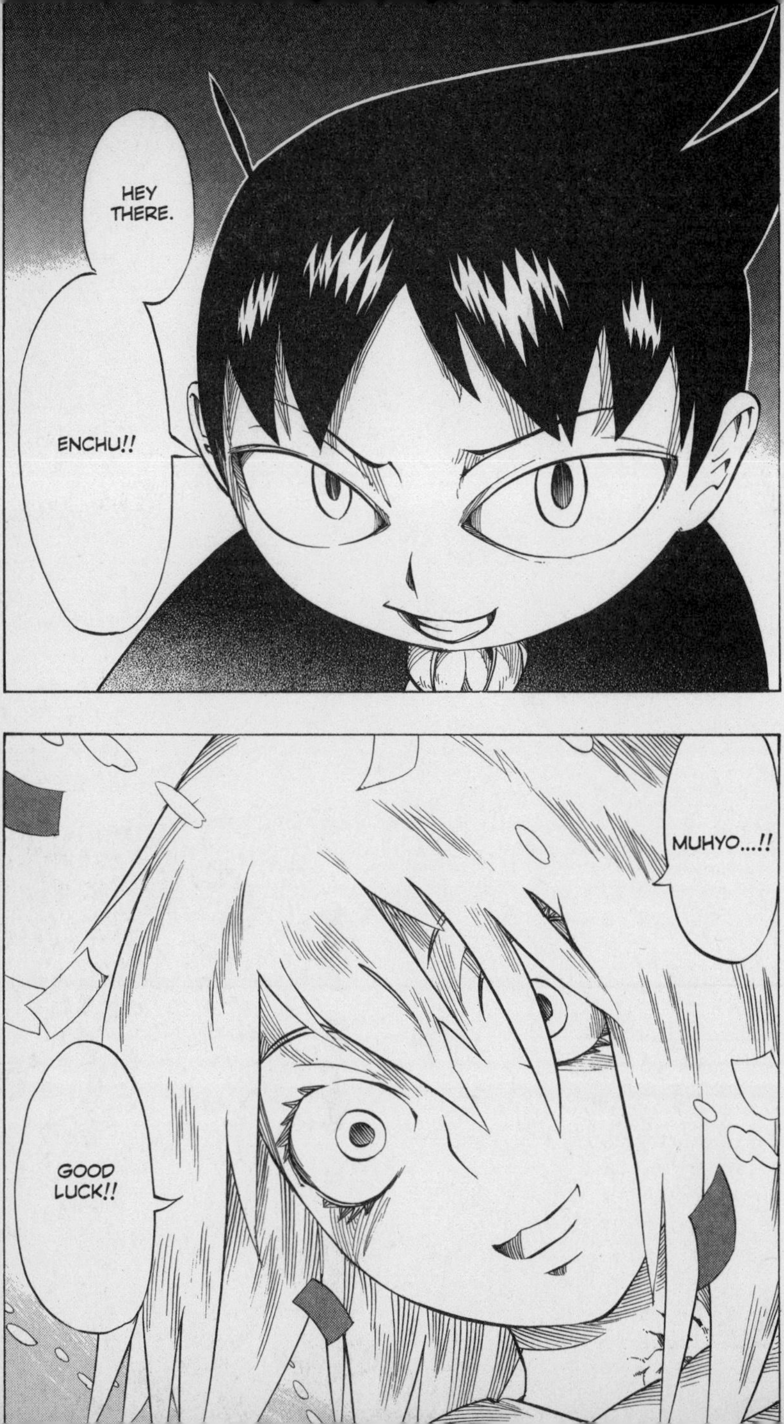
HEY THERE.
ENCHU!!
MUHYO...!!
GOOD LUCK!!

ARTICLE 13
PRIDE

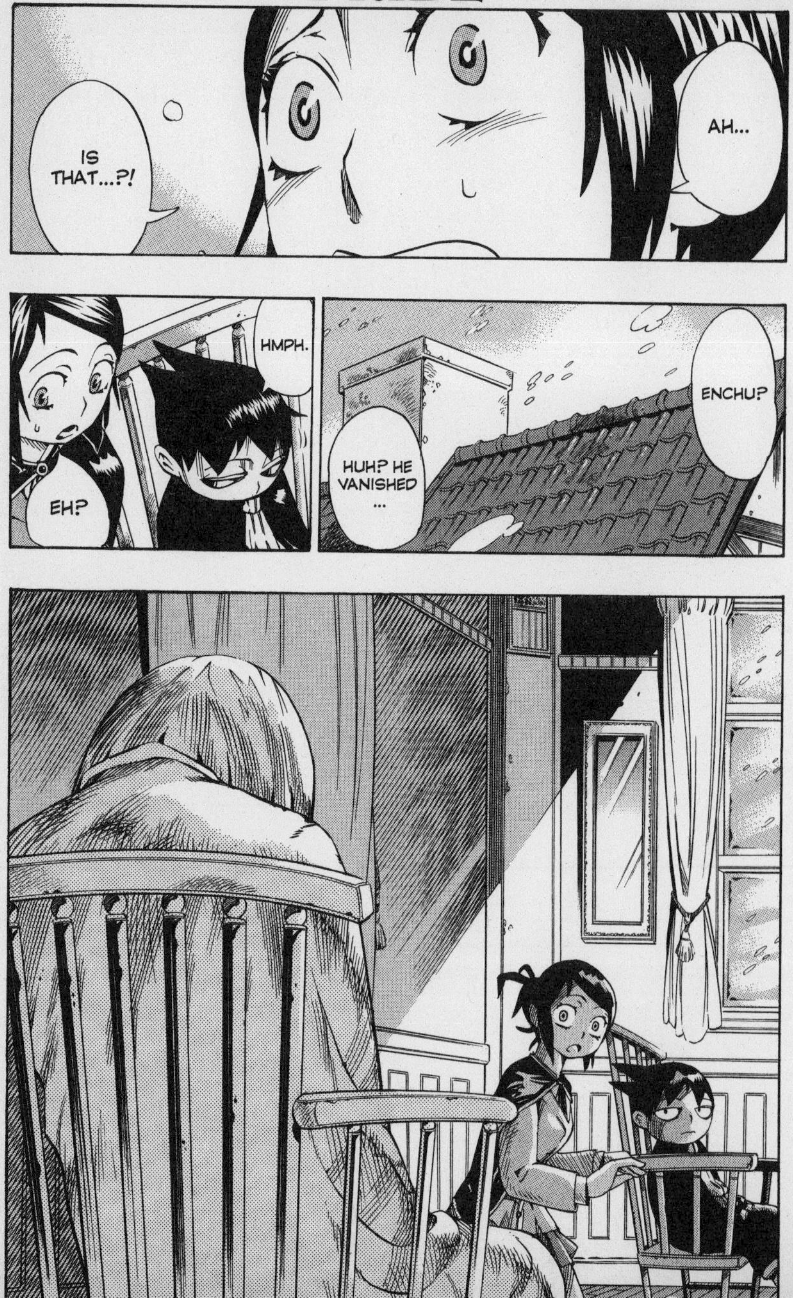
AH...
IS THAT...?!
ENCHU?
HUH? HE VANISHED ...
HMPH.
EH?

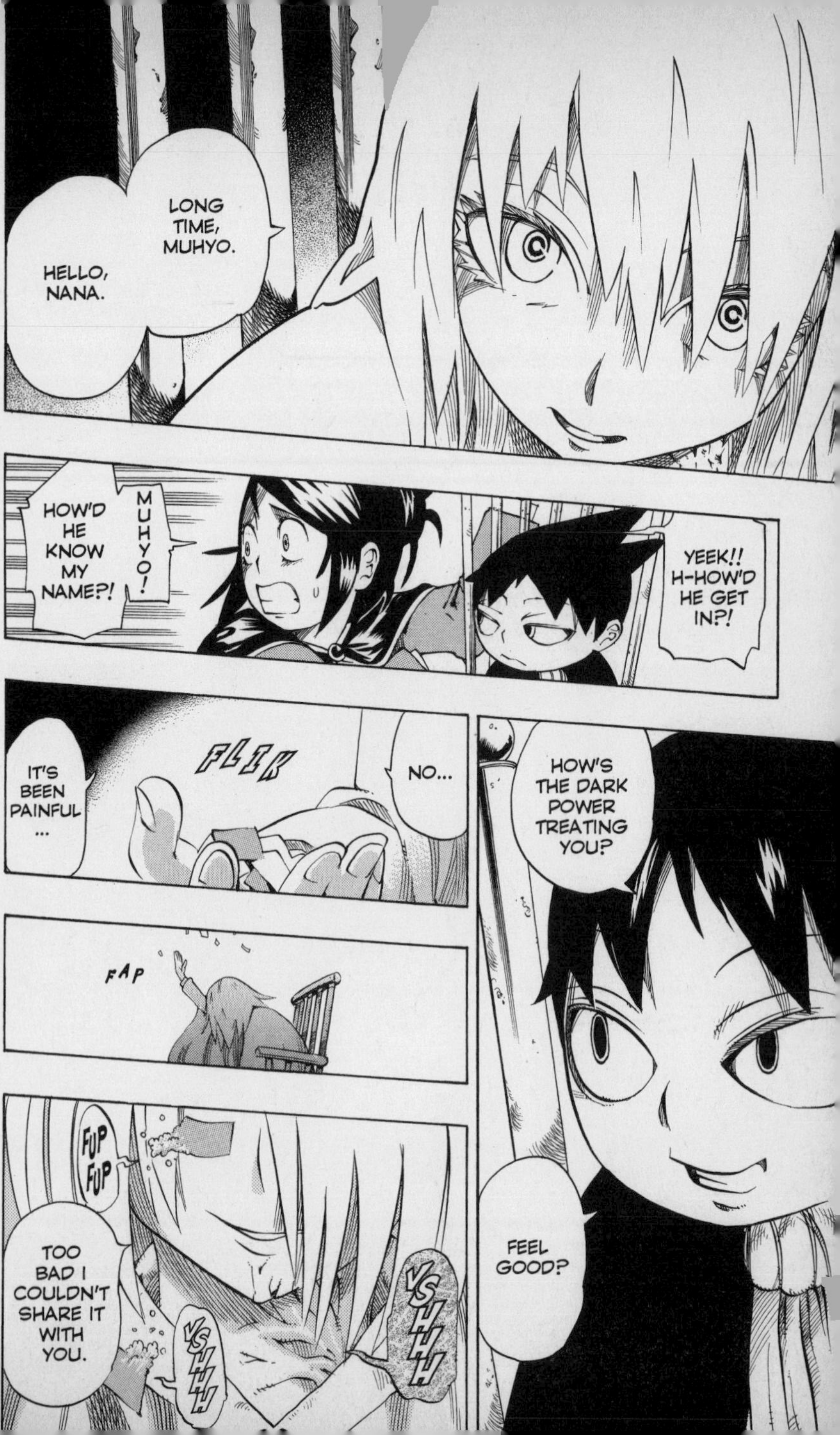
LONG TIME, MUHYO.
HELLO, NANA.
YEEK!! H-HOW'D HE GET IN?!
MUHYO!
HOW'D HE KNOW MY NAME?!
HOW'S THE DARK POWER TREATING YOU?
FEEL GOOD?
NO...
FLIR
IT'S BEEN PAINFUL...
FAP
FUP FUP
VSHHH
TOO BAD I COULDN'T SHARE IT WITH YOU.
VSHHH

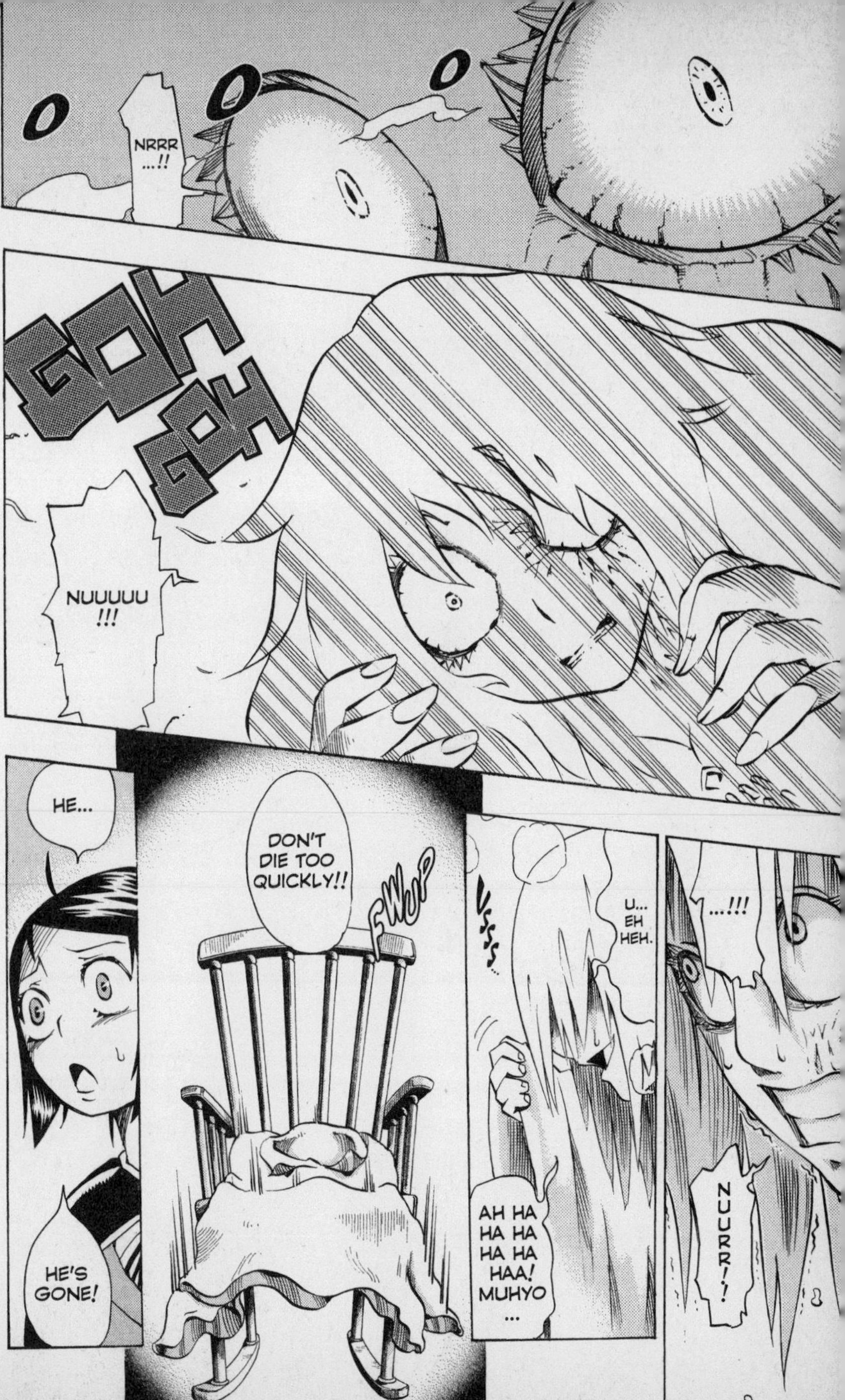
NRRR ...!!
GOH GOH
NUUUUU !!!
...!!!
NUURR!?
U... EH HEH.
VSSS...
AH HA HA HA HA HA HA HAA! MUHYO ...
DON'T DIE TOO QUICKLY!!
FWUP
HE...
HE'S GONE!

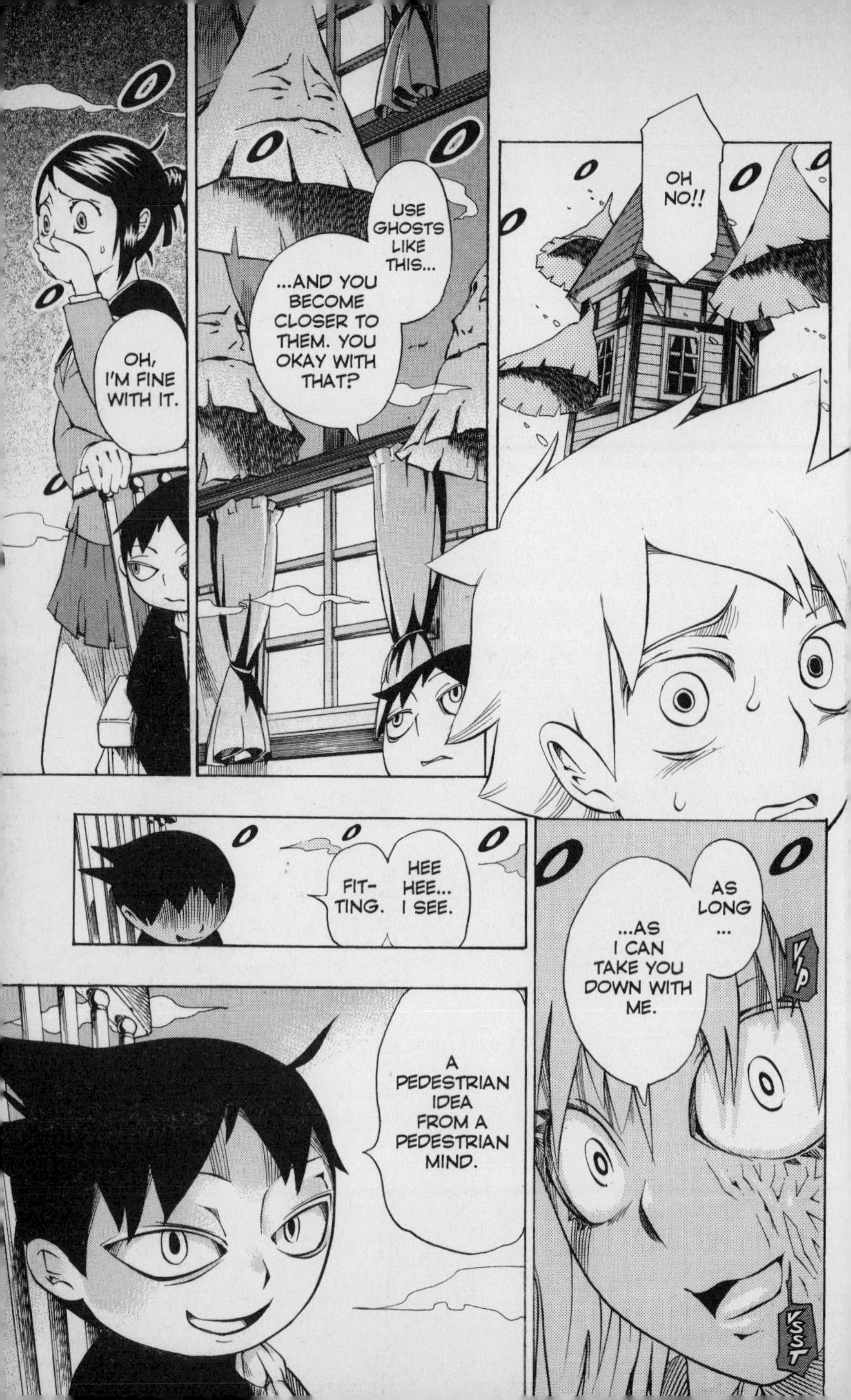
OH NO!!
USE GHOSTS LIKE THIS...
...AND YOU BECOME CLOSER TO THEM. YOU OKAY WITH THAT?
OH, I'M FINE WITH IT.
AS LONG...
...AS I CAN TAKE YOU DOWN WITH ME.
VIP
VSST
HEE HEE... I SEE.
FIT-TING.
A PEDESTRIAN IDEA FROM A PEDESTRIAN MIND.

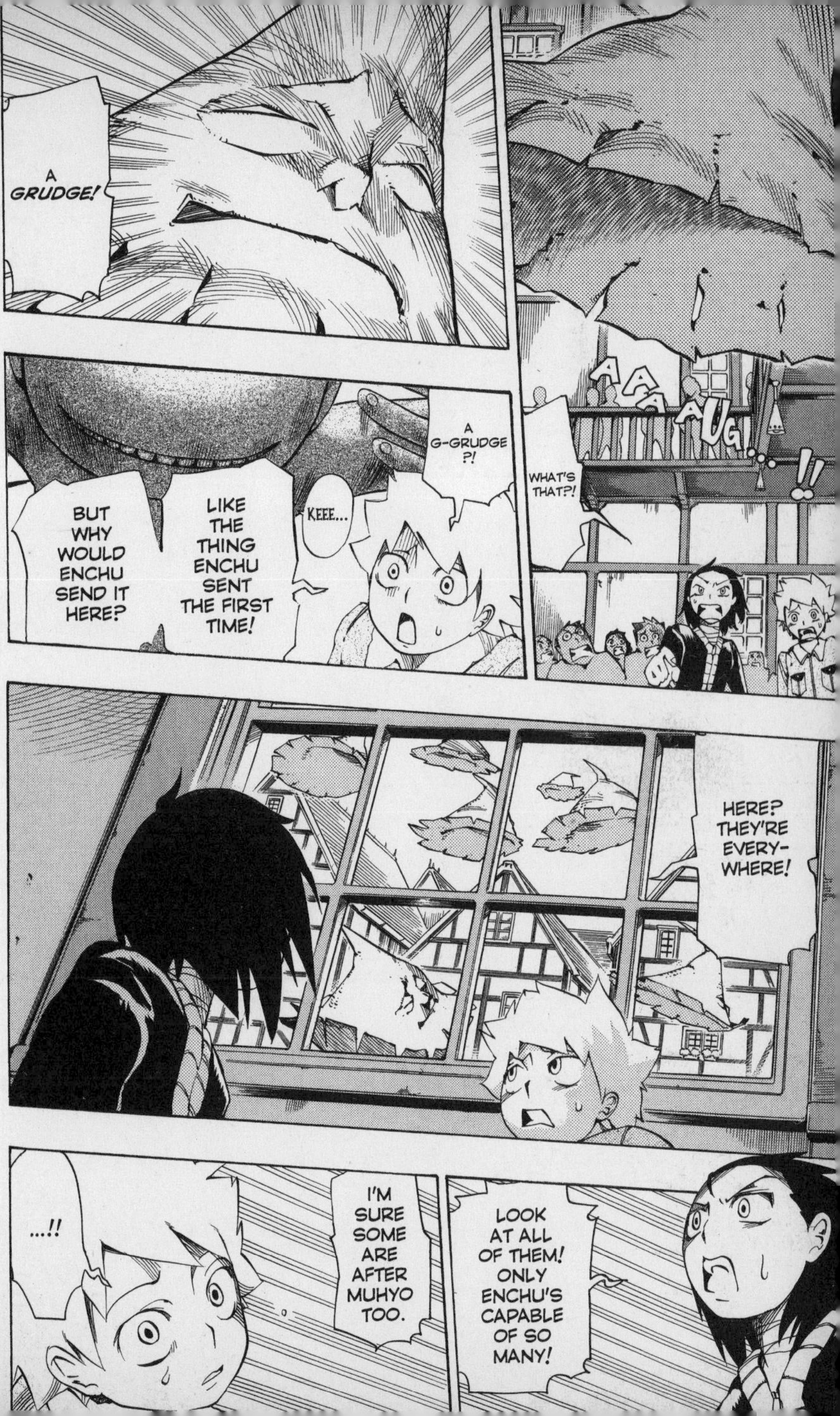
AAAAUGH...!!
WHAT'S THAT?!
A GRUDGE!
A G-GRUDGE?!
KEEE...
LIKE THE THING ENCHU SENT THE FIRST TIME!
BUT WHY WOULD ENCHU SEND IT HERE?
HERE? THEY'RE EVERY-WHERE!
LOOK AT ALL OF THEM! ONLY ENCHU'S CAPABLE OF SO MANY!
I'M SURE SOME ARE AFTER MUHYO TOO.
...!!

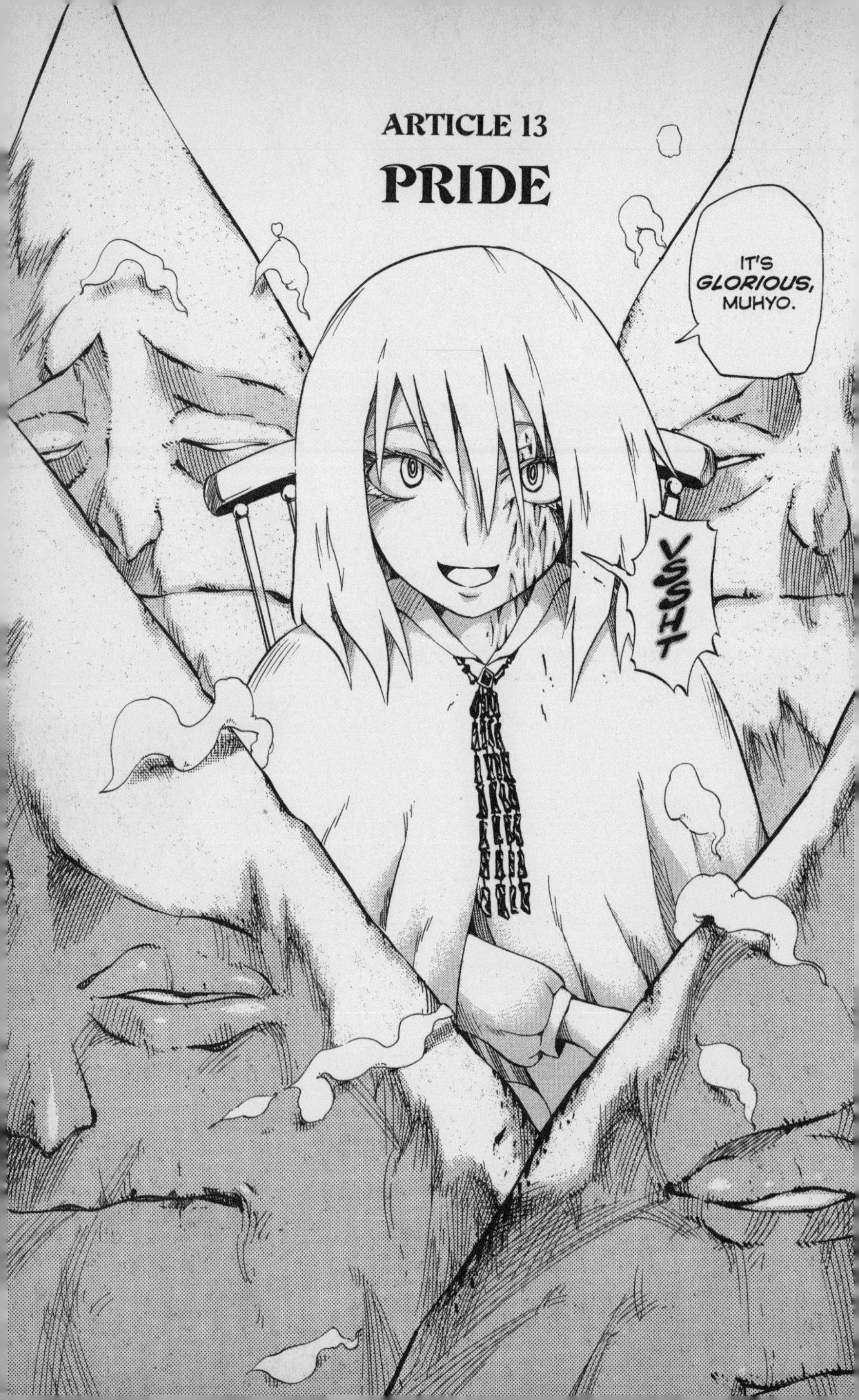
ARTICLE 13
PRIDE
IT'S GLORIOUS, MUHYO.
VSSHT

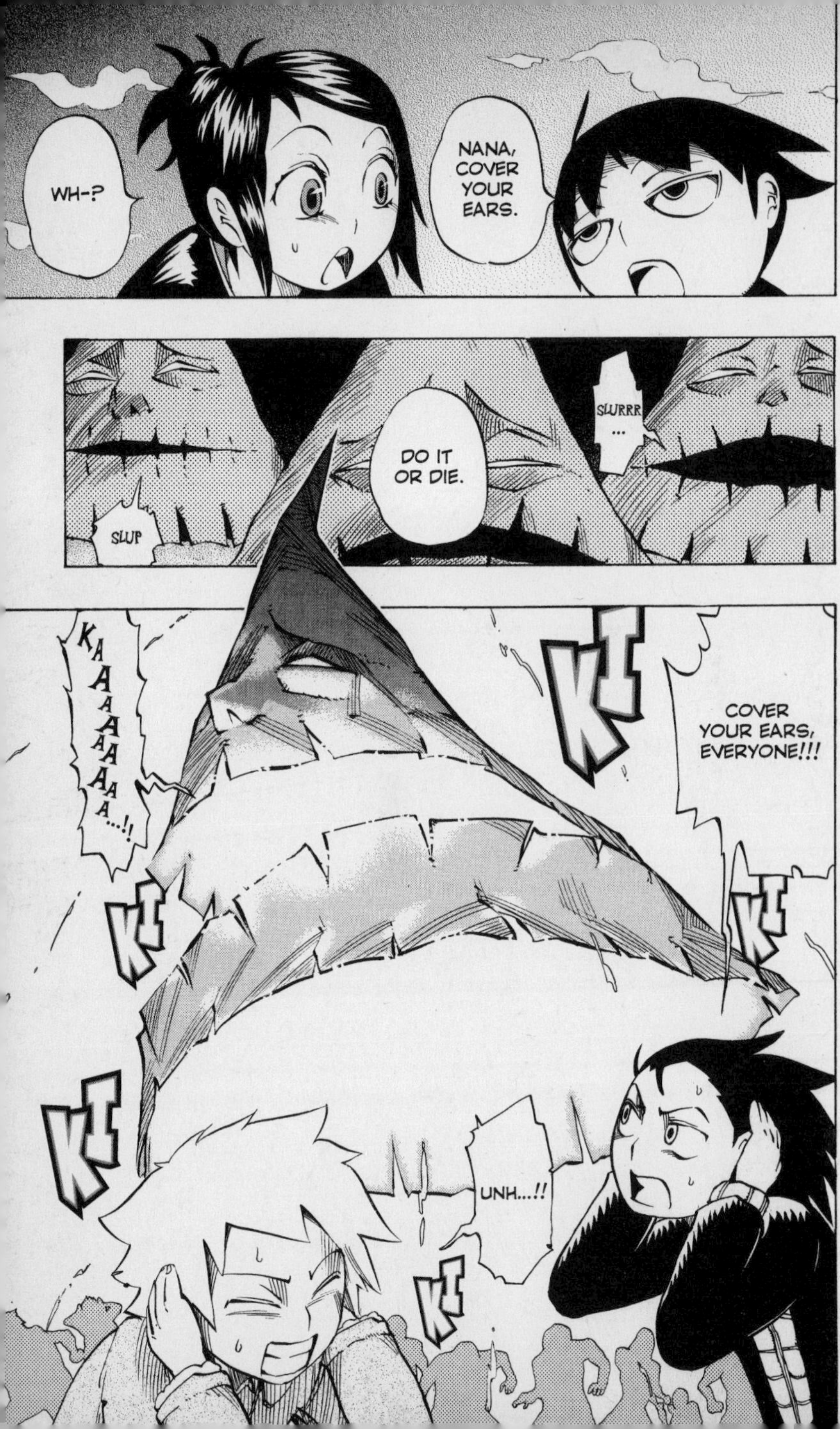
NANA, COVER YOUR EARS.
WH-?
SLURRR...
DO IT OR DIE.
SLUP
COVER YOUR EARS, EVERYONE!!!
KI
KAAAAAAAAA...!!
KI
KI
UNH...!!
KI
KI

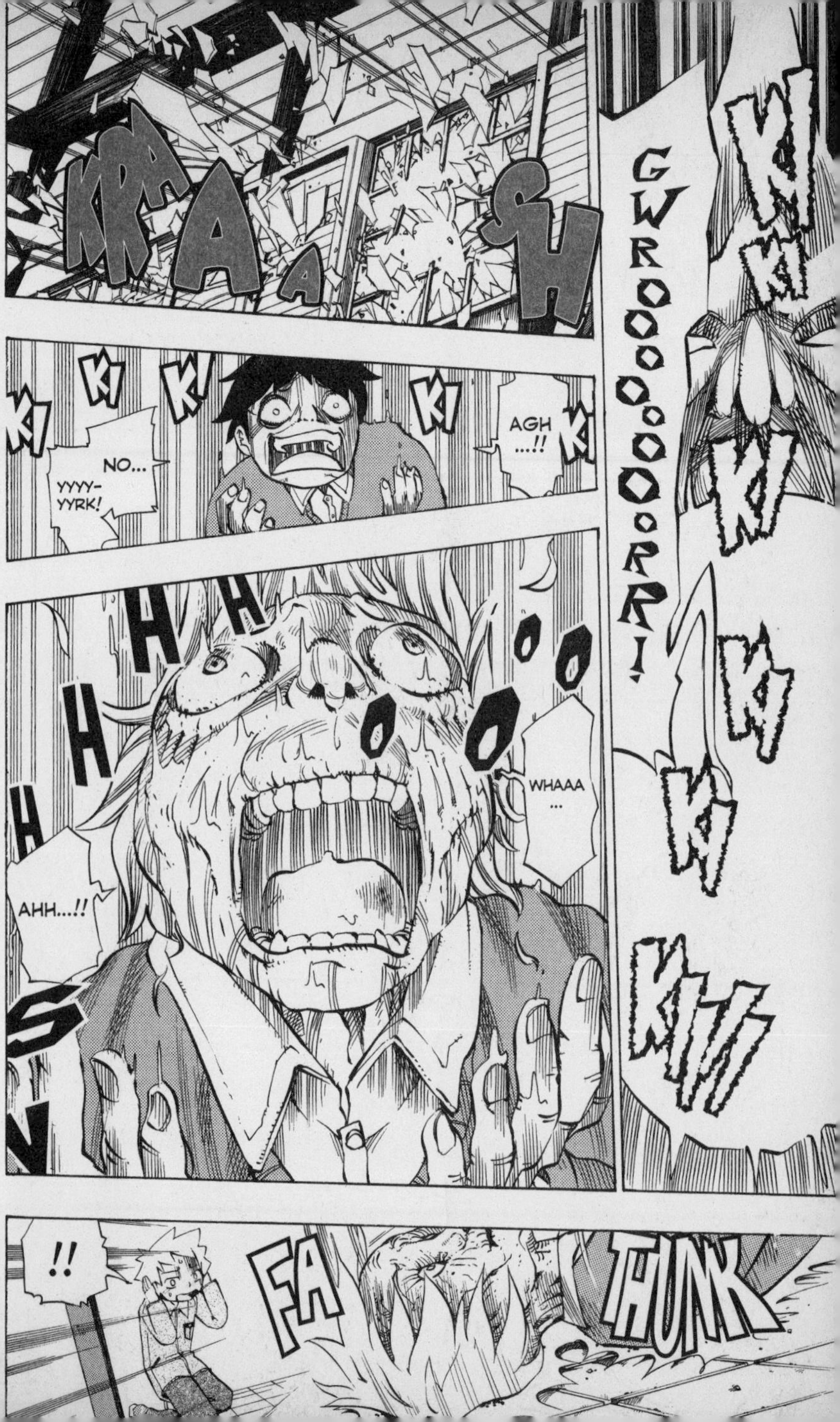
GWROOOOOOORRI!
KI KI KI KI KI
KRAAASH
AGH ...!!
NO... YYYY-YYRK!
KI KI KI KI
WHAAA ...
AHH...!!
!!
THUNK
FA

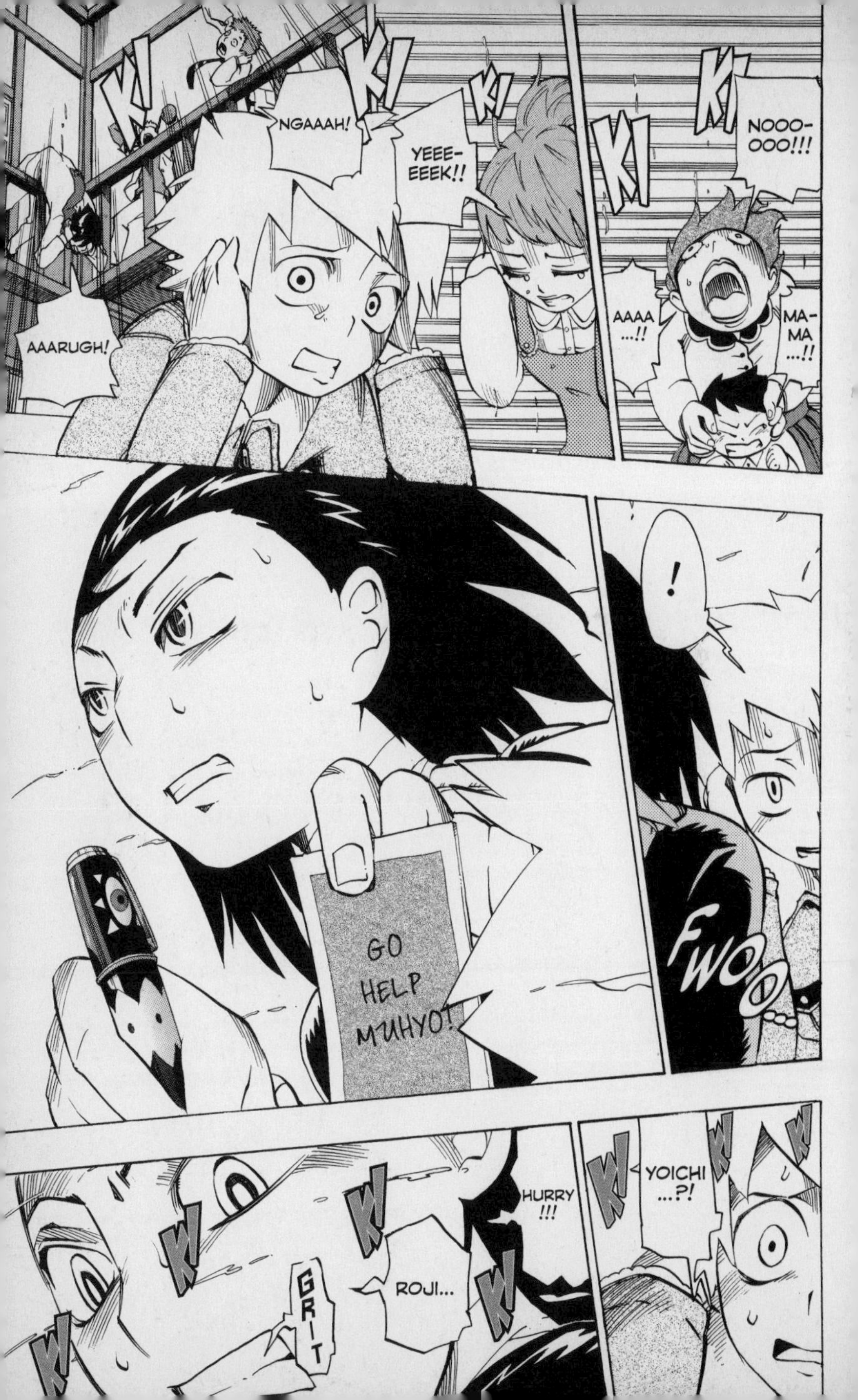
KI
KI
NOOO-OOO!!!
MA-MA ...!!
AAAA ...!!
KI
YEEE-EEEK!!
KI
NGAAAH!
KI
AAARUGH!
!
FWOOO
GO HELP MUHYO!
KI
KI
YOICHI ...?!
KI
HURRY !!!
KI
KI
ROJI...
GRIT
KI
KI

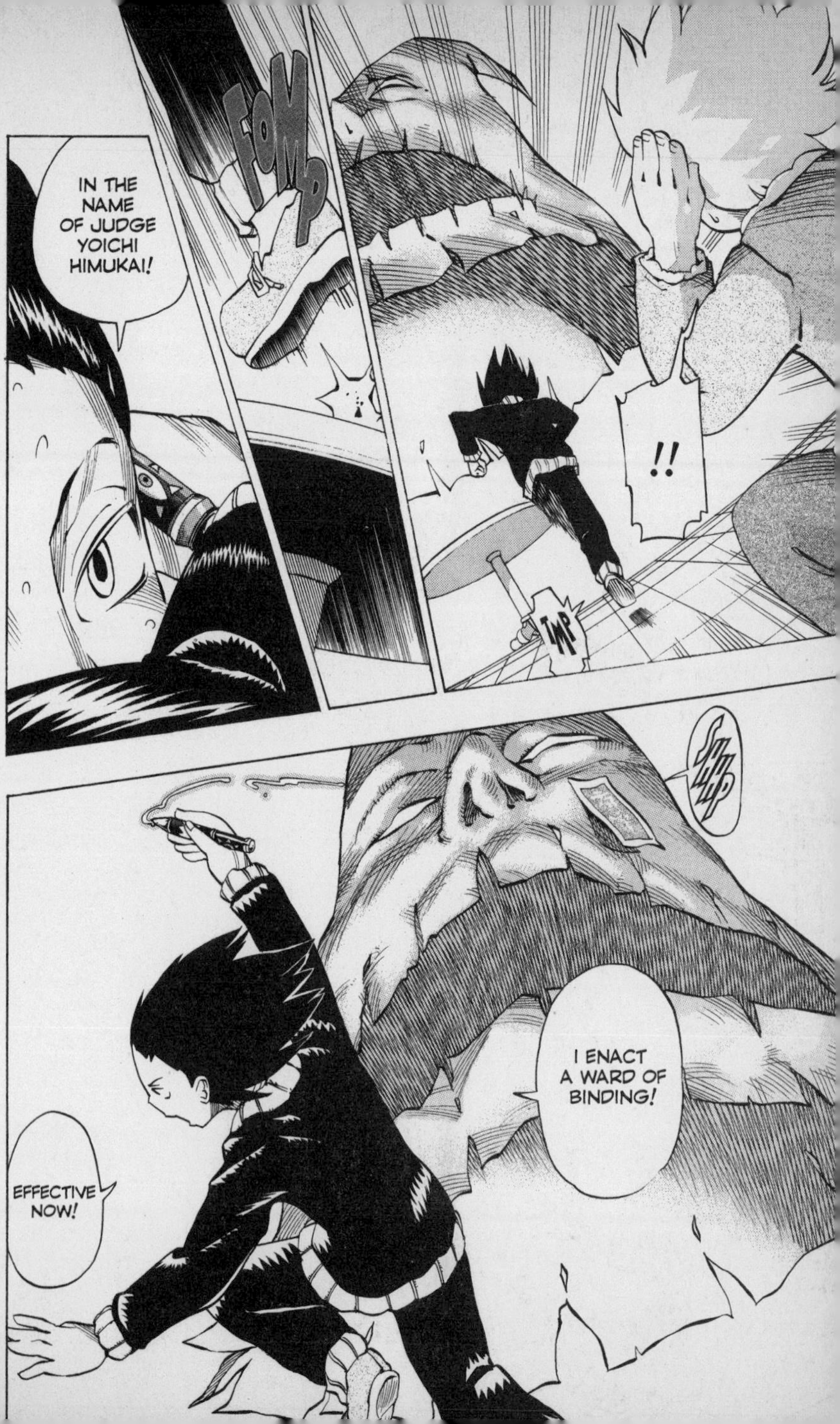
!!
TMP
FOMP
IN THE NAME OF JUDGE YOICHI HIMUKAI!
I ENACT A WARD OF BINDING!
EFFECTIVE NOW!

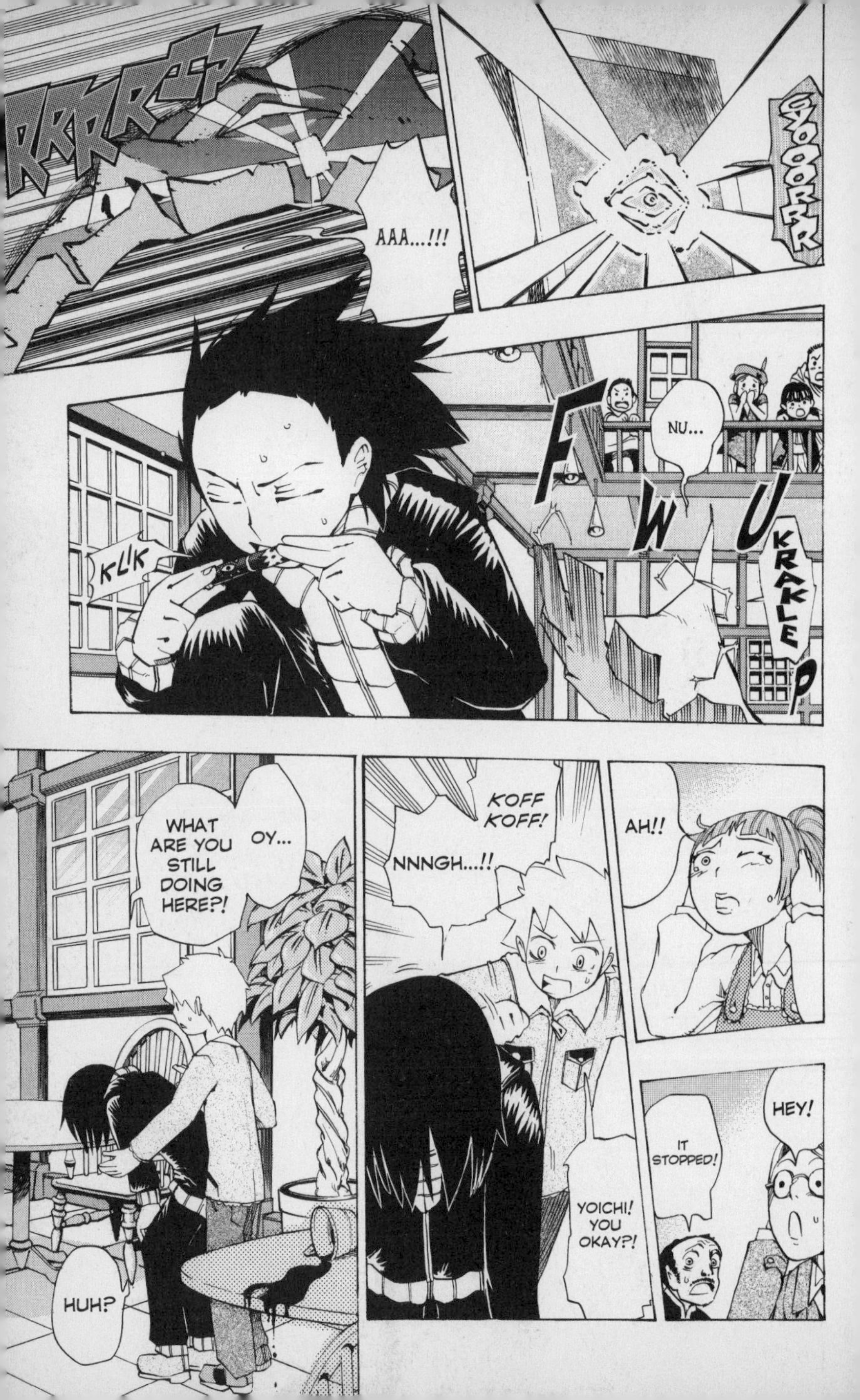
GYOOORRR
RRRRIP
AAA...!!!
NU...
FWUP
KRAKLE
KLIK
AH!!
HEY!
IT STOPPED!
KOFF KOFF!
NNNGH...!!
YOICHI! YOU OKAY?!
OY...
WHAT ARE YOU STILL DOING HERE?!
HUH?

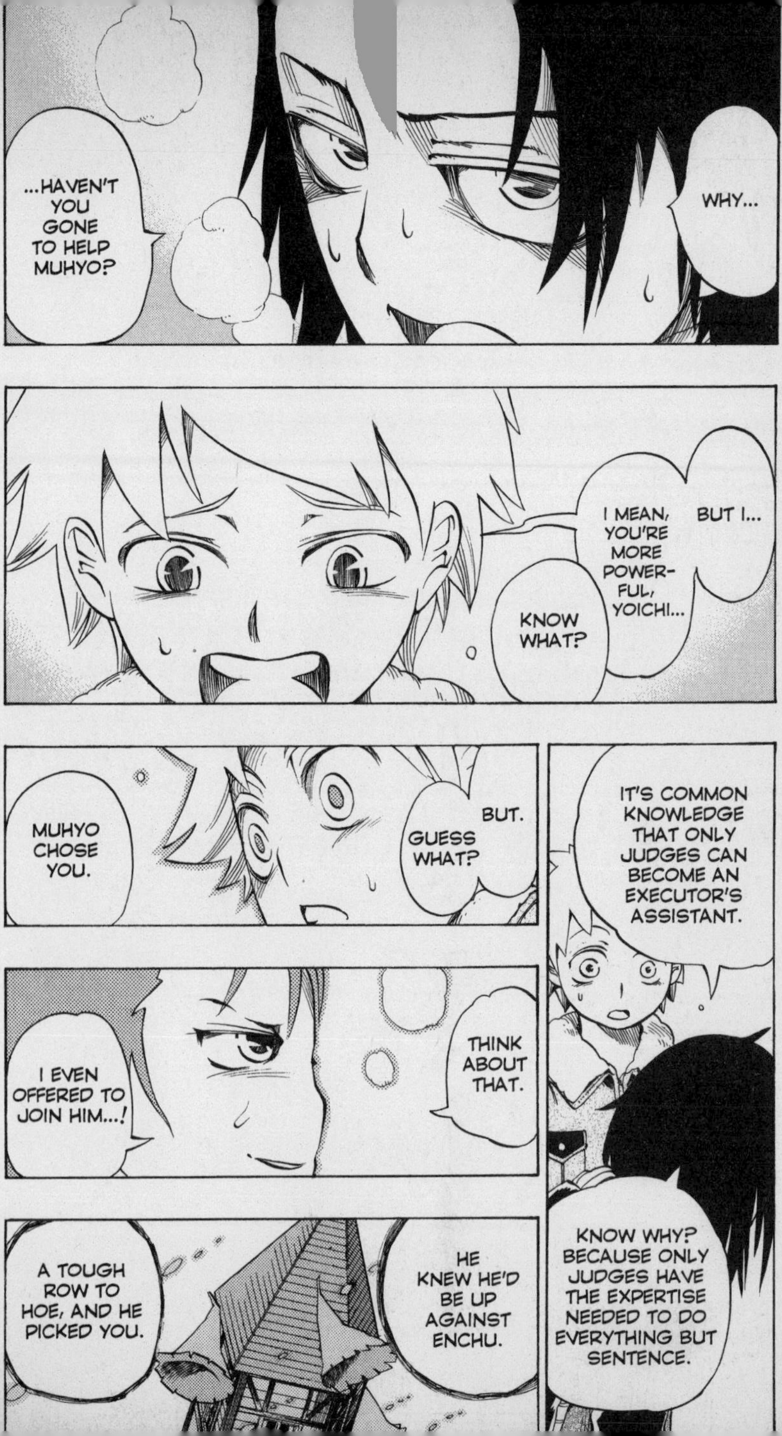
WHY...
...HAVEN'T YOU GONE TO HELP MUHYO?
BUT I...
I MEAN, YOU'RE MORE POWER-FUL, YOICHI...
KNOW WHAT?
IT'S COMMON KNOWLEDGE THAT ONLY JUDGES CAN BECOME AN EXECUTOR'S ASSISTANT.
KNOW WHY? BECAUSE ONLY JUDGES HAVE THE EXPERTISE NEEDED TO DO EVERYTHING BUT SENTENCE.
BUT. GUESS WHAT?
MUHYO CHOSE YOU.
THINK ABOUT THAT.
I EVEN OFFERED TO JOIN HIM...!
HE KNEW HE'D BE UP AGAINST ENCHU.
A TOUGH ROW TO HOE, AND HE PICKED YOU.

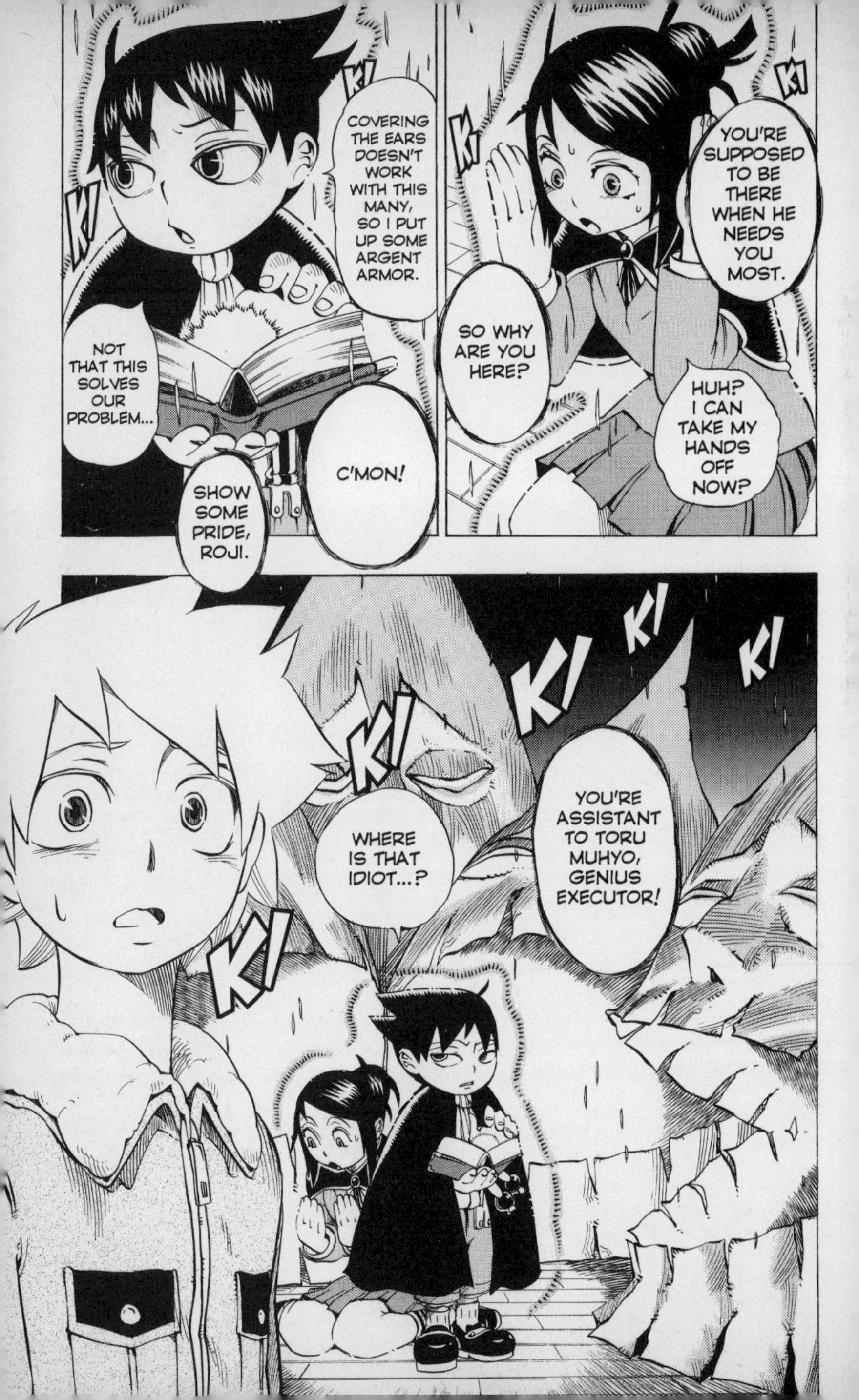

KI
KI
YOU'RE SUPPOSED TO BE THERE WHEN HE NEEDS YOU MOST.
SO WHY ARE YOU HERE?
HUH? I CAN TAKE MY HANDS OFF NOW?
KI
KI
COVERING THE EARS DOESN'T WORK WITH THIS MANY, SO I PUT UP SOME ARGENT ARMOR.
NOT THAT THIS SOLVES OUR PROBLEM...
C'MON!
SHOW SOME PRIDE, ROJI.
KI
KI
KI
KI
YOU'RE ASSISTANT TO TORU MUHYO, GENIUS EXECUTOR!
WHERE IS THAT IDIOT...?
KI

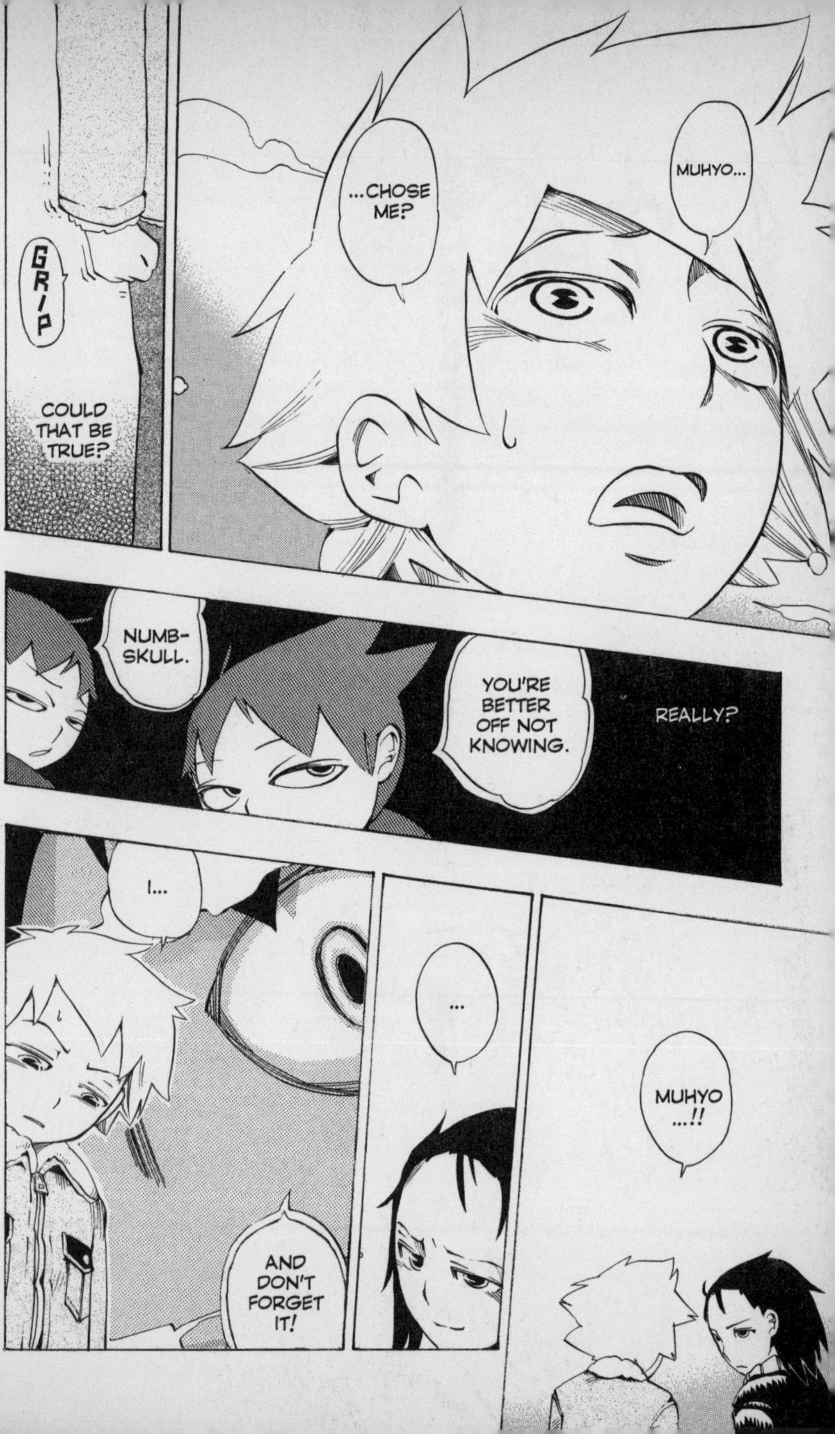
MUHYO...
...CHOSE ME?
GRIP
COULD THAT BE TRUE?
REALLY?
YOU'RE BETTER OFF NOT KNOWING.
NUMB-SKULL.
MUHYO ...!!
...
I...
AND DON'T FORGET IT!

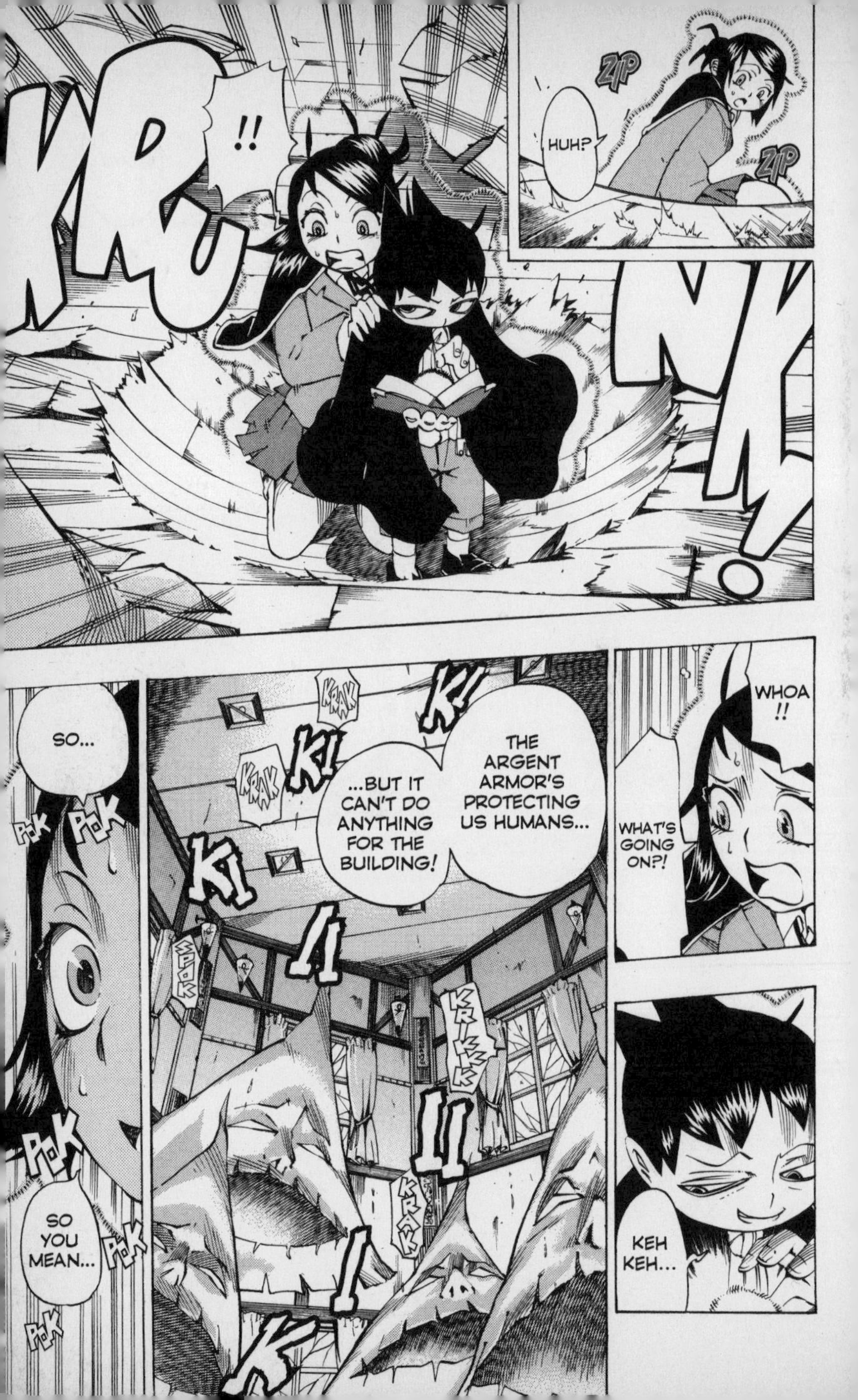
ZIP
HUH?
ZIP
KRUNK!
!!
WHOA!!
WHAT'S GOING ON?!
KEH KEH...
THE ARGENT ARMOR'S PROTECTING US HUMANS...
...BUT IT CAN'T DO ANYTHING FOR THE BUILDING!
KRAK
KRAK
KRIKKK
KRAK
SO...
POK POK
POK
SO YOU MEAN...
POK
POK

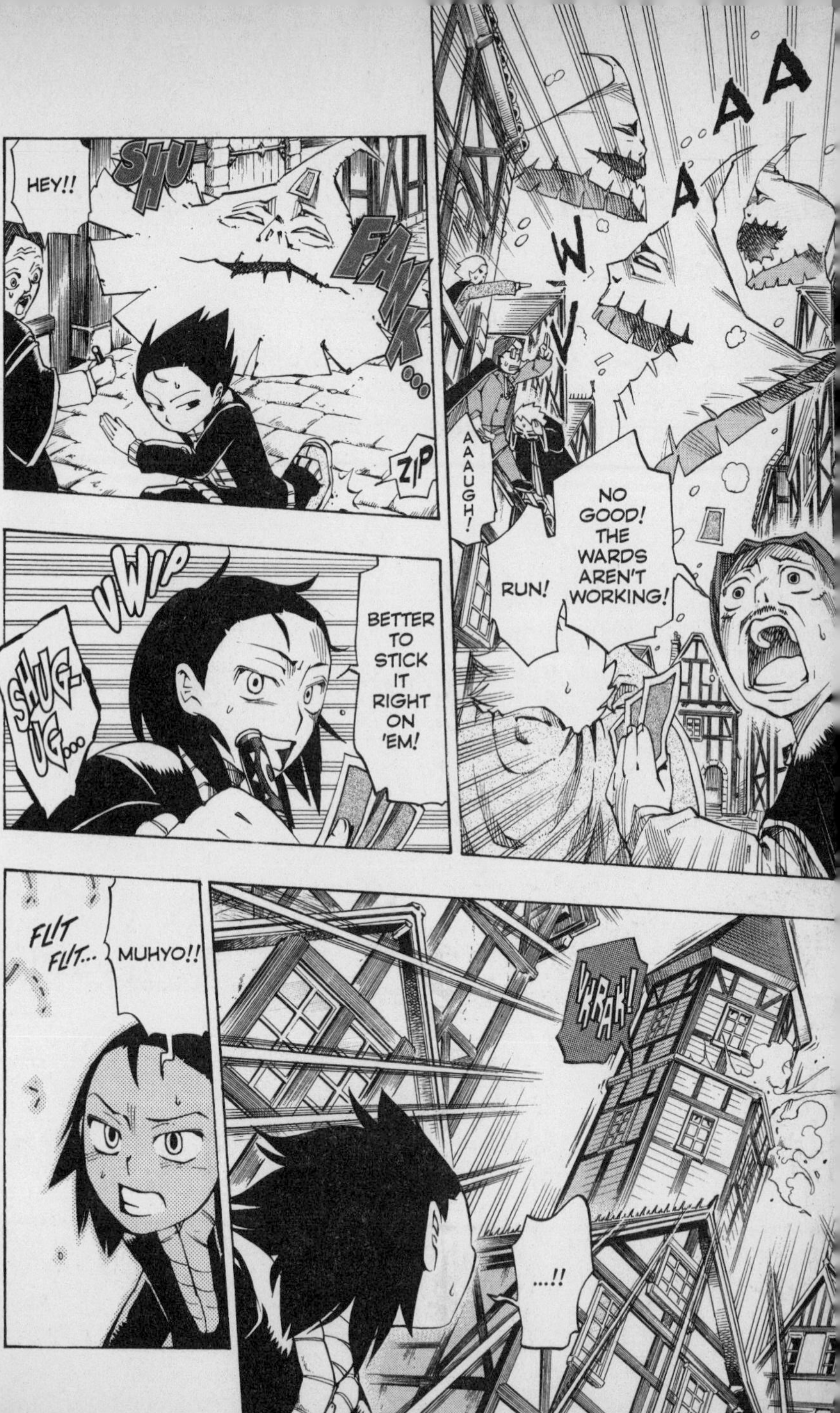
WAAAA
NO GOOD! THE WARDS AREN'T WORKING!
RUN!
AAAUGH!
HEY!!
SHU
FANK...
ZIP
VWIP
BETTER TO STICK IT RIGHT ON 'EM!
SHUG-UG...
VKRAK!
...!!
FLIT FLIT...
MUHYO!!

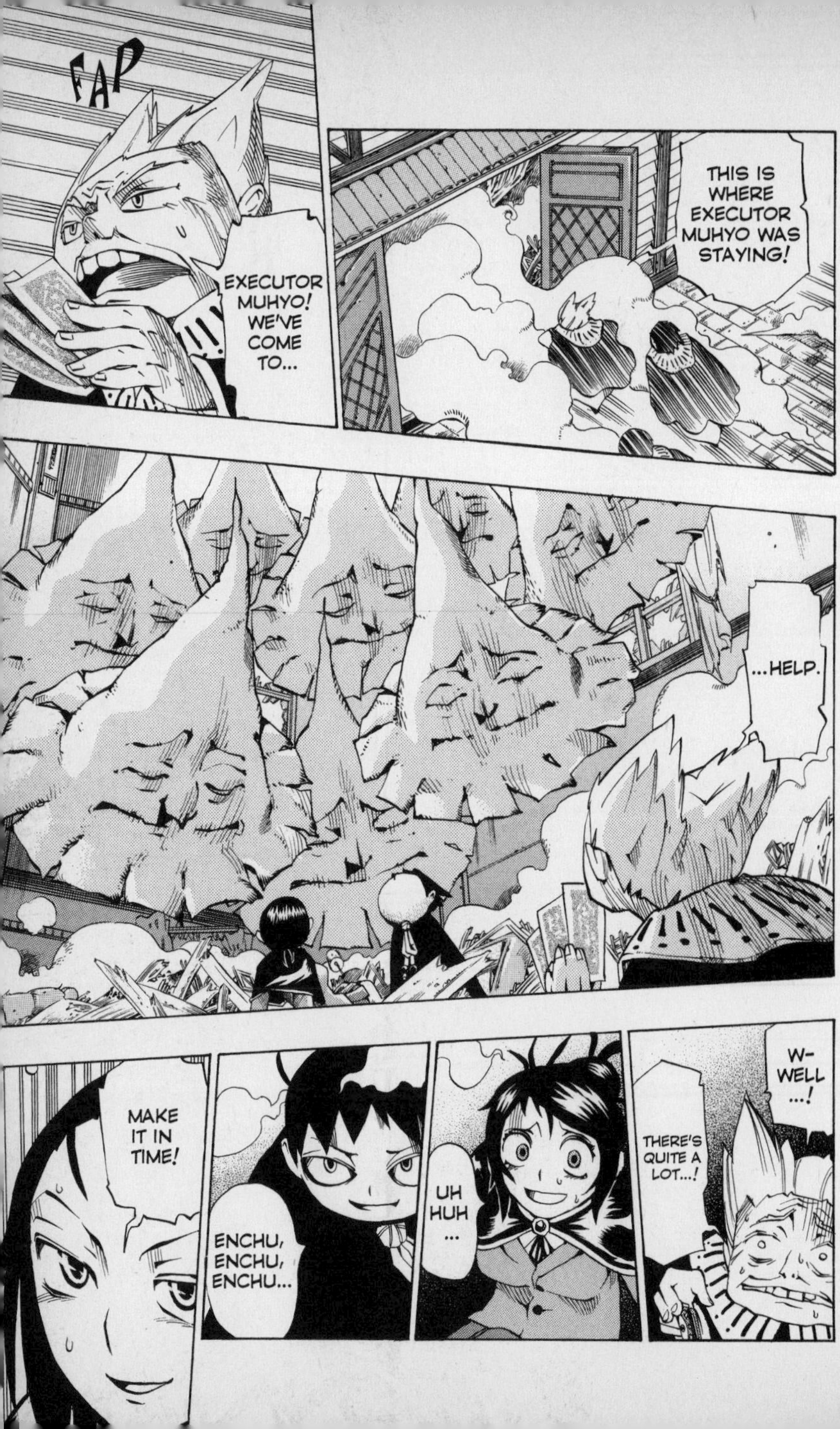
THIS IS WHERE EXECUTOR MUHYO WAS STAYING!
FAP
EXECUTOR MUHYO! WE'VE COME TO...
...HELP.
W-WELL...!
THERE'S QUITE A LOT...!
UH HUH...
ENCHU, ENCHU, ENCHU...
MAKE IT IN TIME!

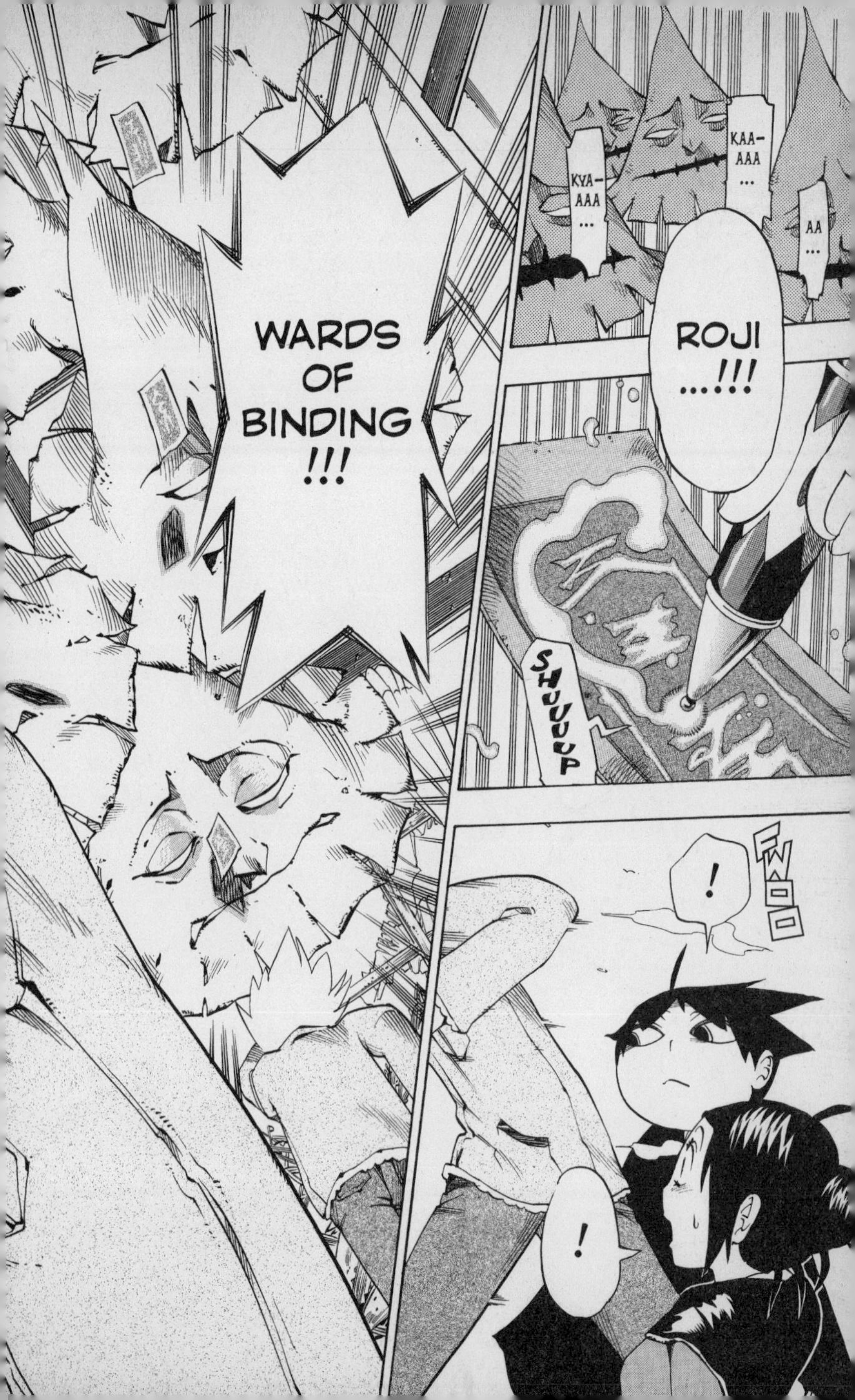
AA ...
KAA-AAA ...
KYA-AAA ...
ROJI ...!!!
SHUUUUP
FWOO
!
!
WARDS OF BINDING !!!

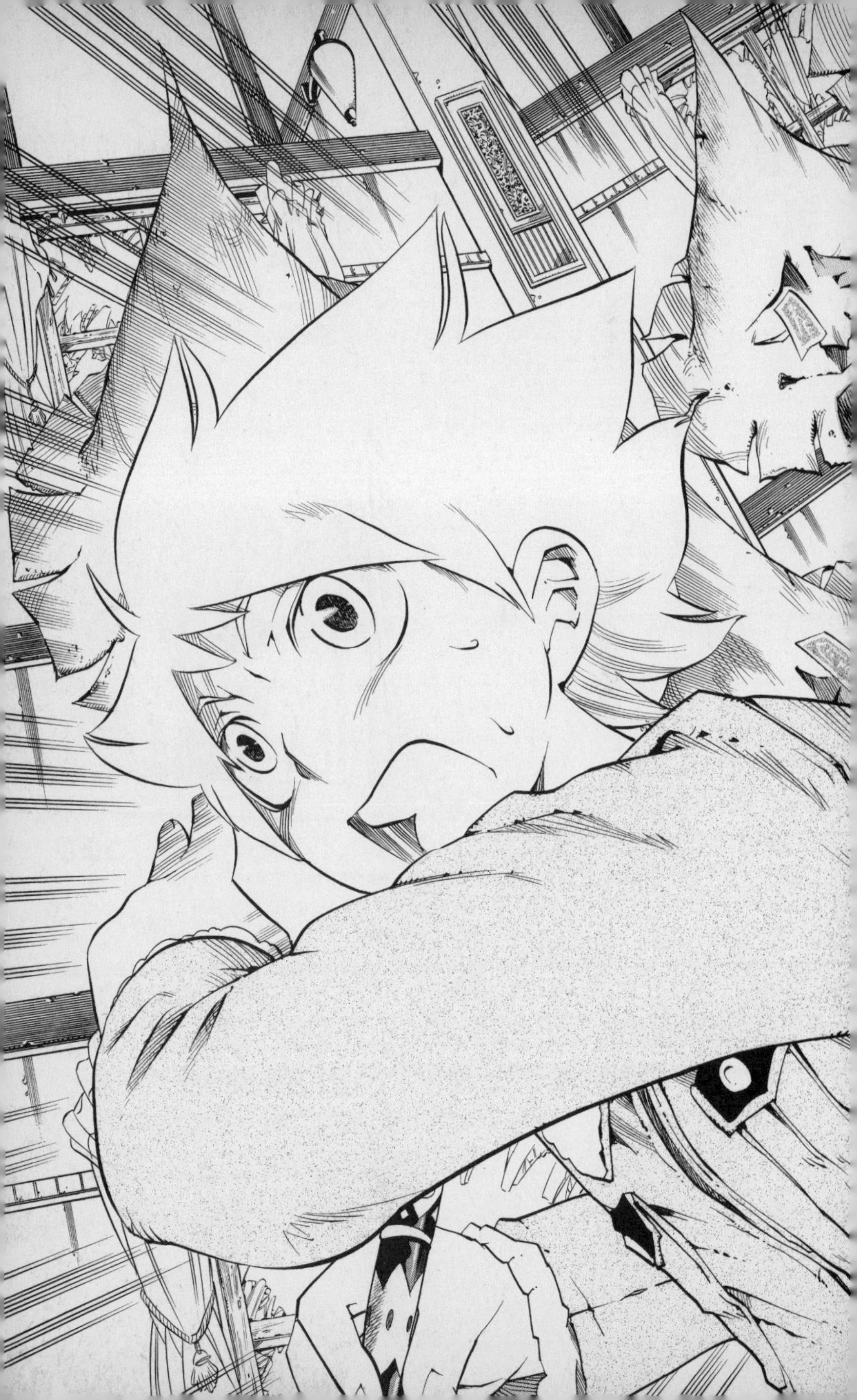

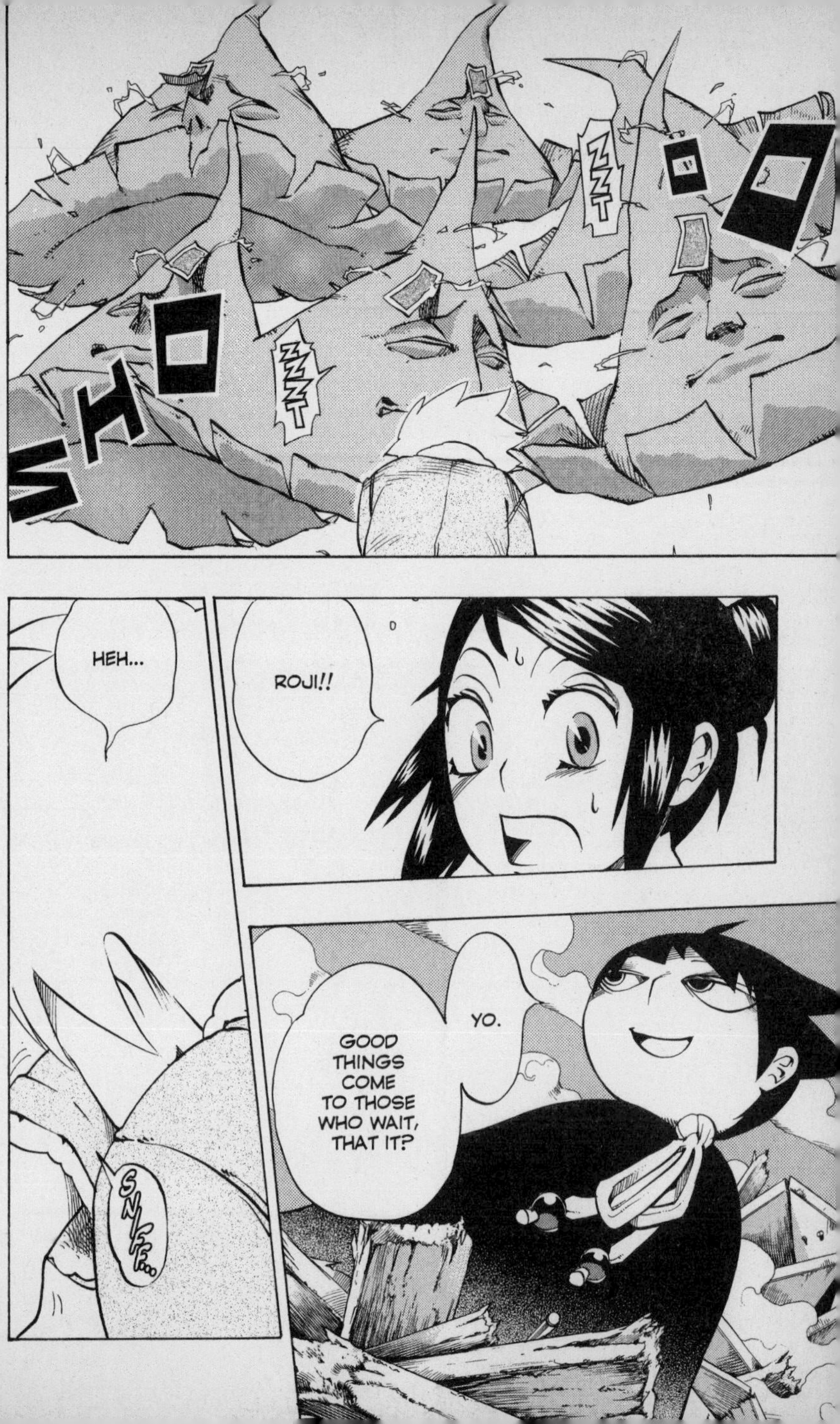
ZZZT
ZZZT
SHOOO
ROJI!!
YO.
GOOD THINGS COME TO THOSE WHO WAIT, THAT IT?
HEH...
SNIFF...

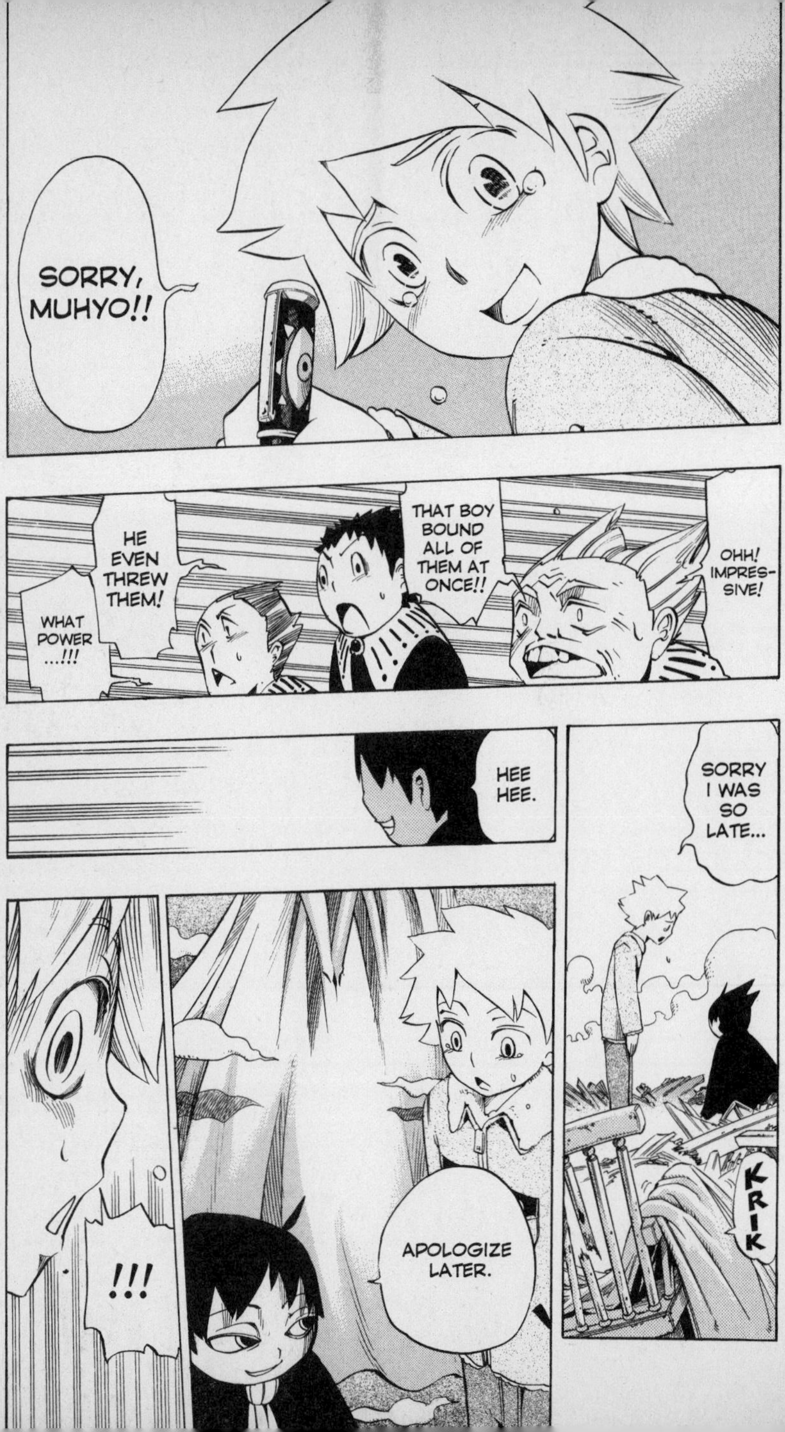
SORRY, MUHYO!!
OHH! IMPRES-SIVE!
THAT BOY BOUND ALL OF THEM AT ONCE!!
HE EVEN THREW THEM!
WHAT POWER ...!!!
SORRY I WAS SO LATE...
KRIK
HEE HEE.
APOLOGIZE LATER.
!!!

YOICHI HIMUKAI

BIRTHDAY: AUGUST 5
HEIGHT: 173 CM

LIKES:
    SANDWICHES
    GIRLS

TALENTS:
    MAKING FRIENDS
    GUESSING CUP SIZES
    ALL SPORTS
    SECRET OPS

NOT GOOD WITH:
    WORK
    CRYING GIRLS

ARTICLE 14
TOGETHER

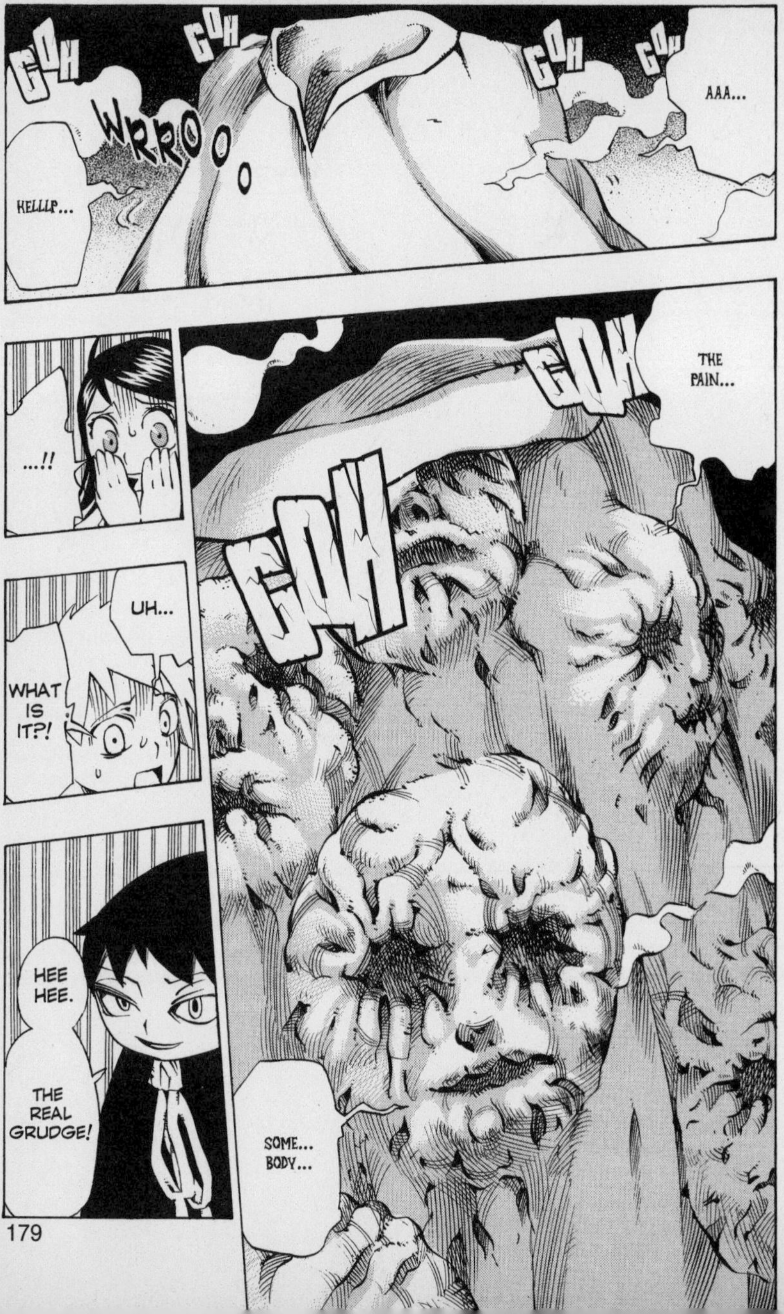
AAA...
GOH GOH
GOH
WRROOO
GOH
HELLLP...
GOH
THE PAIN...
GOH
SOME... BODY...
...!!
UH...
WHAT IS IT?!
HEE HEE.
THE REAL GRUDGE!

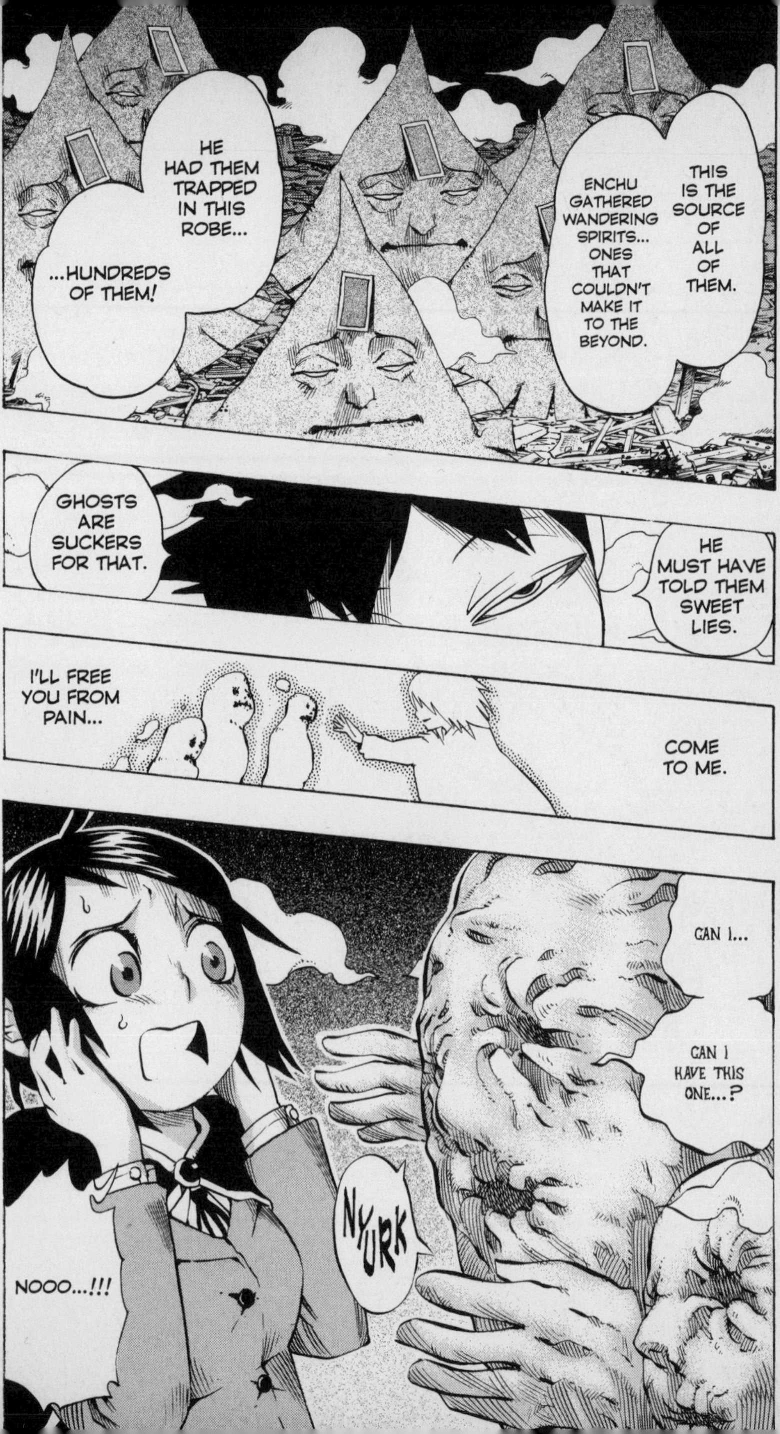
THIS IS THE SOURCE OF ALL OF THEM.
ENCHU GATHERED WANDERING SPIRITS... ONES THAT COULDN'T MAKE IT TO THE BEYOND.
HE HAD THEM TRAPPED IN THIS ROBE...
...HUNDREDS OF THEM!
HE MUST HAVE TOLD THEM SWEET LIES.
GHOSTS ARE SUCKERS FOR THAT.
I'LL FREE YOU FROM PAIN...
COME TO ME.
CAN I...
CAN I HAVE THIS ONE...?
NYURK
NOOO...!!!

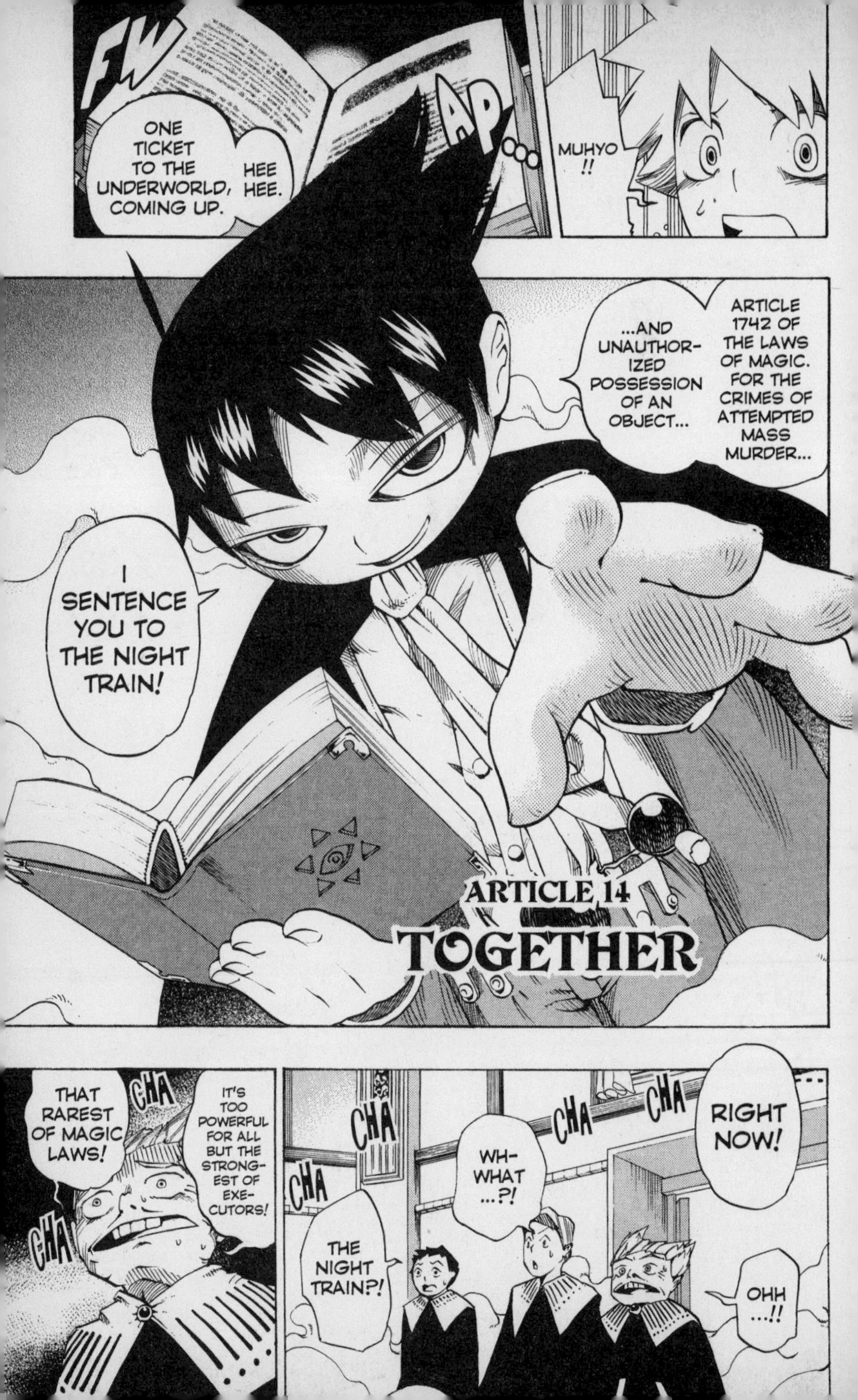
MUHYO !!
FWAP
ONE TICKET TO THE UNDERWORLD, COMING UP. HEE HEE.
ARTICLE 1742 OF THE LAWS OF MAGIC. FOR THE CRIMES OF ATTEMPTED MASS MURDER...
...AND UNAUTHORIZED POSSESSION OF AN OBJECT...
I SENTENCE YOU TO THE NIGHT TRAIN!
ARTICLE 14
TOGETHER
RIGHT NOW!
CHA
CHA
WH-WHAT ...?!
CHA
CHA
THE NIGHT TRAIN?!
OHH ...!!
IT'S TOO POWERFUL FOR ALL BUT THE STRONGEST OF EXECUTORS!
CHA
THAT RAREST OF MAGIC LAWS!
CHA

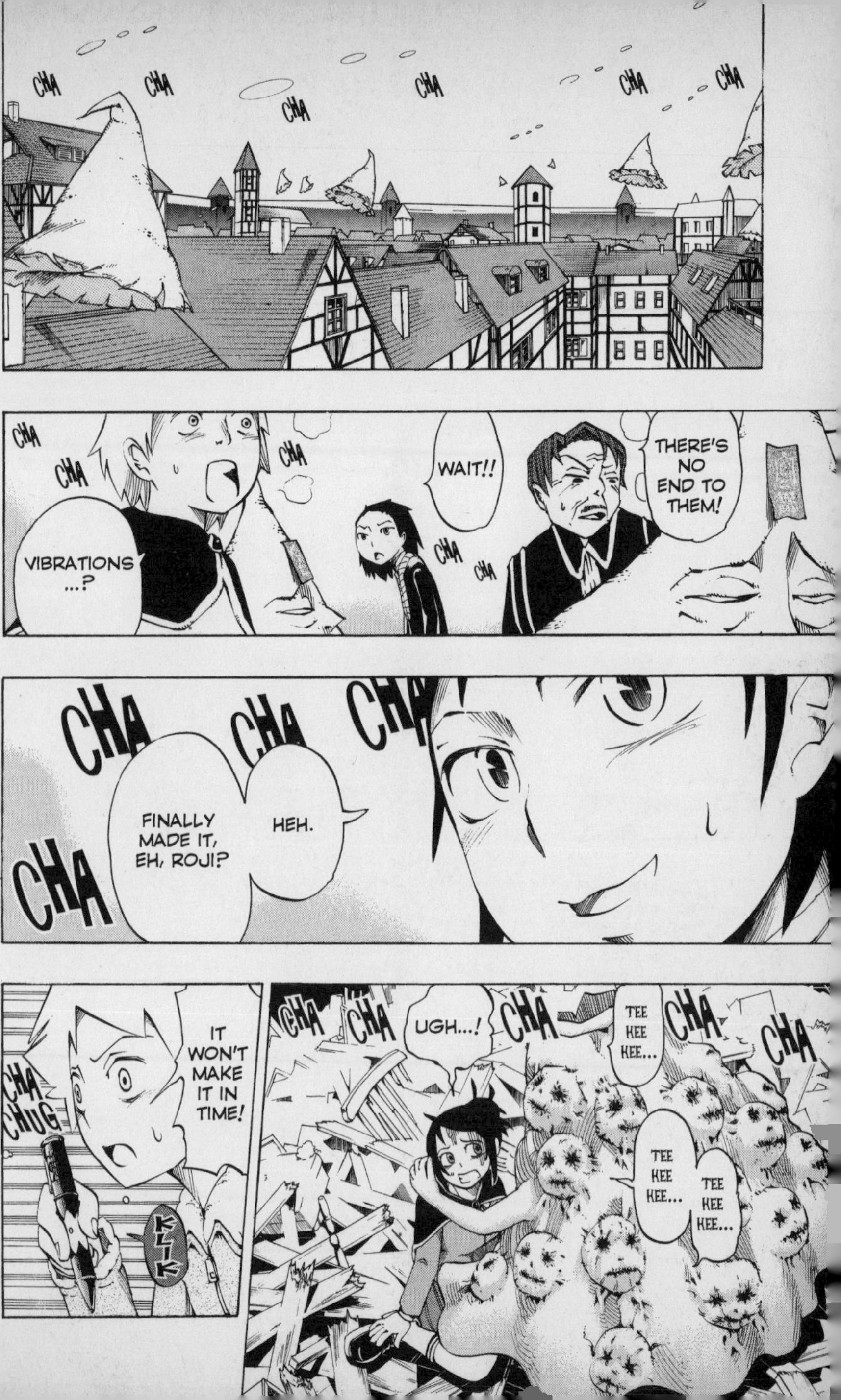
CHA
CHA
CHA
CHA
CHA
CHA
THERE'S NO END TO THEM!
CHA
CHA
WAIT!!
CHA
CHA
CHA
VIBRATIONS ...?
CHA
CHA
CHA
HEH.
FINALLY MADE IT, EH, ROJI?
CHA
CHA
CHA
TEE HEE HEE...
CHA
UGH...!
CHA
CHA
TEE HEE HEE...
TEE HEE HEE...
IT WON'T MAKE IT IN TIME!
CHA CHUG
KLIK

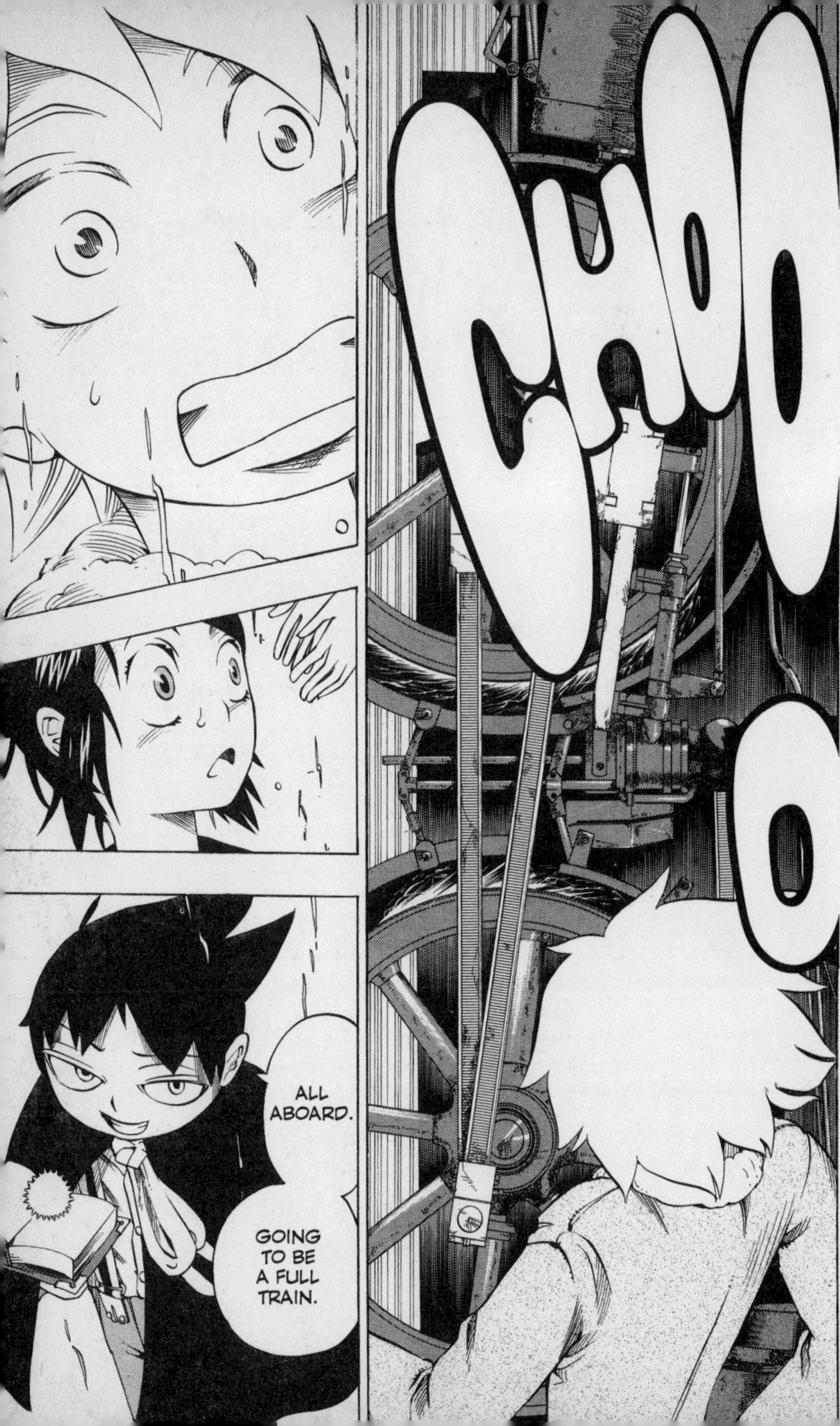
CHOO
O
ALL ABOARD.
GOING TO BE A FULL TRAIN.

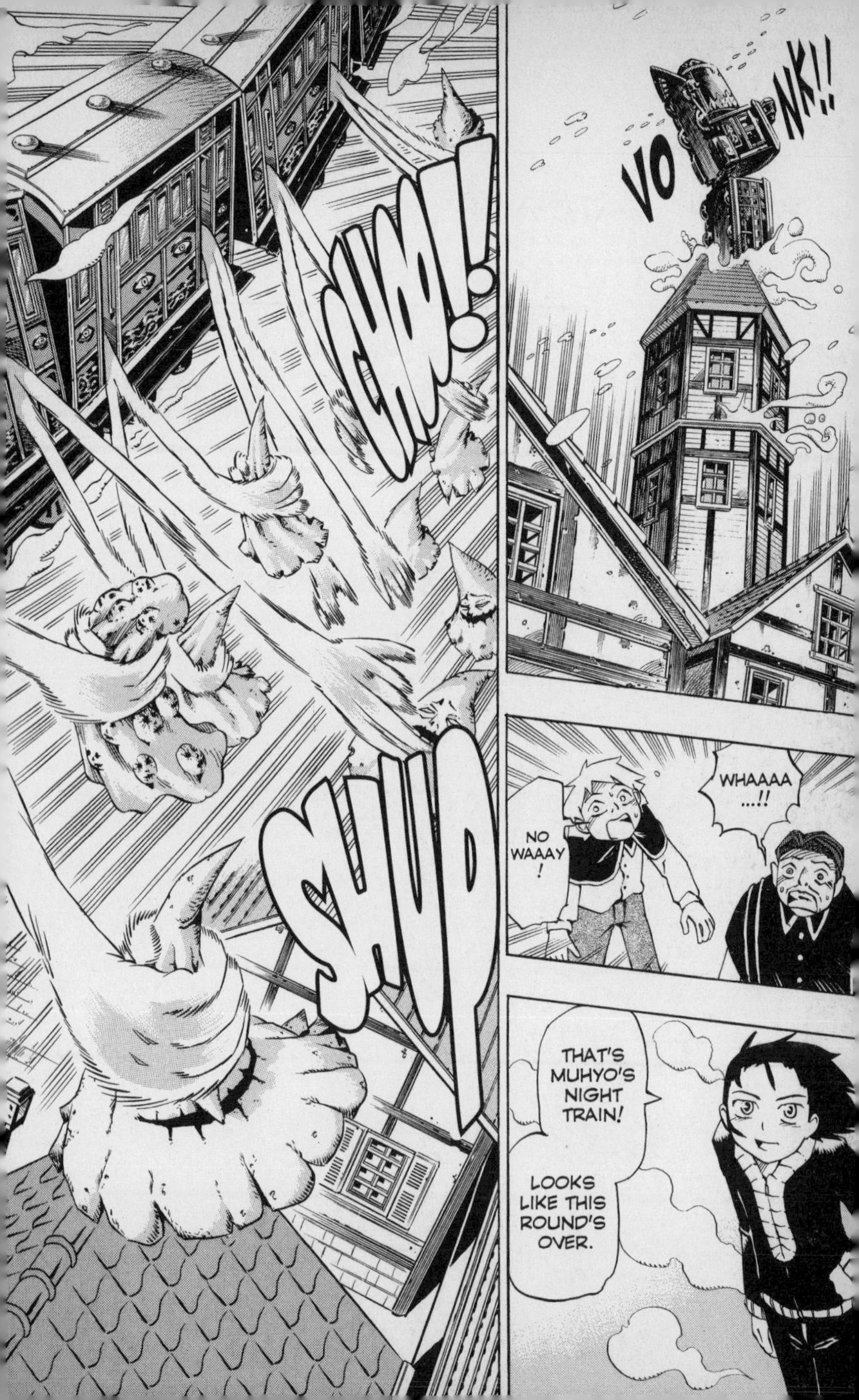
VONK!!
WHAAAA ...!!
NO WAAAY!
THAT'S MUHYO'S NIGHT TRAIN!
LOOKS LIKE THIS ROUND'S OVER.
SHOO!!
SHUP

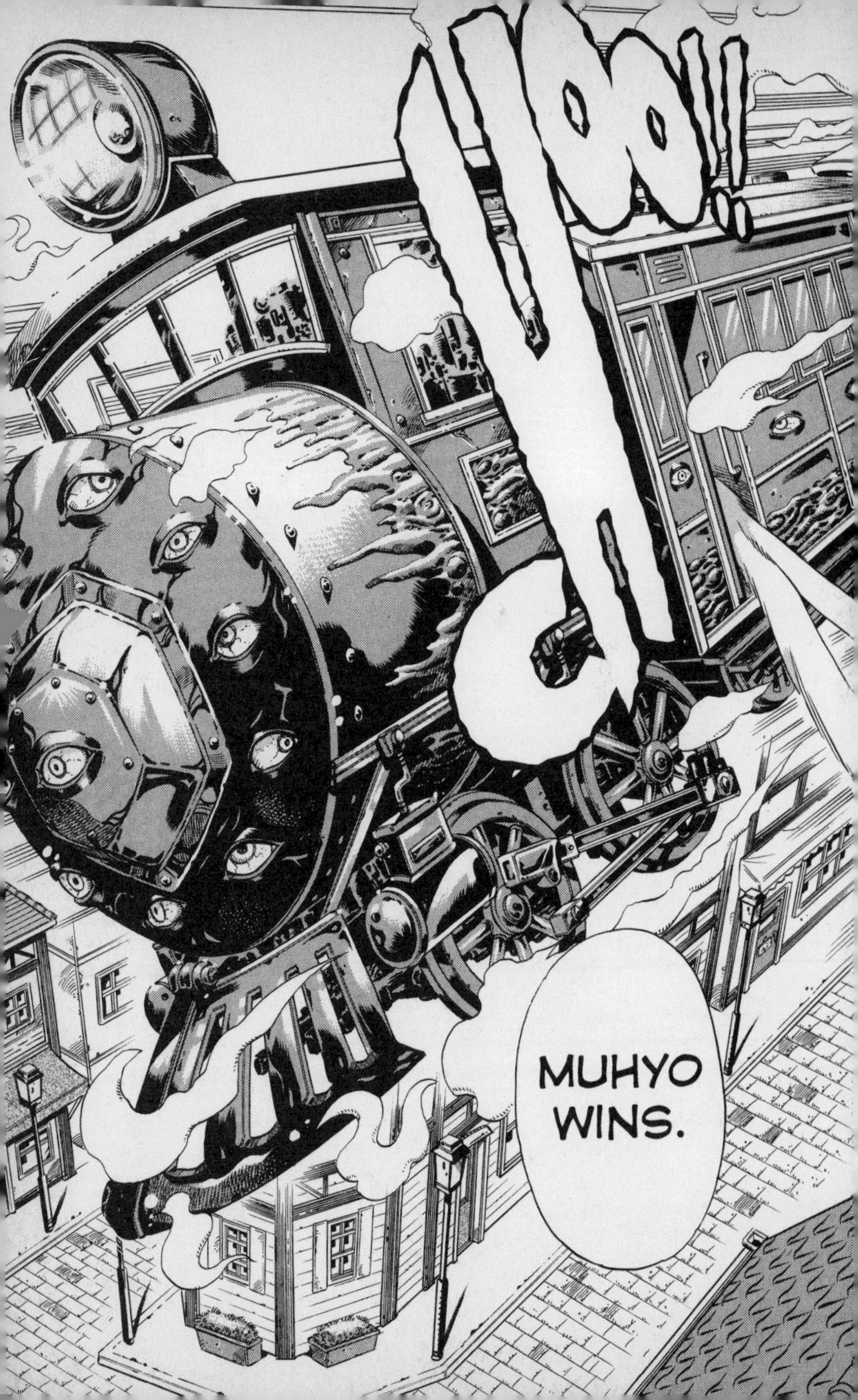
MUHYO WINS.

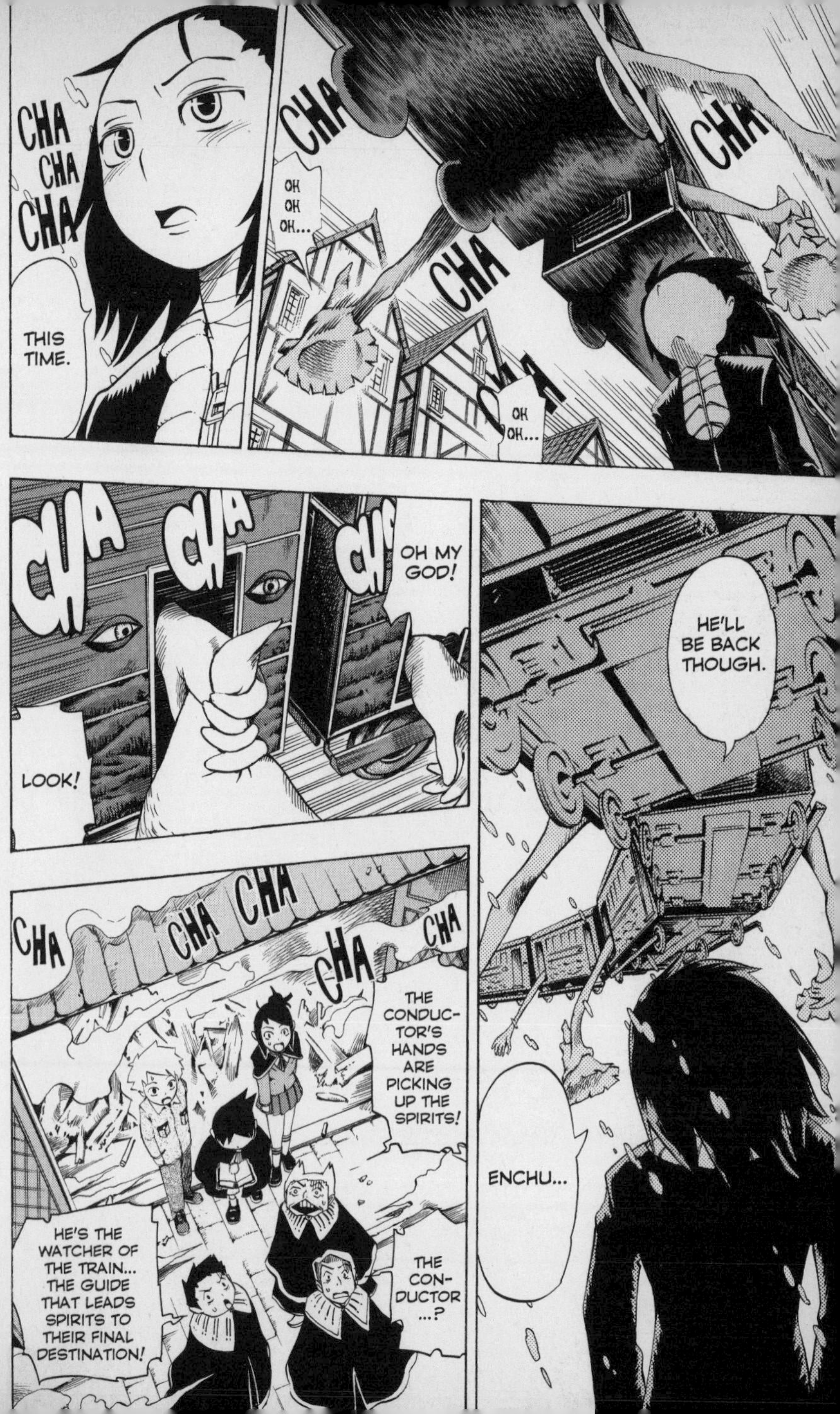
CHA
CHA
OH OH OH...
CHA
CHA
OH OH...
CHA CHA CHA
THIS TIME.
HE'LL BE BACK THOUGH.
ENCHU...
CH
OH MY GOD!
CHA
CHA
LOOK!
CHA
CHA
CHA
CHA
CHA
THE CONDUCTOR'S HANDS ARE PICKING UP THE SPIRITS!
THE CONDUCTOR...?
HE'S THE WATCHER OF THE TRAIN... THE GUIDE THAT LEADS SPIRITS TO THEIR FINAL DESTINATION!

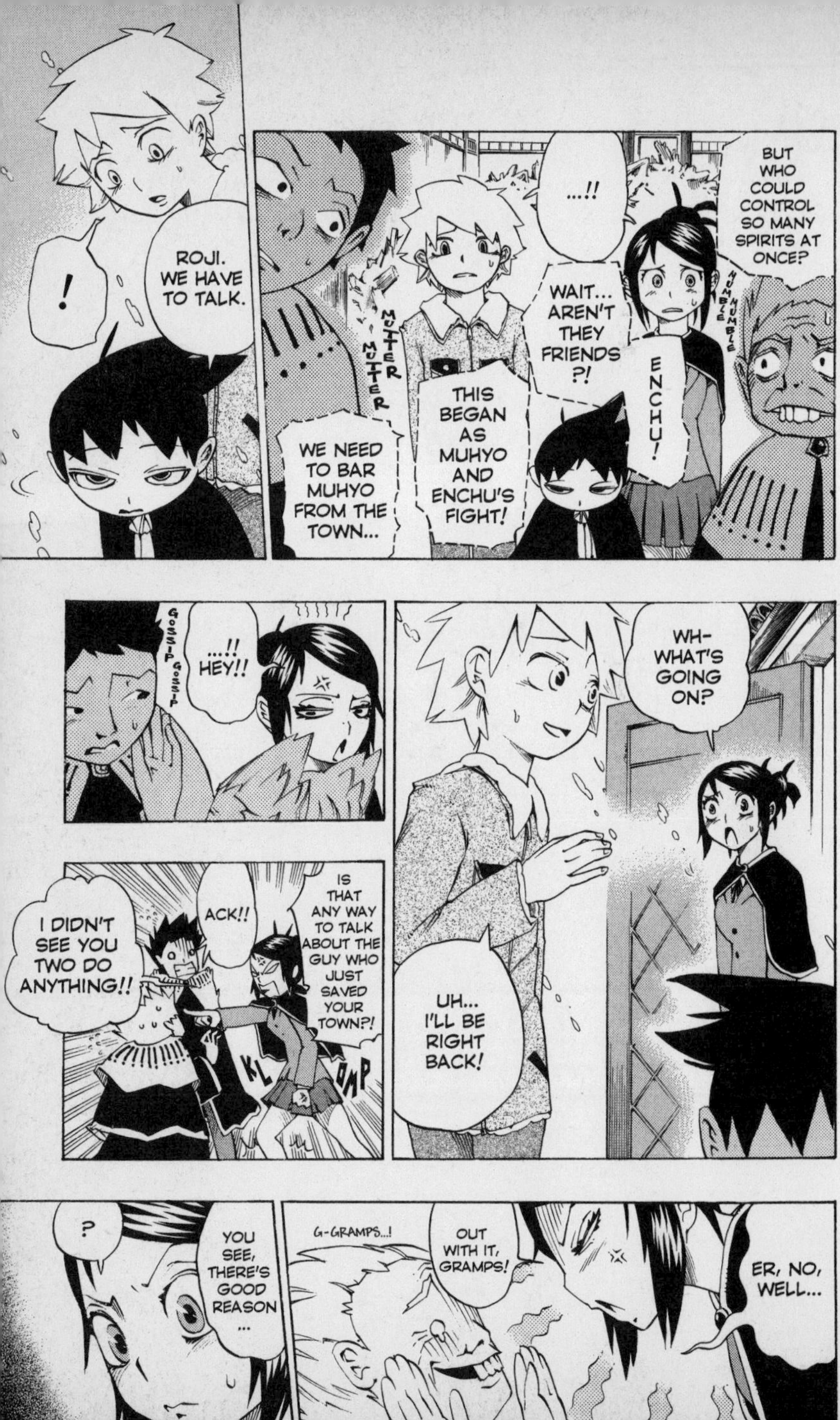
BUT WHO COULD CONTROL SO MANY SPIRITS AT ONCE?
HUMBLE HUMBLE
...!!
WAIT... AREN'T THEY FRIENDS?!
ENCHU!
THIS BEGAN AS MUHYO AND ENCHU'S FIGHT!
MUTTER MUTTER
WE NEED TO BAR MUHYO FROM THE TOWN...
ROJI. WE HAVE TO TALK.
!
WH- WHAT'S GOING ON?
UH... I'LL BE RIGHT BACK!
...!! HEY!!
GOSSIP GOSSIP
IS THAT ANY WAY TO TALK ABOUT THE GUY WHO JUST SAVED YOUR TOWN?!
ACK!!
KLOMP
I DIDN'T SEE YOU TWO DO ANYTHING!!
ER, NO, WELL...
OUT WITH IT, GRAMPS!
G-GRAMPS...!
YOU SEE, THERE'S GOOD REASON ...
?

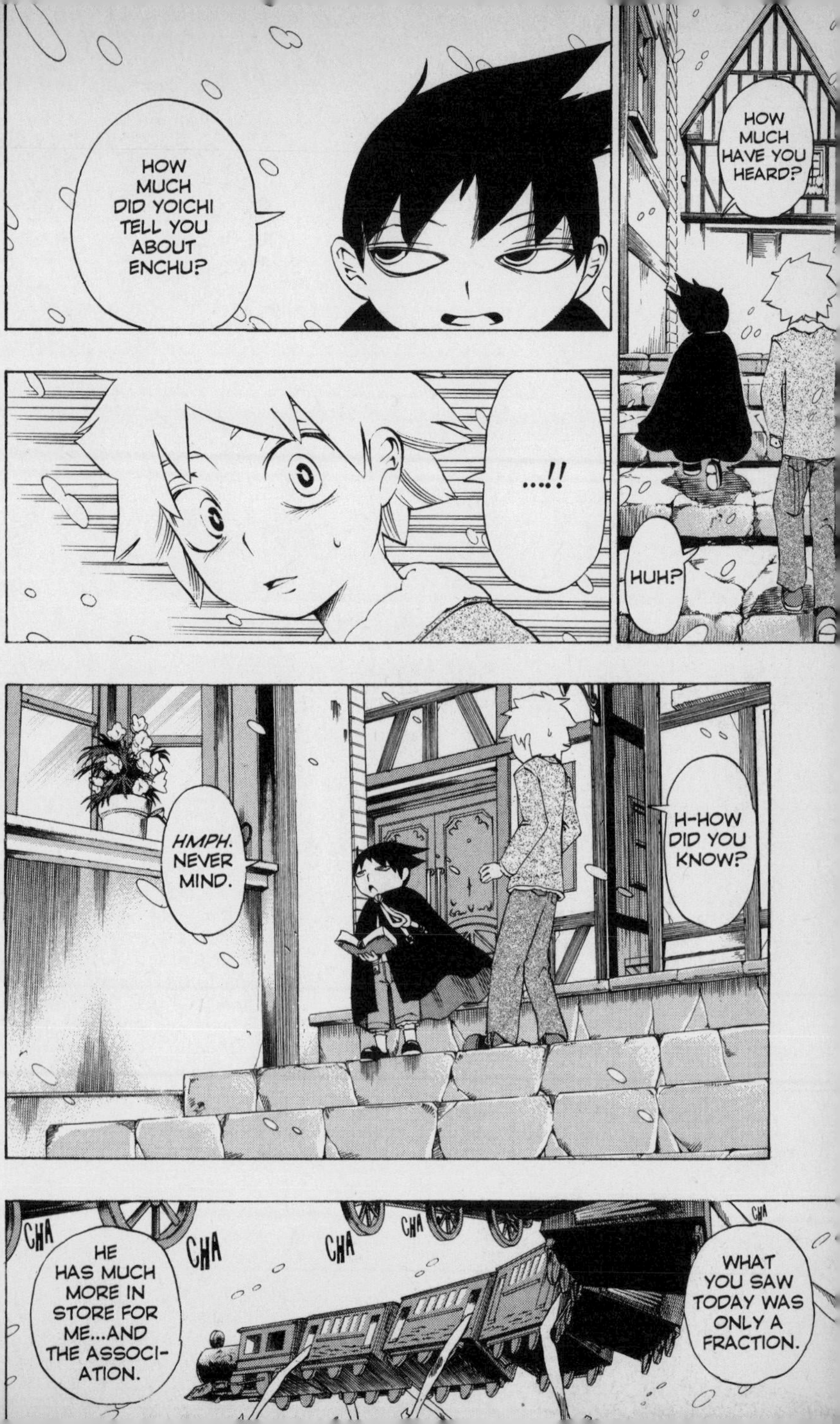
HOW MUCH HAVE YOU HEARD?
HUH?
HOW MUCH DID YOICHI TELL YOU ABOUT ENCHU?
...!!
H-HOW DID YOU KNOW?
HMPH. NEVER MIND.
CHA CHA CHA CHA CHA
WHAT YOU SAW TODAY WAS ONLY A FRACTION.
HE HAS MUCH MORE IN STORE FOR ME...AND THE ASSOCIATION.

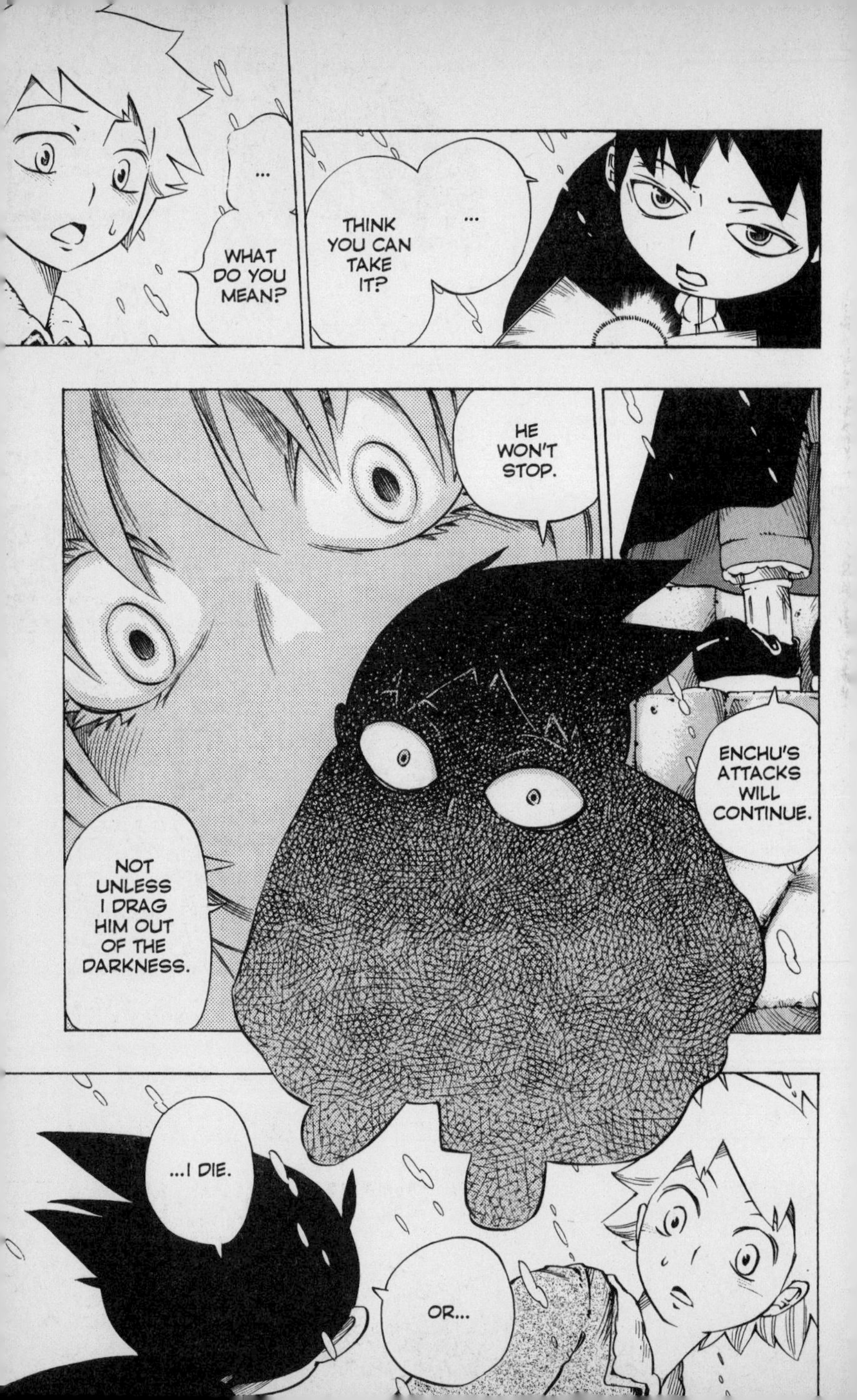
... THINK YOU CAN TAKE IT?
... WHAT DO YOU MEAN?
ENCHU'S ATTACKS WILL CONTINUE.
HE WON'T STOP.
NOT UNLESS I DRAG HIM OUT OF THE DARKNESS.
OR...
...I DIE.

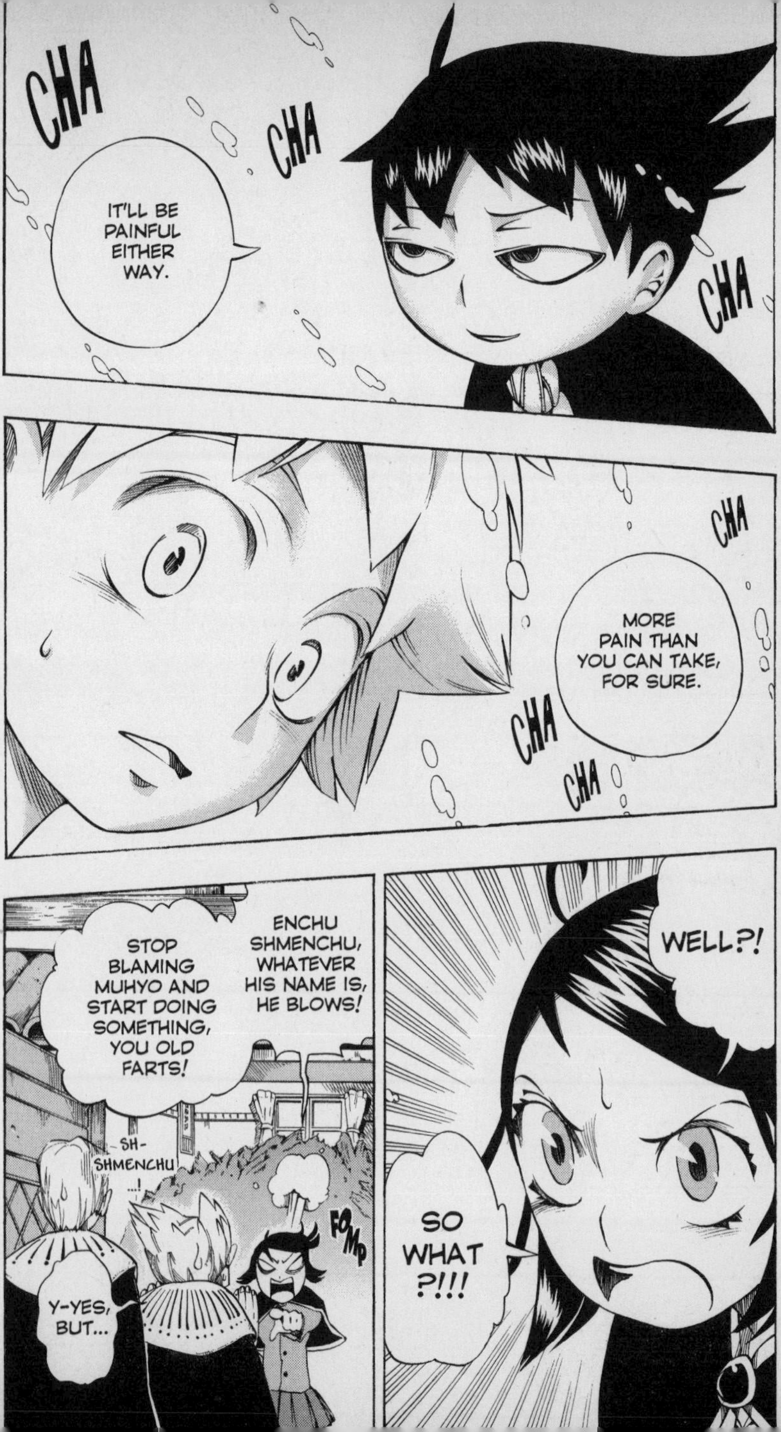
CHA
CHA
CHA
IT'LL BE PAINFUL EITHER WAY.
CHA
MORE PAIN THAN YOU CAN TAKE, FOR SURE.
CHA
CHA
WELL?!
SO WHAT?!!!
ENCHU SHMENCHU, WHATEVER HIS NAME IS, HE BLOWS!
STOP BLAMING MUHYO AND START DOING SOMETHING, YOU OLD FARTS!
FOMP
SH-SHMENCHU...!
Y-YES, BUT...

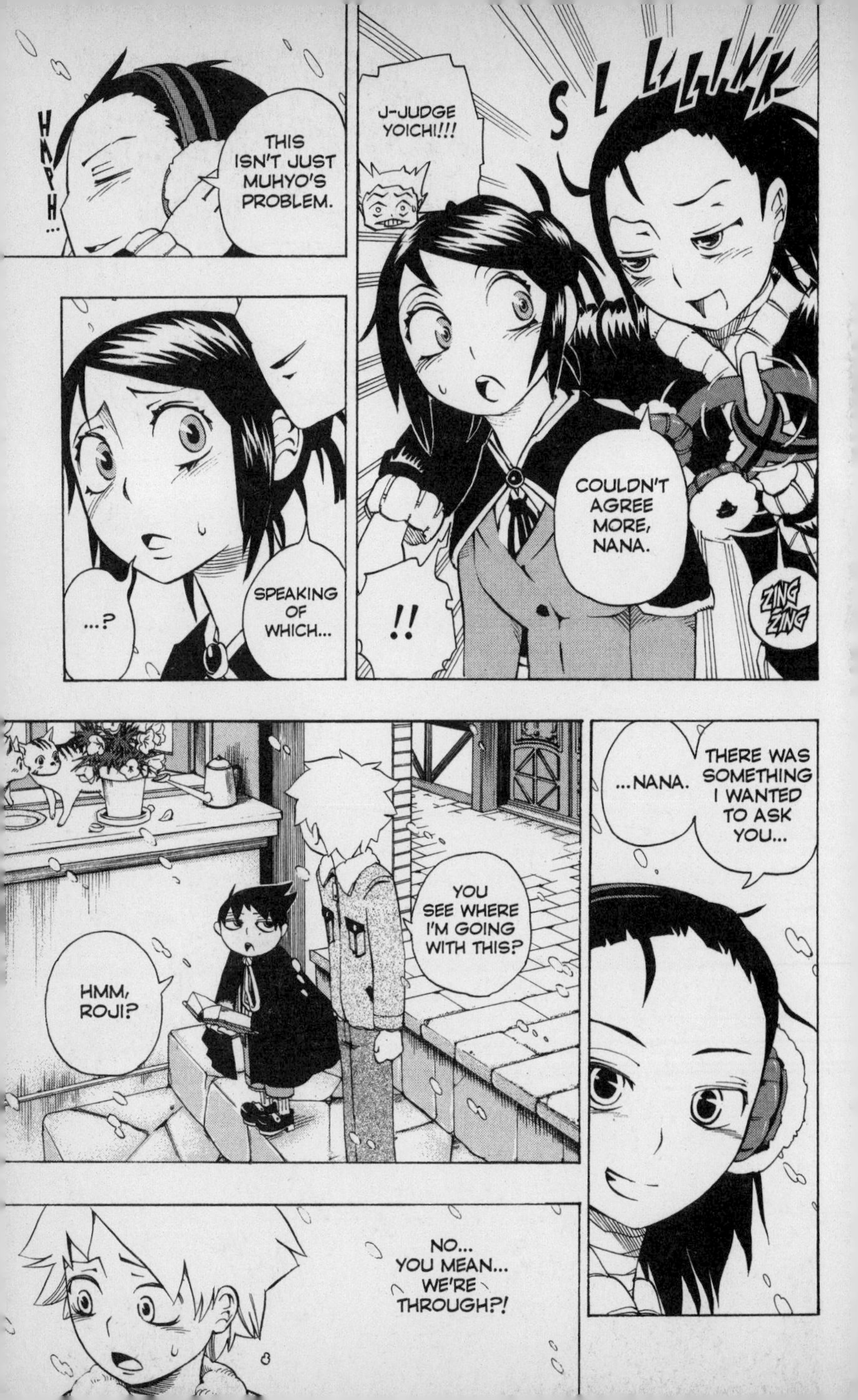
SLLLINK
J-JUDGE YOICHI!!!
COULDN'T AGREE MORE, NANA.
ZING ZING
!!
THIS ISN'T JUST MUHYO'S PROBLEM.
HMPH...
SPEAKING OF WHICH...
...?
THERE WAS SOMETHING I WANTED TO ASK YOU...
...NANA.
YOU SEE WHERE I'M GOING WITH THIS?
HMM, ROJI?
NO... YOU MEAN... WE'RE THROUGH?!

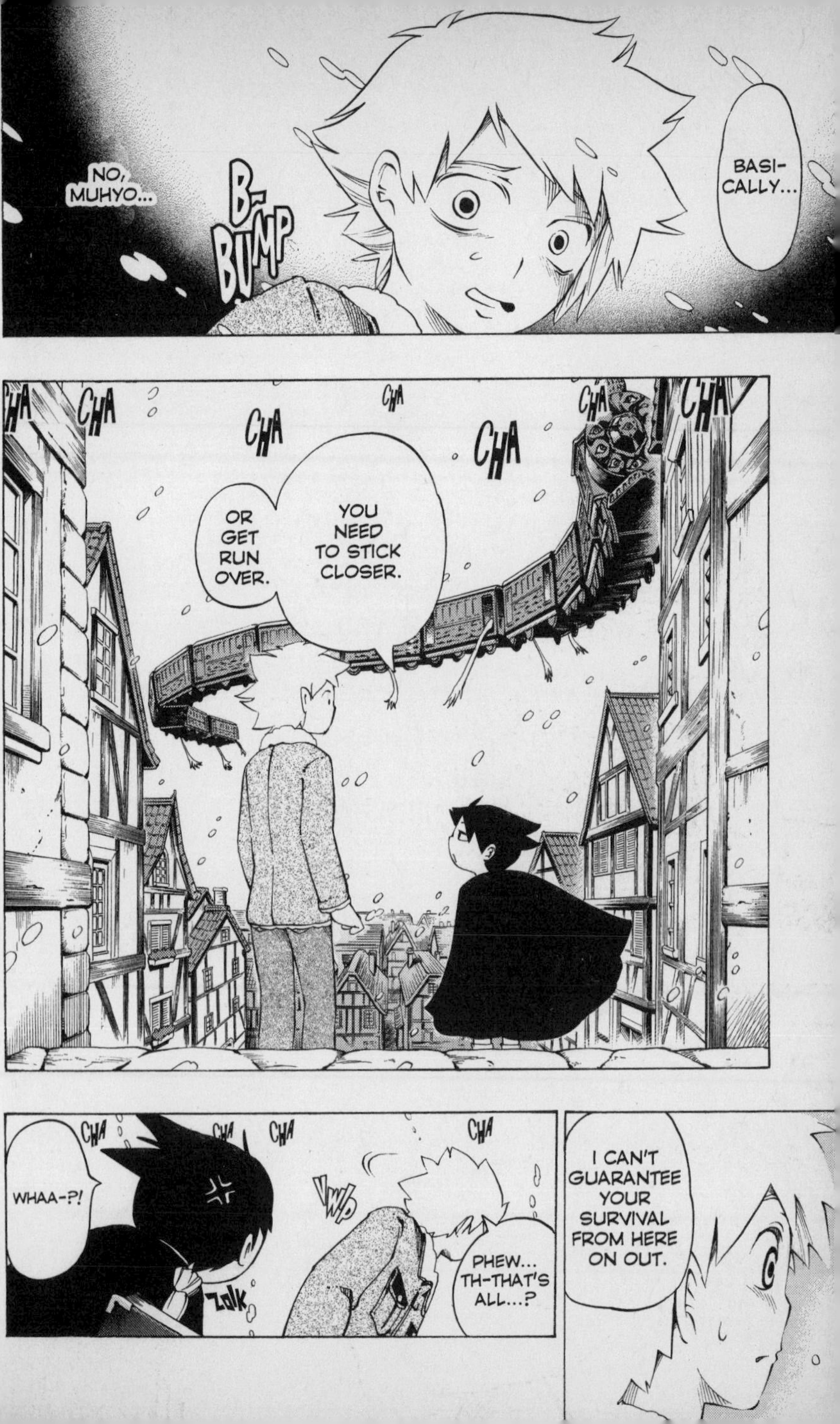
BASI-CALLY...
B-BUMP
NO, MUHYO...
CHA
CHA
CHA
CHA
CHA
CHA
CHA
YOU NEED TO STICK CLOSER.
OR GET RUN OVER.
I CAN'T GUARANTEE YOUR SURVIVAL FROM HERE ON OUT.
CHA
CHA
PHEW... TH-THAT'S ALL...?
VWIP
CHA
CHA
ZOIK
WHAA-?!

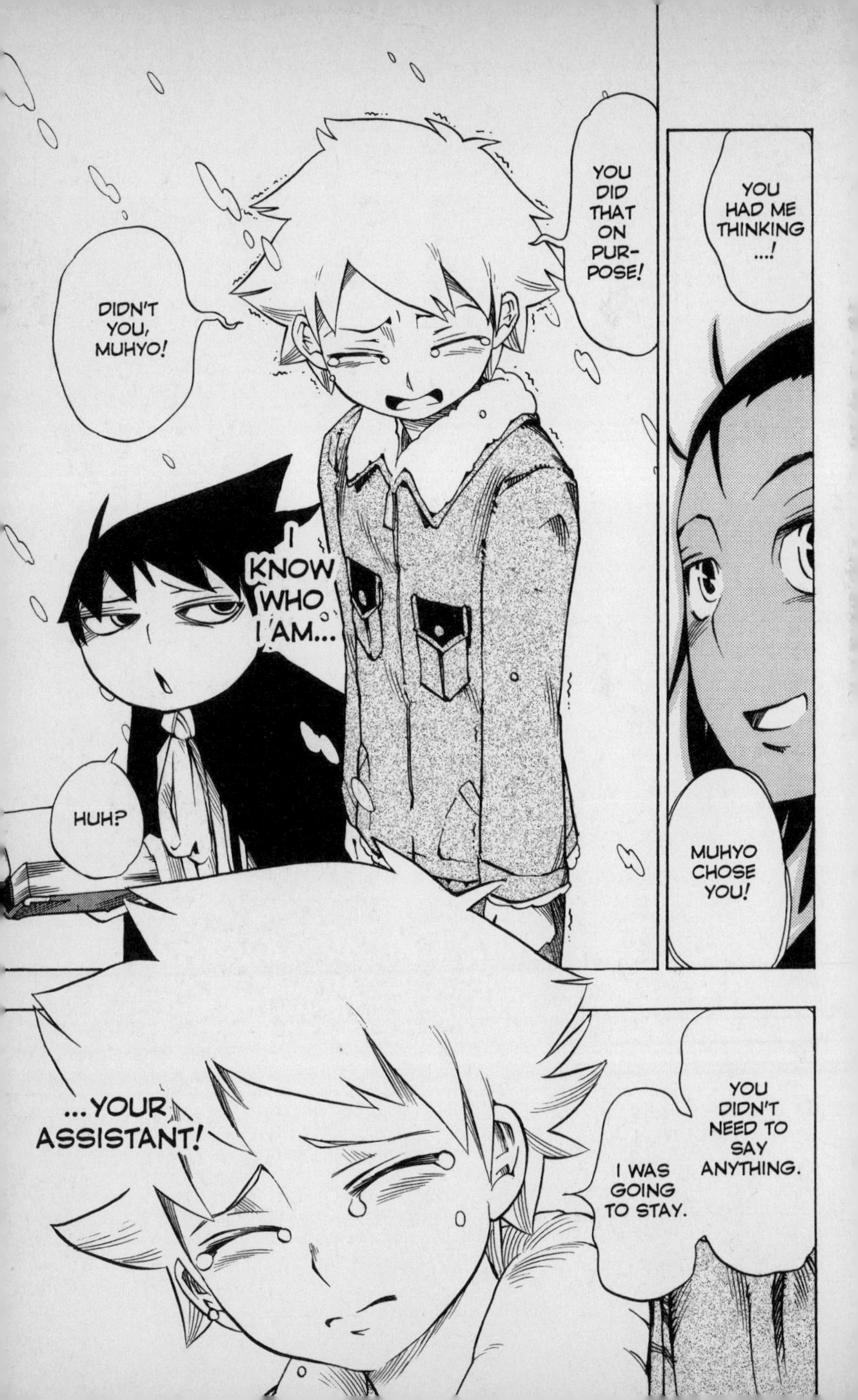

YOU HAD ME THINKING ...!
MUHYO CHOSE YOU!
YOU DID THAT ON PURPOSE!
DIDN'T YOU, MUHYO!
I KNOW WHO I AM...
HUH?
YOU DIDN'T NEED TO SAY ANYTHING.
I WAS GOING TO STAY.
...YOUR ASSISTANT!

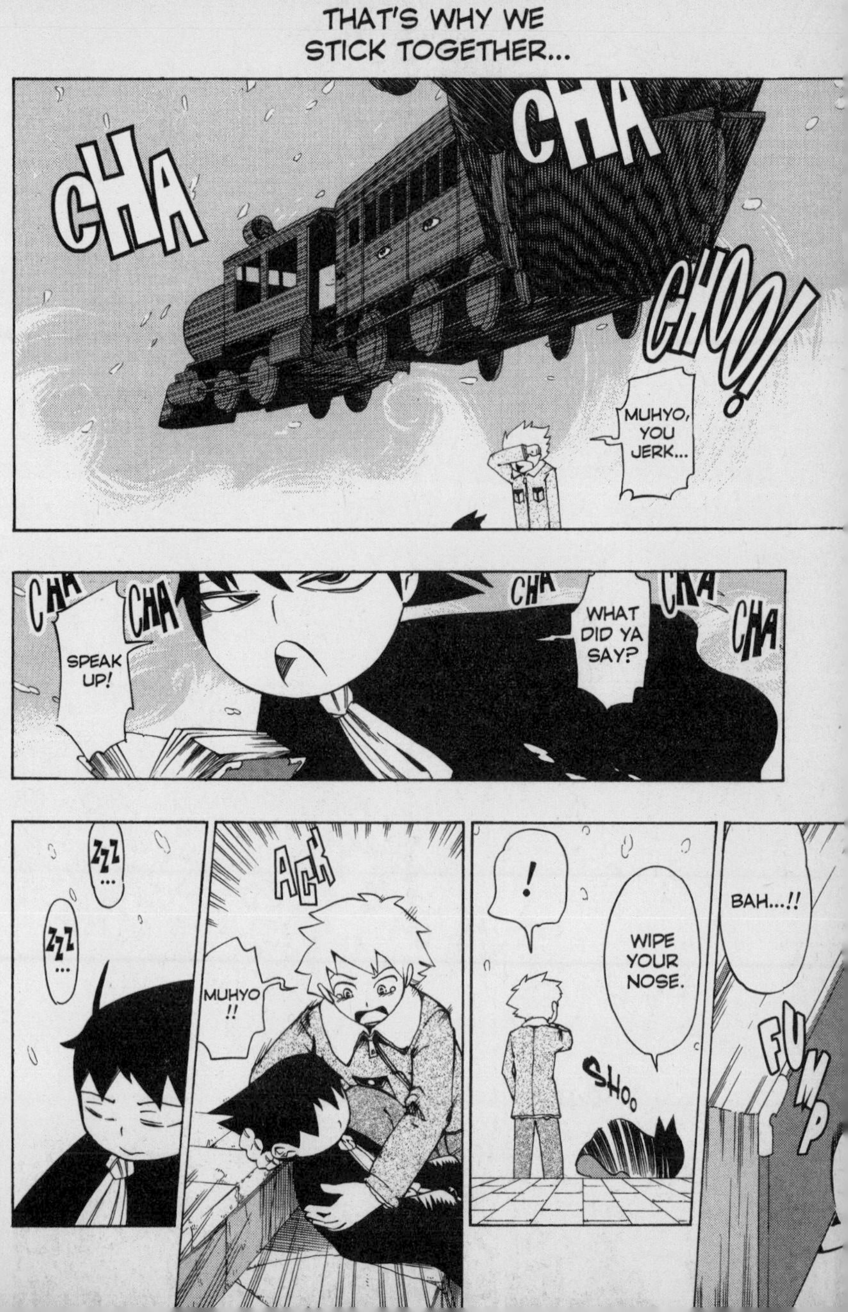
THAT'S WHY WE STICK TOGETHER...
CHA
CHOO!
MUHYO, YOU JERK...
CHA
CHA
CHA
WHAT DID YA SAY?
CHA
CHA
SPEAK UP!
CHA
BAH...!!
FUMP
!
WIPE YOUR NOSE.
SHOO
ACK
MUHYO !!
ZZZ ...
ZZZ ...

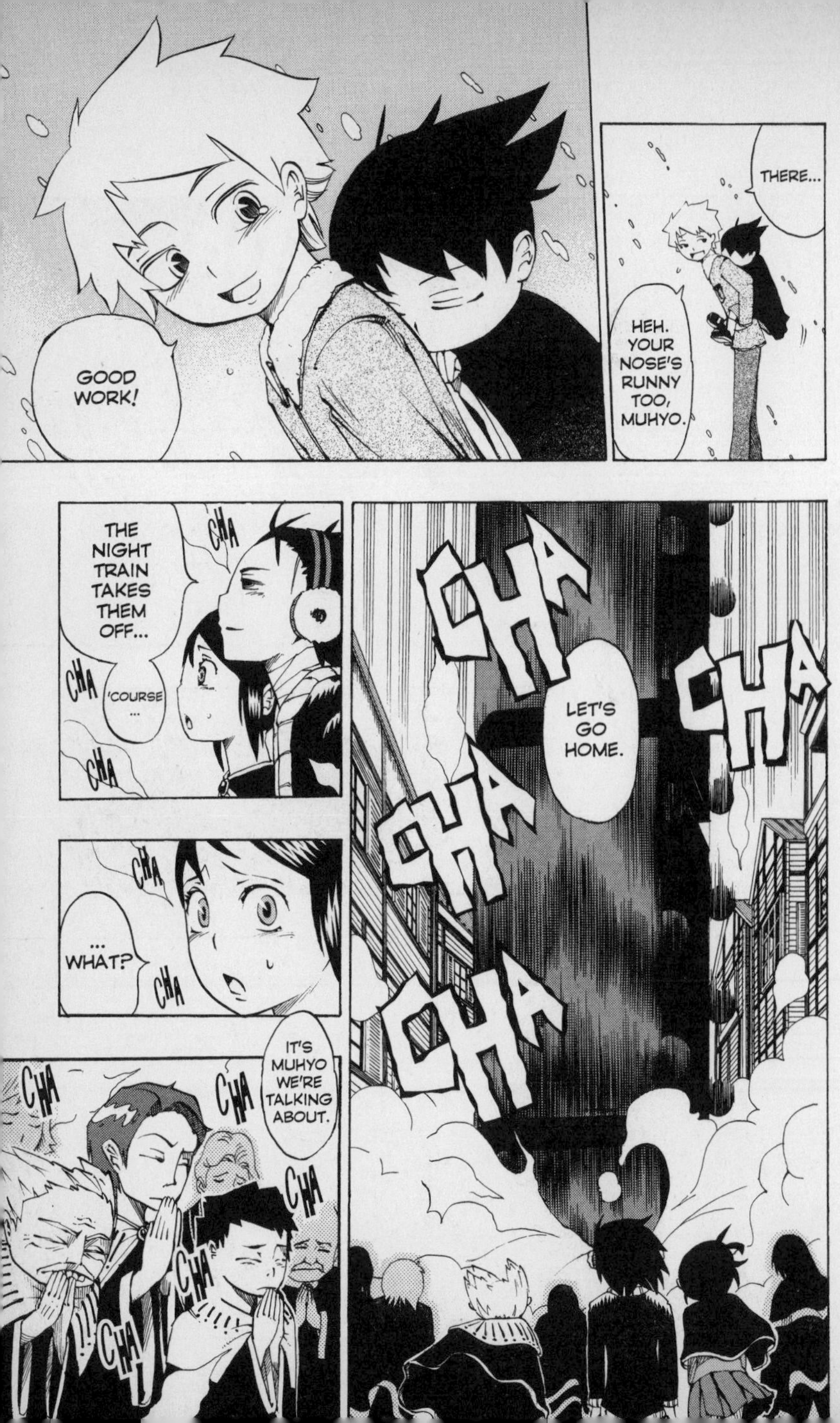
THERE...
HEH. YOUR NOSE'S RUNNY TOO, MUHYO.
GOOD WORK!
CHA
CHA
LET'S GO HOME.
CHA
CHA
THE NIGHT TRAIN TAKES THEM OFF...
CHA
CHA
'COURSE ...
CHA
CHA
... WHAT?
CHA
IT'S MUHYO WE'RE TALKING ABOUT.
CHA
CHA
CHA
CHA
CHA

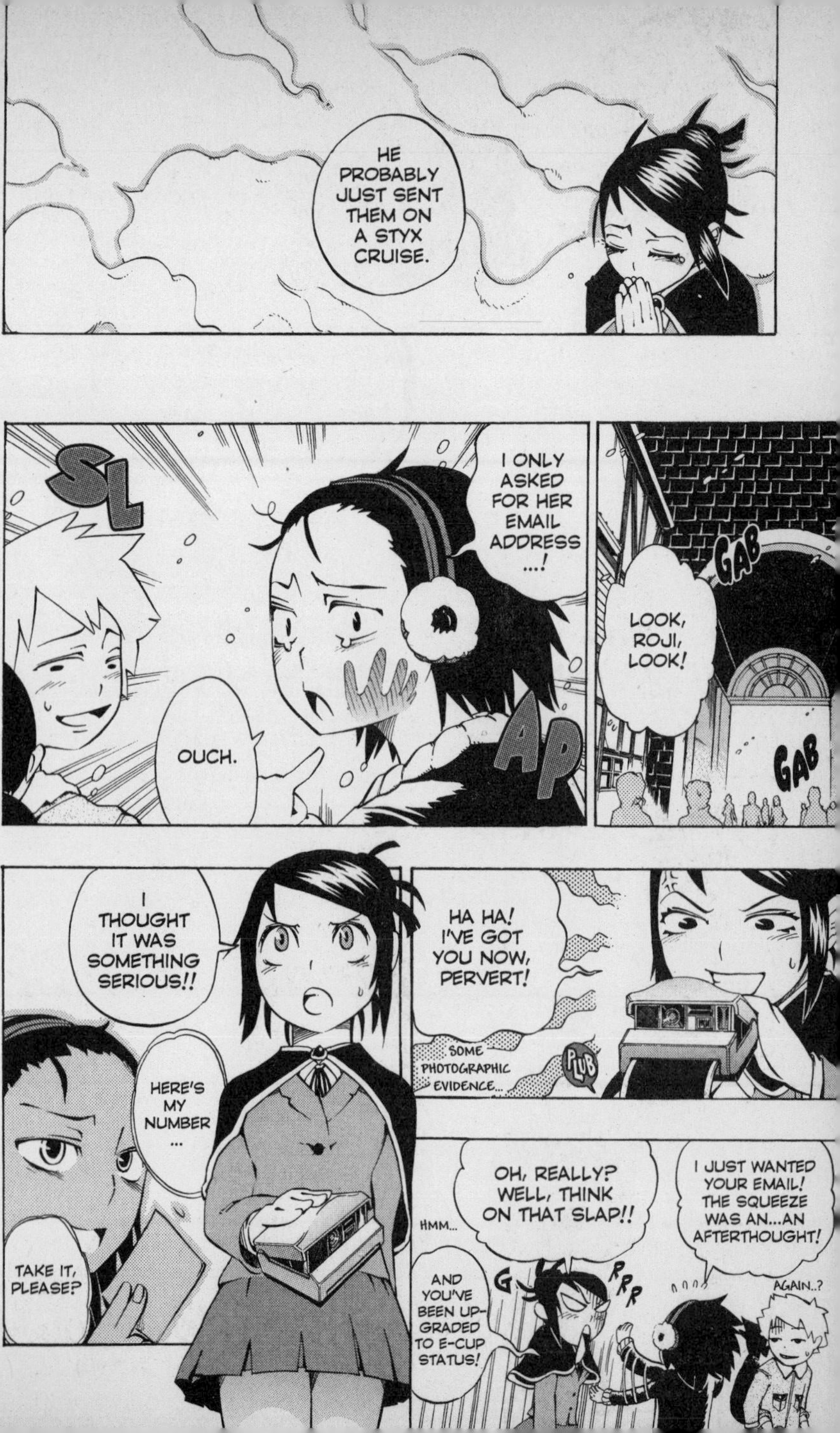
HE PROBABLY JUST SENT THEM ON A STYX CRUISE.
GAB
LOOK, ROJI, LOOK!
GAB
I ONLY ASKED FOR HER EMAIL ADDRESS ...!
SL
AP
OUCH.
HA HA! I'VE GOT YOU NOW, PERVERT!
SOME PHOTOGRAPHIC EVIDENCE...
PLUB
I JUST WANTED YOUR EMAIL! THE SQUEEZE WAS AN...AN AFTERTHOUGHT!
AGAIN..?
OH, REALLY? WELL, THINK ON THAT SLAP!!
HMM...
RRR
G
AND YOU'VE BEEN UP-GRADED TO E-CUP STATUS!
I THOUGHT IT WAS SOMETHING SERIOUS!!
HERE'S MY NUMBER ...
TAKE IT, PLEASE?

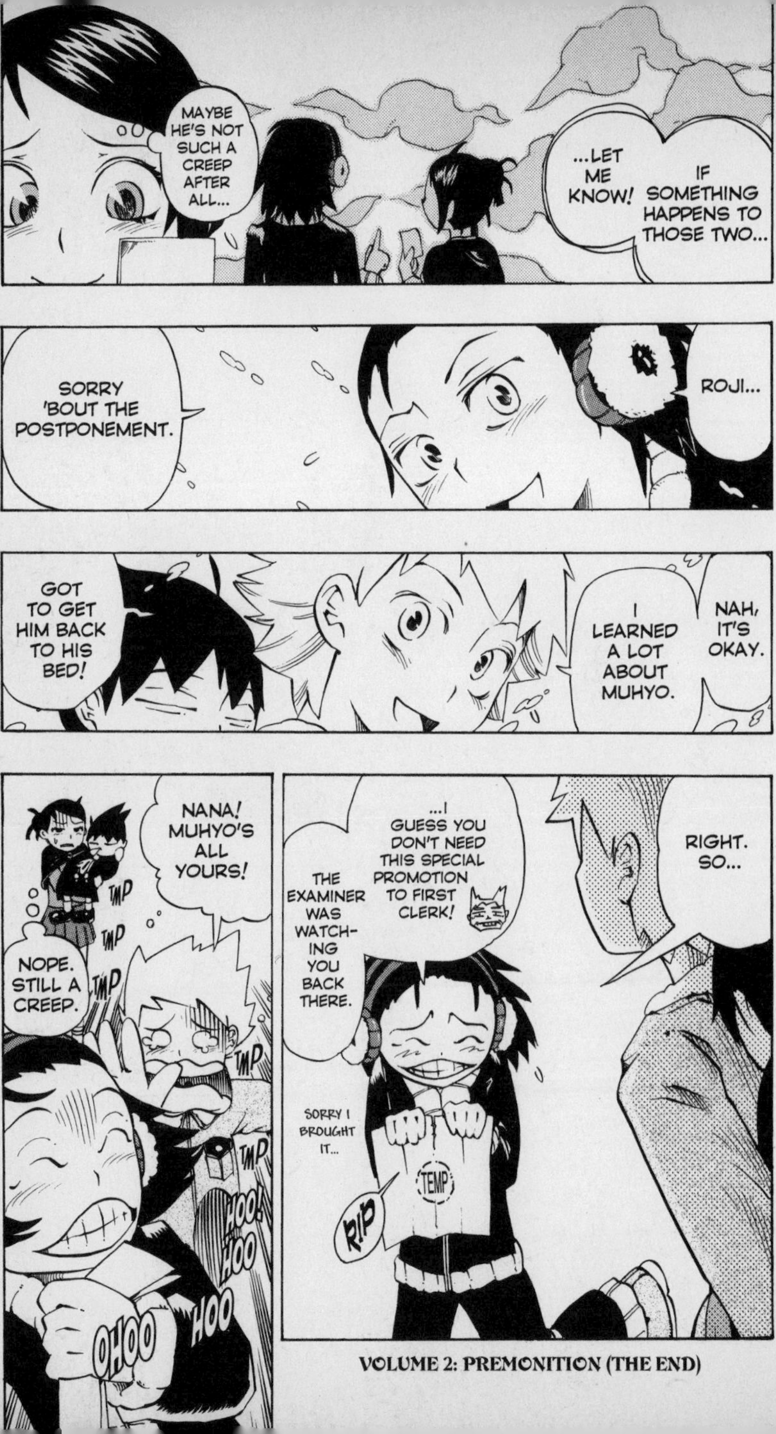
IF SOMETHING HAPPENS TO THOSE TWO...
...LET ME KNOW!
MAYBE HE'S NOT SUCH A CREEP AFTER ALL...
ROJI...
SORRY 'BOUT THE POSTPONEMENT.
NAH, IT'S OKAY.
I LEARNED A LOT ABOUT MUHYO.
GOT TO GET HIM BACK TO HIS BED!
RIGHT. SO...
...I GUESS YOU DON'T NEED THIS SPECIAL PROMOTION TO FIRST CLERK!
THE EXAMINER WAS WATCHING YOU BACK THERE.
SORRY I BROUGHT IT...
TEMP
RIP
NANA! MUHYO'S ALL YOURS!
TMP
TMP
TMP
NOPE. STILL A CREEP.
TMP
TMP
HOO! HOO
HOO
OHOO

VOLUME 2: PREMONITION (THE END)

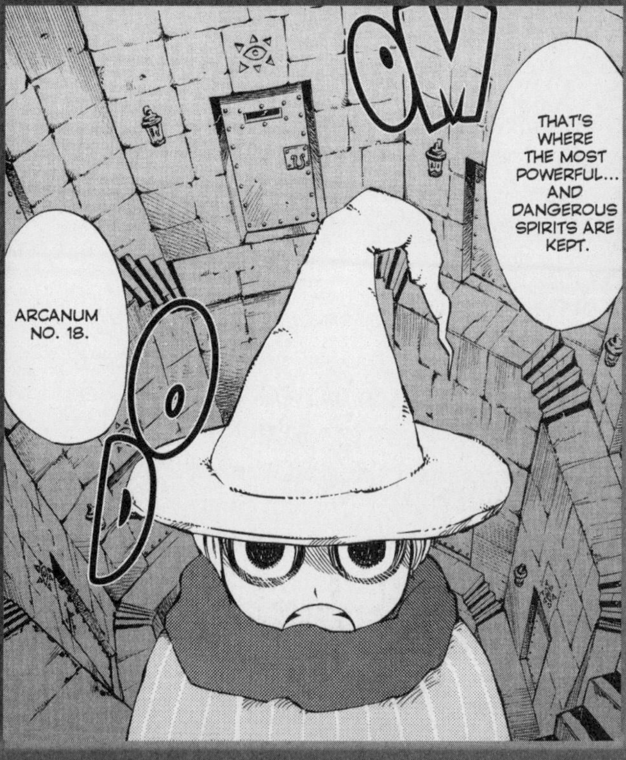
THAT'S WHERE THE MOST POWERFUL... AND DANGEROUS SPIRITS ARE KEPT.
DOOM
ARCANUM NO. 18.

In The Next Volume...

When a magic lock in a top-security prison for dangerous ghosts breaks, Muhyo's old friend Biko shows up asking for help. Find out what happens when our heroes venture to the prison Arcanum!

Available February 2008!

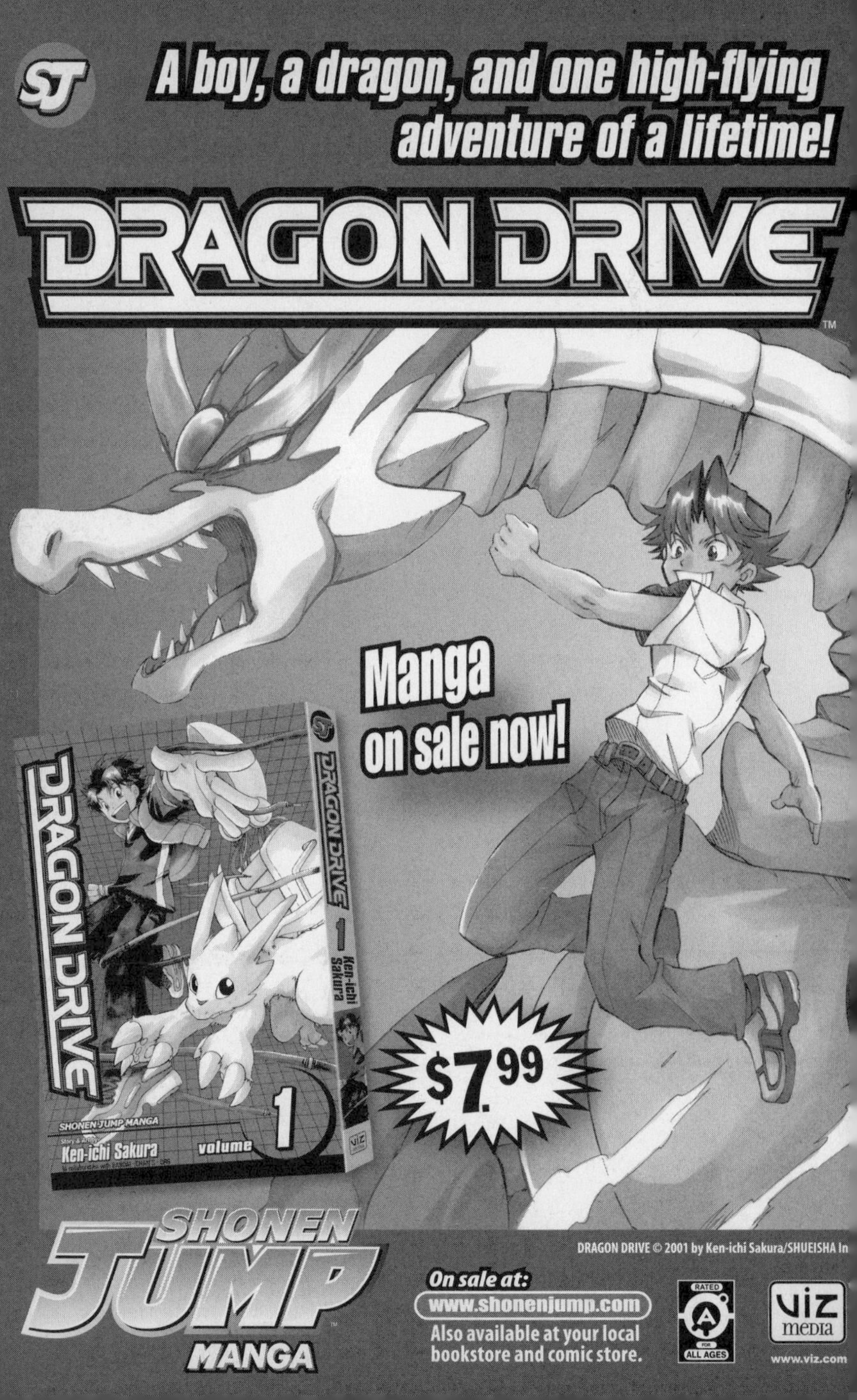
SJ
A boy, a dragon, and one high-flying adventure of a lifetime!
DRAGON DRIVE™
Manga on sale now!
DRAGON DRIVE
SHONEN JUMP MANGA
Story & Art by Ken-ichi Sakura
volume 1
DRAGON DRIVE 1 Ken-ichi Sakura
$7.99
SHONEN JUMP™ MANGA
DRAGON DRIVE © 2001 by Ken-ichi Sakura/SHUEISHA In
On sale at:
www.shonenjump.com
Also available at your local bookstore and comic store.
RATED A FOR ALL AGES
VIZ media
www.viz.com

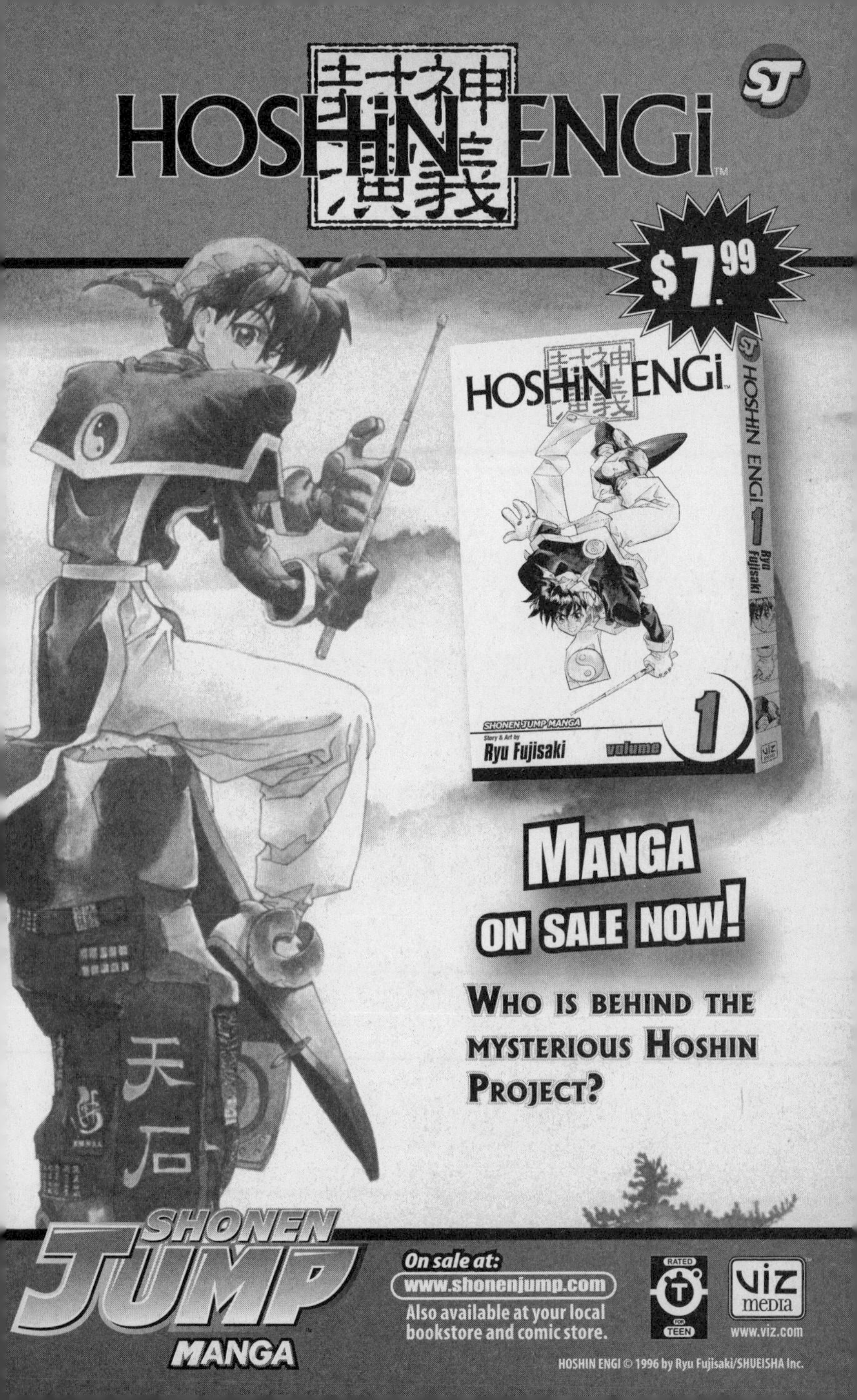
HOSHIN ENGI™
封神演義
SJ
$7.99
HOSHIN ENGI
SHONEN JUMP MANGA
Story & Art by
Ryu Fujisaki
volume 1
MANGA
ON SALE NOW!
WHO IS BEHIND THE MYSTERIOUS HOSHIN PROJECT?
SHONEN JUMP MANGA
On sale at:
www.shonenjump.com
Also available at your local bookstore and comic store.
RATED T FOR TEEN
VIZ media
www.viz.com
HOSHIN ENGI © 1996 by Ryu Fujisaki/SHUEISHA Inc.

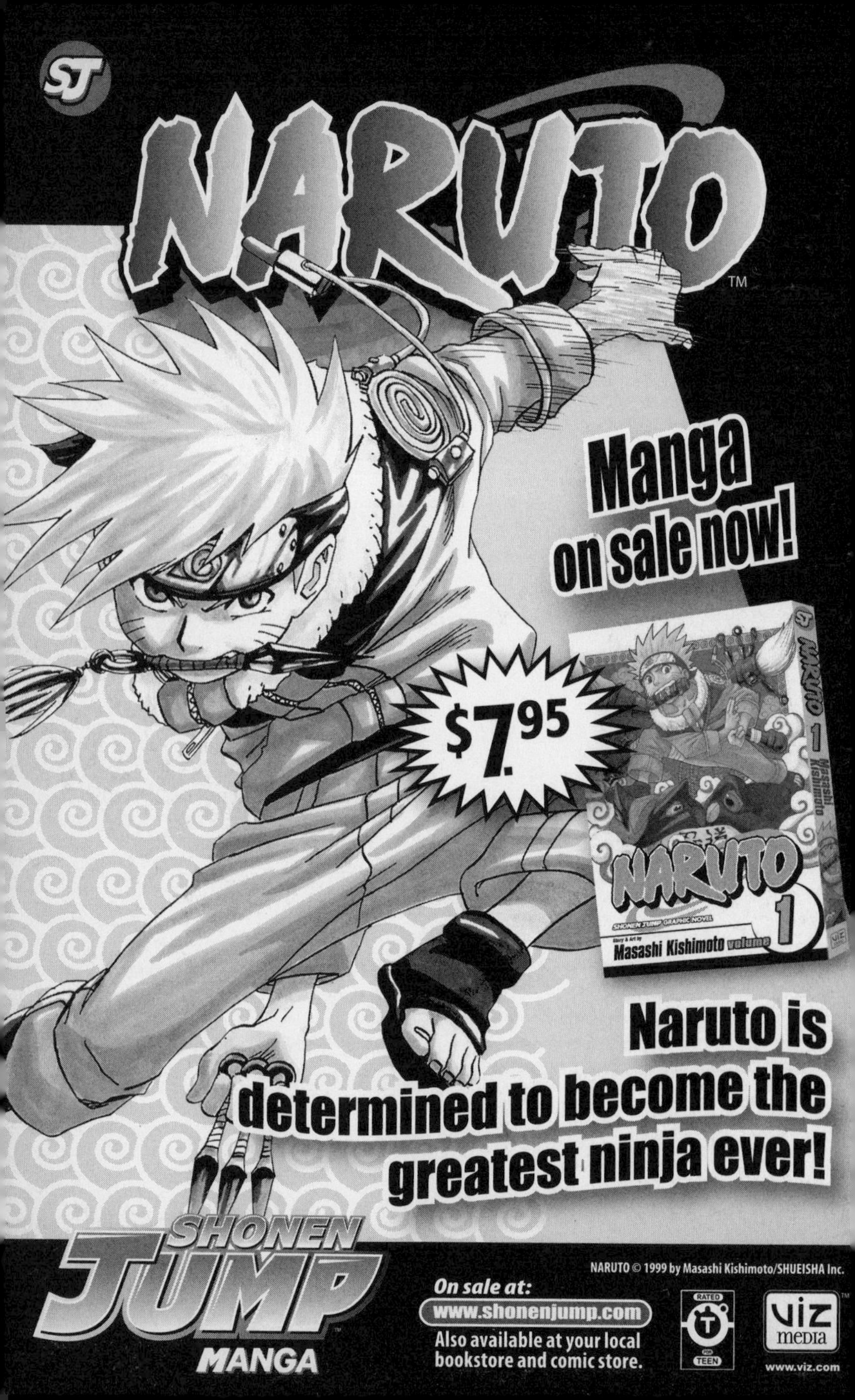

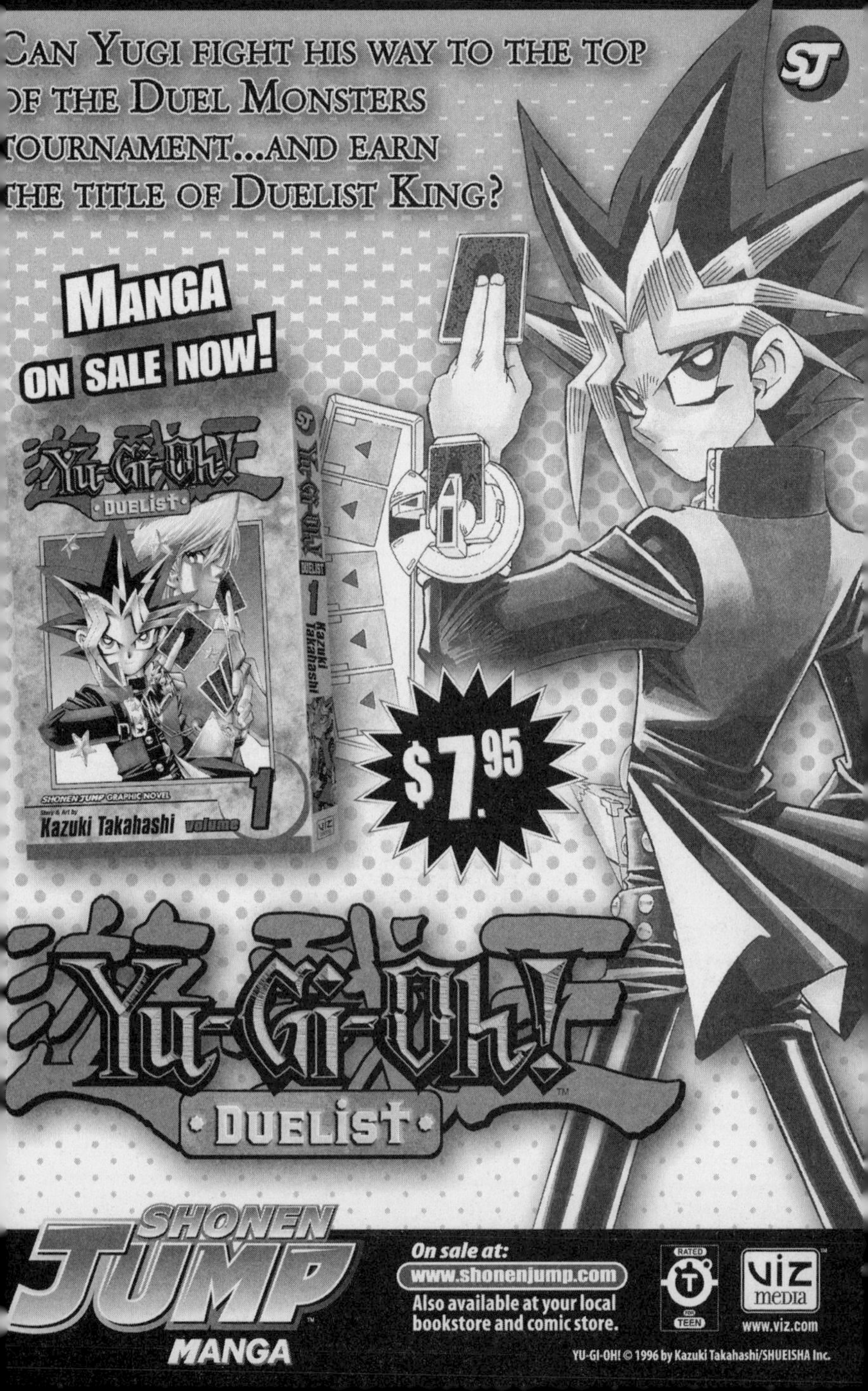
CAN YUGI FIGHT HIS WAY TO THE TOP OF THE DUEL MONSTERS TOURNAMENT...AND EARN THE TITLE OF DUELIST KING?
SJ
MANGA ON SALE NOW!
YU-GI-OH! DUELIST
SHONEN JUMP GRAPHIC NOVEL
Story & Art by Kazuki Takahashi volume 1
$7.95
YU-GI-OH! DUELIST
SHONEN JUMP MANGA
On sale at:
www.shonenjump.com
Also available at your local bookstore and comic store.
RATED T FOR TEEN
VIZ media
www.viz.com
YU-GI-OH! © 1996 by Kazuki Takahashi/SHUEISHA Inc.

$7.95

MANGA ON SALE NOW!

LUFFY HAS VOWED TO BECOME KING OF THE PIRATES AND FIND THE LEGENDARY TREASURE KNOWN AS "ONE PIECE"!

On sale at:
www.shonenjump.com
Also available at your local bookstore and comic store.

www.viz.com

ONE PIECE © 1997 by Eiichiro Oda/SHUEISHA Inc.

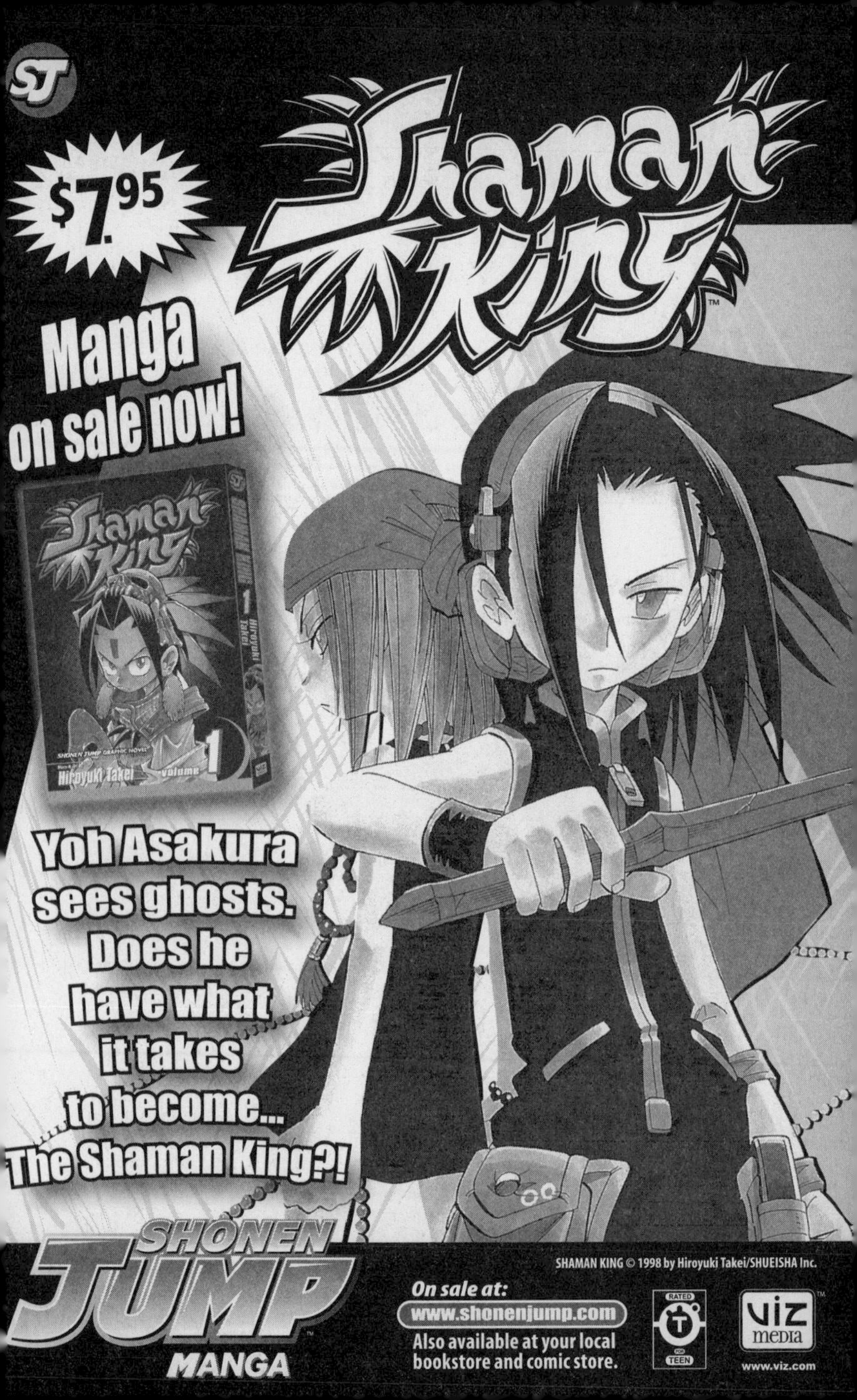
SJ
$7.95
Shaman King™
Manga on sale now!
Shaman King
SHONEN JUMP GRAPHIC NOVEL
Hiroyuki Takei
volume 1
Yoh Asakura sees ghosts. Does he have what it takes to become... The Shaman King?!
SHONEN JUMP MANGA
SHAMAN KING © 1998 by Hiroyuki Takei/SHUEISHA Inc.
On sale at:
www.shonenjump.com
Also available at your local bookstore and comic store.
RATED T FOR TEEN
viz media
www.viz.com

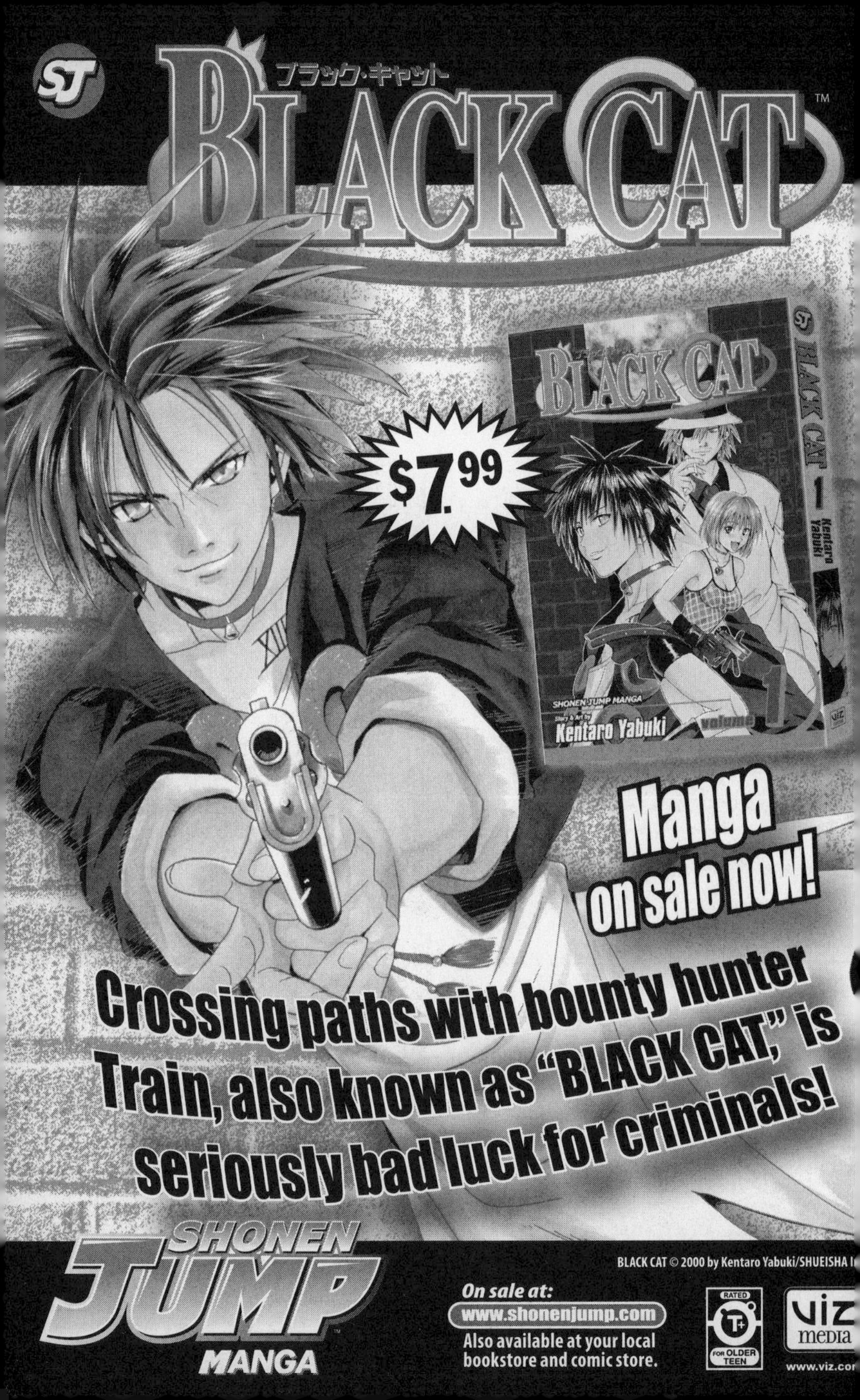
SJ
ブラック・キャット
BLACK CAT™
SJ BLACK CAT 1 Kentaro Yabuki
BLACK CAT
SHONEN JUMP MANGA
Story & Art by Kentaro Yabuki
$7.99
Manga on sale now!
Crossing paths with bounty hunter Train, also known as "BLACK CAT," is seriously bad luck for criminals!
SHONEN JUMP MANGA
BLACK CAT © 2000 by Kentaro Yabuki/SHUEISHA I
On sale at:
www.shonenjump.com
Also available at your local bookstore and comic store.
RATED T+ FOR OLDER TEEN
VIZ media
www.viz.co

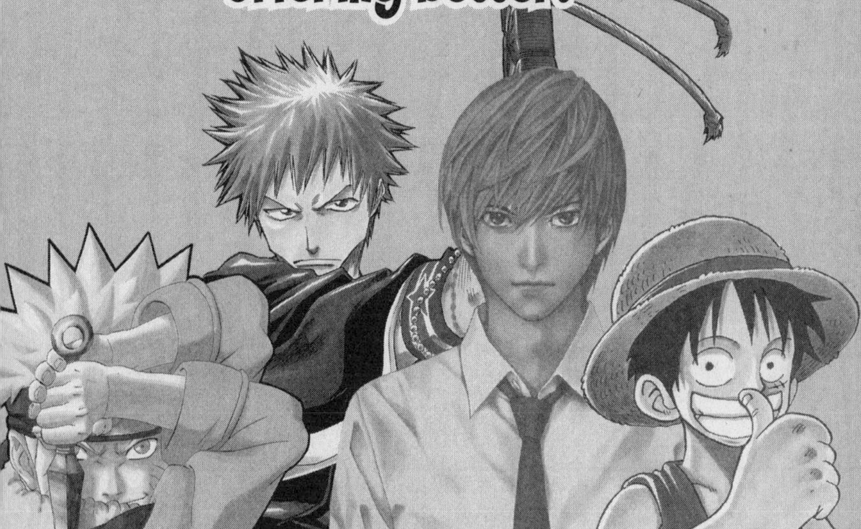

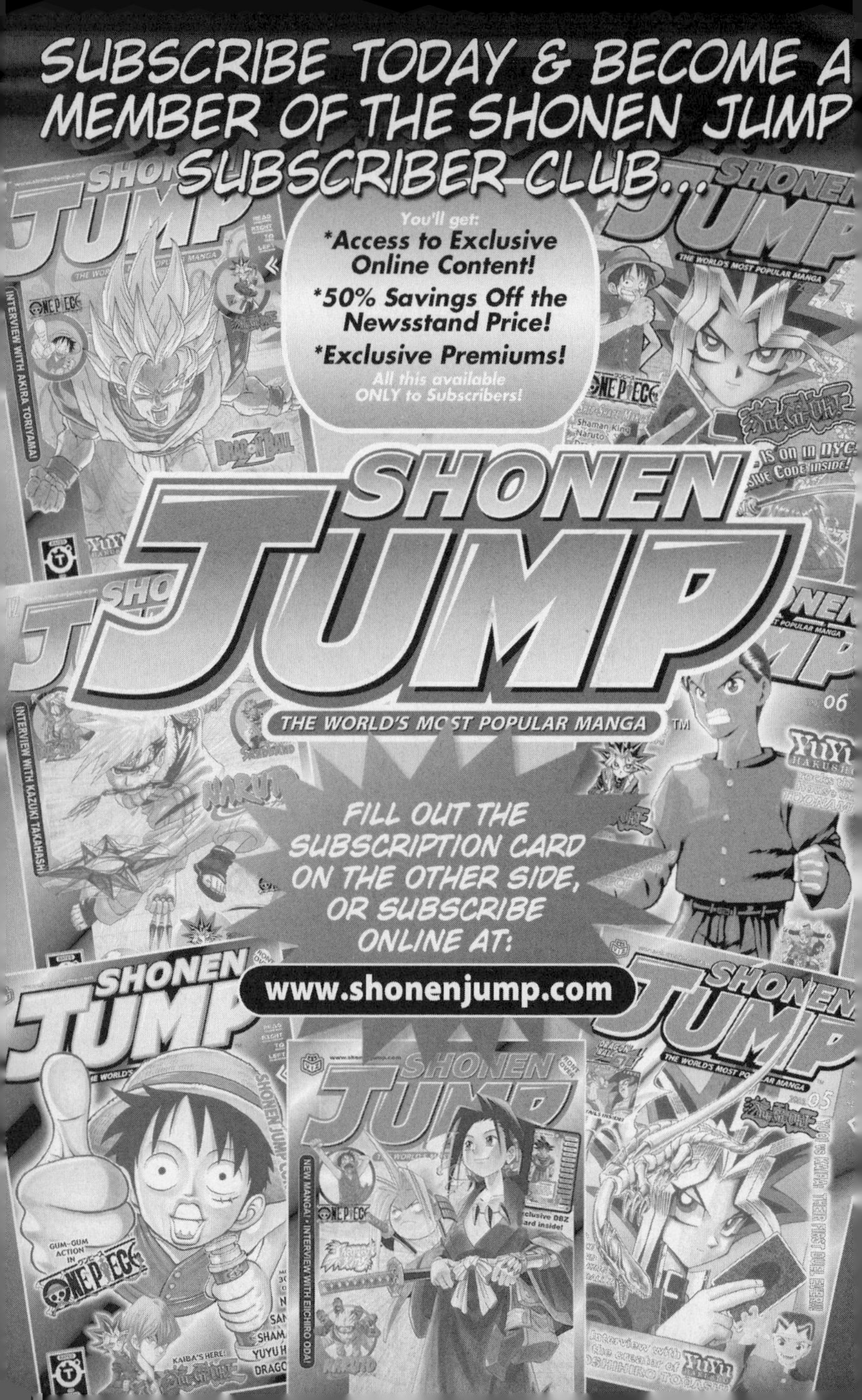
SUBSCRIBE TODAY & BECOME A MEMBER OF THE SHONEN JUMP SUBSCRIBER CLUB...
You'll get:
*Access to Exclusive Online Content!
*50% Savings Off the Newsstand Price!
*Exclusive Premiums!
All this available ONLY to Subscribers!
SHONEN JUMP
THE WORLD'S MOST POPULAR MANGA
TM
FILL OUT THE SUBSCRIPTION CARD ON THE OTHER SIDE, OR SUBSCRIBE ONLINE AT:
www.shonenjump.com
INTERVIEW WITH AKIRA TORIYAMA!
INTERVIEW WITH KAZUKI TAKAHASHI
NEW MANGA! • INTERVIEW WITH EIICHIRO ODA!
GUM-GUM ACTION IN ONE PIECE
KAIBA'S HERE:

Save 50% off the newsstand price!

THE WORLD'S MOST POPULAR MANGA

SUBSCRIBE TODAY and SAVE 50% OFF the cover price PLUS enjoy all the benefits of the SHONEN JUMP SUBSCRIBER CLUB, exclusive online content & special gifts ONLY AVAILABLE to SUBSCRIBERS!

☑ **YES!** Please enter my 1 year subscription (12 issues) to *SHONEN JUMP* at the INCREDIBLY LOW SUBSCRIPTION RATE of $29.95 and sign me up for the SHONEN JUMP Subscriber Club!

Only $29⁹⁵!

NAME

ADDRESS

CITY   STATE   ZIP

E-MAIL ADDRESS

☐ MY CHECK IS ENCLOSED   ☐ BILL ME LATER

CREDIT CARD: ☐ VISA   ☐ MASTERCARD

ACCOUNT #   EXP. DATE

SIGNATURE

CLIP AND MAIL TO →   SHONEN JUMP
Subscriptions Service Dept.
P.O. Box 515
Mount Morris, IL 61054-0515

Make checks payable to: **SHONEN JUMP.**
Canada add US $12. No foreign orders. Allow 6-8 weeks for delivery.

P6SJGN   YU-GI-OH! © 1996 by Kazuki Takahashi / SHUEISHA Inc.